Everybody's War

People who rebuilt their lives,
and enemies who became friends,
in the long shadow of World War II.

by Wim de Vriend
poems by C. L. Grove

Everybody's War © by Wim de Vriend, ISBN 0-9726226-7-5
Fourth edition. All rights reserved, 2013/14/15/17/20.
Golden Falls Publishing, Coos Bay, Oregon.
Order inquiries: costacoosta@coosnet.com

Contents:

Back cover picture by Cliff Roberts

Books by Wim de Vriend

Betsy Boerhave's Diary – T*he translated diary of a 19th century Dutch housewife and shopkeeper.* Illustrated and annotated; 454 pages. Published 2002. List $23.95. Available at iUniverse.

The JOB Messiahs – *How government destroys our prosperity and our freedoms to 'create jobs'.* A history of 40 years of 'economic development' programs that only fostered waste and corruption, while blocking redevelopment in a post-industrial town on the Oregon coast. Lavishly illustrated, fully footnoted, with index, 496 pages; 2nd ed., 2012. $35, with free shipping. Available from the author.

Odd Customers – *Fun, frolic and flippancy at a German restaurant on the left coast, and tales from World War II.* With poems by C. L. Grove. 200 pages, illustrated. 2nd ed., 2012. *Special*: $13. Available at Blue Heron in Coos Bay and from the author. Free shipping.

Everybody's War – *People who rebuilt their lives, and enemies who became friends, in the long shadow of World War II.* 393 pages, illustrated, with poems by C. L. Grove. 4th ed., 2017, list $25; available at the Blue Heron in Coos Bay, from Amazon, and directly from the author with a free bonus. Free shipping.

One hidden little girl – *The story of 'Liesje', the wartime cover name of Betsy Walvis, a little Jewish girl hiding in the Netherlands during World War II.* Many years after the war the author discovered that when he was a toddler 'Liesje' had been living with a farm family across the street, and they'd had many common experiences. He translated her memoirs and added his own wartime recollections to set the stage. Illustrated and annotated, 44 pages, pub. 2015. Free, but out of print; may be reprinted on sufficient demand.

To be published this year: I am working on a book centered on the experiences of German Mennonites in Ukraine, and recent allegations of WWII war crimes by Mennonite individuals.

costacoosta@coosnet.com

WILL BUCK BE BACK?

I'm covering the between-meals shift, and I just served a very nice couple who are gushing effusively about their Sauerbraten and their Schnitzel. How rewarding. The cowbell on the front door rings raucously, due to a chunky chap in his late sixties who bursts in and plops down on the bench in the entry.

"One for lunch, sir?"

"No, I just wanted to come in and listen to your music."

"By all means. You can hear it better if you sit here," I say, pointing at the waiting area. A few months ago we rebuilt our music system, so all of it comes off a DVD with about 700 MP3 songs which include the Blue Danube, Oompa-oompa German brass bands, and the Vilja-Lied from the Merry Widow. Praise *Gott* for technology to enhance our Germanic atmosphere. And thanks also for the extra speaker in the soffit outside, which was meant to charm people into entering. Speaking of which, here's one example.

"No, I can hear it just fine here, if that's alright!" He is kind of loud.

"You betcha, suit yourself." I'm starting to hope this is the last I hear from him. But no such luck.

"Say, how much is it for a beer?" That's a surprise; I had pegged him as a low-income resident of one of the nearby boarding houses.

"What kind of beer?"

"O, any old kind of beer."

We have a big selection of draft beers, imported and local ones. But I sense he's not into fancy suds. "A bottle of Bud is three dollars."

"Dzjeesus! That's outta my budget!" It figures; the convenience store sells them much cheaper, and they give you a brown paper bag too. But couldn't he just be quiet? My paying customers are looking at each other. "Okay, you don't need to buy anything," I assure him. "Just enjoy the music." I hope he translates this as: "Please quit bugging me." But no such luck. He turns up the volume:

"Corriiisst! Looks like nobody cleaned up the place last night!"

Biting my tongue, I manage to ignore this too. But there will be no reprieve; his volume is stuck on HIGH:

"My name's Buck! WHAT'S YOURS?"

Now I find myself pushed to the wall. In "How to Make Friends & Influence People", the manipulation manual that marinated millions of used-car salesmen in cloying kindliness, Dale Carnegie wrote that knowing other people's names gives you power. When they hear someone call them by name, people will mellow and open up to the caller. But I'm dead-set against increasing this caller's power over me. Maybe I should explain that in the time and place that formed me, the exchange of first names was a rare privilege, not a right. When I first went to work in Amsterdam, you called your supervisor Mr. So-and-so, not Tom, Dick or Harry. Violations were met with an ice-cold stare followed by a tongue-lashing. Only if your performance warranted it – meaning after years of good behavior – Tom, Dick or Harry might allow you to call him that. I say *he might,* and even then, not in front of his secretary. In America it's the other way around. A perfect stranger who calls you by your first name sounds triumphant: Notice me! I'm doing you a big favor!

"I cannot deny my past, to which my self is wed …" It's akin to my disapproval of American church pastors who pray with their hands in their pockets. Highly inappropriate while addressing your superiors, and I've been chewed out for it. Way back when, and I wasn't even praying. But this is why, squinting at my own hands-in-the-pants-preacher addressing the Lord in front of the congregation, this congregant halfway expects him to be struck by lightning from on-high. But maybe the Lord is saving his lightning bolts for the worshippers who came to church in shorts and flip-flops. Or for the teenage girls texting each other during the sermon. Or for me, since I'm spying on my pastor during prayer.

So my reply is curt and officious: "I don't give out that kind of information."

Now Buck becomes incredulous as well as loud: "I told you *my* name! You mean you won't tell me *your* name?"

"That's right. None of your business."

Weighed down by this shocking novelty, he stumbles out the door. Ring-a-ding-ding once again, this time in the right direction. Please don't come see us again, sir.

GERMANY ABOVE ALL?

It's about 3:30 PM during my two hour between-meals shift, and the place is empty. Even though we are doing well this summer, people are not wandering in all afternoon and late at night, as they have done in past tourist seasons. Then the doorbell announces the arrival of a motorcycle rider, all clad in black leather. He is a fellow in his mid-thirties, with all the attributes that used to make proponents of Prussian supremacy drool: well-built, with close-cropped blond hair, light blue eyes and slightly raised cheekbones. As a matter of fact, the Aryan racial hypothesis doesn't seem far from the truth: *"Sprechen Sie noch Deutsch hier?"*

"Doch, das ist mir aber heutzutage nicht mehr so geläufig." – Sure, but I'm not as fluent as I used to be.

It's my favorite trick when a show-off spouts German to the waiter; it's guaranteed to silence those whose repertoire does not extend beyond "Sprekken See Doyts?". But this fellow understands me, and he is happy to learn that I studied German in school, just like everyone else in Holland. I even had a girl friend in Frankfurt once. But even though his German is quite good, I detect a certain hesitancy. Then he explains that he is from Ukraine, but of German background. Do we have seafood? I assure him that we do, and soon a second biker joins him. This one seems to have neither German nor English, so they converse in the Ukraine language, which to my ear sounds a bit softer than

Russian. The German speaker has never had clam chowder, and he wonders if it is any good. Ours is the best, I assure him, and it comes with a guarantee, so they order two bowls, and a garlic-scampi dinner to share. When I return with the chowder they have discovered that we serve English hard cider, and ask for two pints. Soon I only have to show my face to see additional items ordered. First a bratwurst appetizer. Then a salmon dinner for the silent friend. Two more pints of cider. After those come oyster shooters, which turn out to be the only new food experience my German-Ukrainian customer does not care for; neither horseradish nor cocktail sauce can change his attitude. I mention that some people make raw oysters palatable by drowning them in vodka, which finds a ready response but still doesn't do the trick. More cider follows. Throughout, the Aryan spokesman expresses his satisfaction at finding an American establishment that serves palatable food. Evidently, since they climbed on their Harleys they have found nothing but fried junk along the road, and they are sick of it; not an uncommon complaint of travelers in these parts. They also praise my judgment in serving hard cider. Because they are headed for San Francisco, I assure them they will find that city full of good food and drink but that, unfortunately, to the average American "seafood" means deep-fried stuff. It's part of the brick-in-the-stomach nutrition culture that's turning into a national millstone.

I've always had a soft spot for people from eastern Europe; history has been so hard on so many generations. In 1944 Polish troops under Allied command liberated my home town in the southern Netherlands; the casualties they took there were really for Poland, but they didn't know that Churchill had already given away their country to Josef Stalin. Roosevelt, that jaunty windbag, had no qualms about such territorial giveaways to his ally "Uncle Joe", a mass-murderer without whose connivance World War II would not have started in the first place.

My local oyster farmer Lilli Clausen was a *Volksdeutsche* who came from Ukraine as a child; as part of the 1939 Hitler-Stalin pact her family had been repatriated to the fatherland. Or, more accurately, they had made it to that part of recently-conquered Poland that Hitler had incorporated in the *Vaterland*, where they were given the property of a recently dispossessed Polish family. As students of World War II know, a couple of years later Hitler attacked his erstwhile ally Stalin, and after a successful counteroffensive a vengeful Stalin moved all the borders westward, chasing away millions of Germans, including Lilli and her family. Now in her seventies, Lilli has done well with her oysters; yet she still speaks wistfully of all they lost in those dictator-orchestrated mass-upheavals. Tragically for Lilli, and ironically for Hitler, in the end he merely achieved "… the reversal of the momentum of the once-mighty German colonization drive eastward from the Elbe. It had begun deep in the Middle Ages; had led, indeed, to the founding of Berlin around A.D. 1230. This *Drang nach dem Osten*, less a conquest than a colonization, meant to Germans what the winning of the West means to Americans. Adolf Hitler, the Austrian who had so glibly preached a Thousand Year Reich, had, in fact, destroyed the honest work and labor of seven centuries of German pioneers and colonizers."[1]

When my two guests are about done I ask the spokesman if he'd mind checking my translation of a 1921 Soviet poster in the other room. It's in Russian, and he confirms that it calls on the people to turn in their weapons. Actually, I have it on display (along with a World War II German poster promising the death penalty for Dutchmen who possessed firearms) because it makes an excellent argument for our Second Amendment. The people of Ukraine suffered from that most terrible combination of handicaps: a murderous, tyrannical

---

[1] James P, O'Donnell: *The Bunker: The History of the Reich Chancellery Group.* 1978: Boston, Houghton Mifflin Company, p. 5.

government, and no weapons to defend themselves. The Stalin-engineered famine of 1933 killed millions of Ukrainians, including children eaten by their parents. Sure enough, when I ask my German-speaking Ukrainian how his relatives fared during that massacre by starvation, I touch a nerve.

"The only reason my two grandfathers survived," he explains, "was the fact that they had bees. Knowing that Stalin's soldiers would come, they had hidden their hives and their honey in the woods."

"Did the soldiers come and take all their other food?"

Yes; and the troops knew that the people had buried some of their supplies. So they probed the ground with sticks. Besides taking all edibles, they seized anything else of value. "There was a baby in the home," he adds, "and they yanked the pillow from under the baby's head." Ah, what a boon Marxism has been to mankind. To each according to his needs... I'm sure Uncle Joe's soldiers had been properly indoctrinated with the idea that social progress occurs through re-distribution of property, if need be at the point of a gun. To make that great Utopian omelet you may need to break a few eggs, in this case by killing an obstinate social class: the Ukrainian peasants.

When I mention the forced wanderings of Lilli the oyster farmer, my guest explains that after Hitler's 1941 attack on the USSR ethnic Germans from eastern Ukraine were deported to Kazakhstan. After Perestroika they were allowed to return. And apparently, throwing off their collectivist shackles has done wonders for them. My guest is an engineer by trade, obviously prosperous, and he visits the United States several times a year on business. For future occasions he plans to leave his Harley at the home of a sister who lives in the Midwest. He has worked on projects in today's Germany as well. But re-discovering his ancient roots inspired him with pessimism. For a nation to maintain itself, people have to have national pride. But the Hitler era has given Germans such a massive moral hangover that they frown on any kind of patriotic feeling. While he approves of brash American patriotism, he despairs of the long-term survival of Germany. He also shows his command of American slang: "The Germans nowadays," he tells me twice, "are wusses."

Their bill comes to about eighty-five dollars. When I bring him the credit card slip he instructs me to add a tip sufficient to make the total $150. His name is Taras; we part like old friends.

This photo of my family's grocery store must have been taken between 1930, when it was built to serve as a grocery and florist shop, and 1936, when my parents bought it, but discontinued the florist business. The name of the former owner is still on the little warehouse behind the house.

AN UNKNOWN SOLDIER'S WAR

It seems that the events we remember from "when we were very young" are those that stood out. Waking up, being fed, playing with toys, being tucked into bed – those experiences fade with time because even though they were happy ones, they were routines are not memorable. But incidents that were unique or puzzling can become life-long memories. At least, that's been my experience.

Of those life-long memories of mine, a couple date from World War II. In the first one I remember standing, two or three years old, between our home/shop and our little warehouse, watching a bunch of strange men in the street. They were running around trying to catch a pig; and the pig didn't want to be caught. It seemed to be our pig, and I never saw it again. Years later I learned that wartime food rationing was behind that incident. Before the war the Netherlands was a land of milk, butter, cheese and bacon, but after the Germans invaded much of the Dutch food supply was shipped to Germany. The strict rationing system imposed in the occupied countries was not just to distribute the leftovers equitably, but also to control the local population. In order to get a rationing book and food coupons you had to be registered at city hall, which also meant the Germans could easily find you if they wanted to arrest you or put you to work in some German war industry, both highly unpopular events. To facilitate that kind of control, the occupiers prohibited producing food on the side, especially keeping pigs, which people in that area had been accustomed to do. They would feed the pig potato peels all year, and butcher it in the fall. My father had secretly kept one in our back yard until somebody squealed on him – or maybe it was the pig – and the Nazis' Dutch helpers – the Dutch make great civil servants, scrupulously above politics – had come to confiscate it. Whereupon my dad got mad, kicked the pig out of his pig-pen, and told the Dutch toadies that if they wanted his pig, they'd have to work for it. That's the kind of man he was.

In the second incident, I walked into our kitchen to find a perfectly strange man shaving there, someone I'd never seen before, and never have since. Evidently he felt enough at home to stand there, scraping off his beard at the kitchen sink. I remember the peculiar shape of his helmet, sitting on the counter nearby. I don't think he paid any attention to me, but he always stayed in my memory. Sometimes he appeared in my dreams, still a mystery.

When I asked my mother about it, many years on, she was surprised I even remembered it. From her memories and from history books written since, it seems that strange man stood in our kitchen in early September 1944. We lived in Terneuzen, in the southwestern part of the

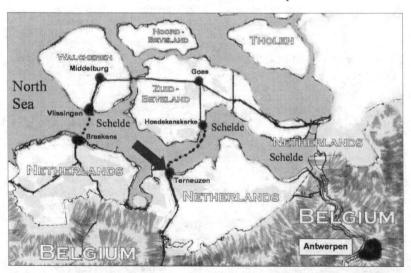

Netherlands, actually in an isolated strip of Dutch territory measuring about 80 km (55 miles) east to west and 20 km (14 miles) north to south. It could be described as northern Flanders, being located west of the large Belgian port of Antwerp and bordered by Belgian Flanders on the south. It is separated from the Dutch islands to the north and from the rest of the Netherlands by the estuary of the Schelde River, which comes out of Antwerp, is several miles wide, and carries a lot of shipping.

Across from our family home and shop was a farm that bore the name *De Moffenschans* – a moniker that translates as "The Kraut Fort", or maybe "The Jerry Fort", where the Den Hamer family lived. Soon after the war the farm fields were covered with row houses, and the big yellow barn burned down in the 'seventies, to be replaced by a store. But the house is still there. So is its name, which memorializes a thousand German mercenaries commanded by Count Philipp von Hohenlohe, who had raised an earthen fortification on that spot during the Netherlands' war of independence against Spain, when this area was highly contested. That was way back in November 1583. The Germans were on the side of the Dutch then, but for a price.

After the conflict their fortification was leveled, which made a choice spot for a farmhouse because it was still a few feet higher than the surrounding flat countryside that was always in danger of flooding. In September 1944 we lived across from the place, that is, my parents, my older brother and I, then three years old. We also had a two-month-old baby in the house, my sister Ella. And that month German soldiers had returned to the Kraut Fort.

After D-Day, June 6 of that year, the Germans had fought tenaciously to contain the Allied invaders in Normandy, and had managed to do so longer than expected. But in the end the vastly superior Allied forces forced a bloody breakout, causing most German armies in France to retreat in easterly or northeasterly directions toward Germany, often in great disarray.

But the routed German troops arriving in our area belonged to just one army, the 15th under General Gustav-Adolf von Zangen; and that one was all by itself. The job assigned to the 15th had been coastal defense, so it had been tasked with building beach obstructions and bunkers and gun emplacements, and manning them against the expected Allied invasion. Because the Germans did not know where that invasion would occur, the 15th had covered a long stretch of coast, from our area southwest into Belgium and northern France, but with much of its forces concentrated around Calais, where Hitler thought the enemy was most likely to invade because it was closest to England.

After the allied breakout in that summer, the 15th Army had withdrawn in a northerly direction. But then it became trapped. To the east, Canadian forces had unexpectedly taken Antwerp and its large harbor, but they had not proceeded further north. But the islands of Walcheren and Zuid-Beveland, north of us, were still controlled by the Germans, who were digging in, by Hitler's orders to maintain control of shipping access to Antwerp. And this meant that the only way for the 15th Army to join the other German forces was by crossing the Schelde and then marching east (see map above). Most of that army would make it across, no mean feat since there was a shortage of ships, a scarcity of Dutch skippers, dangerous shoals, and allied fighters strafing the vessels. So the Germans preferred moving at night if possible, although this increased the risk of their vessels getting stuck on the shoals, where they were sitting ducks for the vengeful Polish troops approaching from the south. Even so, from our town's small harbors and from Breskens,

A requisitioned ferry boat, taking units of the 15th Army across the Schelde. The equipment stored on the back still has camouflage foliage.

further west, an estimated 60,000 to 90,000 of the 15th Army made it to the other side, along with a lot of their weapons.

A sound rule of war says that it is far less important to conquer enemy territory than it is to destroy enemy forces. That doesn't mean you have to kill them all; what you need to do is destroy their ability to fight. If the topography is favorable and you have the resources, you can surround enemy units, cut their supply lines, destroy their food, ammunition and fuel dumps until, starving and powerless, they find surrender their only option. Once that is achieved, the territory will follow. While it is true that in the Pacific war the Japanese had other ideas, this is how things worked in the European theater.

But the Allied Supreme Commander in Europe, General Eisenhower, seemed to be oblivious to all that, including the 15th Army's still-vigorous fighting potential. He was fixated on operation Market Garden which was planned for that same month, September 1944. Market Garden was British General Montgomery's plan to seize the Rhine bridges at Arnhem, in the eastern Netherlands, and from there to roll across the northern German plain, unimpeded by natural obstacles. This was the action later known as "A Bridge Too Far", the largest airborne operation of World War II and an exorbitant catastrophe. Oddly enough General Eisenhower had made the same mistake –

The 15th German Army's chief crossing routes in September 1944 are indicated in this contemporary aerial picture of the Schelde estuary. The shorter crossing in the background followed the peace-time ferry route between Breskens (left) and Vlissingen. The longer crossing in the foreground copied the ferry route between Terneuzen (left) and Hoedekenskerke.

allowing large German units to escape by water – twice before. Toward the end of the Sicilian campaign he had ignored the retreat of 40,000 well-armed German troops across the Strait of Messina to mainland Italy, and a bit later he allowed another 30,000 to sail to Italy from Corsica, while that island was being conquered by the Allies. This occurred despite complete Allied mastery of air and sea, and of course those escaped German troops made the Allies' bloody Italian campaign even bloodier.

The escape of the 15th Army across the Schelde estuary, the third such blunder, was at least as calamitous, because it kept the Allies from using the harbor of Antwerp to supply their armies for the push into Germany. It wasn't until late October, well after the 15th Army's escape and the failure of Market Garden, when amphibious Allied troops invaded the islands on the northern bank of the Schelde. But by then the German garrisons had fortified their positions and mined the shipping lanes. Worse, after its September crossing the still-intact 15th Army had marched east virtually unimpeded to fight the allies again, in Market-Garden that September, at the Battle of the Bulge in December, and during its last stand in Germany's industrial Ruhr area in early 1945.

It was only then when the German war machine finally ran out of steam. Meanwhile it took until the end of November 1944 for the first Allied supply ship to dock in Antwerp, destroying all hope of ending the war that year.

To enhance their mobility the retreating soldiers of the 15th had stolen anything on wheels. This was quite a contrast with their invasion of the Low Countries in 1940, when they had been far more scrupulous. But this time they moved in stolen horse-drawn wagons and other vehicles, even baby carriages, and above all on bicycles. In fact, by this time they had acquired a pernicious reputation for stealing bicycles, although they always did so properly – by giving the owner a signed receipt. Some people still have those receipts, quite a few of which were signed *"Feldmarschall Arschloch"* – Field Marshal Butthole. But they never saw their bicycles again.

So in September 1944, when part of these troops were housed in the barn and in the home of the Kraut Fort across the street, my father snuck out in the middle of the night and stole a bicycle back, but without leaving a receipt. The next morning my mother was beside herself while one of the Germans ran around the neighborhood like a madman, shouting: *Wo ist mein Fahrrad?* "Where is my bicycle?" But his bicycle was well-hidden in our attic. And he didn't run around very long, since he needed to catch a boat.

Before the tired, dirty troops were to cross the Schelde, order must be restored. In good German fashion, this included getting cleaned up and shaved. That's why a German soldier walked across from the Kraut Fort, knocked on our door, and asked if he could shave. Most people did not say no to such requests. So I walked in on him and watched him shave, though I don't know if he noticed me. And my two-month old baby sister Ella must have seen him too, but of course she wouldn't have remembered.

"So he shaved and then he left. Was that all there was to that?" I asked my mother.

"Yes," she said pensively. "But before he left, he asked if he could hold Ella for a moment."

A burgher fell into the Sauer,
as he tried to land a trout –
where the Sauer meets the sewer!
(That was one real sour Kraut!)

C. L. Grove: *River Rhymes*

"A HALF-FLOATING, HALF-SUNK WRECK"

This morning I need to stop at the Fred Meyer grocery store to pick up ingredients for our Dutch meatballs. The Cash & Carry wholesale doesn't have the low-fat ground beef and ground pork we need. Coming in, I spot Jürgen and his wife Carmen in the cafeteria. They are having a Dutch-style breakfast, Jürgen explains. Soft white rolls from the bakery, and sliced cheese from the deli counter. More economical than a restaurant breakfast, too.

"So how's the jewelry business these days?"

"Ah, not too good."

"Neither is the restaurant business, to be honest."

"It couldn't be as bad as the jewelry business," Carmen adds cheerfully. Yes, I suppose right now buying jewelry is even lower on people's must-do-list than is going out to eat. But they've had a lot of good years too, Jürgen and Carmen have. Their primary business is the manufacture of class rings, which they sell all over the country. He is an expert at creating molds for those things, a different one for every high school. A uniquely American business, class rings. I can see why someone would like to advertise on his finger that he attended Yale or Princeton. But Podunk High? But a lot of Americans are mawkishly sentimental about their high schools, as shown by the prosperity of class ring makers and trophy shops and sports gear merchants, along with a thriving internet industry that enables people to track down former class mates from Podunk High. Jürgens Jewelers were doing very well until the price of gold went through the roof, followed by the recent financial blow-up, which made people cut way back on spending. Well, every business has its ups and downs.

I first met Jürgen and Carmen at my restaurant, where he told me his life's story. His last name is Pooch, pronounced "Poagh" in German. The way Americans would pronounce Pooch is similar to the German "Putsch", which is why he doesn't like to use it. He snarls at the canine connotations. Jürgen was quite a wanderer in his younger days. Among other things he was a traveling musician, and he also briefly joined the French Foreign Legion. Very quickly it dawned on him that was a grave mistake, and he got out thanks to a former Waffen-SS officer who had joined the Legion before him. But originally Jürgen was from Danzig, the city Hitler went to war over in 1939, and he claims he is actually of Jewish origin, as were most of the inhabitants of Danzig. But Hitler never bothered the Danzig Jews, Jürgen said, and his father served in the German army like all other Germans. I don't know how true all this is, but if being talkative, multi-talented, and having curly hair are proof of Jewish descent, he's got them all. Then, as he was telling me all this, he got a thoughtful look:

"You know, my father died in Holland. In September of 1944."

"O? Where was that?"

Every European language his its own rules for spelling and pronunciation, so when he said the name of the place, all I heard were perplexing sounds. Then, after several tries on his part, it dawned on me that it was Hoedekenskerke (for English speakers: Hoodakanskirkuh). The locals, who like the Cockneys drop h's everywhere, call it 'Ootyaskahrkah. What it means is, more or less, "Little Hat (or Hatkin) Church", after the shape of the village church's roof. It's located on the north shore of the Schelde, the coast of Zuid-Beveland, and it has a small harbor. (See the map on page 8.) For many years a ferryboat connected the village to Terneuzen, my hometown on the south shore. I was amazed to realize that the way the crow flies, I was living seven or eight miles from Hoedekenskerke at the time Jürgen's father was being killed there. What a small world.

Then Jürgen confided that he had promised his late mother he'd find his father's grave. But he never had done it, so I offered to help. My special investigator in the case was my mother, who still lives near Terneuzen. The Dutch keep very good public records, and soon she was able to send me copies of two pertinent documents. One was a Red Cross letter from 1955, inquiring about the whereabouts of the grave of *"Maschinenmaat Willy Pooch"*, who had gone down near Hoedekenskerke with a bombed German Navy ferryboat, on September 10, 1944. Going by his title, Pooch senior must have worked in the engine room of that vessel, but there was no response accompanying this letter. The other letter had been written less than a year after the end of the war, and was addressed to the widow of Heinz Hoffmann, a petty officer killed on the same boat. Its author was a nameless administrator at Hoedekenskerke town hall, who wrote in a German not entirely grammatical, but clear enough. My English translation is below, followed by a reproduction of the actual letter:

April 24, 1946

Mrs. Annemarie Hoffmann
(24) Hamburg-Lokstedt 2
Friedrich Ebertstrasze 30 I
Germany
British Zone

You ask me in a letter of March 31 of this year to inform you about the death of your husband, who lost his life on Sunday 10 September 1944. On 11 September 1944 he was buried in the municipal cemetery in this municipality, where he lies with about forty other soldiers; as far as I know in an individual grave.

The time of the retreat of the Germans is still quite fresh in our minds, so I am able to tell you quite a bit, including about the particular rocket-bomb attack on the ship on which Heinz Hoffmann was present.

Already as of early September (about the 3rd or 4th) the German army in Belgium had been defeated and was no longer capable of resisting the onrush of the victorious allied troops. Large units gave up the fight, but many tried to flee north. Day and night, all sorts of ships and boats crossed the mouth of the Schelde from Terneuzen to Hoedekenskerke. But the Schelde is about four kilometers wide and often stormy, so at the beginning of the crossing already it was clear to us that many vessels might not reach South-Beveland. On top of that there were the British Spitfires and Mustangs, that were watching the retreat from high in the sky, every day, and often came down when something important showed up.

The entire population was often present, when far from shore one vessel after another was sunk. I hope you will understand that we Dutchmen could feel freedom coming, and therefore cheered in our hearts at every attack, not out loud, because the army, the S.D.[1]) and so forth were still there, but silently in our hearts, because every ship that was sunk and every soldier who fell meant one step towards freedom for us. You simply can't understand when after long and hard years of inhuman terror and slavery finally, finally our long-awaited liberty is coming and the enemies are steadily being pushed back.

Then came Sunday, September 10, 1944. At about 5 in the afternoon a boat came over from Terneuzen. All day there had not been any airplanes, so there were renewed attempts by the Germans at escaping. Also present on the boat was Heinz Hoffmann, petty officer. Slowly the boat approached, and it looked as if all would end well. But

P-47 Thunderbolt being flown at low level over the North Sea by Lt. William Hartshorn, returning from a mission over Belgium and Holland, Sept. 1944.

---

[1]) S.D. = *Sicherheitsdienst* (Security Service), a notorious German secret police agency similar to the Gestapo.

when it was only 50 meters from shore, we saw nine Thunderbolts come rushing up in the western sky. We could tell right away that they were not after the boat, so we remained standing on shore, quite unconcerned.[1]) But then the excited men on the boat made their big mistake. Two or more of the cannons on board fired at the plane that brought up the rear. Now their fate was sealed. After a brief hesitation just one of the Thunderbolts turned back, and after four rocket bombs and some machine gun strafing the entire ship was no more than a half-afloat, half-sinking wreck.

At the very last moment the vessel succeeded in reaching the shore. It was obvious that many dead and wounded were on deck. As soon as possible they were conveyed to the infirmary in the municipality, where a few more of the wounded died. It is not known to me whether your husband perished immediately during the attack, or later on in the infirmary. We are not able to determine this, either. All that is known is that there is a sign at the municipal cemetery, on which also the name Heinz Hoffman has been painted. As far as we know he was not buried in a mass grave but in an individual grave.

I know nothing concerning any personal effects left behind; in addition, German soldiers were never recorded here as having been killed.[2])

This is about all that is known here about September 10, 1944. Should you perhaps have further requests, then I might try to check on something for you, the Netherlands Red Cross might perhaps also be able to communicate details.

I hope to have assisted you to the best of my knowledge. I also want to communicate that you should have had no fear at all that your request might not be answered by us. Certainly, the entire German army was our enemy, but we Dutchmen are always humane. In Holland you will never try in vain to do something for fallen soldiers that have been left behind.

Respectfully Yours,

Hoedekenskerke Municipality

---

[1]) Most likely they were all standing on top of the sea dike, which would have afforded a better view.

[2]) In the Netherlands (as in most European countries) all births, marriages and deaths must be recorded at City Hall.

K 939

GEMEENTE HOEDEKENSKERKE

Telefoon 253   Postrekening 92393

No.

Onderwerp:

HOEDEKENSKERKE, **den 24. April** 1946,

Bijl.

Frau Annemarie Hoffmann,
(24) Hamburg-Lokstedt 2,
Friedrich Ebertstrasze 30 I,
Deutschland.-
Britische Zöne.

   Sie fragen mich in Schreiben des 31.3.d.J. etwas mitzuteilen
über den Tod Ihres Mannes, der am Sonntag den 1o. September 1944 gefallen ist. Er wurde am 11. September 1944 auf dem Gemeindefriedhof
in dieser Gemeinde begraben, wo er liegt mit etwa vierzig andere Soldaten; soweit mich bekannt in einem einzelnen Grab.

   Die Zeit der Zurückzug der deutschen liegt uns noch ganz
fresch im Gedächtniss, sodasz ich wohl ein und ander erzählen kann,
auch über den spezialen Raketenbomben-angriff auf dem Schiffe, worauf sich Heinz Hoffmann befandet.

   Schon vom Anfangs September(etwa 3.oder 4.) war die deutsche Wehrmacht in Belgiën geschlagen und nicht mehr im Stande die
heranstürmende, siegende alliierte Truppen nachzuhalten. Grosze Einh-
heiten beendeten den Kampf, aber viele versuchten zu fliehen zum
Norden. Tags und Nachts überquerten allerhand Schiffe und Boote die
Scheldemündung von Terneuzen nach Hoedekenskerke. Aber die Schelde
ist etwa vier Kilometer breit und manchmal stürmisch, sodasz für uns
schon im Anfang der Überschleussung fest stand, dass viele Fahrzeuge
nicht Süd-Beveland erreichen konnten. Überdies waren noch die Britische Spitfires und Mustangs, die jeden Tag hoch im Himmel die Flucht
betrachteten und oft herunter kamen, wenn etwas wichtiges dabei war.

   Die ganze Bevölkerung war oft dabei anwesend, wenn weit aus
dem Küste die Schiffe der eine nach dem andere versänkt wurden. Ich
hoffe dass Sie verstehen wollen, dass wir Holländer die Freiheit an-
kommen füllten, und deswegen bei jeden Angriff im Herze jauchzten,
nicht laut, da noch immer die Wehrmacht, S.D. usw da war, sondern
still im Herze, da jedes Schiff das versänkt wurde und jeder Soldat
der fiel, für uns einen Schritt zur Freiheit brachte. Sie können doch
nicht verstehen, wenn nach langen und schweren Jahren von unmenschliche
Terror und Sklaverei endlich, endlich die lang erwartete Freiheit kommt
und die Feinde allmählich zurückgedrängt werden.

   So kam Sonntag den 1o. September 1944. Nachmittags um etwa
fünf Uhr kam ein Boot herangefahren von Terneuzen nach hier. Den ganzen Tag waren keine Flugzeuge da gewesen, sodass nochmals von deut-
scher Seite versucht wurde, zu entkommen. Auf dem Boot befand sich
auch Heinz Hoffmann, Unteroffizier. Allmählich kam das Boot näher und
es sah danach aus, alsob alles für sie gut enden konnte. Als aber das
Boot etwa fünfzig Meter aus dem Wall war, sahen wir im Westlichen
Himmel neun Thunderbolts, im rasender Fahrt heranstürmen. Wir sahen
sofort, dass sie das Boot nicht als Ziel hatten und blieben deswegen
ganz Ruhig am Ufer stehen. Da begann aber der grosse Fehler der ver-

schreckten Mannschaften. Zwei oder mehr der sich an Bord befindeten Kanonen gaben Feuer auf das letzte Flufzeug. Jetzt war ihren Schicksal besiegelt. Nur eine der Thunderbolts kam zurück nach einigen Zweifel und mit vier Raketenbomben und etwas M.G.feuer war das ganze Schiff nicht mehr als eine halb treibende, halb sinkende Schicht.

Es gelang das Fahrzeug noch im letzten Augenblick am Ufer zu bringen. Es zeigte sich, dass viele Tode und verwundete sich auf dem Verdeck befanden. Sie wurden am schnellsten befördert zum Lazaret in dieser Gemeinde, wo noch einige der Verwundeten gestorben sind. Es ist mir nicht bekannt ob Ihr Mann schon sofort gefallen ist beim Angriff, oder später im Lazaret. Es ist auch nicht möglich für uns dies nachzuprüfen. Bakannt ist nur, dass sich am Gemeindefriedhof einenSchild befindet, worauf auch den Nahm Heinz Hoffman gemahlt worden ist. Soweit bekannt wurde er nicht in einem Massangrab sondern in einem Einzelnen Grab beerdigt.

Mir ist nichts bekannt über evt. Nachlasssachen; auch wurden deutsche Soldaten niemals als gefallen schriftlich bei uns erfasst.

Dies ist ungefähr alles was hier bekannt ist vom 1o. September 1944. Möchten Sie vielleicht noch etwas näheres wünschen so könnte ich vielleicht versuchen noch etwas für Sie nachzuprüfen, auch das Niederländische Rote Kreuz könnte vielleicht noch Einzelheiten mitteilen.

Ich hoffe also Sie nach besten Wissen geholfen zu haben. Noch will ich mitteilen, dass Sie gar keinen Angst zu haben hätten müssen, dass Ihre Bitte nicht von uns beantwortet würde. Bestimmt war die ganze deutsche Wehrmacht unser Feind, aber wir Holländer sind immer Menschlich. Niemals werden Sie in Holland vergebens versuchen etwas zu tun für Hinterbliebonen gefallener Soldaten.

Wir grüssen Sie, hochachtungsvoll,

GEMEINDNAMT HONDELENSKERKE.

LIESJE AND JAKOB'S WAR

It was during one of our overseas phone calls, in the late nineties, when my mother first told me about Liesje. My mom was still working in the family store then, toward the end of her 64-year shopkeeper's career. That career had begun in 1936, the year she married at age 20 and started a small shop to have something to do (raising seven children was not enough), and it ended in 2000, when my older brother sold the now greatly-expanded store, and she was eighty-five. During all the intervening years her favorite place was at the cash register, partly, I think, because of the opportunities for socializing. Anyway, she mentioned that she was at her usual post, looking out through the big plate glass window, when she noticed some of the Den Hamer children, now in their sixties or older, walking up to the store with a lady she had not seen before.

When they came in, they asked: "Do you remember Liesje?"

She did not remember Liesje, and perhaps that was just as well. For they explained that during the war Liesje had been living with them right across the street, at the *Moffenschans*, the Kraut Fort farm. But it had all

BEKANNTMACHUNG

Wiederholt habe ich die niederländische Bevölkerung davor gewarnt, in irgendeiner Form die Feinde Deutschlands zu begünstigen.

Trotzdem ist wieder ein schwerer Fall von Feindbegünstigung vorgekommen. Am 7. 8. 1941 musste auf niederländischem Gebiet ein britisches Kampfflugzeug notlanden. Der unverletzt gebliebenen Besatzung von 6 Mann wurde bei ihrem Bestreben, zu fliehen, Unterstützung durch Niederländer zuteil durch Hergabe von Geld, Nahrungsmitteln und Zivilkleidung.

Noch am gleichen Tage wurden die Engländer gefangen. Die Begünstiger wurden sofort vor ein Deutsches Kriegsgericht gestellt. Dieses verurteile 5 von ihnen zum Tode und drei weitere zu langjährigen, teilweise lebenslänglichen Freiheitsstrafen.

DEN HAAG, den 14. 8. 1941

gez.: FR. CHRISTIANSEN
General der Flieger
Wehrmachtbefehlshaber in den Niederlanden

Public Notice

I have repeatedly warned the Netherlands population not to give any kind of aid and comfort to Germany's enemies.
Nevertheless another serious case of aid and comfort for the enemy has occurred. On August 7 1941 a British warplane had to make an emergency landing on Dutch territory. The 6-man crew which had remained uninjured received support in its efforts to escape from Dutchmen by means of money, food and civilian clothes. The Englishmen were caught the very same day. The supporters were immediately brought before a German Court Martial. This condemned 5 of them to death and three more to long, partly life-long prison terms.

The Hague, August 14, 1941

Signed: Fr. Christiansen
Air Force General
Army Commander in the Netherlands.

---

been very hush-hush; Liesje was a little Jewish girl, and my mother, if she had even noticed her, never knew she was not a Den Hamer child.

Today, when personal memories of World War II are eagerly recorded before they are forever lost, it may seem strange that during those years people didn't exchange much information. The explanation: "Loose Lips Sink Ships." Even without having been told, a mean old retired farmer living across the street had figured out the den Hamers' secret, and had threatened to turn them in. That he never did so may prove he knew which way the wind was blowing, but above all, people HAD to keep secrets, even from trusted friends. That self-protective habit took decades to lose. That's why even we, their friends and neighbors, never knew about Liesje, not even after the war was over. And for his part, Mr. den Hamer never knew about my dad's participation in an underground railroad that had moved downed Allied airmen south into Belgium and on through France into Spain, hopefully to fly back to Britain. The only secret each man knew about the other was that during the war they met regularly at our house to listen to a radio hidden under an upstairs floor, to hear the news from London; that was illegal too. Many years later I discovered the secret compartment, because my dad was now using it to hide liquor he was selling without a license. If you expect people to resist an enemy occupier, don't count on the most docile, law-abiding citizens.

Later on Liesje, like many Jewish children who had survived the war, emigrated to Israel. When my mother finally met her at about age sixty she had come back for a visit.

All of these actions: hiding Jews, helping Allied flyers, and listening to the radio, were offenses that could get you shot, or thrown into prison, or hauled off to a concentration camp, and/or all of your property destroyed. MI9, the semi-secret British organization that oversaw the return of Allied airmen, reckoned that for the 2,000 who made it back to Britain, 2,000 helpers on the Continent had lost their lives.[1]   Survival, therefore, required stony taciturnity.

It was for such reasons that all through the war years a pall of silence hung over our town, as over every other town in the occupied countries. And for a considerable time after the war, few people except blowhards talked about the things they had done. It had all been very unpleasant, and people would rather get on with their lives. They wanted to create careers, businesses, homes and families, and most Americans were of the same mind: hence the baby boomer years. And so were the Germans, and the surviving Jews too. This may explain why, once peace returned, the den Hamers never told my parents about Liesje.

And for his part, my dad said nothing about his risky activities on behalf of the allied pilots.

We didn't find out until almost thirty years after his death. The one who brought it up was a Mr. Eekman, a man in his late eighties, the age my father would have been had he lived longer. My mother took me to

[1] I.C.B. Dear and M.R.D. Foot: *The Oxford Companion to WORLD WAR II.* Oxford University Press, 1995: p. 747.

A photo of Axelsestraat before the war. On the right is the house of the *Moffenschans* farm, on the left are the 19th century houses in one of which the hostile retired farmer lived.

visit him, and he related his story. It included some juicy details, like the time the underground railroad north of us had accumulated a large number of downed Allied flyers who needed to get across the Schelde to continue their journey south. There was a ferry running, but it was of course being watched. So the airmen became taciturn farm laborers in charge of a herd of cows traveling on the ferry.

When the Germans asked why it took so many hands to drive the cows, the farmer told them that the cows were sick, and might act up.

As Mr. Eekman talked it dawned on me that one reason for my dad's silence about all this must have been that in war or in peace, he didn't want my mom wondering what he was up to. He was of the old school that considered it undesirable for wives to know everything, and no doubt some of his wartime activities would have nearly scared her to death. Mr. Eekman said he'd seen my father carrying an Allied pilot on the back of his bicycle once. He also remembered that at least one airman had spent the night in our little warehouse behind the store, shown on page 7.

Once during an internet discussion about the Jewish Holocaust I related the Liesje story as proof that some Europeans really had tried to save Jews, only to be furiously attacked by a Jewish girl who thought they could and should have hidden far more Jews than they did. Maybe so, but such attacks risk painting the attacked as purposely callous, and the attacker as uninformed. What, for instance, did the bulk of the population really know about the fate of the Jews who had been rounded up and transported east, to 'labor camps', which was the Nazis' cover story? And if everyone did know what was really going on, that poses an unavoidable question about the *Judenräte*, the Jewish Councils that were established by the Germans and composed of some of the country's most prominent Jews: judges, scientists, physicians, industrialists. The Jewish Council in Amsterdam performed the dirty work of rounding up fellow-Jews for deportation, and of the twenty members only two resigned. So why didn't the others? Perhaps because, as highly educated 'notables', it was not in their nature to swim against the stream. When after the war, survivors of the Dutch-Jewish community tried to hold them accountable for their meek collaboration, the councilors became quite indignant and broke off all contact.

Human nature is not a simple thing. It should mean something that the number of Dutchmen honored at the Yad Vashem memorial in Israel, for their efforts to protect Jews from extermination, 5,413, is exceeded only by the number of Poles who did so: 6,532. Still, it's morally hazardous to draw simple conclusions from these numbers because conditions varied greatly in the occupied countries. Pre-war Poland contained over 3 million Jews, some 10% of the Polish population; and in accordance with Nazi racial ideology the non-Jewish Poles were treated very badly too. As a result, equal numbers of Jewish and non-Jewish Poles were killed: some 3 million each. But the percentages were reversed: while 10% of the 30 million non-Jewish Poles lost their lives, 90% of the Polish Jews did. The pre-war Netherlands, with a population of under 9 million, contained some 140,000 Jews, of whom more than 100,000 lost their lives.

What may help put these figures into some perspective is what it took to hide Dutch Jews from their murderous persecutors. Food was a big obstacle because it was restricted, due to requisitioning by the Germans, and rationing for the Dutch. Without the required food coupons plus money, most people could not feed another mouth. But the Den Hamers owned a farm, so they had an easier time obtaining food. Secondly, Dutch houses were small, Dutch cities were compact, and the country had no real wilderness like France or Poland did; all of that made it hard to hide people. A typically Dutch solution was the hiding place of the group of Jews that included Anne Frank, in the very heart of Amsterdam. They hid in an *achterhuis*, literally an "after-house". An *achterhuis* was invisible from the public street because, during past centuries when building sites were scarce in Amsterdam, it had been built in the backyard of an existing house. Of course, in the end even

Anne Frank's *achterhuis* proved inadequate because the group stayed in one place too long: over two years. It was more common for *onderduikers* ("underdivers": people who stayed below the surface) to keep moving from one hiding place to another before drawing attention.

The Den Hamers had a different solution, one that could be compared to hiding a pebble on a beach. They had a large house and nine children, many of whom had dark, curly hair. So as the tenth child, Liesje would not stand out much.

Many Jews and other *onderduikers* could never be seen outside. But Liesje could, which is why she described her arrival at the den Hamers as "I came from hell into heaven. All of a sudden I'm allowed to walk outside, talk and laugh. But I am still alone without my own family. They endanger their entire family, nine children, in order to save me." [1]

In 1942 Liesje had been taken to her first *onderduiker* address, a family living in a walk-up apartment in Amsterdam. The family's two boys, 8 and 10, bullied the little girl, threatening to turn her in to the Gestapo if she didn't do what they wanted. That included surrendering what few toys she had:

> I was little, and I had no choice and nobody who would help me. No one was supposed to find out that I was there. So I was not allowed to cry, to laugh, to look outside and of course not to walk outside. Their home had no place to hide me but the mother had a brilliant solution. They had a Murphy bed with two belts across its width. Once in a while I would be tied to that bed, fastened with two belts and put against the wall folded up.
>
> I would hang there for a couple of hours to "get used to it", as they said. No need to mention that I was not allowed to make any noise and certainly not to cry. . . .
>
> I felt very humiliated. Despite everything I do know they saved my life.
>
> After almost a year, I am five and a half by then, I was transferred late at night to a different family. I remember we were traveling all night. . . . . So then I end up with the family Den Hamer in Terneuzen . . . They had nine children (six daughters and three sons) and took me into their family as the tenth child. Later on they told me that when I arrived I had stiff legs and had trouble walking. I arrived with a false

---

[1] This quote and others that follow are from my booklet *"One Hidden Little Girl,"* which is my translation of *"De SHOA – De Tweede Wereldoorlog 1940-1945 en ik"*, written by Elisheva Polak whose name started out as Betsy Walvis, lived under the false name Liesje (Liesbeth) Huistink during the war, and changed her name to Elisheva after emigrating to Israel in 1951. Polak was the name of her late husband, who had come from Romania.

From left to right: David, Kees, Koos, Gillis, Truus, Tannie, Jeannie, Nellie & Alie den Hamer.

identity card. They could use this to have me entered in the population registry and get ration cards for me.

Over there I was able to just walk outside like normal, and later on I was registered at school for first grade.

On this document all data were false. My name, my last name, birthplace and my parents' names. The only information that is correct is my birthday. Thanks to the latter my mother is able to find me after the war.

I came from hell into heaven. All of a sudden I'm allowed to walk outside, talk and laugh.

What must have made her first *onderduiker* experience especially vexing was that she had been a rambunctious, enterprising toddler quite unlike her older sister who had been an 'easy child'.

At the Den Hamers' most of the children had regular assigned duties such as cooking, cleaning and milking; the younger ones were merely expected to behave and to play. David, the youngest, who was about a year and a half older than Liesje, was delighted with his new sister, and she loved her 'youngest brother'. David was quite upset when after the war Liesje's mother came to collect her. Liesje herself had mixed feelings about leaving; she described her war experiences as 'being uprooted twice', first by being taken away from her family and then from the den Hamers, whom she truly loved.

As I read the memoirs Liesje sent me, I realized that we had so many experiences in common:

> On Sundays we went to church. Aunt Den Hamer (that's what I called her) inspected us one after another, whether we were clean and properly dressed and wearing shoes. During the week we walked around on wooden shoes. Every child got two peppermints and money for the collection . . . We sat in church in one long row. When you were nudged you could eat the candy. After that came the collection bag and the money for the church had to go into that. A couple of times my youngest brother and I put the candy into the collection bag and kept the money for ourselves. But then we would be a bit scared all week long. Would the dear Lord have seen that? And if so, what would happen to us?

Since confession is supposed to be good for the soul, I admit having engaged in the very same petty larceny. This church embezzlement was enabled by two cultural peculiarities. One was that Dutch peppermints were hard, round tablets more than an inch in diameter and almost a quarter of an inch thick, that would make the same clinking sound as a coin being dropped; and coins were what people used, back when they were worth more than now. And instead of collection plates, common in America, Dutch protestant churches used a double-handled, black velvet bag, at least half a foot deep, that made it impossible to see what exactly your neighbor was dropping into it; you only hear the sound.

> Evenings before going to sleep aunt Den Hamer came to pray with every child separately. Sometimes very softy (so nobody could hear) I would ask if I had a sister with ringlets. Her reply always was: "Sweetie I don't know." And they really knew nothing about me. Only what had been written on my false document. And so I stayed with them for two and a half years until my mother found me in August 1945. I was happy at the Den Hamer family's. They were very good to me. I felt at home. When David got new shoes or something else, I got it too. Until this day I consider them my own brothers and sisters.
>
> A few months before the liberation the Den Hamer family home was requisitioned by the Krauts. The family was forced to go live in two rooms. One day I was walking outside when one of the Krauts picked me up and held me in his arms and put me back down. Aunt Den Hamer saw that and told her husband that evening. They thought it was too dangerous for me, but also for them personally.

"A few months before the liberation" (of that part of the Netherlands) was an overstatement; at most, two or three weeks may have passed before the arrival of the Polish and Canadian troops. And the incident with the German soldier may have been perfectly innocent, as had been my own encounter with the German in our kitchen. But the Den Hamers didn't want to take the risk, and decided to send Liesje and four of their own children to stay with relatives in a hamlet not far out of town, until the German menace was gone.

> I was part of the Den Hamer family. During the war Mr. and Mrs. Den Hamer celebrated their 25th anniversary. They placed an ad in the paper with all the names of their children and my name was there too. It caused a cousin of Mrs. Den Hamer to send a letter congratulating her on the birth of her tenth child.

After the local liberation, on September 20, 1944, the allies still faced the task of clearing the rest of the southern bank, and all of the northern bank, of the Schelde estuary. Without that, their recent conquest of the Antwerp harbor was useless. What became known as the 'Battle of the

October 13, 1944: A column of amphibious vehicles known as Alligators (on the right) passing others called Terrapins near Terneuzen. Crewed by Canadian troops, they are preparing to cross the Schelde to clear German troops still dug in on the northern bank.

Schelde' or Scheldt became a bloody, muddy hell, because both sides used the fact that much of the land was below sea level to flood it, in order to frustrate their opponents' mobility. During several raids in October 1944 British bombers breached the dikes of the still-occupied island of Walcheren, furthest to the west. Gradually the entire island was flooded, albeit not to any great depth, and the tactic was fairly successful because the Germans retreated to the few spots remaining above water. Next, amphibious allied forces landed on November 1, and the Germans surrendered a week later. Mrs. den Hamer's parents

lived on Walcheren; she herself once showed me a centuries-old cabinet that had come from their house. The bottom three or four feet of that beautiful wood had turned a dull grey from standing in salt water for over a year. Liesje recalls:

> Everything was covered with water. Mrs. den Hamer's parents . . . came to live with us. Grandfather still wore the traditional costume. Grandmother was paralyzed. In the evening she was washed, dressed and put into a chair, and the boys brought her to the living room so we could all be together. I remember there always was a very long table in the dining room with a lot of people coming to eat. We the family, laborers and other visitors. Also there was an elderly aunt who taught me to knit with matchsticks.
>   There were a lot of bombings, and when we heard the sound of the airplanes, we ran towards the cellar. They said that I was always one of the first in the cellar.

Using the false papers that the Underground had supplied, Liesje had been registered for first grade, at the same old, war-damaged Christian

school I would attend a few years later, shortly before it was razed. To get there we walked about a kilometer north along Axelsestraat, crossed a bridge called the Axelsebrug, and turned left a block or so to the school. 'Brug' means bridge, 'straat' means street, and the Axelsestraat was called that because it ran about 10 kilomerters south to the town of Axel. Back to Liesje's story:

> We lived on one side of the bridge and the school – I attended first grade – was on the other side of the bridge. When you were late for school you always had a good story: the bridge was open. It happened one time that I was alone at the table for lunch. Aunt Den Hamer asked me where the other children were, to which I answered: "They are waiting 'cause the bridge is open." Then she asked me how I had come home. O, I answered, I ran and climbed across the locks, which of course was deadly dangerous. That was a very narrow little bridge with ropes and pipes. Aunt became very angry. And it was the only time I got a spanking (which I deserved) because I had made a big mistake.

In the picture above, left is south and right is north, and the school, not visible, was a block or so to the west of the opened part of the bridge. But the little bridge she crossed, from which the picture was likely taken, was not 'deadly dangerous'. It felt rickety, and it was scary for a child because it ran above a set of lock gates for the barge basin that were usually discharging a strong gusher of water in one direction or the other, right below your feet. But there was no danger as long as you didn't climb over the railing, and my parents never told me not to use it. My interpretation is that Mrs. den Hamer, as a mother of many children, was simply more safety-conscious than average, and "Liesje" was an enterprising, spunky little girl.

Instead of walking across the opened Axelsebrug, Liesje would have walked east a few hundred yards to cross the rickety little bridge, on the left, that ran above one set of lock gates of the Oostkolk, the eastern barge basin.

Terneuzen was liberated by Polish troops, of the First Polish Armored Division, on September 20, 1944, but most of the rest of the country had to wait until May 5 the following year, 1945.

But before that happened a lot of water had to pass under the bridge, and the first cargo ship with allied war materiel didn't arrive in the port of Antwerp until November 28. After Canadian forces had cleared both sides of the estuary, which took until November 8, British minesweepers still had to get rid of the mines that the Germans had sown; the German navy even employed one-man mini-subs to sow more and to launch torpedoes at vessels trying to navigate the ship channel. Most of those mini-subs became coffins for the intrepid sailors inside, but one of the British minesweepers hit a mine, which killed most of its crew. The picture below shows Liesje at the Terneuzen cemetery, placing flowers on the crewmen's graves. She is accompanied by a number of local farm folk including Tannie, one of the Den Hamer daughters, all in traditional local farm dress, which was still common then even though the Den Hamers had abandoned it. The picture was used for war propaganda publications.

After the Netherlands' national liberation on May 5, 1945, which is still a big holiday, surviving Jewish parents tried to find their *onderduiker* children, which was no easy task, even with the help of the Red Cross. In accord with the Underground's secrecy rules the Den Hamers never knew Liesje's real name, and the only truthful information on her identity card was her birthday. But in the end that prompted an inquiry from her mother, who had survived along with Liesje's sister. Her father had been murdered in Auschwitz in November 1942, and 90% of her family had suffered the same fate. Her inquiry caused the Den Hamers to have a picture made of Liesje, which led her mother to travel to Terneuzen, in August.

Their return to Amsterdam was no glorious homecoming. Many returning *onderduikers* found that neighbors had stolen their furniture, and the government offered no resettlement help except that they could engage a bailiff to retrieve their property.

> When I came back to Amsterdam after the war, my mother sent me to a Christian school close to home. The Jewish school was too far away. I was in fourth grade when I told my mother that the history teacher had said that it was the Jews' fault that the Second World War had started. In the middle of that school year I was transferred to the Jewish school. When I stood before my new classroom I saw that there was a place available next to a girl in a dark dress. She drew a line across the school bench so we would not touch each other. For three days we looked at each other without saying a word. Then suddenly she said: "You're not Betsy Walvis but Liesje Huistink." To which I said: "You're not Ruth Salamon but Elsje Verschieren." Then it turned out that we had been *onderduikers* in the same village and had been together in the same classroom for some time.

In the early 1950s Liesje, her mother and her sister Sophia emigrated to Israel, where at first they lived in a *Moshav*, a cooperative farm, in rather primitive conditions. When they arrived, Jews with non-Hebrew names were required to change them. Given a choice of Batya, Bat-sheva or Elisheva, she chose the latter. School was an immersion experience, where for about three months she understood nothing until she had absorbed enough modern Hebrew, also called *Ivrit*. And gradually things improved. Liesje/Elisheva married Haim Polak, a Romanian Jew, in 1957. They had two daughters, but Haim died quite young, in 1968. Two years earlier the Den Hamer children had funded a reunion trip for Elisheva on the occasion of Mrs. den Hamer's' 70th birthday. And in 1978 Jacobus and Adriana den Hamer were honored at the Yad Vashem grove, as 'righteous gentiles'. Tannie, the Den Hamers' fourth-eldest daughter and her husband, plus Elisheva and her aunt Saar planted the tree.

The photo that was sent to Liesje's mother.

Reunited; Liesje/Elisheva and Mrs. den Hamer on her 70th birthday, October 29, 1966.

When I contacted Elisheva in Israel, she sent me a copy of a book about her experiences that she had published in 2010, and I sent her a copy of "Everybody's War". After losing a few tears while reading her story, I offered to translate her book into English, a proposal she received with enthusiasm:

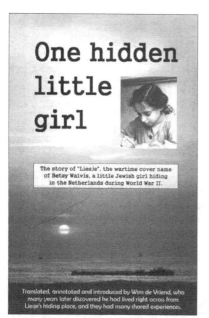

One hidden little girl

The story of "Liesje", the wartime cover name of Betsy Walvis, a little Jewish girl hiding in the Netherlands during World War II.

Translated, annotated and introduced by Wim de Vriend, who many years later discovered he had lived right across from Liesje's hiding place, and they had many shared experiences.

My granddaughter of 26 who lives in Australia is here on vacation, and says how nice if it were in English, so her boyfriend Dan will be able to read it too. This contact with you has to be a miracle.

She also wrote that she did not want me to change anything in her book, nor add anything, a request I fulfilled except for including an introduction and some explanations of unfamiliar concepts in Dutch and Israeli society. And I readily agreed to her condition not to sell copies of my translation. As a document of less than fifty pages it would not cost much to print, anyway. So I sent her a stack of the booklets and gave away the rest.

I never asked my friend Jakob Jakobs how he had made it through the war; he was my age, so he must have been in hiding too. In college he seemed like a happy-go-lucky, cheerful guy. But one time after college in the 1960s, when he wandered into my attic room in Amsterdam, he was positively gloating. Unlike me, Jakob was a natural athlete, a fast boxer and a clever soccer player. Rubbing his hands, he told me that he had just come off a train where he had found a German, sitting alone in a compartment. And he had beaten him to a pulp. Not because he knew him, but because he was German, and thanks to the Germans Jakob had lost his entire family. The Dutch trains, he had discovered, were good German-hunting territory. What fun.

I did not criticize him for it; frankly, I didn't know what to say because I had not walked in his shoes. I suppose I could have asked how he knew that this particular German had contributed anything to making Jacob an orphan. He might even have helped Jews. At the time Jakob was getting his kicks in train compartments, the Israelis were honoring such 'righteous' Germans, and at present the record at Yad Vashem counts some 600 of them. In 2008 a museum on the subject opened in Berlin, a city in which (as cited by Yad Vashem) 5,000 to 7,000 Jews became *U-Boote* (submarines), a variation on the Dutch *onderduiker* moniker. Only a quarter survived; the rest were either discovered or killed in the massive allied bombings of Berlin.

Did the majority of Germans help Jews? No, but neither did a majority of the population in the occupied countries. It's human to crave safety, so wherever you go, only a minority of the people will swim against the current, provided they have the chance, the principles and the courage. The Den Hamers, besides being economically advantaged, were serious conservative Protestants. They would have remembered God's promise to Abraham's descendants in Genesis 12:3: "I will bless them that bless thee, and curse him hat curseth thee; and in thee shall all the families of the earth be blessed." Anyway, beating up Germans seemed to be therapy for Jakob. And he didn't seem to doubt the justice of his violent hobby.

In recent decades a Dutch-Jewish researcher, Dr. Bloeme Evers-Emden, has found that of the Jewish children who survived the war in hiding, many emerged emotionally deficient. Her research confirms something most of us might have guessed: you can't tear a small child away from its family and plunk it into a strange home or, worse, a series of strange homes, without causing emotional harm. Even if, after the war, such children were reunited with their natural parents – and Jakob had not been so lucky – many had learned to 'turn off their feelings' in their new environment. While hidden in those strange wartime homes they had to behave, and by and large they did; but afterward, whether or not they were able to re-join their families, they had no switch to turn those feelings of unconditional trust back on. This led to what Dr. Evers-Emden describes as an 'emotional deficiency', a lack of human empathy that inhibits healthy relationships and may even transfer to the next generation. As adults, many formerly hidden children recognized that they were cold, emotionally unresponsive people who had trouble loving anyone. Besides their parents (if they had survived) this often included their own children. As a trenchant example Dr. Evers-Emden cited the case of one Jewish man, born in 1936, who during the worst of the Jewish persecution had been hidden at nine different addresses in the Netherlands. Now living in Haifa, he had five daughters, the eldest twenty-nine – and none was married, which is unusual for an Orthodox family. When Dr. Evers-Emden explained her findings that survivors like him seemed to lack the capacity to love, he seemed both relieved and sad. "I must have transferred it to my daughters," he decided.

When I attended a reunion of my Dutch college class in the 'nineties, I heard that Jakob Jakobs had not stayed in Holland but had moved to Israel also. And not long after that he got cancer and he died there, at quite a young age.

Dunking people in a pond or in the nearby river was an important part of my college experience. Jakob Jakobs is the boy on the right; I'm on the left.

The Song of the Eighteen Dead by Jan Campert (1902 - 1943)

During World War II, Dutch journalist, writer and poet Jan Campert wrote 'The eighteen dead' to honor 15 Dutch resistance fighters and 3 communists, executed by the German occupiers. During the war Campert helped about 20 Dutch Jews escape to Belgium. While crossing the Dutch/Belgian border on July 21, 1942, he was arrested with a companion and a 21-year old Dutch Jew. The Jew committed suicide that same day; Campert died on January 12, 1943 in the notorious Neuengamme concentration camp in northern Germany, of pleurisy.

Het lied der achttien dooden

Een cel is maar twee meter lang
en nauw twee meter breed,
wel kleiner nog is het stuk grond,
dat ik nu nog niet weet,
maar waar ik naamloos rusten zal,
mijn makkers bovendien,
wij waren achttien in getal,
geen zal den avond zien.

O lieflijkheid van licht en land,
van Holland's vrije kust,
eens door den vijand overmand
had ik geen uur meer rust.
Wat kan een man oprecht en trouw,
nog doen in zulk een tijd?
Hij kust zijn kind, hij kust zijn vrouw
en strijdt den ijdlen strijd.

Ik wist de taak die ik begon,
een taak van moeiten zwaar,
maar't hart dat het niet laten kon
schuwt nimmer het gevaar;
het weet hoe eenmaal in dit land
de vrijheid werd geeerd,
voordat een vloekb're schennershand
het anders heeft begeerd.

Voordat die eeden breekt en bralt
het miss'lijk stuk bestond
en Holland's landen binnenvalt
en brandschat zijnen grond;
voordat die aanspraak maakt op eer
en zulk Germaansch gerief
ons volk dwong onder zijn beheer
en plunderde als een dief.

The song of the eighteen dead

A cell is just two meters long,
two meters square all told –
and smaller yet the spot of ground
that soon enough will hold
what's left of me, and left of them;
we will be eighteen friends
buried together, without names,
before tomorrow ends.

O loveliness of light and land,
of Holland's coast so free;
I could not bear the gruff commands
of our foul enemy.
In times like this, what's left to do
for men whose hearts are real?
They kiss their wife and child, they fight,
and soon their fate is sealed.

When I joined up I knew full well
my life would be in doubt;
but 't was my heart that said I should
defend what made me proud;
it knew that freedom had a place
of honor in this land,
before 't was trampled and defiled
by a brutal, bloody band.

A band that broke their solemn oath
of friendship and of peace,
invaded Holland's fertile space,
like locusts from the east.
They brag of honor and of race,
that robbing, raucous rabble;
our streets resound with stomping boots,
our air with Nazi-babble.

De rattenvanger van Berlijn
pijpt nu zijn melodie, -
zoo waar als ik straks dood zal zijn,
de liefste niet meer zie
en niet meer breken zal het brood
en slapen mag met haar -
verwerp al wat hij biedt of bood
die sluwe vogelaar.

Gedenkt die deze woorden leest
mijn makkers in den nood
en die hen nastaan 't allermeest
in hunnen rampspoed groot,
gelijk ook wij hebben gedacht
aan eigen land en volk -
er daagt een dag na elken nacht,
voorbij trekt ied're wolk.

Ik zie hoe't eerste morgenlicht
door 't hooge venster draalt.
Mijn God, maak mij het sterven licht,
en zoo ik heb gefaald
gelijk een elk wel falen kan,
schenk mij dan Uw gena,
opdat ik heenga als een man
als 'k voor de loopen sta.

The sly pied piper of Berlin
still plays his melody;
as sure as I will soon be dead,
my love no more to see,
no more to share my bread with her,
no more to share her bed -
reject whate'er he offers you,
and do not be misled.

Remember, all who read these
words,
my comrades soon to die,
and help their loved ones, even as
their troubles multiply,
since we too staked our very lives,
for freedom we were pining –
darkness always precedes the light,
clouds may have silver linings.

I see the early morning light
touch on the windowpane.
My God, make this an easy death,
and if I die in vain,
we are all failures; please bestow
your pardon and your grace,
so when the rifles are lined up,
a man is whom they face.

The month following Jan Campert's death his poem was printed in underground resistance newspapers, and reprints (like the one shown on page 39, with the illustration) were sold to raise money for Dutch families who were hiding Jewish children.

A PACKAGE FROM AMERICA!

In January of 1992 a letter was delivered in Coos Bay that had been
mailed 42 years before. Its three yellowed pages had been written in
1950, in what was then the French sector of occupied Berlin. The letter
and a picture of the writer, torn from a photo album, arrived inside an
envelope made from an old German map. That envelope was nearly
falling apart, due to the deterioration of the glue during decades in limbo
– wherever limbo was. The postmaster said it could not have been on
American soil. Some people speculated that with the complicated
political situation in Germany of that time, the letter may have been
stuck in some cubbyhole, only to be found and forwarded after East
Germany was re-united with West Germany, in the fall of 1990. But
we'll never know. Much more important were the contents of the letter,
which was a thank-you for a CARE parcel received by the young
woman in the picture, whose name was Frieda Kunkel.

Back in 1950 post-war Germany's *Wirtschaftswunder* – its economic
miracle – had barely started to bear fruit, and poverty was still severe;
for one piece of evidence, check Frieda Kunkel's clothes, which
obviously represented her Sunday best. But more important than the
shortage of textiles was the continuing shortage of food; many people
were still on the edge of starvation. An organization called CARE

(Cooperative for American Remittances to Europe) had started emergency food deliveries to Europe and to occupied Germany, at first with unused military food kits prepared for the American invasion of Japan that never happened, thanks to the nuclear bomb program. This campaign continued for many years. For ten dollars, individual Americans could have a CARE food parcel made up and delivered, and many such food drives were organized by churches. In the end a CARE package became a household word, like aspirin. And from then to this day, parcels sent by American parents to their college-attending children are called 'Care packages'.

Frieda Kunkel

Frieda Kunkel's CARE package had been sent by the Christian Science Church of Coos Bay, the then clerk of which was Gladys Lyon, but the mailing had been handled by the Church's headquarters in Boston. No doubt it was more economical to send a load of standard parcels from the East Coast than from churches spread all over the country. CARE parcels contained what we'd consider run-of-the-mill staples: rice, beans, coffee, tea, flour, sugar, lard, various canned meats and canned fish, and chocolate. And after so many years, Gladys Lyon didn't even recall her involvement.

When she wrote her letter, Frieda Kunkel's circumstances were much closer to poverty than what passed for that condition in America. In his 1949 book "Behind the Curtain" journalist John Gunther described Berlin's atmosphere in 1948/49, the time of the airlift:

"Berlin has about as much vitality as a mass of putty. The very grass has grown over the streetcar tracks on Kurfürstendamm. People walk slowly, with hunched and sagging shoulders; an almost suffocating dreariness hangs over the community; the food shops are scraped bare; except for the pulsating throw of air lift planes overhead, the city is almost soundless."

But Frieda Kunkel's spirit was not filled with "suffocating dreariness". To preserve the flavor of her letter in my translation below, I stuck closely to the flowery formal ways of the German of those days, which were in fact quite similar to Dutch customs back then:

Berlin, February 1, 1950

Esteemed, kindhearted Mrs. Gladys E. Lyon!

On Thursday, January 26, with great joy and gratitude, we received your dear parcel. We only received your dear letter today, but I have to write you immediately how happy you made us. To truly understand how much love you brought us, I would like to tell you briefly our life history so that you, our goodhearted benefactor, can imagine how much joy we experienced thanks to you, and what it meant to us to receive such a loving present. I am the daughter of a poor working man's family, out of 13 children I was the only girl. Eight of the children died when they were small. My father was a drinker, he died in 1920. My dear mother was left alone, her entire life was trouble, work, worry, suffering and want. I myself was ill for many years due to malnourishment and became an invalid, and so Mother and I have had to run our household with very little money. We never experienced so much goodness as we received through your love, we can pamper ourselves, o how wonderful it is! . . .

If the cruel war had not come, with all of its horrors and suffering, we might have started having a better life, but the suffering was not over, two dear brothers I lost through death in this war, another brother with a family lost his entire home, only ruins were left. Our road in this life was hard and sad. But now we have our church back, she is our only joy, God our only

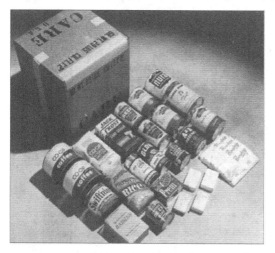

comfort and help! . . . Right now there is a lot of unemployment here, but I have found a small cleaning job.[1])

Our dear, goodhearted benefactor!

What the mouth cannot say, what only the heart experiences, we felt your presence - God the father alone can give you what you gave us – LOVE, the love that is so comforting and merciful!

When it was announced in church that we could expect a parcel from America! There was a shout for joy, and sleepless nights of gladness, what beautiful things might be in it, and all for us? O, too wonderful! Receiving parcels is not just rare in our lives, but it has never happened. The first parcel! And from America! We were completely beside ourselves and could hardly eat anything from excitement, when the day to receive it finally came . . . an entire parcel. Mother and I stood before our table rich with presents, quietly flowed tears of joy, melancholy and gratitude. My thoughts went into the wide, far world, where the generous hand was that made it all ready for us. O, if only we could embrace you and press your dear hands, *Thank You, Thank You so very kindly!!!...*

For those who know German, and to give wider circulation to this historic piece, I reproduce it in full on the next pages.

Received from CARE, the following:

_____ 4 packages

Miss. Frieda Kunkel. _____ Name

① *Prinzenallee 81. Berlin N. 20. Franz Sektor* Address

Germany,   am 26. Januar 1950. Date

WA-32

---

[1]) "*Aufwartestelle*", the word she used, could mean cleaning in an apartment house in lieu of rent, but also a job waiting tables. The former seems more likely.

Berlin, den 1. 2. 50.

Hochverehrte Herzensgute Mrs. Gladys E. Lyon!

Ihr liebes Paket haben wir am Donnerstag den 26.1. mit sehr sehr großer Freude dankend erhalten, Ihren lieben Brief erhielten wir erst heute, aber ich muß Ihnen sofort schreiben, wie glücklich Sie uns gemacht haben. Um wahrhaft verstanden zu werden wie große Liebe Sie uns getan haben, möchte ich Ihnen kurz unsere Lebensgeschichte erzählen, damit Sie Gütige Spenderin sich ein Bild vor Augen führen, wieviel Freude wir durch Ihre gütige Hand erleben durften, und was es für uns bedeutete so liebreich beschenkt zu werden. Ich bin die Tochter einer armen Arbeiterfamilie, von 13 Kindern war ich das einzige Mädel. Acht Geschwister starben klein. Mein Vater war Trinker, er starb 1920. Meine gute Mutter blieb allein, ihr ganzes Leben war Mühe, Arbeit, Kummer, Leid und Entbehrung gewesen. Ich selbst war viele Jahre durch Unterernährung schwer erkrankt und Invalidin geworden, und so haben Mutter und ich mit sehr wenig Geld haushalten müssen, soviel Gutes wie wir nun durch Ihre Liebe empfangen haben, haben wir noch nie erlebt, wir dürfen uns nun auch mal pflegen, ach wie wundervoll ist es!!! Nach vielen Trübsalen, die man als Christlicher Wissenschafter ja nun nicht mehr i. Erinnerung rufen möchte, fanden wir Christian Science, seit 1929 sind wir treue Anhänger der vierten Kirche in Berlin.

Wenn nicht der grausame Krieg gekommen wäre, mit all seinen Schrecknissen und Leiden, so hätten wir nun anfangen dürfen endlich unser Leben glücklicher zu gestalten, aber das Leid war noch nicht aus, zwei liebe Brüder verl... in diesem Krieg durch den Tod, ein ander... mit Familie verlor sein ganzes ..., es blieben nur Trümmer. Unser bisheriger Lebensweg war hart und traurig. Jetzt aber haben wir unsere Kirch wieder, sie ist unsere einzige Freude, Gott unser einzigster Tröster und Helfer! Ich habe durch Christian Science meine Gesundheit bis auf kleine Schwächen ... erlangt, mein liebes altes Mütterchen sie ist jetzt 7.. Jahre, hat ebenfals viele große Krankheitsprobleme gelöst. Gottlob ich bin wieder arbeitsfähig geschrieben. ... herrscht hier große Arbeitslosigkeit, doch ich habe eine kleine Aufwartestelle gefunden. Immer mutig im Kampf gegen den Irrtum; denn wir wissen ja nun, es gibt kein Leid, das Liebe nicht heilt!

Unsere geliebte herzensgute Spenderin! Was der Mund nicht aussprechen kann, was nur das Herz empfindet, wir fühlten Ihre Nähe - Gott der Vater allein kann Ihnen geben, was Sie uns gegeben - <u>Liebe</u>, die sowohltuende barmherzige Liebe!
Als uns in der Kirche gesagt wurde, Sie können ein Paket aus Amerika erwarten! Da gab es ein Jubelruf, und schlaflose Nächte der Freude, was wohl alles für schöne Dinge dortdrinn sein mögen, und alles für uns? Ach zu herrlich! Pakete zu bekommen ist in unserm Leben nicht nur etwas seltenes, sondern noch nie dagewesenes. Das erste Paket! Und aus Amerika! Wir kamen ganz aus der Fassung, und

konnten vor Aufregung so gut wie nichts essen, als
der Tag zur Abholung endlich da war. Ich habe in der
Kirche schon zweimal einige _____ Galen an Lebens-
mittel erhalten, auch bekam ich schon ein paar
Kleidungsstücke; aber nun sollten wir ein ganzes
Paket auspacken, Mutter und ich standen vor unserm
reichen Gabentisch, still, flossen Tränen vor Freude,
Wehmut und Dankbarkeit. Meine Gedanken gingen
in die weite ferne Welt, wo jene gütige Hand uns
dies alles bereitete. Ach könnten wir Sie umarmen,
und die lieben Hände drücken, haben Sie Dank,
soviel innigen Dank!!! Gedanken durchdringen
eiserne Mauern, sie gehen über Land und Meer.
    Geliebte Wissenschafterin mögen Sie die Wärme
unserer Gedanken empfunden haben, und Seien
Sie aufs herzlichste gegrüßt, grüßen Sie auch unsere
                Mutterkirche!

                In Liebe und Dankbarkeit
                Ihrer gedenkend
                        Ihre
                Frieda Kunkel und Mutter.

Hoffentlich können Sie Liebe Miss Gladys,
meinen Brief lesen, ich kann leider kein Wort englisch.

Anbei ein kleines Bildchen von mir, es war im Album
eingeklebt, daher ist es so unsauber, und läßt
sich nicht gut beschreiben.

THE WIENER SCHNITZEL

"So, what part of Germany are you from?" asks the man paying at the cash register. He and his wife have just finished a Rouladen with Spätzle and a Wiener Schnitzel, and are feeling quite content.

"Actually, I'm not German. We just put on a good show."

Usually I leave it at that, but he looks puzzled. And although I don't speak with much of an accent, he may have an ear for accents. So I finally reveal: "Actually, I'm from the Netherlands."

"Isn't that kind of odd, a Dutchman serving German food?" Evidently he thinks that after all these years, a Dutchman would rather spit on German food than serve it.

"Well, time heals all wounds," I explain soothingly. "For example, just a couple of blocks down this road, there's Koreans serving sushi."

"Huh. I had not thought of that." Well, we will always have people living in a time warp. I've heard Americans predict that the German nation will forever be militaristic, and that only Germans can be Nazis. Ha. If the Nazis – God forbid – ever take over, some Americans I know will be the first to join them. Besides, every German with whom I talk politics these days sounds like a militant pacifist. And according to media reports, today's German army is a very far cry from the *Wehrmacht*, let alone the *Waffen-SS*, since it seems to be oversupplied with overweight soldiers who are much better at consuming beer and sausages than at doing push-ups. Even the Germans' élite troops seem to have no great taste for shooting people, according to a 2008 report on the departure of a company of German commandos from Afghanistan. During their three-year stay, these high-end warriors had never even left their base camp for action in the field. In 2009 General Schneiderhahn, the *Bundeswehr's* inspector-general, was telling politicians in Berlin that the successors to Germany's mighty military machines of the past needed "a better feeling for discipline and . . . a greater readiness to serve the state." Among the many things exasperating the general were complaints about sleeping bags. "Are our soldiers too soft?" wondered the popular German newspaper *Bild*.

Yet if we look back a few centuries, we see that such drastic changes have happened before, and the German reputation for militarism is of fairly recent origin. Back in the Middle Ages the English were the most feared warriors on the continent, followed in the 15th and 16th centuries by the Spanish. In time the Spanish war machine lost its reputation for ferocity, not to the Germans but to the French. From Louis XIV through Napoleon, French armies invaded and ravaged various parts of present-day Germany no less than eleven times. It was not until the Franco-German war of 1870-71 – which Napoleon III started – that the Prussians' decisive victory over France solidified German military renown. Even so, not all Germans were enamored of that kind of progress, which was one reason millions came to America. Some of my wife's Prussian ancestors jumped ship in San Francisco because they wanted no part of Bismarck's army.

Earlier on, in 1741, a group of Mennonite emigrants from the Rhineland had arrived in Philadelphia. Like the Amish who still farm west of that city, they were fervent pacifists. One of the group, Hans Nicholas Eisenhauer of Elterbach, bought a 168-acre farm near Harrisburg, Pennsylvania, on January 20, 1753. Exactly 200 years later Hans Eisenhauer's great-great-great-grandson Dwight D. Eisenhower, the famous World War II general, would be inaugurated President of the United States. Despite Eisenhower's military fame, most of his ancestors had lived their lives as pacifists. His mother even belonged to the Jehovah's witnesses, a denomination that still refuses to bear arms. During the Nazi era, thousands of German Jehovah's witnesses were killed or hauled off to perish in concentration camps because they refused to renounce their religion and join Hitler's armed forces.

It's true that by the time of Hans Eisenhauer's arrival in America, Germans and German-speaking Swiss had gained some military notoriety. But much of that was militarism by necessity. Many German-speaking lands were extremely poor, so they exported mercenaries to fight other people's wars. The 18th-century principality of Hesse (north of Frankfurt-on-the-Main), for instance, is described by the historian Frederik Ohles as 'a land of indigence in good years, hunger in bad.' Things were so bad for 18th century Hessians that slavery and soldiering were equivalent options. One Hessian ruler, Count Friedrich II, sold several thousands of his subjects to the British, who sent them to America to fight the revolutionary colonists. And they lost.

"When the military man approaches," George Bernard Shaw observed, "the world locks up its [silver] spoons and packs off its womankind." It was his way of observing that when masses of soldiers of any nationality are on the march, bad things will happen. It has not been publicized much, but a substantial number of murders and rapes were committed by members of the American armies liberating Europe. In addition American soldiers committed astronomical amounts of theft, most of it unpunished. This included pilfering stuff from newly-liberated Europeans who had thrown open their homes to them. And to show that no warring nation has a monopoly on atrocities: shortly after their liberation from the Germans in World War II, the Netherlands sent troops to suppress the independence movement in the Dutch East Indies. Some of those men had barely recovered from their stay in a Japanese camp, or from the Dutch wartime famine. But I know that some of the tactics they employed in Indonesia would have done the SS *Einsatzgruppen* proud.

As far as the WWII German crimes are concerned, especially the Jewish Holocaust – Robert Jackson, the chief prosecutor at the Nuremberg war-crimes trial, said in his opening statement that he did not plan "… to incriminate the whole German people. … If the German populace had willingly accepted the Nazi program, no storm troopers would have been needed … or concentration camps or the Gestapo." Adding absurdity to the proceedings, the henchmen of a dictator as bad as Hitler (or worse) sat in judgment at Nuremberg. They were Russian judges whose leader, Josef Stalin, had eagerly made a deal with Hitler to wipe Poland off the map in 1939, thereby starting World War II. And then there was the matter of the Katyn massacre of tens of thousands of Polish officers, which the Soviets had included in the Nuremberg indictment as a German war crime. There is no doubt that Stalin was the real perpetrator, but the Nuremberg tribunal gingerly stepped around that conclusion.

Even the historian Gitta Sereny, no apologist for the Nazis, acknowledges that "… the German army has traditionally far more often than not respected the law; German soldiers who committed offenses against either property or human life risked dire disciplining and even death." In the part of the Netherlands where my family lived, the victorious invading German soldiers of 1940 did not loot civilian homes. By the time they arrived, those homes had already been looted and vandalized, by poorly-led French and Belgian troops present in our region to 'defend' it. One of the first things the Germans did was to put on a public concert for the town people. But of course, as time went on relations did not remain so positive.

While over 75 percent of the Jews in the Netherlands perished during World War II, only a minority of the Jews in neighboring Belgium did. One major reason was that the German governor for Belgium was a military man, General von Falkenhausen, who responded to pleas from Belgian leaders by ordering Belgian Jews exempt from deportation. In 1944 Von Falkenhausen was recalled to Berlin, to spend the rest of the war in Nazi concentration camps himself. The Netherlands, on the other hand, was run by a fanatical crony of Hitler's, Arthur Seyss-Inquart, a fanatical anti-Semite who was hanged by the allies at Nuremberg, for having wiped out all thoseDutch Jews.

So, to wrap up a story that's growing long, why does a Dutchman serve German food in a small Oregon town? Well, I like German food, as do quite a few Americans, many of whom have a German family background, have served in the U.S. military in Germany, or enjoyed travel there. Moreover, in the food business you need a clear identity, so people have a reason to come to your place. And I didn't want to do Chinese, Mexican or fast food, like everyone else in this town.

But also, growing up in the Netherlands it was hard not to be impressed by our big eastern neighbor who, in addition to periodic fits of dubious behavior, had contributed so much to civilization. Aside from hearty, flavorful food and drink, consider music: German-speaking people are responsible for two thirds of the world's classical repertoire – by Bach and by Handel, Haydn, Mozart, Beethoven, Schubert, Brahms, Wagner, Schumann . . . And if you don't care for classical stuff, check out the immortal repertoire of German *Volkslieder*, on Youtube – wonderfully singable pieces, often written by the greatest of German poets and musicians: *Im wunderschönen Monat Mai – In einem kühlen Grunde – Ännchen von Tharau – Auf Flügeln des Gesanges – Am Brunnen vor dem Tore – Die Lorelei* . . .

In literature, German has a reputation for ponderousness. But a language is a lot like food in the restaurant business; it all depends what you do with it. Take my youthful idol Heinrich Heine, whose wit and brevity made the German language sing:

> *Du bist wie eine Blume,*
> *so hold und schön und rein.*
> *Ich schau dich an, und Wehmut*
> *schleicht mir ins Herz hinein* ...

At the risk of being criticized by the real literati, I translate this as:

> You are so like a flower,
> so sweet, and pure as gold.
> I look at you, and sadness
> gently slips into my soul ...

Rotterdam after the May 1940 German bombing

Heine, that incorrigible wit who described the German nobility as *"Esel die nur von Pferde reden"*: asses who only talk of horses. Who, when the German censors were giving him a hard time, published a work consisting of blackened lines interspersed with the word *Dummköpfe*.

And who, on his deathbed in Paris in 1856, assured the world: *"Dieu me pardonnera; c'est son métier."* God will forgive me; it's His profession.

I realize, of course, that Heinrich Heine was of Jewish descent, as were many prominent German artists, writers, politicians, scientists and businessmen. With his simple-but-o-so-effective use of the language, Heine was part of an already-existing German tradition that included Goethe and other great writers. But the genius of the Jewish people shows in their ability to internalize the best of local cultures in order to contribute to them, wherever they get half a chance. You can make the case that if Hitler had not chased away so many Jewish scientists – Einstein in particular – he might well have won World War II – he would have had the BOMB! Still, even without the Jewish contribution, the achievements of German science and industry command respect. Towards the end of the war they were producing submarines, airplanes, tanks and rockets that were far superior to anything the Americans had; they just couldn't make enough of them. (Plus, they ran out of gas.)

And finally, an important attraction for me are Germany's ancient towns; I love traveling there. I like traveling in France too, but too much of that country looks like it never gets a coat of paint. Not true of Germany, which has always been, and still is, an immaculately kept, well-organized place.

I admit that in the days of my youth, after listening to my family's World War II stories, I was uneasy about traveling in Germany. In this respect, some Germans were their own worst enemies or, in today's parlance, they lacked "sensitivity". For instance, when a Dutchman visiting post-war Germany struck up a conversation with a German, it usually went like this:

German: "*Ach*, you are from Holland! That's a nice country. I've been there."

And then came the punch-line: "*Im Kriege.*" – "during the war." Yeah, thanks for dropping in, pal.

Along this line, during the 'fifties a story made the rounds about a German who came to the airfield near Rotterdam, to rent a small plane. He explained that he wanted to re-experience May 14 of 1940 when he flew one of the bombers that destroyed the city center. The owner of the plane decked him.

Another behavior that has cost the Germans is their noisy way of conducting business. Not many years after the war my parents took a bus trip into recovering West Germany. One of the passengers had spent time in a concentration camp, and when the bus was boarded by the German customs agents, he completely lost his composure and had to abandon the trip. He couldn't take the border officials' shouting at each other. I'm sure what they shouted was quite innocent; it was the volume and the pitch, not the contents, that brought back his nightmares.

Talking of which, to this day I have never forgotten one shouting experience I had in a German public restroom. As is customary in Europe, such restrooms were arranged very sensibly, with an attendant who punctiliously cleaned the stalls after each use, and who for her trouble (most were elderly women) expected the customer to deposit something in a conspicuously placed dish. I mean money. In recent years the attendants seem to have been replaced by automated, coin-operated systems. If Americans could be persuaded to accept either system – human or coin-operated – we would avoid a lot of repulsive roadside experiences. But I doubt that in the U.S.A. this can ever come about; somebody will sue on behalf of the constitutional rights of restroom vandals and perverts.

Anyway, here I am in the early sixties in Dortmund or Cologne or Frankfurt, I don't remember which, in a restroom stall in a large public facility, bothering nobody, just doing what I need to do, when all of a sudden loud shouting erupts on the other side of my latched door. For an instant I wonder if I have done something wrong, but no: this row is not about me. It's a raucous dispute between attendants, one male, one female:

"Passen Sie auf, diese sind meine Toiletten!" (Watch out, these are my toilets!)

"Nein, die gehören nicht zu Ihnen!" (No, those don't belong to you!)

"Ich bin ja seit lange für diesen Toiletten zuständig, Mensch!" (These toilets have been my department for a long time, woman!)

"Nein, Sie sind gar nicht dafür zuständig ..." (No, those are not your department ...)

Etcetera, at a very high volume. Preferring neutrality, I cleared out before the artillery started up. But it left me wondering if the German soul didn't have some innate craving for territory after all, be it ever so humble. Territory to be gained by making a raucous racket.

Now it so happens that there is a connection between these tales of noisy verbosity and the origin of a common Dutch word that describes a German: *mof* (plural: *moffen*). It's a derogatory term, roughly equivalent to the American word *Kraut*, the origin of which is obvious, or to the French *boche*, which more or less means "blockhead". But *mof* has a much longer history than either of these: the farm called *De Moffenschans* (loosely translated as *The Kraut Fort*), across from our house in northern Flanders, gained its name not from the retreating Germans who briefly camped there in the fall of 1944 but from a thousand German mercenaries stationed at the site in 1583, during the 80-year Dutch war of independence, when they fought on our behalf. So the word *mof* has been in common use for at least four centuries. It seems to be a Dutch version of the German word *Muff*, which is still in use to describe a sullen, sulky person – in one word, a grump. *Mof* is also related to the Middle-Dutch verb *moffelen*, which means being a loudmouth. Curiously, the English word *German* (according to Dutch sources, for which I cannot vouch) was derived from a Celtic verb that meant yelling and shouting, which is *gairm* in old Irish and *garm* in Welsh. In Anglo-Saxon use, *gairm* or *garm* became "German".

So, considering all the loudmouth-connotations insinuated by *German* and *mof*, plus my relatives' World War II experiences – *Licht aus! Ausweis bitte! Mach schnell!* – "Lights out! Papers please! Hurry up!" – my sentiments toward the German people were not wholly favorable. But around the time of my toilet-tale I also ended up in Frankfurt, flat-broke, trying to find the way to my pen-pal girlfriend's home, on *Kiebitzpfad.* Some people I accosted explained where it was, but they recommended taking the streetcar.

"I'll just walk. I don't have the money to spend on a streetcar," I explained.

"*Dann gebe ich Ihnen die zwanzig Pfennig,*" said one gentleman, pulling out his coin purse. "In that case, I'll give you the twenty cents."

And with those few words, he rehabilitated his entire nation.

Nevertheless, even today some people still hold Germans in low esteem because of two terrible wars, for which they got all the blame. The victors write the history books. And politics relies too much on emotions. Given the right combination of popular emotions and populist demagogues, Nazism can pop up anywhere. And it has, especially the kind of native Nazism that accuses anybody it doesn't like of being Hitler.

It's been several years since we had a difference of opinion with a customer who complained about his Wiener Schnitzel. The meat was not right, he claimed, and he didn't want to pay for it. Sometimes people who complain have a case; sometimes they are just whiners. But whiners who have eaten most of their meal don't get it for free, so I insisted he pay half price, or else. I don't always do that, but I was irritated. He left irate.

A bit later the phone rang. The voice on the other side said: "I understand that you make your Wiener Schnitzels from the meat of Jewish babies. Is that true?"

A DRINKING WAR

It's about 3:30 in the afternoon, the beginning of June. There's nobody in the place, but the summer trade should pick up after the middle of the month, if the good Lord's willing and the oceans don't rise. Our president promised he would do something about the oceans but so far he seems to have only applied himself to the economy, and not with great success. A lot of people are hard-up, and it's spreading. Late last night Adam called me in a bit of a panic: "How do I add a five-dollar tip on a one-dollar charge? The machine won't let me do it."

"What's with the one-dollar charge? Didn't that woman have a dollar cash?" I assume it was a woman, because a lot of women act as if we've already transitioned to a cashless society. Turns out I'm right about the woman part, but it's worse:

"She had a fifteen-dollar gift certificate," Adam explains. "And she had a sixteen-dollar dinner. So then she charged the one dollar on her credit card, and added a five-dollar tip."

"Good grief." She's gone so we can't do anything about that. "There's a special code you need to enter for the tip," I explain. It's written on the instructions for the machine. Look behind it."

Rummage, rummage at the other end. After first entering the code wrong, he gets it done. So this morning I explain the facts of life.

"About that one-dollar credit card charge, if at all possible I'd like you to avoid that kind of transaction, Adam. It's hardly worth it."

"It's a dollar," Adam says. He doesn't mention it's five for him.

"Here's how it works. Say, was that a paid-for gift certificate?" We rummage through the tickets, and it was not. It was one of the many free ones we give out to an endless list of local charities.

"For every credit card charge I pay an average of 23 cents. Plus about 2.35% of the total, on top of that. In this case that's 2.35% of six dollars, because it comes off the tip part too ..." – I'm hitting buttons on the calculator – "That's 14 cents on top of the 23. So all told, out of that one dollar I pay 37 cents for the privilege of having some dimwit use her free gift certificate. Count your profits, my dad used to say."

"I've got a better one yet," Adam says. "The other day I have these two people come in. They are like: 'Is it Happy-Hour yet?' And it was about a quarter to four, so I'm like, 'No, it starts at four.' And they go: 'We'll be back.' Sure enough, at four sharp they're back. They order one glass of wine – "

During Happy Hour, 4 to 6 PM, drinks are a dollar off, but the food is what brings 'em in. With that one drink you get your pick of all kinds of appetizers for $2 each, which averages about half the regular price.

"– and then," Adam continues, "they order exactly enough $2 appetizers to use up their free gift certificate. And they're out of here."

No doubt never to be seen again. Adam leaves on his break, but a minute after he walks out, the front door rattles. Is he back? No; it rattles a lot these days; it's the combination of early-summer ocean winds and a worn-out set of doors. We can't do anything about the former, but in a month or so we'll have the doors replaced; in the meantime we keep one of them locked. The doors rattle again, a bit harder. Is somebody coming in? By gum, somebody is. A stocky fellow in his late forties, wearing a brown jacket, no hat, and a graying crew-cut. Crew cuts are not too common these days, and he has a somewhat lost look.

"Hi. One for lunch, sir?"

"I–guess–so." Instead of stepping to one of the booths he moves towards the bar, but slowly. I put a menu in front of him and turn around to get him a glass of water.

"Rum-Coke," he says quickly before I get a chance. OK; why not; he looks all right. O crap, I only have Coke in cans now, because we're getting rid of the soda machine, and regular Coke has run out. But we still have some Diet Coke in the machine. I pour a shot of house rum, top it off with a little Diet from the spigot, and set it before him. He has a ten-dollar bill on the bar. I put down six dollars change.

"Can I get anything else for you?"

First he takes a deep swallow. "Sir," he says next, and I suddenly see that his light blue eyes are very watery: "Can you point me to any bars around here, where a guy can do some real drinking?" Evidently our bar doesn't qualify, but I don't mind.

"Why, yes. Did you try the Witches' Pot?" I point north and west, adding: "It's right around the corner."

"Nah," he says. "Didn't work."

"I thought they'd be open."

"Nah. No good." This is a bit vague. I wonder now if they were closed or he's already been there and they got rid of him. In that case he's getting a second load here. Or a third. We've seen that before, and it's usually bad news. Suddenly, he bellows: "Now, Sir! Do you know of any drinking bars around here?"

"Well, there's the one in the old city hall. It's on Central Avenue, the next street. Are you walking or driving?"

"W–walking." That may be good news for public safety.

"You walk down Central Avenue four blocks, and the old city hall building will be on your left. There's a bar in there."

"Huh. What's the name?"

"I – don't know. It changed hands recently." I omit that after a long stretch of running a disorderly establishment, the previous owner got his license pulled. But before he went out of business, I hear he made a ton of money. You can do that simply by ignoring all the rules of the

Oregon Liquor Control Commission. Don't worry about serving minors, don't worry about serving drunks, don't worry about anything. Serve 'em till they drop, and then serve 'em some more. Even if the OLCC fines you, it can be a winning financial strategy. As if they're all on a mailing list, all the local alcoholics, experienced masters or mere journeymen, show up *en masse*. That's why there's always one bar like that in town; the location changes, but word gets around fast. In the meantime the owner keeps promising he will clean up his act. By the time the police get sick of being called out for disputes and fights and public dispersal of bodily fluids, and the city council votes to close the place down, the public nuisance has filled a Scrooge McDuck warehouse with gold.

"S—Sir," he says precipitously. "I'm an officer!" And, elaborating. "I'm doing a report on bars. For the enlisted men!"

That sounds great, his own private version of the USO. I wonder if we measure up. But it seems he didn't like the sound of the old city hall. Maybe city hall suggests the presence of liquor control officials.

"So, you're making a guide to drinking bars for the men?"

"That's right, you got it. Sir! Is there another drinking bar nearby?"

"Well, yes, there's also the Drunk Duck, down the street." At this his ears perk up. When a bar carries the name The Drunk Duck, it seems to broadcast to the world that it's a serious bar; and this one always has been. Dark and dirty, a hardened drinker's home away from home.

His rum & Coke is almost gone, not quite. He doesn't seem very steady now; funny I didn't notice it before. My best recourse is to get him out of here, although I'm not about to take away his drink, as the OLCC suggests in these cases. He has the build of a hardened drill sergeant.

"The Drunk Duck is six or eight blocks down the street," I explain. "You can't miss it. It's on your right. It's a real drinking bar, has been around forever."

He gets up.

"Sir!" he shouts. I'm going down to inspect that place! And you're all right! Here's your tip!" Leaving the six dollars on the bar, he stumbles toward the entrance and tries to leave through the locked left door. "Something wrong here!" he shouts accusingly. "Why is this locked?"

"It's broken. Here, this one works." I obligingly open the right-hand door for him.

"Hey, Sir!" he bellows. "You're all right! But I need to do some real drinking. In a real drinking bar. For my investigation. For the men!" And he's gone.

In about twenty minutes Adam comes in for his evening shift. I tell him about my serious drinking activist. "The old city hall opens at 5," he says.

"That's all right, I think he went down to the Drunk Duck."

"A good place for him," Adam agrees.

"Yeah, he didn't want to go to the Witches' Pot. I wonder."

"He probably got thrown out of there," Adam says.

Before heading for home I walk around the corner to the Witches' Pot. They are doing a pretty good business. I wonder why my customer didn't think it was a real drinking-bar; it has all the standard requirements. No windows, just a few dim lights, plenty of TVs, video poker, a pool table. Plus a couple of real drinking-bar-tenders, meaning fortyish females with smoky voices and few illusions left about the world. I pull back an empty stool. One of the bartenders hitches up the corners of her mouth into the standard bar smile.

"I just wanted to ask you a quick question."

"OK?"

"About half an hour ago, was there a guy in here with a crew cut, drinking rum & Cokes?"

"O yeah," she says. "O yeah. He wore a leather jacket. Had two rum & Cokes. Then I told him: 'You better leave.' "

"I think I just had him at my place." Elucidating: "I'm from the Blue Heron, around the corner."

"The Blue Heron!" one of the guys to my right says. "That's not much of a drinking-bar."

"The food is good, though," says his mate.

"What did he do?" I ask the barkeep.

"Talked too much, shouted at people, and then he bit them."

"Bit them?"

"Yeah, he bit the guy sitting next to you."

I look to the left; the bitten guy seems to be trying to stay out of it.

"Where did he bite him?"

"On his arm," the barkeep says.

"I'd let him bite me on the ass," the guy to the right of me offers helpfully.

"Well, I supposed it was a clean bite. Disinfected by alcohol," I speculate. "All right, thanks. I know enough now."

YANKEE BEETLES GO TO WAR

On a sunny day in 1948 or 1949, my entire first or second grade class – I'm not sure which – was marched off to the sea dike along the Schelde estuary, with a patriotic, lethal mission: to search and destroy *Coloradokevers* (Colorado beetles) by drowning them in jars of oil. I believe our teachers were in charge of the oily part, while we had

That's me in the front row, on the right. This must have been in first or second grade, maybe at a birthday party. Despite the poor quality of the picture you can still see war damage to the building.

to collect the critters. The reason for our mobilization was the threat that a population explosion of this striped bug posed to the nation's potato supply. Just how vital that was I learned from a story my mother told when returning from vacation in Italy, in the 1950s. An Italian peddler was hawking nylon stockings to tourists, but he had no need to know her size: *"Ah, Holländer! Dicke beine! Viel Kartoffeln essen!"* (Ah, Dutch! Fat legs! Eat lots of potatoes!!)

With the Netherlands being a water-rich country, Colorado potato beetles often floated to new chomping grounds, and even in salt water they survived for days. So we were under orders to grab any that had floated ashore, before they invaded the potato fields behind the dike. I don't remember if I found any beetles or not; I seem to recall it was a rather disorganized expedition, but we didn't mind getting out of Miss Rijnberg's classroom for the day.

Coloradokevers were a serious concern all over Western Europe back then. Their presence was blamed on American World War II food transports, even though isolated European infestations had been found as early as the 1870s. In 1947 the Dutch government's agricultural service launched a big anti-*kever* campaign which included, besides the mobilization of school kids, tons of American DDT and propaganda films with orators that sounded just like the Nazi bosses we had recently gotten rid of, calling for 'total war' and 'complete mobilization' while threatening draconian punishments for conscientious objectors to their War On Beetles. The only thing missing seemed to be the threat of the concentration camp. And at our tender age we'd been made the storm-troopers of the Potato-Beetle Eradication Movement.

Fast-forward about five decades, when after the collapse of East Germany (what the communists called the "German Democratic Republic", or GDR), and its absorption by West Germany, a lively German trade sprang up in *Ostalgie* – objects of nostalgia for the not-so-good-old-days in the East (*Ost* in German).

"FIGHT THE COLORADO BEETLE – he chomps on harvest and foreign exchange." Part of the 1940s Dutch campaign.

Besides pieces of the graffiti-covered, torn-down Berlin wall, people were selling uniforms and medals of the hated former border guards and of the GDR "people's army," along with helmets, field manuals, ammunition, awards, posters, and all other manner of self-glorifying but ultimately futile totalitarian trinkets. The trash and *Kitsch* left by the repressive régime had acquired historical, even sentimental value, perhaps fostered by the knowledge that the creeps were safely gone. The GDR's bosses had been as controlling and as ruthless as the Nazis, and possibly worse.

Among those GDR leftovers being dumped on the internet market, a little booklet caught my eye. It didn't cost a lot, but to me it was priceless. That's because it made a connection between two events stuck in my memory. The first was a bunch of little Dutch kids wandering all over a Dutch dike, not to put their fingers in it but to catch potato beetles. The second event was what was called, with considerable respect, *die Luftbrücke* by the Germans, and *de luchtbrug* by the Dutch: "the air bridge". The Americans called it the *Berlin airlift*, and it was a massive demonstration of air power that defeated Josef Stalin, the Russian dictator. The little booklet was the Russian's way of putting the best possible face on his defeat, by claiming the American cargo planes' real mission was to infest the GDR with Colorado beetles.

First, a little background for the younger generation. Prior to the end of World War II it had been agreed that conquered Germany would be divided into four zones, each one supervised by one of the four major allies. Different parts of what would later become West Germany would be run by the Americans, the British and the French, while the eastern part of the country would be run by the Russians. A few years after the war the Russian zone became the GDR, another mid-European "satellite" of the Soviet empire.

Germany's former capital city, Berlin, was located far inside the GDR. In the cockamamie kind of arrangement that can only work among good friends, the wartime negotiators had divided the city into four occupation zones also. In practice this meant that after the war the eastern section of the former German capital became part of the Soviet-dominated GDR while West Berlin, run by the Americans, British and

Two pieces of GDR propaganda: on the left, a poster celebrating the country's 30th anniversary, in 1979. 10 years later it all fell apart. On the right, another piece of state-worship: *"GDR – My State"*

French, became a conspicuous island of western influence. This, of course, soon became a thorn in the Russians' side, and we have to bear in mind that in those pre-internet, pre-TV days, totalitarian governments considered it not only desirable but feasible to shield their subjects from foreign information. To the Russians, West Berlin was an annoying gap in their control system, and a threat to the viability of their east-German satellite. Every day people from the Russian zone voted with their feet by moving their families to West Berlin, from where they could travel freely to West Germany and build a better future. The construction of the Berlin wall in 1961 would be the final answer to what had by then become a population drain that threatened to empty the GDR of everybody with any skills or enterprise. But that wall was yet to come.

To reach West Berlin, the allies had been promised road and rail access across East German territory, but this had never been put on paper. Soon after the war ended Stalin started a campaign of harassment against Berlin's western zone, hoping to make life in West Berlin so difficult for the allies that they would up and leave the place to them. This campaign included a refusal to ship any food grown in Russian-controlled East Germany to West Berlin, so everything had to be brought in from the west. Then, in June 1948, the Russians blocked both road and rail access from the west. Evidently they believed that

without trucks and trains, the western powers would have to leave, due to the impossibility of supplying the needs of 2 million Berliners.

In the U.S. considerable sentiment rose for a military confrontation, but instead it was decided to call the Russians' bluff and supply Berlin by air. Through three air corridors over East Germany, which had been agreed upon earlier, American and British planes brought in everything the West-Berliners needed. This was no small matter, nor was it economical. For instance, most of the city was heated with coal. By weight, coal is a low-value product that is best shipped by rail or by water, because other means of transportation will multiply its cost. The same can be said of bulk commodities such as flour, potatoes, salt, building materials, and so on. But economy was hardly a consideration; the Western allies felt strongly that to keep the support of the Europeans and to stop Russian expansionism, they could not afford to abandon West Berlin. During almost a year of operations, airlift planes delivered over 2 million tons of food and other supplies, or an average of 6,000 tons a day. Twin-engine C-47 aircraft of those days could only carry 3.5 tons, and soon they were replaced by the four-engine C-54s which could carry 10 tons. But that still meant 600 flights a day. Planes followed each other so closely that pilots who missed their landing in Berlin were forbidden to try again; they had to return to their West-German base and get back in line.

Politically the operation was a complete success; after nearly a year even the Russians could see that too, so they re-opened the highway and the railroad. Their obstreperousness had backfired, not only because the allies had demonstrated their determination and their airlift capacity, but because an increased awareness of Russian aggressiveness had accelerated the reconciliation between the West Germans and their WWII enemies, easing the formation of the West German state and its integration into NATO and other international organizations.

But while all those planes were flying over their territory, it stands to reason that East Germany's rulers wanted to provide an explanation to their people, preferably one that would fortify their own position. The booklet I found was supposed to do that by presenting evidence that the real purpose of the American flights was to infest farms in the Eastern zone with Colorado potato beetles. It all looks very official: vertically along the publication's spine runs the text: *DOKUMENTE ZUM KARTOFFELKÄFER-ABWURF,* meaning "DOCUMENTS ON THE POTATO BEETLE DROPS". The back cover explains how to tell potato beetles (left) from beneficial ladybugs (right). And the picture on the front cover shows the striped potato beetles, artistically enhanced to operate as stars-and-stripes beetles: *HALT* (STOP) to the *Amikäfer* (= "Ami-beetles"; during the war the Germans commonly called American troops *Amis*).

On behalf of East German farmers and peace-loving progressives everywhere, the page shown nearby demands that the U.S. dollar-imperialists behind the potato beetle plot be tried as war criminals, along with the traitor Adenauer (the

Kartoffelkäfer
unter der Lupe

Zeichnung des bekannten sowjetischen Karikaturisten Kukriniksi

sozialen Fortschritt und für den Frieden in ihrem eigenen Land zum Schweigen zu bringen versucht, will mit dem abscheulichen Mittel des Atombomben- und Bakterienkrieges die ganze Welt unter die Herrschaft des Dollarimperialismus zwingen. Seine Beauftragten in der amerikanischen Regierung, seine Söldlinge und Befehlsempfänger, die sich um die Bonner Separatregierung des Landesverräters Adenauer scharen, gehören — und das verlangen die deutschen Bauern und mit ihnen alle Vertreter des Friedens und des Fortschritts auf der ganzen Welt mit Recht — auf die Anklagebank für Kriegsverbrecher.

**Kartoffelkäferabwurf
durch amerikanische Flugzeuge**

recently-elected, first Chancellor of West Germany, who would serve until 1963 and himself had been persecuted by the Nazis). The cartoon, drawn by a Soviet artist, shows sneaky beetles crawling under a magnifying glass: Beetle-in-chief Harry Truman crawls in the middle, and below him Beetle General Lucius Clay, the military governor of the American zone, who has been honored as the "father" of the Airlift.

Maps like the one below sought to prove connections between population explosions of potato beetles on East German farms and alleged overflights by American planes. Regardless of whether the beetle reports were accurate, it's unlikely that the flight observations were, because American and British planes were strictly limited to flying through their designated flight corridors, and even then they were often harassed by Russian flak, Russian searchlights, Russian radio signals, and Russian fighters shooting at random. One Russian fighter that was buzzing a British plane even collided with it, killing all aboard. So it's hardly likely that allied planes would have been allowed to fly in the patterns drawn on these maps without being attacked.

With regard to the Colorado potato beetles themselves, it's true enough that they came from America, but apparently they originated in Mexico. In the 19th century they were observed in the Rocky Mountain area, feeding on a thistle of the nightshade family. When cultivation of

Die Einflugstrecken der amerikanischen Flugzeuge

potatoes, another nightshade plant, spread from South to North America, the beetles switched to eating potato leaves. Though they don't eat the potatoes themselves, those will die and rot if they lose too much foliage. The leaves of other members of the nightshade family (tomatoes, tobacco and eggplant) are also attractive to the beetles.

Potato beetles overwinter in the soil, to surface in spring when the weather warms up. They then feed on emerging potato leaves, and they breed; the hatched larvae also feed on the leaves, and then they burrow into the soil, to emerge as fully-grown beetles ready to breed and chomp on more potato foliage. The entire process, from egg to adult, can occur within three weeks. Because one female can lay 800 eggs, weather can make a huge difference. If conditions are favorable, meaning a mild winter that kills few beetles followed by a long summer, potato beetles can breed three times, which in the USA happens in the Southwest but not in northern Maine where one generation a year is the norm. It figures that in a more variable climate, annual beetle populations may vary enormously. This seems to be the case in Western Europe. For instance, well before the current hoopla about global warming, in the Netherlands the summer of 1947 was the warmest in a record kept since 1700. Such exceptional weather is bound to have boosted the Colorado potato beetle population.

Anyone who objects that no government could be as mendacious as this, and that there must have been something to the potato beetle charges, should check the GDR régime's attitude toward the truth of other matters. In 1986, they decided to celebrate – that's right, *celebrate* - - the 25th anniversary of the Berlin wall, the wicked concrete eyesore and adjacent people-shooting-range that had turned their country into one giant concentration camp. The theme of this celebration was: "1961-1986: TWENTY-FIVE YEARS ANTI-FASCIST PROTECTIVE WALL". Shown below is a commemorative stamp. They had similar celebrations for their other horrors, such as the border guards who shot to kill. Little did the celebrants know that they had only 3 years left; they must have missed the handwriting on their protective wall.

After completing my chapter about the imaginary potato beetle

bombing campaign, I related my findings to my friend and German sausage maker Gary Saks.

"O yes," he said. "During the war the British planes did that to us also."

AL KAMPEN'S WAR

One recent afternoon Pastor Gary, the minister at a local Baptist church, dropped in to bring me some papers. Gary and his wife had been in before, for bratwurst and strudel. Before entering the ministry he had served several years in Germany as a US military man, so we got to talking, and after the usual preliminaries: "What part of Germany are you from?", he told me the story of Al Kampen, a parishioner of his at a church in Waterford, California, where he served about ten years, until 1999.

In World War II, he told me, Al Kampen was a teenager hiding from German forced-labor press-gangs in the Netherlands. During the day he and his fellow-*onderduikers* hung out in an area that was difficult for the occupiers to control, a mish-mash of lakes and swamps in the northern province of Friesland.

One day an American B-24 "Liberator" bomber returning from Germany crash-landed in the swamp where they were hiding. They set out in rowboats to retrieve the crewmen, most of whom had survived, and to help them get started on their way back to England. One of the crew gave Al (whose real Frisian name was Auke) his .45 pistol.

Soon after the war Al/Auke's dad, who like his ancestors had been a Frisian dairy farmer all his life, decided to emigrate to southern California, where he had relatives who would sponsor the family. After arriving in early 1948 the Kampens ran dairies in parts of the Los Angeles area that were still rural then – Gardena, Paramount and Artesia

Klaaske (Clara), Auke (Albert), with birthday cake, and Feitze (Fritz) Kampen

– and prospered a great deal more than they had in Friesland. But son Al suffered a hip injury while serving in Korea, so he could no longer milk cows. He built a small restaurant called Kampen's Kitchen in the orchards near Waterford, south of Modesto in the Central Valley. One day in 1983 a chatty man about his age walked in for pie and coffee. He noticed a map on the wall and Al's accent, asked where he was from, and got to talking about his own experiences as a crashed bomber crewman in Friesland. His name, he said, was Doug Fairbanks. And then they agreed that he was the one who had given Al his .45 pistol.

Intrigued by an interesting World War II story with a feel-good ending, I was eager to dig into the papers Gary had brought. But it was only after I had been digging for some time when I realized the lengths to which historians must go to sort fact from fiction. Al Kampen's assistance to the B-24 crew was not in doubt. He had received two official Certificates of Appreciation, one signed by General Eisenhower on behalf of the United States (nearby), the other by the British general in charge of allied strategic bombing sorties from England. His younger brother John told me the B-24 crash was not the only occasion on which Al and his friends had helped crash-landed airmen. I also found newspaper articles from Friesland that reported the incident. And Gary had brought two undated American newspaper articles about the chance reunion at Kampen's Kitchen, plus the memoirs of Al's father, Feitze Tjeerd Kampen (1898-1985), who went by the name of Fritz in America. Fritz's recollections had been typed by his youngest daughter Clara, who also sent me a copy of the memoirs of her sister Margie, the Kampens' third child after Ted and Albert. Even though at times they contradicted each other,

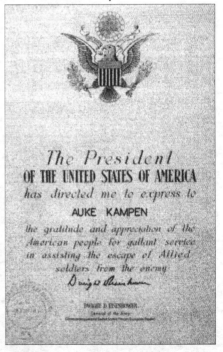

The President
OF THE UNITED STATES OF AMERICA
has directed me to express to
AUKE KAMPEN
the gratitude and appreciation of the American people for gallant service in assisting the escape of Allied soldiers from the enemy

DWIGHT D. EISENHOWER
General of the Army

all confirmed the bomber-story from 1944, and added a lot of life to it. What misstatements the writers made about the history of the time were correctable by means of the public record. But it seemed safe enough to trust those parts that described their own experiences. After all, who would know better?

Kampen's Kitchen (now called Cathy's Coffee Shop) in Waterford; interior view below.

One passage from Feitze Kampen's memoirs may serve as an example. Feitze wrote: "In 1939 World War II started. Soon after Hitler conquered Belgium, the Dutch soldiers came and put search lights in the back of our farm pasture … they also stationed 10 soldiers and a captain to operate the search lights, and we had to house and feed them." Historically, the first part was wrong; Belgium didn't surrender to Hitler until 13 days *after* the Netherlands had already done so, in May 1940. Instead of the conquest of Belgium, Feitze Kampen must have been thinking of Poland, which had fallen to Hitler well before May 10, when he invaded the Netherlands, France and Belgium all at once. Aware that the Netherlands was at risk, the Dutch government had mobilized its military in August of 1939, right before Hitler's invasion of Poland, which lighted the fuse for WWII; and this mobilization would have included anti-aircraft searchlights. So while Feitze's grasp of world history was imperfect, I saw no reason to doubt his word about the searchlights and the Dutch soldiers operating them in his pasture. And this was the way I dealt with most of the personal recollections.

To set the stage for Al Kampen's story, let's first get a feel for the country into which he was born in 1924, and where he grew up. I've always found the old saw that truth is stranger than fiction meaningless because 'strange' is a matter of opinion, and there is some awfully strange fiction out there. But I do believe that reality beats fiction for being surprising as well as interesting, which is why I read very little fiction. And the Kampen family's story is a wonderful piece of reality.

The province of Friesland is a remnant of the once-powerful Frisian nation, which from the 6th through the 8th century controlled the entire North Sea Coast of the present Netherlands along with parts of northern Germany and lower Denmark. Incidentally, parts of the Frisian empire were the source of the Anglo-Saxon migrations that conquered large parts of England during the early Middle Ages.

Back then communications between the originally Frisian part of western Holland, north of Amsterdam, and the present Dutch Province of Friesland, to the northeast, were easier because the Zuiderzee, a shallow, 2000 square mile bay of the North Sea that makes a big hole in the middle of the Netherlands, did not yet exist; it didn't form until violent storms started washing away much of the coast in the 13th century (See map a couple of pages down). As a people, Frisians have long been known for being exceptionally tall, with blue eyes and blond hair, and many of the men have prominent noses. Typical Frisian family names end with, –ga, –ma, or –stra: Huizinga, Dantuma, Terpstra. But in several northern Dutch provinces including Friesland the single most common family name is still *de Vries*, which simply means 'the Frisian'.

The contrast between Waterford's orchards and the Frisians' water-logged land is stark. For centuries they had lived precarious lives on artificial mounds called *terpen,* surrounded by water much of the time, thanks to centuries of rising sea levels and sinking lands during the first millennium AD. In the mid-19th century the location of the Kampens' dairy farm was so water-logged that a geographer's description of a nearby village, Eernewoude, reads: "It is a small and remote place with 55 hectares [135 acres] and over 200 inhabitants, mostly fishermen, skippers and sailors, while in addition good peat land can be found. Since it is only accessible on foot during dry summers, it is obligatory to always come get the preacher with a suitable vessel and to return him, whenever he may have to conduct any services. ... [The little Reformed church is located] on a tidy, clean churchyard, planted with tall trees, which is the only place available to the residents for a stroll." [1]

---

[1] My translation, from A.J. van der Aa, *Het Aardrijkskundig Woordenboek der Nederlanden.* After the crash-landing, the B-24's survivors were first taken to Eernewoude.

Once, setting out in a rowboat across their flooded farm, young Feitze found their sheep standing on a high spot, their heads barely above water. He managed to coax them to higher ground. Finally the never-ending threat of flooding induced several dairymen including his father (Al's grandfather) to form a *waterschap*, a drainage district that funded dikes, locks and pumps to bring down the water table and prevent future floods. They pledged their farms as security for the lenders. All went well until the Great Depression, when diminished dairy revenues could no longer cover the payments to the *waterschap* and for the farm, which Feitze was now buying in installments from his dad. In November 1934 the farm was sold in foreclosure, dispossessing them both. But before that happened Feitze had some adventures in that watery region that ended better. Here are two, in his own words:

"Every week a lady would come to the farms to bring bread and bakery goods. She carried these in two baskets hung from a yoke which was on her shoulders. Often she would put her baskets in a boat and row to the farms. Her name was Willemke van der Werf and she was in her 60's. Once she put her baskets in the boat, untied the boat and was going to step into it; but the row boat moved away from the canal side and she stepped into the water, luckily she held onto the boat. She had on a huge black heavy skirt, which most of the women wore, and the air underneath it kept her afloat. She floated upright across the canal and down a ways until she reached the northeast side and then her skirt got soaked and she started to sink. All the time, of course, she was calling for help because she didn't know how to swim. We finally heard her when she neared our house and all ran out to help her. We pulled her out and she was alright."

"Also one event I remember well was when I, with God's help, saved a man from drowning in the icy water of the Rakken. It happened one winter after a hard frost. Most of the water ... was frozen solid except on the bends ... there were soft spots ... Every Tuesday Foeke de Koe came to the farms to bring petro oil which he also carried in containers which hung from a yoke on his shoulders. I saw him coming from our home and thought already, "I hope he doesn't try to cross at the bend it's too soft even though it looks hard," but he did. I ran as fast as I could ... And there he surely was in the water, grabbing on to bits of chipping ice ... the ice I was standing on started to break so I had to back up. I told Foeke to put his arms through the loop [of a line I had thrown him] and he finally managed to do so. ... I called to him to try and put his knee on the ice ... Then we were able to pull him out and up onto heavier, thicker ice ... Praise the Lord he was safe, but he couldn't stand or move. We brought him to the house where it was warm and put dry clothes on him and gave him warm coffee and brandy. He finally improved. That evening his son came to take him home."

After they lost their farm and couldn't
find another one to rent in Friesland, the Kampens found one in a
dairying area southeast of Amsterdam. Milk prices were still low; money
was still tight. Tired of wearing cast-off dresses that didn't fit, Margie
taught herself to sew at age 13. Feitze's parents, who had also lost their
home, came to live with them, and as we know, after the Dutch army's
mobilization in August 1939 the Kampens had to house and feed the
crew who operated anti-aircraft searchlights in their pasture. During
those years of hardships, Feitze's wife Klaaske 's hair turned white.

But when in the spring of 1940 the owner sold the place out from
under them, they found another dairy farm to rent back in *heitelân*, the
Frisian fatherland. It had 60 acres, half of them unprotected by dikes,

which might be flooded some winters. Their move back to Friesland was planned for May 1940. On May 9 they loaded their cows, horses, sheep, goats, pigs and chickens, their household goods including Feitze's organ, the farm equipment and eight children, on a 170-ton barge in Ouderkerk, on the river Amstel just below Amsterdam. The barge owner, Sjied Visserman, insisted on leaving right away, so the Kampens would need to milk their cows on board. Feitze hated doing that but he complied, they sailed north on the Amstel through the city of Amsterdam and by 6 PM passed through the harbor locks into the Zuiderzee, now called the IJsselmeer.[1] But in the end their reluctant, hasty exodus evoked another "Praise the Lord" from Feitze because the next day, May 10, turned out to be the date of the feared German invasion. He wrote that three hours after their barge had exited into the lake: "At 9 PM that night [of the 9th] the Germans took control of the … locks and no one was allowed to pass through from then on until 1945 until the war was over. God rescued us again, and just in time." About the underlying cause he was wrong. As soon as the Germans invaded, the Dutch military had sunk ships to block access to locks like these, which were considered strategic. But it came to the same thing: a few hours later their passage would have been impossible.

To reach Friesland they sailed in a northeasterly direction across the big lake, which made for a harrowing trip: "During the night on the IJsselmeer, we saw search lights, bombers, heard bombing and fighting. The war was going on all around us, no one slept; we all prayed."

But reaching the coast of Friesland was not the end of their troubles. Due to local fighting and the Dutch military's flooding of the low-lying land to stop the German advance, they couldn't access Friesland's inland waterways. Finally skipper Visserman managed to enter the town of Workum, barely inside the province, but he would go no further because he did not want to lose his barge to the approaching Germans. All the Kampens' goods were unloaded, the town let them use some land to run their cows, their furniture was stored in a friend's barn, and most of the children were lodged with local friends and relatives. The improvised arrangement lasted the better part of a week, during which they were able to sell their milk to the local dairy plant.

---

[1] The IJssel river, a branch of the lower Rhine, empties into the former Zuiderzee or Zuyderzee; *Meer* means lake. As a make-work project during the Depression the Zuiderzee had been turned into a freshwater lake by the 32 kilometer (20 miles) long *Afsluitdijk* (Close-off-dike); hence the name change.

Because they were still far from their new farm, Feitze tracked down another barge skipper, Hilka Prins, whose main business had been to haul manure from Friesland across the IJsselmeer, the reverse of the trip they had just made. At the moment Prins was trapped inside the province, unable to get his barge out due to the military situation, so he gladly took on this new cargo. Begging and bribing their way through the locks and bridges of the inland waterways they finally made it to their new farm by midnight, May 17th:

> "We then put the cows in the pasture and tried to sleep some before the 5 a.m. milking. In the morning we sailed around to the farm house and unloaded our belongings. What an experience. We left ... May 9 and arrived [at the farm] May 18. We had moved right in the middle of the Dutch army's efforts to stop the Germans invading their country ... Through it all the Lord was leading us each step of the way, and now he would shelter us in [this] remote area ... Skipper Prins stayed with his boat for three or four months or more in the *rietvelden* or swamp areas with tall reeds to avoid having his boat confiscated. He often stopped in to see us and stay with us."

At this time all Dutch barge owners were worried about losing their vessels to the German military, which had plans to convert all the ones it could find to landing craft for an invasion of England. This invasion, operation Sea Lion, was called off later that year, but not before quite a number of barges had been rounded up and fitted with front gates.

The Kampens' new farm was even more isolated than their original family farm. Although it was no more than two miles southeast of the small town of Wartena, where school and church were located, Margie wrote that getting there took 45 minutes because they had to row across two small lakes and one large one, followed by a 20-minute hike through the fields. Their farm had neither electricity nor running water. Because of the lack of electric power, a wind-powered, American-style steel windmill helped control the water level in their fields. But, she observed, their isolation was a blessing in disguise because it provided some safety from the searches and man-hunts by the Germans.

During this period two more children were added to the Kampens' eight, including in 1943 Clara, the youngest daughter who later on typed Feitze's memoirs. They now had five sons and five daughters. Fortunately the first year the family received a sizable sum from the Dutch government for water damage to their land, due to the military flooding that had temporarily ruined their grass: "The Lord blessed us in many ways. We had a real good, dry summer in 1940; thus soon after we arrived we could start harvesting the hay. It grows year after year by itself with good weather permitting. Our *schuur* [barn] was soon full of hay." It was a sizable barn, too.

In recent years a large part of the area where the Kampens farmed

Water on both sides: the Kampens' dairy farm during World War II.

has been turned into a national park called *De Alde Feanen* – The Old
Fens – in Frisian which is linguistically closer to English than is standard
Dutch, for reasons found in British history. *De Alde Feanen* could
remind a visitor of the Everglades, with abundant swamps, lakes, bogs,
and small woods, but no alligators or palm trees because many winters it
is completely frozen over. *Feanen* is a reminder of how much of this
landscape was created out of fen, by peat diggers in the 19th century,
when dried *turf* (peat) was a popular fuel before coal and oil became big.
Sometimes the peat diggers re-filled the holes they had dug with soil, but
often no one had any soil to spare. In time this caused new bodies of
water to be added to the already-ample supply of lakes and waterways.
A happy result was that in time the region became a magnet for people
who enjoyed sailing, swimming and fishing. This was even more the
case during the war, because no one was allowed to travel very far.

During those years the area also attracted a new kind of residents:
onderduikers, or 'under-divers', people who wanted to make themselves
scarce. Many were young men evading forced labor in the German war
industries, which was not only miserable work but dangerous due to the
intensifying allied bombing campaign. Of Frisian men put to work in
Germany during the war, about a thousand never came back. When five
onderduikers came to stay at Feitze's farm in the summer of 1941, he built
them a small room in the barn. They were the first of a group that kept
growing all through the war. Feitze's oldest sons, including Al, were
also in danger of being rounded-up, so they often slept in the barn too,
or on a hay barge. In his memoirs Feitze Kampen did not mention Jews
but Margie and John Kampen mentioned that Feitze sheltered a number
of Jewish *onderduikers* as well; many years later he was honored for it.

During the year 1944, 200 people may have stayed at the farm for
various lengths of time. Summer was busiest, with 30 to 50 lodged on
any one day. While quite a few were *onderduikers*, most were vacationers
to whom Feitze had assigned different parts of his barn, one for men,
one for women. But everyone paid him a Dutch quarter a day. As a
result: "Through the summer of the war years, we were able, with the
Lord's grace, to earn quite an amount of money … We were able to pay
off all our old debts." And the Kampens' kids had fun to boot. Margie
remembered: "… the campers brought their own musical instruments.
We had a party, singing and dancing – and everyone had a great time."

Then, one night in May 1944, they were startled out of their sleep by
jackboots stomping through the house. N.S.B.-ers, Dutch Nazis, had
barged in to search for prohibited radios and *onderduikers*.

"I said, "No, I just have a few vacationers." It was early for vacation season. I only had four girls who slept in the ladies section [of the barn]. Fortunately, the girls and the *onderduikers* also heard the N.S.B.-ers. Three of the young men hid under the hay in the ladies section and the girls laid down their heads on them and pretended to be asleep. The N.S.B.-ers searched the barns and asked the girls if they had seen any *onderduikers* and they answered, "No." Two other *onderduikers* hid themselves in the loft. Eventhough they searched the hay, they didn't find them. Ted, Albert and Henry were sleeping in a room at the end of the hay loft. Ted heard the commotion and hid above the room, but Albert and Henry slept on. Fortunately they never saw the room. The Lord must have blinded their eyes ..."

That's a distinct possibility, even if the Lord's work was facilitated by a shortage of light. For a week afterwards Feitze's three older boys slept on the moored hay barge, hidden under fences covered with straw. They still showed up for the early-morning milking. But then,

"... in the summer of that year, 1944, in the *buitenland* [the land outside the dikes] there was an airplane crash. Usually the planes flew over us and went northeast toward Germany and we did not see much air warfare. Often so many bombers passed over us that our barn doors rattled and the youngest children were scared and cried."

By this time, one Allied bombing mission overflying the area could include hundreds, sometimes more than a thousand bombers, in formations up to sixty miles long. John Kampen recalled that when the bomber traffic toward Germany was so heavy that you could hardly hear yourself and the small children were crying, Father Feitze would sit down at the organ and play great Christian hymns for everyone to join in, as loud as they could. Feitze continues:

"We don't know what the problem was but the plane was trying to land in a field, and in the process hit a windmill. One of the wings flew off and the crash jolted the plane so severely that the pilot was killed and another had a broken leg, nine others were unharmed. We and neighbors hurried down to the site and were there in 5 to 10 minutes. Albert took the nine men in two boats and hid them in the *rietvelden* [reed fields], before the Germans could come and capture them. The Germans also saw and heard of the crash and were there from Wartena with their motor boats within an hour. The pilot and the man with the broken leg were captured. They asked everyone where the other crew members were, but no one told them. The Germans searched everywhere for the nine, but never found them. After Albert hid them, they . . . hid with different farmers and later we heard they were transported to Rotterdam in hearses, hidden in coffins, and then boarded ships and returned to England."

The windmill hit by the plane was not a traditional Dutch mill, the kind you see in the tourist ads. It was the wind-driven, American-style mill that pumped water out of the Kampens' fields. According to another eyewitness, the rescuers needed boats to reach the crew.[1]) Water surrounded the plane they were crawling out of, either through a hatch or through holes in the fuselage, since B-24s did not crash-land very well.

Both of Pastor Gary's newspaper articles had reported the chance 1983 meeting at Al's restaurant, and both included a description of the crash-landing in 1944. The less well-written article carried the caption: "Al Kampen Reunited With American He Saved In WWII". I'm assuming that it appeared in a small local weekly, the *Waterford News*, although this could not be verified because its archives were lost in a fire. In this article Al confirmed that the U.S. Air Force B-24 Liberator " . . . first hit a large windmill before it hit the ground so I thought there would be no survivors." But they found that ". . . six out of the eight airmen lived through the crash, many with injuries."

So according to this piece the B-24 had a crew of 8, by Feitze's count it had a crew of 11, and according to the better-written article it had a crew of 9. (This article, titled "Two War Vets Meet Again", is reproduced on the next page. No one had written a source or a date on it, but thanks to a very helpful Modesto librarian I found that it appeared in the Modesto Bee on May 29, 1983.) In any case, these diverging numbers show how easily historical facts can get muddled, but it turns out that Feitze had the right number for the crewmen. Although most B-24s had 10-men crews, U.S. Air Force records confirm that this one had 11.

While these errors may seem trivial, they reflect poorly on small-town journalism. And there were many more mistakes, possibly due to the writers' eagerness for drama. According to the *Modesto Bee* article:

---

[1]) "Hans Kloosterman, nu bedrijfsleider op een Amerikaanse boerderij" *Leeuwarder Courant*, May 24, 1947, and "Op een middag in maart 1944", *Leeuwarder Courant*, June 5, 1947.

Two war vets meet again

WATERFORD — Raked by German fighter planes and hit by flak going and coming, the four-engine B-24 had dropped its bombs on the submarine pens at Bremerhaven and was headed back toward England when two engines went out and it began losing altitude.

Among the crew of nine was Doug Fairbanks, then a 19-year-old Texan on his seventh mission as flight engineer.

The plane started to lose altitude in Friesland, a low-lying area of southern Holland, where another 19-year-old, Auke Kampen, was dodging the Germans.

Kampen was not an active underground fighter, but with his brother and other youths lived in what they considered a sanctuary from the Germans, thanks to its lowland geography with many small islands, lakes and waterways. They didn't want to be rounded up by the Germans and forced to work in their factories.

Fairbanks' plane, one of a giant armada on a saturation raid into Germany's heartland, was flying at 18,500 feet when, badly shot up, it started to nose dive. The pilot chose to crashland rather than parachute because there were wounded and dead aboard. Some crew members, including Fairbanks, decided to parachute.

Meantime, Kampen had heard and seen a plane going down, and he went into action. It was March 31, 1944.

Since then, many of those wartime memories faded into the distant recesses of their minds.

Until a few days ago, that is, when a chance meeting in a Waterford restaurant revived memories.

Fairbanks, now an outside representative for a Sonora bank, had completed his Waterford task when he stopped in at Kampen's Kitchen for a cup of coffee and a piece of pie. Kampen, who changed his name to Al when he came to the United States, greeted him, and as they visited, Fairbanks remarked on his accent.

"Yes, I was born in Holland," replied Kampen. Fairbanks then said his plane had gone down there, and their recollections brought out their wartime experiences.

Al Kampen

The B-24s had started the raid from England before dawn. There were "a million" Allied planes, going and coming on the bombing run, said Fairbanks, and the Germans were using all the ammo they had. Before his plane started down, half his squadron of 10 planes had been lost.

"Our airplane was only about 1,000 feet when I jumped. I no sooner opened my chute than I splashed."

Meant me, said Kampen, he was less than a mile away when he saw the plane going down. "We had rowboats, and I took the biggest I could find. As soon as I got there, I could see some guys walking around. A couple were wounded. Two didn't make it."

"They picked me up right away," said Fairbanks. "I was in the mud, trying to stagger around, cold, miserable, scared." The details of what followed were hazy. It seemed to him, and still does, that he was in a boat with two rescuers.

"I know it was cold, stinking, rotten. I might have had a case of shock from going into ice-cold water. I could have hit my head going out of the plane, or maybe I hit it when I landed."

Kampen could not speak English and the air crewmen could not speak Dutch, but by gesturing and saying, "Kom, kom, kom," they quickly followed him into the boat. There were four sets of oars, he said, and some of the six rescued helped row three to four miles to a farmhouse where he knew the underground would take over.

One of the young crewmen, said Kampen, handed him his .45 pistol. Fairbanks, who said he cannot remember what happened to his sidearm, does recall worrying about it. "The first thing I remember, I couldn't find it. I don't know whether I handed it to someone, or someone took it from me, or I just lost it. I was in a fog. Very possibly I could have had a concussion."

For Fairbanks, the details continued to be fuzzy. He does remember being put into a small basement area — a "kelder, where they kept their milk and butter cold," explained Kampen. There, Fairbanks' muddy, wet clothes were taken for cleaning and he was given a bed. Overseeing him was a young Dutch woman who could speak a little English.

In the night after the second day, Fairbanks was loaded into a wagon, covered and moved to the coast where he was taken aboard a small boat to England.

The blanks continued. "I remember when they tried to debrief me, they were asking questions I just could not answer."

Puzzling, too, was the fact he never made contact with any of his crewmen again. "I never saw them again. I don't know whether they lived or died." His contact with Kampen left him wondering if they were discussing the same episode or two very similar ones.

After the war, Kampen received a framed citation from Gen. Dwight Eisenhower for his rescue. He brought it with him when he came to the United States to work on an uncle's dairy in Gardena. Later, he was drafted and spent 15 months in Korea. He moved to Waterford and built his restaurant in 1966.

Fairbanks had returned to Texas and was a private detective before moving to California 17 years ago.

"Raked by German fighter planes and hit by flak going and coming, the four-engine B-24 had dropped its bombs on the submarine pens at Bremerhaven and was headed back toward England when two engines went out and it began losing altitude. Among the crew of nine was Doug Fairbanks, then a 19-year old Texan on his seventh mission as flight engineer. ... *[The article from the weekly states: "It was the 7*th *mission of the Air Force in Europe that came down," which makes no sense.]*

The plane started to lose altitude in Friesland, a low-lying area of southern Holland *[wrong bearings; it's at the opposite end]*, where another 19-year-old, Auke Kampen, was dodging the Germans. ...

Fairbanks' plane ... was flying at 18,500 feet when, badly shot up, it started to nose dive. *[sic]* The pilot chose to crashland rather than parachute because there were wounded and dead aboard. Some crew members, including Fairbanks, decided to parachute. ... It was March 31, 1944. *[The other article cites the same date]* ... Before his plane started down half his squadron of 10 planes had been lost.

"Our airplane was [at] only about 1,000 feet when I jumped. I no sooner opened my chute than I splashed."

Meanwhile, said Kampen, he was less than a mile away when he saw the plane going down. "We had rowboats, and I took the biggest I could find. As soon as I got there, I could see some guys walking around. A couple were wounded. Two didn't make it."

"They picked me up right away," said Fairbanks. "I was in the mud, trying to stagger around, cold, miserable, scared." ...

Kampen could not speak English and the air crewmen could not speak Dutch, but by gesturing and saying, "kom, kom, kom," they quickly followed him into the boat. There were four sets of oars, he said, and some of the six he rescued helped row three or four miles to a farmhouse where he knew the underground would take over.

One of the young crewmen, said Kampen, handed him his .45 pistol. Fairbanks, who said he cannot remember what happened to his sidearm, does recall worrying about it. "The first thing I remember, I couldn't find it. I don't know whether I handed it to someone, or someone took it from me, or I just lost it. I was in a fog. Very possibly I could have had a concussion."

Contradicting this last paragraph, the article presumably from the *Waterford News* (reproduced on the next page) stated:

"Fairbanks said that he remembered handing the weapon to a young Dutch boy who was part of the rescue team. "It had to be me," Kampen says assuredly. "It was even the same day and the same flight mission," he said.

As incredible as it may seem, Al has a memento of the occasion ... Al Kampen showed the Eisenhower plaque to Fairbanks who read it with amazement. ...

Al Kampen now expects his new friend to visit occasionally remarking, "it's really hard to believe."

Sometimes people who say something is hard to believe are itching to believe it. And to be fair, you could hardly blame Al Kampen. My first perusal of the materials had made me a believer too. If the articles sounded a little contradictory or overly dramatic, that was to be expected of eyewitness reports about stressful events from long ago. Besides, there could be no doubt that in 1944 a disabled American B-24 had crash-landed near the Kampens' farm, and that one of the crew had given Al Kampen his pistol. That incident is re-confirmed in Feitze's memoirs, where he mentions that in April 1945, the Germans returned to their farm for one last man-hunt. That would occur a year after the B-24's crash, with the war's end mere weeks away. As Feitze recalls:

Al Kampen Reunited With American He Saved In WWII

Al Kampen was only nineteen years old when he rescued American soldiers from Nazi invaders in his native Holland. That was thirty-nine years ago. So when one of Al's customers came into Kampen's Kitchen two weeks ago it came as a big shock to him to learn that the man drinking coffee at his counter was an American who's life was saved by Kampen.

It was March 31, 1944 near Wartana, Holland when Auke Kampen (later he "americanized" his name to Al) saw an American Air Force B-24 crash land into a swamp. "The airplane first hit a large windmill before it hit the ground so I thought there would be no survivors." By Auke and friends investigated and found out the six out of the eight airmen lived through the crash, many with injuries.

It was the 7th mission of the Air Force in Europe that came down.

The group of Dutch men took the survivors to the underground where they were harbored from Nazi Germany soldiers. According to Al, Nazis were at the scene of the crash within thirty to fourty minutes later and the Americans probably would have been taken prisoners and possible executed.

The story has stayed in Al Kampen's head for thirty-nine years. Only until two weeks ago did the story take on a different meaning.

Al reports that a man came in several weeks ago to have coffee at Kampen's Kitchen. His name was Doug Fairbanks of Sonora and he was in the city to repossess a mobile home. As Al and the customer began talking, they soon realized that they had met earlier in life, the man at the counter being one of the Americans rescued by Kampen behind the counter.

"You might say that it was incredible but the more we talked, the more definite it was that he was one of the guys I rescued on that plane," Al remarked.

"One of the Americans that survived the crash gave me a .45 pistol," Al recalls. Fairbanks said that he remembered handing the weapon to a young Dutch boy who was part of a rescue team. "It had to be me," Kampen says assuredly.

"It was even the same day and the same flight mission," he said.

As incredible as it may seem, Al has a memento of the occasion of his participation in World War II. It is a plaque from the General of the U.S. Army Dwight D. Eisenhower expressing thanks to Al for his assistance in giving refuge to allied soldiers in Europe. Incidentally, Al Kampen showed the Eisenhower plaque to Fairbanks who read it with amazement.

"Being a rescuer of American soldiers was risky business than as some Dutch undergroud men were discovered and shot," the owner of Kampen's Kitchen remarked.

Kampen recalled the time he was captured, along with his brother, by German Nazi soldiers. Soon afterwards, the soldiers who were detaining them drank excessively and became drunk. Kampen and his brother overpowered their captors and escaped.

Al Kampen now expects his new friend to visit occasionally remarking, "it's really hard to believe."

"I was ordered to go and show them the hay loft . . . Our children had built a small house in the hay and had laid a blanket in it. The officer asked me who was sleeping there, he spoke Dutch. I told him my children used it for a playhouse. He believed me and we went down. There were other soldiers everywhere, and they searched everything possible. They looked especially for radios, guns, and ammunition. I had one revolver *[sic]* hidden high up in the barn on top of a beam; Albert got it from the American-Canadians *[sic]* who crashed. Of course, they didn't find it."

Next a German 'higher ranking officer' questioned him about two men, suspected *onderduikers*, whom he had spotted in a rowboat on the lake. When Feitze feigned ignorance he slapped him and threatened to shoot him. After Feitze gave in, the officer went into the house to verify the information with his wife who was surrounded by the youngest children, all of them crying. Then he came back outside:

"He surprised me because he gave me a cigar and asked me to forget what had happened. I agreed that we had to forget and forgive each other. I think he must have been a Christian, because he changed after he went in our front room. I think he saw the two texts we had hanging on the wall: *"God zorgt voor u"* [God Takes Care of You] and *"De Here Zegene U."* [May the Lord Bless You]. I told him that after World War I

The Kampen family in 1947, shortly before they left for America. On the right is the skipper of the boat. Back row, left to right: Ted, Henry, Albert and father Feitze. Middle row: Fred, grandpa, grandma, mother Klaaske and Ann. Toward the front: Jane, John and Grace

my family took care of a German girl from Hamburg, an Elza Saffen, and my uncle took in a German boy from Bremen. These children were orphaned and undernourished and Dutch people took care of them for several years . . . the officer agreed that war was terrible and said he had not seen his wife and children in over four years. He told me he was also a farmer and lived not too far from the Dutch border. He then asked me to see the cows, and then he ordered all the soldiers to leave and later left himself. God had wondrously taken care of us, and we praised and thanked Him for it."

Despite Feitze's confirmation of the pistol-story, I felt a need to obtain further information from Al Kampen's surviving relatives and from the most reliable source: public records. War is partly a bureaucratic endeavor. Good documentation is essential to justify vast expenditures, enormous property destruction, and the loss of thousands, sometimes millions of lives. Moreover, the natural tendency of men in a top-down hierarchy is to accumulate enough paperwork to support every decision they make. But today, many years after the events, such records are priceless to an amateur historian trying to separate fact from fiction. And that's what I felt compelled to do, because some versions of the story disagreed to the point of putting essential facts in doubt.

Soon my job became like peeling an onion. You remove the outer skin, thinking this is all, only to discover there's another layer hiding the truth. And another. Finally I arranged my conclusions by the story's major elements, which were: (1) Fairbanks' pistol, (2) the date, and the bomber's mission, (3) the crew's injuries, and (4) their escape.

DOUGLAS FAIRBANKS' WAR

1. Douglas Fairbanks and his pistol

While according to the *Modesto Bee* article (pp 60/61) Fairbanks was vague, even clueless about what had happened back in 1944 to his pistol and to himself, the *Waterford News* reported that "Fairbanks said that he remembered handing the weapon to a young Dutch boy." But that was the only part of that article associated with Fairbanks, who in the *Bee* article had been as talkative as he was vague about everything, including the fate of his gun. So while there can be no doubt that the *Bee* had spoken to both men, it is possible that the *Waterford News* only spoke to Kampen, and that Fairbanks' statement was second-hand, relayed by Kampen, who might have embellished it.

I thought at first that the *Waterford News* writer, who was no Pulitzer Prize material, must have quoted Fairbanks (or Kampen, speaking for him) wrong. But that part of the article did not sound in the least ambiguous, and neither did the pistol-report in the Bee. The problem was that they were opposite stories. Did Fairbanks contradict himself, or had an excited Al Kampen done it for him? One peculiar element in Fairbanks' alleged statement in the Waterford paper was the description of Al Kampen as "a young Dutch boy." In 1944, according to both articles, Kampen and Fairbanks were the same age, 19. On the other hand, this could show a cultural difference supporting Kampen as the source. Dutch people may address acquaintances of all ages as *jongen*, literally 'young one' or 'boy' in English. But while in America addressing someone as 'young man' will create no problems, calling them 'boy' sure might. Al Kampen may not have been so sensitive.

In 1983 in Waterford, Fairbanks' .45 pistol had become crucial to his identity. But both articles had weakened the evidence, the Modesto Bee by reporting his vague forgetfulness, and the Waterford News by quoting his confident recall, either an odd contradiction by Fairbanks or erroneous hearsay by Al Kampen. Hence three scenarios are possible. The first two assume Fairbanks *was* interviewed by both journalists:

1) If his first interview was with the *Modesto Bee*, Fairbanks started out being very noncommittal about the pistol, and when that interview made him realize how much his credibility depended on it, he told the other reporter something far more definite.
2) Alternatively, Fairbanks' first interview had been with the *Waterford News*, and he realized that by being so definite about the pistol he was going out on a limb. So in an attempt to back-track he became vague and evasive with the *Modesto Bee* reporter.
3) Instead of 1) or 2) having occurred, Fairbanks never spoke to the *Waterford News* at all, and his statement in that article about giving the pistol came second-hand, from an over-excited Al Kampen who was interviewed by the *News* some time later.

At the end of the day and after much pondering, I would call scenario #3 the most likely, and #2 the most unlikely. For one thing, weekly small-town papers can't afford much independent reporting, so they often follow leads already published in a local daily. Besides, the *Waterford News* article mentions several times that the 'reunion' between Kampen and Fairbanks happened at least two weeks earlier.

Both scenario #1 and #2 would make Fairbanks a shifty character. But if I'm right about scenario #3 being the right one, meaning the *Bee* was the only paper that interviewed him so he did not contradict himself in the article, that doesn't make him any less shifty. Besides the vague pistol-story, Fairbanks described war conditions that would have brought the entire strategic bombing campaign to a halt. Then he told the *Bee* that he escaped back to England by boat, which is highly implausible. On top of that he was strangely vague about his debriefing there, while also claiming he had no idea what happened to his crew mates, from whom he never heard again. He even suggested he might not have been part of that particular crash-landing but a similar one.

Let's start with the tail and work our way up. How likely is it that two different B-24s hit a windmill during a crash-landing in Friesland in 1944? And next, how likely is it that crew mates who lived through several dangerous bombing missions plus a crash would never attempt to contact each other? Even today, when most World War II vets have already left us, the internet brims with memories and arguments by crews of bomber groups, squadrons and planes – and their descendants. If Fairbanks had never contacted his crew mates after the war, some of them would certainly have tried to contact *him*. You could be charitable and decide that his hard parachute landing had given Fairbanks a concussion and a memory blackout, and that he misspoke. Or, less charitably, you could conclude that he lied to cover his butt, and his memory-blanks and his foggy debriefing-story were part of that.

As I found more inconsistencies, I wondered if I should really throw cold water on a heart-warming tale, one of those cosmic incidents that do occasionally happen. The human craving for such stories is what creates markets for novels and movies, but this one was supposed to be fact. Yet too many contradictions were piling up.

When I told Al Kampen's brother John that Fairbanks might not have been on the crashed bomber at all, he disagreed because years ago he had spoken with Allen Seamans, the B-24's navigator, in Pueblo, Colorado, and Al, who was deathly ill at the time, had talked to Seamans by phone for over an hour. John had also talked to another crew member, Anthony de Benedictus from Brooklyn, NY, who told him that since his rescue by Al and his friends he had prayed daily for their safety. He knew they had taken great personal risks. And when he heard that the Kampens and their big family had done well after coming to America, he happily said he could now stop praying; they were safe.

The crew of B-24 #42-99975, "Yankee Bell Harmony"		
Pilot	KENDRICK, John M. Jr.	Wounded; P.O.W.
Co-Pilot	JUDD, Stephen P.	K.I.A.
Navigator	SEAMANS, Allen E.	P.O.W.
Bombardier	OWEN, Robert H.	P.O.W.
Radio Operator	STANCZIEWICZ, Stanley A	P.O.W.
Top Turret	OWENS, John W.	P.O.W.
Ball Turret	SHERMAN, Robert R.	P.O.W.
Right Waist	MINEER, William E.	Escaped
Left Waist	GRAHAM, James C.	P.O.W.
Tail gunner	KETTNER, Frank J.	P.O.W.
Nose turret	de BENEDICTUS, Anthony J.	P.O.W.

I do not doubt John Kampen's word that had spoken to de Benedictus and to Seamans, and that both had been on the B-24 that crash-landed near the Kampens' farm. Besides, the Air Force's crew list of the mission, on this page, lists Seamans and de Benedictus among the crew. But that did not prove that Fairbanks had been on board too, and as you can see, he is NOT listed. Fairbanks had said (in the *Modesto Bee* article) that he was the B-24's flight engineer. This particular list does not mention a flight engineer as such, but on B-24 Liberators (and on B-17 Flying Fortresses) the flight engineer usually doubled as the top turret gunner, a position occupied on this B-24 by John Owens.

There was a famous Douglas Fairbanks, or rather there were two. Douglas Fairbanks Sr. (1883-1939) and his son Douglas Jr. (1909-2000) were prominent American movie actors. Douglas Jr. was also a highly-decorated Navy officer in World War II. If some fast talker was trying to think of a snappy name to attach to a heroic but fictitious World War II record, "Douglas Fairbanks" might have come naturally.

I was very glad to find out that AFHSO, the U.S. Air Force's Historical Section, has Missing Air Crew Reports (MACRs) for all aircraft lost during the war. One such MACR was the source of the crew list above. As I became increasingly frustrated by the contradictions between the initial story and the documentation that should have supported it, I finally asked AFHSO about the mysterious Fairbanks himself:

"Was Douglas Fairbanks (not the movie star, apparently) among the crew members reported as MIA? . . . Can you give me Fairbanks' bomber group numbers and the airfield they operated from? . . . Is there a record of Fairbanks' debriefing after his return to England? . . . Do you have a way to find out if he is still alive and, if so, where he could be contacted?"

Remarkably fast – overnight, in fact – I received a response:

"The only Douglas Fairbanks listed on the name index of Missing Aircrew Reports went down in Italy.

There was no accident report filed with a crew member by the names of Douglas Fairbanks or D Fairbanks." [1]

2. The date of the crash, and the bomber's mission

The article from the *Modesto Bee* supplied dramatic, plausible-sounding details of the doomed bomber's flight. They included that the B-24 had bombed submarine pens at Bremerhaven, not a huge distance east of Friesland. Fairbanks MUST have been the source of this information. Given the language barrier, Al Kampen back in 1944 would have been unable to banter with the bomber crew about their targets. According to both articles, the raid occurred on March 31, 1944.

Submarine pens were heavily-fortified concrete structures that protected moored subs (popularly known as *U-Boote*, from *Unterseeboote*, meaning under-sea-boats) from bombing raids. But there were two problems. The first one was that on March 31 there had been no American bombing raid on Bremen or on Bremerhaven. In fact, according to easily-found public information, all of 1944 saw only a handful of American raids on the greater Bremen area. Most were done by B-17s. The one raid by American B-24s that year was on June 18, when as part of Mission #421, 106 (or 107) American B-24s bombed Bremerhaven, but there is no mention of U-Boot pens being targeted. If they had been, the record would have mentioned it.

---

[1] Some time after receiving this information I came across a mention of a C. D. Fairbanks, who had been a tail gunner on the 492nd B-24 bomber group, one of the B-24 groups that had bombed Bremerhaven on June 18, 1944. Some people prefer to use their middle name as their first name; could D. have stood for Douglas? My first thought was correct but not my second one. Charles Donovan Fairbanks of Cincinnati, OH (not Sonora, CA) went by Don Fairbanks. Following his stint as a B-24 tail gunner, he made a lifelong career as a pilot and flight instructor.

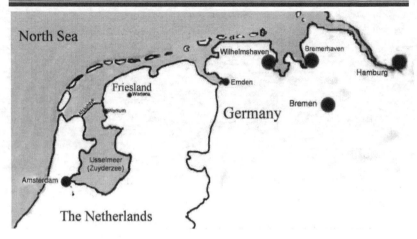

There is a reason for that: Bremerhaven had no U-Boot pens worth bombing. The allies were aware of one such pen, the Valentin, but it was under construction, so they waited until March 1945 to bomb it.

During my searches I was happy to discover that the Province of Friesland has a registry of all known World War II military plane crashes in the province which caused at least one death. Created by combining local records and military ones, Allied and German, this registry has a search feature by location and by crew members' names, and provides dates, causes of the crash, and each crewman's fate. According to this source, during the entire war four plane crashes involving a fatality occurred in the vicinity of Wartena: a British bomber in 1942, a German fighter in 1943, and two American planes in 1944. One of the American planes was a P-38 Lightning that crashed on May 24, 1944. The other was a B-24 that crash-landed near Wartena on March 8, while hitting a

windmill. Bingo! It belonged to the 564th Bomb Squadron, 389th Bomb Group, and was Serial # 42-99975, nicknamed "Yankee Bell Harmony", although an internet registry of bomber nose-art says that the crew had baptized it "The Latrine Rumor". Bombers' nicknames could be changed; they were a morale-boosting privilege of the crews, but the Army Air Force itself did not use them to identify planes.

According to the Frisian registry and U.S. Air Force records, this B-24 was not returning from Bremerhaven, but from bombing Berlin:

"Above the target area the right inside engine was hit by Flak, which made it necessary to feather it. A little later the left inside engine was hit, which caused the B-24's engine power to diminish greatly. The aircraft became separated from its formation and was flying at a very low altitude. Above the northern Netherlands an emergency landing was decided on. Although in principle the flat land near Wartena was suitable, the emergency landing failed. The aircraft became unbalanced and hit a windmill, which caused it severe damage. Due to this co-pilot Peter Judd lost his life; pilot John Kendrick was severely injured." [1])

During a landing with a disabled No. 2 engine (the left-inside engine mentioned above), a sharply-decelerating B-24's flight deck was at risk of being hit by that engine's propeller flying off its shaft and plowing into it, if the crew had been unable to feather it as they had done with the #3 engine. The record is silent on this, but a flying propeller could have been one cause of the pilot and co-pilot's injuries. Another obvious possibility is the jolt from the B-24's high wing being ripped off the plane by its collision with the windmill.

And whichever one of these men was landing the plane, Judd or Kendrick, he deserves our respect because B-24s were harder to fly on course than the better-known B-17s, and even more so when they lost engine power. Moreover, unlike the B-17, the high placement of the wing reduced the crew's chances of surviving a belly landing. Perhaps Judd and Kendrick were overly optimistic about their chances of making a successful landing, or perhaps they didn't spot the slim windmill in that often-hazy country. In any case, they paid a heavy price. Reportedly Kendrick lost both legs but survived the war in a POW camp. Judd, the co-pilot who died either on the way to or in the German military hospital in Leeuwarden, the provincial capital, posthumously received the Air Medal and the Oak Leaf Cluster. Buried on March 10 in Wartena, he was later reburied at the large Netherlands-American war cemetery at Margraten, in the province of Limburg. His grave is in section B, row 11, number 26.

One of Al Kampen's fellow-rescuers, another 19-year old by the

"Everything that deceives can be said to enchant."

Plato

---

[1]) My translation, from http://www.luchtoorlogfriesland.nl/.

name of Hans Kloosterman, made it a point to attend Judd's funeral in Wartena. He wrote to his parents in Cannonsville, N.Y., promising that he would take care of the grave. After the war the Judds invited him to come to America, and gave him a job managing a farm they owned in Binghamton. [1])

3. The on-board injuries and the bail-out

Almost certainly again with Fairbanks as its source, the Modesto Bee article talked of the B-24 being "raked" by German flak and fighters that shot out two engines, and of losing altitude over Friesland. Fairbanks got the part about the two engines right (an easy guess) but, also according to him:

> ". . . badly shot up, it started to nose dive. The pilot chose to crashland rather than parachute because there were wounded and dead aboard. Some crew members, including Fairbanks, decided to parachute. . . . Before his plane started down half his squadron of 10 planes had been lost.
> "Our airplane was [at] only about 1,000 feet when I jumped. I no sooner opened my chute than I splashed."

To begin with, it's no mean feat to turn a nosedive into an emergency landing. But on the off-chance that Fairbanks had been on 1944's only B-24 raid on Bremerhaven (the one on June 18, mentioned on page 89) and that he merely got the date wrong, I took a short detour to see if American aircraft losses on that day had been at all like his description ("Half his squadron of 10 planes had been lost.").

On June 18's Mission #421, a total of 1,378 American bombers, the majority B-17s, hit a couple of dozen dispersed targets. Of 107 B-24s that were to bomb Bremerhaven, 3 were lost, and one landed near Göteborg, in neutral Sweden. The Air Force's MACRs (Missing Air Crew Reports) show that the 3 lost aircraft (4 if you include the one that flew to Sweden) were from 3 different bomb groups. A bomb group consisted of 2 or more squadrons, usually of 12 planes each that stayed in formation as much as they could, for defensive purposes. So whether Fairbanks' squadron consisted of 10 or 12 planes, there is no way that half his squadron (5 or 6 planes) could have been lost before his own B-

---

[1]) *Leeuwarder Courant, op. cit.,* May 24, 1947, and June 5, 1947. The once picturesque small town of Cannonsville no longer exists. After the war it was flooded to create a drinking water reservoir for New York City.

24 went down. But of course, that's assuming his plane had been part of the Bremerhaven mission on June 18. None of the MACRs on the B-24s lost that day lists him among the crew. Fairbanks may have had a talent for high drama, but not for telling the truth.

The *Modesto Bee* reporter had also written: "The pilot chose to crashland rather than parachute because there were wounded and dead aboard." After his release from a German POW camp, Anthony de Benedictus stated on a 'Casualty Questionnaire' about his fellow-crew members: "All were O.K. until we crashed." He also stated: "No one bailed out." Four Casualty Questionnaires filled out by other crew members confirm that no one bailed out, either because at first the pilot thought he could make it back to Hethel base in England or, next, because an emergency landing looked feasible or, finally, because they were already flying too low to bail out safely.

4. <u>The escape</u>

The article from the *Waterford News* reported that if the Germans had gotten to the crashed B-24's crewmen before Al Kampen and his friends did, they might have executed them. That was a highly dubious yarn too. Furious fighting men do violate the Geneva Convention in every war, on every side, and during World War II there were even instances – on both sides – of irate civilians lynching survivors from crashed enemy planes. But ordinarily the German military observed Geneva towards POWs of signatory nations, which meant the western powers, not necessarily Russia; and the Luftwaffe in particular deserves some credit for protecting crashed allied crew members. The Germans' priority, and a completely legitimate one it was, consisted of holding captured allied airmen in POW-camps. This would reduce the allies' capacity to fly sorties against Germany because training air crews took a lot of time. If anyone ran the risk of being executed, it was the crew's Dutch helpers. Or if caught they might have ended up in a concentration camp, which was not a great deal better.

According to Fairbanks' story in the *Modesto Bee*, after hiding for two nights in the cellar of a local farm he was taken to the coast, from where a boat took him to England. By itself that didn't invalidate Feitze Kampen's story about the crew members being smuggled to Rotterdam in hearses and traveling by boat from there to England; Rotterdam might have been just one wrong detail. But that story may have been no more than a purposeful deception. The underground was trying to help

9 airmen still at large evade capture. They would have been tight-lipped about their escape routes, and if they gave out any information it would likely be false, in order to throw the Germans off the track. In any case, all these stories of traveling to England by sea were far-fetched. Sure, the distance from the Netherlands to Great Britain is not huge by water, but the Germans knew that too, and they were very good at controlling ship traffic in and out of the occupied countries. That was why the most common escape route for allied airmen ran not by sea but by land, south by way of Belgium and France to neutral Spain and Portugal, or to British-held Gibraltar, from where they were flown back to England.

Caught allied airmen were imprisoned in more than 15 German POW camps called Stalag Luft, which were run by Luftwaffe personnel and weren't near as much fun as portrayed in Hogan's Heroes. Most of those camps were located quite far to the east, many in what today is Polish territory; one can imagine that was done on purpose, to make successful escapes less likely. I have seen estimates that over 50,000 allied airmen were interned in these camps. Because it is known that only about 2,000 managed to make it back to England from the continent, it seems clear that the average crashed airman's chances of pulling that off were tiny, no more than one in twenty-five. It wasn't just that many were downed in Germany proper, where chances of getting help were negligible in the first place, but in the occupied countries they faced formidable hurdles too. Staying hidden, although it was chancy, was not the worst problem; traveling was. Even if they had proper clothes and all the right papers, they might be identified during one of the constant train checks, bus checks, traffic stops, and street *razzias*, where the Germans simply closed off a city street to investigate everyone trapped between the roadblocks. And then there was the language problem: few flyers knew a foreign language, so as soon as they opened their mouths the game was up.

In a purely statistical sense the crew of B-24 'Yankee Bell Harmony' a.k.a. 'The Latrine Rumor' did a little better than one in twenty-five. According to both the Frisian registry and AFHSO records, of the nine walking survivors one made it back to England. That was William E. Mineer, the right waist gunner. The others spent the dreadful winter of 1944/45 in Stalag Luft camps.

The Germans were conscientious about providing translated reports on the whereabouts of caught allied airmen, I assume through the Red Cross, which functioned as a neutral intermediary between the warring sides. Hence AFHSO was able to supply copies of prisoner's transfer

Hotel Ketelaar in Workum. Notice the "stalling" (stabling) for bicycles, on the left.

documents on several crew members. One, on Anthony de Benedictus, and undated, delivered him to the German Army War Prison in Antwerp, Belgium. Another one, dated August 11, 1944, delivered Frank Kettner, the tail gunner, to a prison in Brussels, Belgium. One more transferred Jim Graham, the left waist gunner, to the same Antwerp prison that received de Benedictus, on the same day as Kettner. This suggests that de Benedictus, Kettner and Graham, and possibly 6 more crew members, were at large for roughly 5 months, from March 8 until August 11. After hiding out for some time they must have traveled south, and all but one were caught, not long before those August 11 transfer documents were made out. And these men missed being freed by allied troops by about three weeks. Brussels was liberated on September 3, Antwerp on September 4 of 1944.

After the B-24's crash-landing Allen Seamans, the navigator whom John Kampen had talked to, had spent 3½ months in Workum, at an ancient establishment called Hotel Ketelaar, run by Gerben Bonnema:

> "Bonnema was already sheltering an *onderduiker* Jewish couple and a fugitive railroad station master [1] and now, having added an American flyer, he was certainly eligible to be shot dead five times and

---

[1] Towards the end of the war Dutch railroad workers went on strike, refusing to forward trains hauling Jews to extermination camps, and went into hiding; but this greatly worsened that winter's famine in the cities.

1,000 years in a concentration camp. But since he was also taking care of fourteen German soldiers as regular guests, he thought he had adequate cover for not worrying too much!

"I still remember well when coming back from Makkum I learned that we now had an American besides. I thought it would be best to say hello to the Germans first, so that's what I did. And then I went to the kitchen where Seamans was sitting around."

Seamans, then 23 years old, was made to play a deaf-mute. Naturally he'd had civilian clothes for some time, but of course one English syllable at the wrong moment would have blown the entire situation sky-high. . . . Mr Bonnema: "Only the baker had it figured out, I thought. He said: "When I come in the back door he looks up right away. That doesn't add up." But then I told him that of course those poor deaf-mutes have extra senses to be aware of what they can't hear – and that explanation satisfied him."

During his stay Seamans peeled a lot of potatoes, watched local soccer matches, and joined other Americans hidden in town for a swim near the local lighthouse, where the Germans lodged at the hotel were pulling guard duty. Added Mr. Bonnema: "Those Germans must have heard the swimmers speaking English, but they never did anything about it. Maybe they thought they were being teased, or something." Maybe, but ordinary German soldiers didn't know English in those days, and they may just have assumed the men were speaking Frisian.

After those 3 ½ months in Workum the underground arranged a transport down to Spain for a group of airmen including Seamans, but ". . . somewhere outside our borders treason occurred, and the Americans were picked up. They sat out the war in a POW camp but miraculously their arrest had no consequences whatsoever for any of their helpers in our country."[1]

But what was he after, that fellow who walked into Kampen's Kitchen in May 1983, called himself Douglas Fairbanks, and pretended he was the one who gave Al Kampen his pistol, back in March 1944? One or more of humanity's seductive yearnings, I suppose: a moment of fame, or the secret glee of having fooled a gullible stranger, or some easy money, or a free meal. Today still, it's not unusual for people with an agenda to invent heroic service records; a number of slimy American politicians have been caught doing it. Very likely the possibility never occurred to Al Kampen who, given his solid background, must have been a straight shooter. Still, as a restaurant owner he must have met

---

[1] "Bonnema's en Allen Seamans zagen elkaar na 31 jaar terug", *Leeuwarder Courant*, July 4, 1975, my translation.

people with bogus stories long before Fairbanks came along. I certainly have, and some cost me money.

But being gullible, although it can be expensive, is not a blot on one's character. Al Kampen died in 2005 at age 80, following a year of painful suffering from cancer of the jaw. He was a lover of freedom who had aided the allied war effort at the risk of his own life, and after coming to the U.S. he had served his adopted country in Korea. Al didn't deserve the con job by Fairbanks. But if he died believing in his reunion with the U.S. airman who had given him his pistol, so be it. There was such an airman, Al Kampen had risked his life to help him, and he had given Al his pistol. But he was not Douglas Fairbanks, or whatever his name was. And – shame on Fairbanks, or whatever his name was, for thinking it was a great lark to pretend to have been one of those who were ready to make the ultimate sacrifice, and so often did.

Feitze at the organ, with the Kampen family singing. Behind Feitze stands Jane, next to her John Bylsma, husband of Margie, next Margie, Ann, and Albert holding Emmy Bylsma. Mother Klaaske in foreground. Picture taken about 1950-51 in Paramount, California.

In 2016 I contacted the foundation that arranges 'adoptions' of the more than 8,300 American war graves at Margraten cemetery, about 5 miles east of Maastricht. That ancient, picturesque city is the capital of the Dutch province of Limburg, which as a southeasterly appendage of the Netherlands is bordered on the east by Germany and on the west by Belgium. The foundation put me in contact with a Belgian young man by the name of Tim Ubags, who had wanted to take care of one of the graves ever since he had visited Margraten with his school class at age 11. Tim lives in Eigenbilzen, some 6 miles west of Maastricht. He sent me a picture of him and his sister Isabell, taken on August 23, 2016, at Stephen Judd's grave.

POLITICAL OFFICERS

It's a rainy Wednesday morning the sixteenth in downtown Eugene, Oregon, a place I had not planned to be at. Yesterday I drove to the Eugene train depot to pick up Trudi from the Amtrak arriving from Sacramento at 2:44 PM. She had spent several days visiting her three sandbox buddies in California, all of them now closing in on retirement age. Well, being Amtrak the train arrived about fifteen minutes late, but that issue paled against the fact that she seemed not to be on it. I marched up and down the full length of the very long train, asked some of the attendants, and as soon as the choo-choo puff-puffed out again I went to the station window to check if she was actually on the passenger list. Yes, she was, the man confirmed. What could have happened? Robbed, murdered and dumped along the track? Nah, let's keep the lid on the dramatic flourishes. I could try to call her, but I haven't had a cell phone for some time; didn't use it enough and got tired of paying the monthly charges. I guess that dates me, too. Maybe this is the right time to head over to the Eugene Costco, buy a phone, and call her. But there's something about driving that leaves most of your brain free to ruminate and sort things out, and halfway there, common sense kicks in. First, if she simply missed the train, I need to find out when she can get on next. Second, I noticed that the depot had a pay phone, and using it must be cheaper, even if remaining without a cell phone makes me sooo 20th century. Even if I'm wrong about the pay phone being cheaper, that's what I think, so I make a U-turn.

Back at the depot nobody is using the single pay phone. It figures; even people who look like they just graduated from Greyhound to Amtrak are yakking and texting constantly, all over hell's half acre, in church during the sermon, in restaurants while the waiter is trying to take their order, and I don't know which is worse. I just overheard one character answering his phone with the exclamation that it's been ringing off the hook all morning. Talk of obsolete figures of speech. Cell phones don't have hooks, and hardly any ever ring. Another Ma Bell-inspired phrase, "On your dime", is equally obsolete. Pay phones no longer take coins, and even if they did, dimes would never do. But enough of the idiomatic nitpicking. Using my credit card I call Trudi's cell phone. After some time – I'll bet it's buried in the very bottom of her purse again – she answers: "Hello-o?".

"Hi, my love – uh – where are you right now?"

"We're just coming down the hill, on the way to Sacramento," she announces cheerily.

"I was at the train just now, and you were not on it."

"O?"

"Would you look at your ticket, to make sure what date it's for?"

(… silence …)

"O Lord o' mercy …"

"What's the date?"

"The fifteenth. It's the fifteenth. I somehow had the idea I had to get on the train the sixteenth." The train trip takes a good twelve hours. To arrive around three pm she had to get on at two in the morning, on the same day. She doesn't seem to have realized that every calendar day starts at 12 midnight. I mean, I'm sure she knows that, but it didn't click. Or it was lost in the chatter-din of four old sandbox buddies.

"Well, better go on to the station right away, before you stop for dinner somewhere. And see if they have a spot on tonight's train. Oh, and I don't have a phone. Call Maarten to let him know what's going on, and I will call him in a couple of hours to find out, so I'll know when to pick you up. OK?"

As I hang up the pay phone it comes to me: why can't *I* make her new train reservation myself? So I head back inside, to the Amtrak window. To my pleasant surprise, the friendly man behind the glass acts as if my predicament is nothing unusual. After spending several minutes tapping his keyboard, he announces that everything is in the bag; she will be on tomorrow's train, and there will be no extra charge. By Gum, even if all this taxpayers' money spent on Amtrak adds to the national deficit, it's paying off for me. After thanking him profusely I make a bee line for the pay phone. Trudi still has not reached the Sacramento station, and she receives the news with near-audible overtones of a damsel in distress, saved by a long-distance knight in shining armor.

"I'm just going to stay here overnight," I tell her, "and I'll see you tomorrow." I can't face driving back to Coos Bay right now, and back again in the morning. And it's not that I'm worried about my carbon footprint. I simply hate driving, especially on roads I must have seen a thousand times. And I need some dinner. Maybe I should start with a drink at the wine bar in the nearby 5th Street Public Market. Yes, that might be a proper prelude to an idle interlude. After ordering a nice, full-bodied Italian red, I discover they also have a soup & salad bar, a facility I normally disdain except that this one is done right. Besides the obligatory leaf lettuce mix they offer chilled Brussels sprouts in a marinade; celery root remoulade; marinated red beets and green beans, plus a whole lot more that amounts to a Great Leap Forward from the dowdy salad bars of the 'eighties.

Thus intestinally reinforced I get a room in a modest downtown motel. Now I curse my failure to bring the book I've been reading lately, a 1980 tome called MIG Pilot by John Barron. An interesting and easy read, it's the story of Soviet air force lieutenant Viktor Belenko, who defected from the communist people's paradise in 1976 by flying his highly-secret MIG-25 from the Chuguyevka air base, 120 miles northeast of Vladivostok in eastern Siberia, to northern Japan, landing with only 30 flight seconds of fuel in his tanks. The MIG-25 had greatly worried western defense experts, and Belenko's defection allowed them to investigate it before the Japanese returned it to the USSR, which they felt obligated to do to keep the peace during the Cold War. But the investigation's results were astonishing. The plane, which was loaded with obsolete technology, amounted to no more than two gigantic, fuel-guzzling engines that enabled a quick jump to about 70,000 feet, plus an equally quick descent. All told, the MIG-25's 14 tons of fuel allowed it to be airborne no more than 20 minutes. As a fighter to oppose the U.S. Air Force it would have been no match at all; its combat radius was only 186 miles, and it didn't turn well. In fact, the Russians had built it only to act as an interceptor for the high-altitude U.S. spy planes they had been obsessing about, like Gary Powers' U-2 that they managed to shoot down in 1960. But American reconnaissance methods changed, and the vaunted MIG-25 became useless except as the mythical threat it had been until Belenko's defection.

So much for the technical parts of MIG Pilot, which amount to an interesting example (and far from the only one) of misjudging the enemy's capabilities. But the part of Belenko's narrative that struck me the most was his massive contempt for the little tyrants known as political officers. In that now-expired system they were the enforcers of ideological conformity, constantly bugging people like Belenko, whose job as a fighter pilot put him in the upper echelons of Soviet society, to think the right thoughts and say the right words, and pressuring him to take refresher seminars in Marxist-Leninist doctrine so he could show his 'ideological purity' by regurgitating their pet platitudes.

Too tight to go out and buy another book, I settle in for an evening of TV-watching. TV has become almost a novelty for me, what with my house having been unplugged from it for years. But my re-acquaintance merely reminds me of why we got unplugged. Even on the History Channel, and on the Learning Channel too, programs that promise interesting stuff merely present fluff that never goes anywhere, except to expertly-placed commercials. I finally give up and go to sleep.

Stumbling into the bathroom next morning, I am greatly alarmed at finding this printed message:

> **SAVE OUR PLANET**. Dear guest – Every day, millions of gallons of water are used to wash towels that have only been used once.
> **YOU MAKE THE CHOICE**: A towel on the rack means "I will use again."
> Thank you for helping us conserve the Earth's vital resources.

Don't tell anybody, but since I'm skipping my shower, I can smugly bask in the satisfaction of having saved the Earth's vital resources. Hence I, Superman's secret child, am entitled to reward myself with a leisurely breakfast. The motel room directory recommends the Keystone Café, which sounds vaguely familiar, but its chief attraction is that it's only a two-block walk. That way I may make a further contribution to saving the planet, provided I avoid exhaling CO_2 on the way. But as soon as I step outside it starts drizzling, and I didn't bring a jacket. I guess I'll just walk faster, never mind the CO_2, and as soon as I enter the Keystone it all comes back to me: I've been here, back in the seventies or eighties. Neither the décor nor the menu seems to have changed. It's an old Eugene hippie joint, big on tofu and vegan stuff, its single concession to animal-flesh eaters being turkey ham. I wonder if they even have it; who would want to eat turkey ham? I end up ordering the Feta cheese, spinach and tomato omelet with home fries and some coffee from the waiter, a skinny character with a goatee so wispy, you'd think the billy-goat was not wholly committed to his act of procreation, back at the collective farm on that sultry day in 1985.

"You can serve yourself coffee against the wall," says goatee, nodding towards a cabinet that holds a number of air pots. Against the wall I go, and the coffee is great. When the omelet comes it's only so-so. Could have gained some zest from a little basil, or pesto, or a few salty olives. And the home-fries turn me off, because they're not real. They seem to be pre-cooked potatoes which have been o-so-briefly tossed with a little oil and a lot of paprika to make them look browned. This too may be an inheritance from the seventies, when wordy restaurant menus talked of "gently sautéed", but more likely it's a lazy cook's shortcut. Still, for seven or eight bucks you can't expect Wolfgang Puck standards, so I refill my coffee, finish my breakfast, and get up to leave. Now I notice that the waiter never wrote my coffee on the bill. Being in the restaurant business myself, that bothers me:

"Say, you need to charge me for my coffee."

"We only ask afterwards," he explains. "We don't want to put pressure on people."

Pressure on people? I knew Eugene was a touchy-feely place, but this seems a bit far-out, if you'll pardon the jargon. I'd better not complain about my potatoes, or he may run off to his grief counselor.

Back at the motel I decide next to visit Jerry's, a big local home-improvement center like Home Depot. I'm curious to see if they have any attractive designs for the new front door I'd like to install at the restaurant this summer.

The sales clerk at Jerry's is very helpful; prices for a 3-foot, wood-grained Fiberglas front door with a decorative half-window and two matching, full-length side-lights are between $1,700 and $2,000. That's without hardware and installation, so I may be looking at $3,000, maybe a bit more. Handing me a colorful door-manufacturer's catalog he adds: "And when you're through with that you can bring it back here, and we'll recycle it for you."

Whatever happened to the idea of just putting stuff in the trash? Speaking for myself, I find it rather convenient. More so than making a trip to Jerry's to return a free catalog, and easier on the gas besides. I make a few more stops until finally, along Coburg Road, I notice a Borders bookstore. I've still got a couple of hours to kill, and I've heard Borders is slipping into Chapter 11. So maybe I can pick up a cheap book to read during the rest of my time here. The dynamism of the American retail business never ceases to amaze me; it's a prime example of Schumpeter's concept of creative destruction. Before you realize it, yesterday's sure winners are today's hapless losers, pushed aside by a better idea or a change in consumer preferences, or both. Lately, even mighty Wal-Mart's business is being cut into by the dollar-stores. Borders was slow to see that internet-marketing of books might turn big, brick-and-mortar bookstores from assets into albatrosses. Take the book I forgot to bring along, MIG Pilot. I saw a reference to it, found it on Amazon, and had it in three days. All that took was maybe five minutes, and even if I had traveled to the biggest brick-and-mortar bookstore in the world, there's no guarantee they would have had it.

I walk in through Borders' glass-and-oak doors, which look badly in need of refinishing. Accumulated human skin oils have replaced the vanished varnish, so I try not to touch the dark parts. I check the discount tables. Not much there unless you're looking for coffee-table books about intensely trivial topics. Finally I spot a paperback copy of the late Stephen Ambrose's D-Day book, reduced to 3.99. That will work. I also spot a coffee bar, further back in the store.

"An Americano with soy," says a skinny Eugene goatee, the only other customer at the counter.

"I'd like a short latte," I say. "Not much milk."

"Would you like one of our scones with that?" I have to give her credit for cheerful demeanor, in a store that may close soon.

"No, but I'd like one of these lemon tarts."

"May I have your name?" Evidently fixing two cups of coffee takes so long, you have to go on the waiting list.

"My name is Adolf."

"OK, Adolf." She doesn't bat an eye. No sooner do I sit down with my book when Adolf is summoned from his bunker, to be given his coffee and lemon tart. The coffee could use a little more kick, and the lemon tart tastes more stale than lemony. But I'm not going to complain. This being Eugene, they may save the stale tarts for people by the name of Adolf. Next time I'll try being Napoleon. Or better yet, Vladimir. Vladimir Lenin.

After spending the better part of an hour reading D-Day it's time to head for the train station, so I abandon the premises through oak-and-glass doors whose most conspicuous feature remains that they badly need refinishing. I try again to avoid touching the dark, greasy-looking parts. On this trip I used Trudi's car, a bright-red Camry, and I left it close to the building. Down the row nearest the doors I spot a small red car. It's a Toyota alright, but wrong model and wrong color. Hmm. Maybe I forgot where I left it; wouldn't be the first time. Wait, here's a car the right color, down a row further out into the parking lot. As I said, I'm forgetful about where I put things. Sometimes in my basement, on top of a beam somewhere I find a tool that's been there all these thirty years, patiently waiting to be reunited with its inattentive master. Through an intensifying drizzle I quickly march down the perpendicular row of cars: finally, a red Camry. Problem is, the license plate is wrong. Dang; every second now I'm getting wetter and wetter. Taking a deep breath, I steel myself to conduct a complete walking survey of the parking lot, checking every row of cars until I find the right one. I'm getting waterlogged, but you gotta do what you gotta do. Despair sloshes in with heavy feet when, having once again failed to find the right car, I retreat for shelter under Borders' eaves. If I don't find that car soon, I'm going to be late for the train. These doors through which I walked out – they are the same worn oak doors saturated with hand grease through which I entered, right? They certainly look the same, but – wait, wait, Borders may have more than one set of doors. Of course they do. Big stores always do. I re-enter Borders, and in the distance I spot an identical set of doors – same oak and glass, same greasy edges where the varnish rubbed off. On my way I recognize the bargain tables too, the ones where I found the D-Day book. I exit, and – deliverance! I have wheels after all!

When I find Trudi at the station I'm treated to the warm hugs and ardent kisses donated by a devoted damsel delivered from dreadful distress. We also thank the Amtrak man who made it all possible. But neither one of us feels like spending any more time in Eugene, so we head out to the coast. The next morning Kevin is working the kitchen at the restaurant. This winter, with business slow and a pregnant wife at home, Kevin took a second job at the movie theater, a new opportunity to confirm the universality of weird consumer behavior. For instance, the other day I was proclaiming my opinion, based on decades of observations, that people who drink Diet Coke secretly believe that it neutralizes every calorie in whatever fattening food they wash down with it. "They may deny it," I clarify, "but I will bet money they believe it. People believe a lot of things they hope are true."

"Ha," Kevin says. "The other night this woman came back out of the movie for a free refill for her bucket of popcorn. And to refill her giant Diet Coke. So I ask her, I suppose you think the Diet Coke cancels the popcorn? So she stands there and thinks for a second, and then she says: 'Yeah.'"

This morning he has another story. "This black guy came to the movie with his girl friend. He buys their tickets and they go in. Pretty soon he comes back out to buy a soda. Then he comes out again, to go to the bathroom; I've got several people waiting in line for snacks. He comes out of the bathroom and walks back into the theater. So this one woman standing in line says: 'Hey! I just saw this black guy walk into the movie without paying!'

And then, a guy standing behind her says: 'That wouldn't be racist now, would it?' So she gets beet-red in the face, and runs back into the theater."

I'm getting the feeling that a lot of Americans today would rather enjoy being political officers.

WALLOWING IN WAR

*"Zey say ve Germans loff to go to wahr. A shmall misunderstandink!
We're all friends now. So let's zelebrate Oktoberfest!"*

That's from one of our TV commercials, which we ran to promote
our German cuisine. I wrote the scripts, my wife and I 'starred' in them,
and you can see them on Youtube, under <u>user/blueheronbistro</u>. They
were meant to be funny, and most people took them that way, but one
day, a female customer became offended when she saw a still from one
of the commercials on our menu (the same picture shown on this page).
So she called me over:

"You know, I am offended by this. I'm Jewish, and I'm related to
Holocaust survivors."

In addition, she fired glances as contemptuous as they were smug.
Well, how should a hapless German restaurant owner respond,
especially one who is not even German? "Excuse me, ma'am? How *did*
you ever manage to survive watching *Hogan's Heroes*? People back in the
'sixties didn't have any problem with it, you know? How about that
little German soldier on *Laugh-In*? Remember:: 'Verry interresting!'?"

But I kept my mouth shut, and probably for the best. Too many
people today crave the thrill of victimhood, and if skeptics tell them to
get a life, their craving may turn into ranting and raving. This lady –

victimhood does seem to appeal quite strongly to ladies – had no foreign accent, and she was far too young to have experienced the horrors of the Jewish holocaust herself. But she enjoyed living them in safe mode: second-hand. Vicariously. It's a huge irony that for years after history's most terrible war, even the worst-treated survivors – and I have known some – were not particularly eager to publicize what they went through. That only became stylish later, when time had given it an undeserved patina.

Think about it: here are people who have integrated well in an advanced, civilized society, Germany. They have contributed to German science, medicine, literature, politics, business, entertainment – and they've prospered as a result. Most see themselves as German patriots first and Jews second; many fought for their adopted country. (Anne Frank's father, Otto Frank, had served as an officer in World War I, and gone to great lengths to follow the German officer's honor code.) Then a rabble-rouser seizes power and starts a 12-year-long train of persecutions. It starts with officially-encouraged slander and harassment, then proceeds to humiliation, vandalism and assault, dismissals from public jobs and destruction of livelihoods, confiscation of property, denial of public services and other civil rights; next come arson, random mob-killings and forced emigration; next, slave-labor, induced starvation and disease by means of the ghetto system; and at last the "final solution", the annihilation camps. Who in his right mind would want to re-live such nightmares? People who never did live through them, that's who. Thanks to other people's suffering, they can wallow in *faux* indignation, safely and pompously.

There's money in it too, since this latter-day craving for *faux* woes and *ersatz* agonies has raised a small army of literary swindlers peddling *faux* memoirs. Actually, the genre seems to have been pioneered by Alex Haley's 1976 book about the victimization of blacks called *Roots*. Claiming it was based on ten years of research, Haley presented it as his own family history, starting with an African ancestor who was kidnapped and sold into slavery. *Roots* created a worldwide sensation, was turned into a TV mini-series, won Haley a Pulitzer Prize and made him a multi-millionaire, history's best-selling African-American author. But a couple of years after *Roots'* publication author Harold Courlander sued Haley for plagiarism, for having used large parts of Courlander's novel *The African*. After claiming he had never read *The African*, Haley ended up buying Courlander's silence for a great deal of money. Next, in the early 'eighties genealogists and historians proved that his historical facts were all wrong. Basically Haley had sold a work of fiction as history, shrewdly cashing in on a popular mania for victimhood.

And unfortunately, Haley's template has been copied by writers of *faux* Holocaust memoirs. Binjamin Wilkomirski's 1996 book *Fragments*, a memoir of his survival as a Latvian Jewish orphan in a concentration camp, turned out have been made up by Bruno Doessekker, a Swiss writer. But it sold very well, which may explain why it is still being hawked on Amazon.com as "unadulterated terror … the words of a courageously honest man." Another best-seller, 1997's *Misha: A Mémoire of the Holocaust Years*, the tale of a Jewish childhood spent running from the Nazis and living with wolves in the forest, also turned out to be fiction, concocted by a Belgian writer. In 2008 yet another attention-grabbing Holocaust book was about to be published by Herman Rosenblat of Florida. It would tell the story of his first meetings with his future wife, back when he was a Jewish boy imprisoned in a Nazi concentration camp. A Jewish girl disguised as a Christian farm girl, she used to toss food at him over the fence. Purely by chance they met again years later, in New Jersey, and married. Oprah Winfrey swooned over their love story, calling it the greatest ever. But the book and a planned $25 million movie were abruptly scuttled when historians objected that the food-throwing story could not possibly have happened, given the known layout of the camp. Finally Rosenblat admitted he had made it all up.

Then there is the small fry, the ones not looking to get on the New York Times' bestseller list. In the 'nineties many visitors to the Dachau concentration camp, not far from Munich, met Martin Zaidenstadt, an elderly Jewish man who made himself their uninvited tour guide. Claiming he had been a prisoner at Dachau himself, he would talk passionately about the camp's gas chamber where, he said, many prisoners were killed. (NYT, 10-26-1997). His audiences lavished sympathy and money on him. To be sure, Dachau was a dreadful place where a lot of people perished; from a 12-year total of 200,000 prisoners 23,000 died of disease, malnutrition, maltreatment and from simply being executed. But the Nazis' most notorious, industrial-style gas killings happened in specially-designed camps that were all located in present-day Poland, of which the best known are Auschwitz-Birkenau and Majdanek. A journalist discovered that Zaidenstadt's claim of having been a prisoner at Dachau was false. But, claiming that Zaidenstadt was not breaking any laws, the museum management put up with him. Making an issue out if it in th current political climate, they may have reasoned, was not worth the commotion.

Also looking for a payoff – financial, emotional, or both – are the hate-crime hoaxers. Again, blacks may have led the way, as in the shady Tawana Brawley case. Homosexual hoaxers have been active too. And with regard to anti-Semitic hate-crimes, we saw a big one play itself out right here, of all places. It's been quite some time, but on the lightly populated Oregon coast it raised a lot of eyebrows.

One April morning in 1994, three new residents of Reedsport, a town of about 4,500 then, and 25 miles north of Coos Bay, complained that their home and their vehicles had been defaced with spray-painted anti-Semitic German slogans and swastikas. A year earlier they had been in the news for their re-conversions to Judaism. Next they had rented a vacant former hotel in Reedsport, to serve as their place of business as well as their common residence. When they reported the anti-Semitic vandalism, they also told of anti-Semitic hate-letters left at their building, and of hate-calls on their unlisted telephone. Shortly afterward they made a shopping trip to Coos Bay, and reported that while they were in a local store their vehicle had been vandalized again by unseen anti-Semites. Their complaints created a big stir, all over the state.

What I noticed about the many press pictures was that the anti-Semitic taggers were no craftsmen. Granted that fluency in foreign languages is not among America's great strengths, the spray-painted German was unusually bad. *Nein juden* for "No Jews" is wrong for more than one reason. And the swastikas were reversed (they pointed counterclockwise instead of clockwise), a pitiful show for fervent neo-Nazis. Moreover, as my friend, the poet C. L. Grove then living in Reedsport noted, prior to the Jewish trio's arrival there had been no signs of skinheads or neo-Nazi groups in Reedsport.

Still, to the mayor the incidents were "a slap in the face of all the citizens … we cannot allow people like this to go unpunished." The small town formed a Human Relations Task Force. School children were ordered to study "Tolerance". Politicians issued high-minded condemnations of "Hate". Jews from the Eugene Reform Temple came over for an Anti-Hate candle-light-vigil, and the Anti-Defamation League B'nai B'rith offered a reward. Despite this avalanche of support, the victims told the FBI that the Reedsport police, the town judge and the county sheriff were all in cahoots with the unknown anti-Semites. (The FBI had been called in because it looked like a federal civil rights case.) While their accusations lacked proof, they also seemed unfair because Reedsport's police chief had already called the incident "a sick, deplorable crime" which had "affected the whole community".

In June the victims reported yet more anti-Semitic threats. Then in late August an arson fire broke out in their building. It was only thanks to a water pipe burst by the heat that it didn't burn to the ground. But a few days later the embittered Jewish trio announced they were leaving Reedsport for good. They blamed their continuing persecution, complaining that many in town were whispering that they had committed the 'hate-crimes' themselves. "We had nothing to gain from the fire," the woman in the group, Sherry Armstrong, argued. Reportedly, when the conflagration started they were in Portland, looking for jobs because their business had failed. But their claims of being driven away from Reedsport sounded overdone, one reason being that they had been evicted, having never paid the rent.

It also turned out that when smoke started pouring out of their building they were not yet in Portland, a four-hour drive, but had barely left Reedsport. One minute earlier, as recorded by hidden FBI surveillance cameras, they had driven away, right after Sherry Armstrong had briefly gone inside. And not long before the fire they had taken out fire insurance and moved personal belongings to a storage space rented in Armstrong's maiden name. All this while their other bills went unpaid, though afterwards they filed $85,000 in insurance claims.

In June the following year they were arrested, and charged in federal court with arson, interstate mail fraud, wire fraud, and making false statements to law-enforcement. Two years after their first hate-crime reports they were convicted on all 21 counts. They cried, objecting that their devotion to Judaism prohibited them from staging hate-crimes. Perhaps they should have spent more time studying the Torah, which quite frankly relates an awful lot of incidents of Jewish people doing things that were dishonest or prohibited. Each conspirator went to federal prison for about ten years. Sherry Armstrong continued to maintain her innocence until October 2008, when she finally admitted setting the fire. But she still claimed that the 'hate-crimes' had been real. "Living with that kind of hate caused some poor judgments to be made on our part," she stated. Though the Reedsport trio's tale made big waves in our area, on the national scene it

> "Men stumble over the truth from time to time, but most pick themselves up and hurry off as if nothing happened."
>
> Winston Churchill

was hardly unique. Seeking to cash in on our contemporary persecution-obsession, so many hate-crimes are staged in the U.S.A. that they have created a full-time job for Laird Wilcox of the University of Kansas, who publishes works like *"Crying Wolf – Hate-crime Hoaxes in America"*, a compilation of fraudulent but attention-grabbing incidents staged by blacks, homosexuals and Jews, with some individuals representing more than one victim-group. Because of the sanctimonious deviousness of the perpetrators these stories make fascinating reading. Naturally, established victim-groups like the Jewish ADL and the NAACP abhor fake hate-crimes. But since most of the hate-crimes compiled in those organizations' annual reports remain unsolved, you wonder how many of those were hoaxes too, only done more competently; and like most organizations, professional victim-groups want to prosper and grow. Wilcox quotes the journalist Debra Nussbaum Cohen:

> "The reality, experts say, is that Jews no longer face serious discrimination in American society – not in the community, the workplace, politics or academia.
> But American Jews are convinced more than ever that anti-Semitism remains a serious threat, although few have encountered any real bias themselves."

"Remember the Holocaust, but don't exploit it. Learn from the Holocaust, but don't let it define who you are. Recognize the evil of what happened, but don't lose hope." These warnings came out of a conference entitled "Ethics after the Holocaust", held at the University of Oregon at the time of the Reedsport hoaxers' convictions. Debora Lipstadt, a professor of Jewish studies, confirmed that today's intense interest in the Holocaust didn't emerge until decades after, because the survivors just wanted to live normal lives. But today, "Persecution and suffering have become the keystones of Jewish identity," she observed, while warning: "We need to find a balance between remembering the Holocaust and living as Jews."

All the more so because Jews carry out God's promise in Genesis 12: "… and all peoples on earth will be blessed through you." Jews have given us great insights and great progress and great pride and joy – and lots of fun, too. Starting with Nobel prizes for science, the number of Jewish winners is phenomenal. Or take literature, music and film: so many Jewish authors, composers and filmmakers have brought out the best and highest in whichever country they made their homes. Without *die Lorelei* by Heinrich Heine, a cruise on the Rhine would carry less enchantment today. Without *The Radetzky March* by Joseph Roth, the charms of the long-dead Austro-Hungarian Empire would not draw as many people to old Vienna as they do. And in America George Gershwin has blessed us with *Porgy and Bess*, while Leonard Bernstein gave us *West Side Story*, Irving Berlin wrote *White Christmas* ... and all the grand movie images that defined the United States and made us proud – the lonesome cowboy, the war hero, the pioneer on the prairie – were fashioned by Jewish filmmakers.

O, I forgot about the fun part. The Three Stooges, Jerry Lewis, Jack Benny, Groucho Marx, Victor Borge, Peter Sellers, Tom Lehrer, George Burns, Danny Kaye, Goldie Hawn, Mel Brooks, Woody Allen, Rodney Dangerfield, Jon Stewart ... The list is near-endless. While Jews make up a mere 3 per cent of the American population, they seem to account for 80 per cent of our professional comedians! But being a good comedian requires the ability to laugh at yourself, and that kind of spirit is scarce among people wallowing in victimhood.

> *Interviewer on German TV:* "Why do you think there's not so much comedy in Germany?"
> *Robin Williams:* "Did you ever think, because you killed off all the funny people?"

Yesterday my friend and sausage maker Gary (Gerhard) Saks dropped in. In his teens he was apprenticed to a German butcher, and until he moved to the Oregon coast twenty-five years ago, meat was his main business. Today, at his RV park an hour and a half down the coast, he still has a small butcher shop and serves German-style dinners. He also offers his dinner customers entertainment, both music and jokes, in which he participates himself. I've told him that his reason for going to such efforts is his secret wish to be a star. He didn't deny it.

"Are things picking up, Gary?"

"O yes," he says, "but you wouldn't believe what happened the other day. Those people ended up staying for free."

"Which people?"

"They threw a fit about a joke I told. They were terribly offended, they said, because they were Jewish. Frankly, I didn't even know they were Jewish. But I didn't think it was a bad joke, either. But Jeannette gave them their money back. Three days' stay."

"Good grief. About a joke? I don't think I would have comped them."

"Well, that's how she is. She doesn't like unhappy people."

"OK Gary, now you got me curious. What was the joke?"

"O," he says, "like I say, I thought it was pretty good. See, this Jewish mother has been after her son to start dating, because he's over thirty already, and she wants grandchildren. So one Saturday evening he finally takes out this girl for a date. And of course the next morning his mother wants to know all about her. "Was she good-looking?"

"O yes mom, a real pretty blonde. With light blue eyes."

"So what's her name?"

"Her name is Schmitt."

"Schmitt? What's her first name?"

"Her first name is Edeltraud."

"Edeltraud Schmitt? Stay away from her! She's German! She'll tell you what to do, morning noon and night! She'll scream at you and make you stand at attention! *Achtung!!* She'll never leave you in peace! I'm warning you!"

So like a good boy he takes her advice and the next Saturday evening he takes out a different girl. And the next morning she wants to know all about it.

"She was pretty too, mom. She had vivid red hair and green eyes. I've never known a girl like her."

"Of course you haven't. So what's her name?"

"O'Hara."

"And her first name?"

"Maureen."

"Maureen O'Hara! An Irish girl! Watch out for her! She'll have a terrible temper. When she doesn't get her way she'll beat you with a frying pan, without even cleaning it first! You have to be more careful with your dates!"

So, OK, the next Saturday evening he's got a date with somebody else, and he doesn't come home for a couple of days. And when he finally shows up, he gets the third degree again. But he's prepared:

"O, we had a great time, mom! You wouldn't believe all the things she has. She lives in a great big mansion, and she has a personal chef, and an Aston-Martin, and she has a yacht, and her own private airplane, and . . ."

"That sounds wonderful, son! So what's her name?"

"Her name is Goldberg."

"A Jewish name! Now we're getting somewhere! And what's her first name? Sarah? Rachel? Ruth? Bathsheba?"

"It's Whoopi."

AMSTERDAM HUMOR

The elderly-but-fit looking couple walking in is accompanied by a blonde girl in her mid-twenties who carries a couple of take-out coffee cups. "Do you have a garbage can?" she asks.

"Sure, let me take care of those," I say, having barely suppressed the urge to respond: 'Nope, no garbage cans here; we just throw everything out the window.' That would have been an Amsterdam gag, but I have found that Amsterdam gags don't stroke Americans in a good way.

I dispose of the paper cups, they sit down, and the elderly gentleman pricks up his ears at the music. Then he asks: "*Is dat Willy Alberti of Johnny Jordaan?*"

"I'm not sure which singer that is," I respond in Dutch. "One of those Jordaan characters." The Jordaan was a poor section of old Amsterdam that produced a lot of popular songs, back in the 'fifties, and their performers had names that ended with Jordaan, I assume to establish the genre. *Johnny Jordaan, Tante Sjaan uit de Jordaan . . .* All of their hits had a touch of twang and a waft of wailing. American Country-Western fans can relate to Jordaan-songs, as long as they accept that nobody except the Dutch understands what they are about.

"I thought you'd be playing German music," he says, looking around the room.

"We do, but I needed a few more hits on my disc. And to Americans it's all the same, anyway. *Allemaal één pot nat.*"

They chuckle; he orders a sandwich, and his wife and daughter go for the soup & salad combo. Like well-Americanized females, they insist on getting the dressing on the side. From this, and from the girl's American English, I decide that they are not tourists from Holland.

"So, where do you live?"

It turns out that they live in Eugene, a couple of hours east of here, and they sort of expected me to know that because we talked before, several years ago. I don't remember it; a restaurant owner talks to a lot of people, most of whom remember him much better than the other way around. My customer has spent a lifetime in the textile business, until he retired from Pendleton woolens. Even Pendleton, an Oregon institution famous for its Indian-style blankets, finally outsourced its production to cheap-labor countries. But that has been the history of the textile business, since forever. He started his career in the Amsterdam textile district. That's long gone now, also.

"You know," I confide to the girl, "when you asked me if we had a garbage can I was tempted to say 'No, we just throw everything out the window.' But that would have been Amsterdam humor, and I found that Americans don't always take it well."

She giggles and tells me that while working as a waitress at a Marie Callender's in Eugene she found that out for herself. "One time a party of four had been seated at a table set for only two, so they told me they'd need two more place-settings. And when I said that eating with your hands was the latest thing in natural living, it went right over their heads."

Aha. She did pick up the habit, probably from her parents.

"And just like you asking if we have a garbage can, Americans will ask: 'Do you have a rest room?' Every restaurant has to have a rest room. But if you say: 'Hell no, everybody does it behind that tree out there," you better add 'Ha-ha, just kidding,' real quick."

General laughter ensues. The girl relates how a Dutch friend of hers hasn't been able to find a job. He decided that the way to connect with his interviewers was to use Amsterdam humor, but it fell flat every time.

I imagine his interviewers scribbling on his application: "Seems to think he has to entertain his employer."

Successful humor is, indeed, specific to occasions, but also to times, places, politics, and more. Once when I was working on my house I found a San Francisco Examiner from 1898, inside a wall. Just like any American paper today, it had a whole page of comic strips: the Katzenjammer Kids and lots more I'd never heard of. But I found them incomprehensible. They must have contained lots of plays on long-forgotten news items from the 1890s.

Amsterdam humor, which includes a sizable dose of Jewish humor, doesn't depend on the latest news much. But it contains little barbs, always at the expense of the listener. So while Amsterdam gags aim to show up the listener as silly/ignorant/ungrammatical/uninformed ..., they also aim to show up the speaker as especially clever. This is why it will not succeed in America, least of all if practiced by people in service occupations. People in this country expect waitresses, desk clerks and sales ladies to strictly stick to business. No smart-alecks wanted.

Once during a short visit to my native country I needed to hold some papers together, so I asked a server at a ferryboat lunch counter if he might have a rubber band somewhere.

"Nope," he said. "You better fish that rubber band out of your underpants."

LEAVE IT TO THE BEAVER

On my supply rounds this morning I need to stop at the grocery store, for parsnips and leeks. Due to the winter season, we've been cutting it close on the veggies. Order too much from the wholesaler, and you lose in spoilage what you gain in price. So here I am at the Fred Meyer store, collecting five or six pounds of parsnips and the same amount of leeks, for our winter vegetable *mélange*. I usually have bad luck judging the speed of check-out lines, but this time I hit bull's eye. One checker is almost done with her single customer, a female whose golden years are a distant memory. Quickly I move in and plunk my basket on the conveyor belt. The aged shopper has paid, and is collecting her stuff.

"Are these turnips?" the checker asks.

"Parsnips," I correct her. She looks up the code for parsnips and next arranges the leeks, which are wet and muddy, on her scale.

"What *are* you gonna do with all those leeks?" asks the elderly lady, still collecting her stuff.

"Ah – I thought I'd create some work for the plumbers," I explain. "Construction work is slow right now, so they could fix a few leeks."

They look at me strangely. Multiculturalism has failed to create a market for Amsterdam humor. Even so, what business is it of hers? Do I ask perfect strangers: "What *are* you gonna do with all that Ex-Lax?" or: "What *are* you gonna do with all those Depends?" Huh?

The checker slips the soggy leek arrangement into a separate plastic bag, and I hand over the cash. The other shopper is still there, loitering.

"Now really, what *are* you gonna do with all those leeks when you get home?" she demands, still hoping for enlightenment.

"Soon as I get home I'm gonna call the plumber, because with that many leeks, we're bound to have water problems." I say, heading out.

Thanks to the profound scientific mystery of Global Warming, we're having a cold snap right now. Nothing like the hard freezes in the Midwest and back East, but chilly enough for me to wear my tall black Russian fur hat, the one that still carries a Soviet Navy emblem. Say what you will about the Russians, but they do know about warm hats. Besides, there is a positive side to the failure of Amsterdam humor to make inroads in the USA. Wear an unusual hat in Amsterdam, and you're likely to see people openly snickering. At a minimum you will have a gang of little kids pointing fingers and running after you, jeering. You see none of that here. Americans are discreet.

As I walk in through the front door of the restaurant, Adam and Tamera are sitting in the waiting area, taking a break. Tamera is chatting, while Adam scans the classifieds for cars and guns. He looks up at my hat, with an Amsterdam-level disdain.

"That's the biggest beaver I ever saw," he scoffs.

"O, I don't think you've seen a whole lot of beaver yet." It was on the tip of my tongue; it had to come out, and Tamera cracks up. Adam gives me a blank stare, which after multiple seconds becomes a blush. So far his relationships with the opposite sex can be described as more mercenary than biblical. To him, the primary use of girls is as co-conspirators in minor commercial corruption. In the morning he's likely to saunter in holding one of those huge, overpriced coffee drinks with ten flavors, gobs of whipped froth, and more corn syrup than coffee. But when asked why he spends such outrageous amounts for a mere drink, he'll grin and explain he got it free from one if his many female admirers working in a drive-thru espresso. Similar story in the afternoon, when he walks in carrying a big submarine sandwich.

Still giggling, Tamera starts sweeping, and I take my veggies to the kitchen. While he starts chopping them, I tell Adam about the nosy shopper. "Did you know her?" he asks.

"I wouldn't know her from Adam. Or Eve."

"Then maybe she was putting the make on you," he ventures.

I hadn't thought of that. Now I'm the one who's slow on the uptake. She was not my type, and well past pull date. But then, I'm no spring chicken either. Predators lurk in unexpected places, ready to jump the unwary.

"You know, Adam," I say, "You might have something there. Years ago I decided once that the canvas on our awnings needed to be washed. They were filthy, but they were too big, so I dragged them down to the laundromat behind Safeway, where they have these oversized washers and dryers. There was only one other customer there, a woman, and she was all smiles, for some strange reason. You know, "How you doin'? You got enough quarters?" And then it dawned on me: laundromats are places where boy meets girl."

"That's right," says Adam. "Married people don't go to laundromats."

So, laundromats are hunting grounds for females on the prowl. And for males too, I suppose, although I can't see how laundry can be conducive to romance, dirty or clean. I mean, the laundry. And the same hazard may await single males shopping at the supermarket. "Why isn't the wife doing this for you, huh? You need some help?"

"Grrr – get away from me."

"WE GOT THREE ABUNDANT MEALS A DAY"

"Is everything satisfactory?" I ask the elderly couple. The portly husband has been brutally attacking his Oktoberfest plate, which consists of three German sausages – Bratwurst, knackwurst and a long, thin wiener – plus a slice of sauerbraten with tangy gravy, accompanied by warm potato salad, sauerkraut and red cabbage. It's similar to what Frenchmen call *choucroute garni*, sauerkraut with stuff, and the Germans *Schlachtplatte* – a butcher's platter.

"Good food," he sighs contentedly, waving his fork long enough to cool it slightly, "and plenty of it." While the fork resumes the attack I move on to the next table, to refill one coffee cup and two ice waters.

"Just fill mine with coffee also, will you?" says the faded woman across from the coffee refill. She holds out her almost-empty cup of hot chocolate. I comply, make sure everything else is satisfactory too, and go on my way reflecting that twenty years ago I might have charged her for the cup of coffee, besides charging for the chocolate. But I won't, just like long ago we quit charging for refills of sodas and iced teas. Europeans expect to pay for every cup and for every glass, and you can still forget about getting free ice water in the Old Country. Which is odd, considering how Americanized they have become, with McDonald's and all. I suppose their reason for skipping the free ice-water custom is purely economic. But it might be cosmetic, too. Back in the 'sixties in Amsterdam, an old sailor explained to me once that it's their habit of drinking ice water all day long that gives elderly American women such wrinkly faces.

Whatever be the truth of that, American restaurant customers expect abundance of both food and drink, without being nickel-and-dimed for refills. And guilt-mongering Malthusian moralizers can preach to satiation about eating smaller portions, but the typical American restaurant can't afford to have people walk out the door grumbling that they didn't get their fill. Except in a few anorexic enclaves in New York City and in Beverly Hills, L.F.B.B. *(Little-Food- for-Big-Bucks)* has few devotees in America.

I suppose this is why the one customer who ever took exception to the amount of food on his plate was a foreigner. An elderly British gentleman, he waxed outraged at the size of the Beef Stroganoff I placed before him. Sputtering that he couldn't come close to finishing it, he made an impression. Not because he belonged to a large flock, but because he was such a rare bird. Almost everyone in America likes big meals, and if they can't finish them they like bringing the leftovers home, thereby proving that there is such a thing as a free lunch.

This expectation of abundant food has long and strong roots, I've discovered. This past winter I assisted with the publication of a book containing the memoirs of my sister-in-law's grandfather. Born in 1887 in my hometown of Terneuzen, in the southwest of the Netherlands, Jan Geensen was a sailor who traveled in these parts over a century ago, back in 1906-1907. Born in 1887, he died in 1967, after finishing most of his memoirs, which must have been based on notes or on a diary, since they are quite detailed.

Jan Geensen's early youth was typical of that era: hard work, poverty, and numerous siblings, about half of whom died in infancy, followed by the mother. In 1901, at age 14, Jan decided he wanted to be a seaman, so he started working as a deck hand on a sailing barge, in spring and summer hauling rock for local diking projects, and sugar beets in late fall. From the barge he advanced to short-line freighters and tramps,

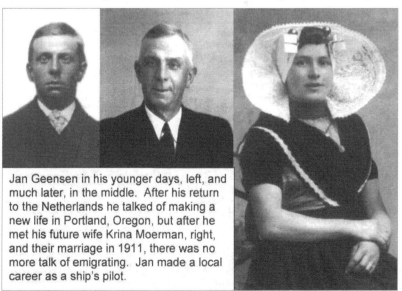

Jan Geensen in his younger days, left, and much later, in the middle. After his return to the Netherlands he talked of making a new life in Portland, Oregon, but after he met his future wife Krina Moerman, right, and their marriage in 1911, there was no more talk of emigrating. Jan made a local career as a ship's pilot.

nearly all sailing vessels too, which he preferred over the steam ships that were slowly replacing them. For one thing, he felt that for the crew having to climb the masts to the various yards, raising and lowering the ship's sails together, enhanced solidarity and friendships. And for another, a sailing ship making its way across the ocean had incomparable charms for a sailor who was also a romantic. The translated quotes that follow are from the book:

"From on top of the yard you had a beautiful view. All around you'd see the sea with its foamy heads, the ship plowing through at a slant, due to the pressure of the sails. While stomping back and forth through the waves and with the bow hitting a breaker, the bow-spray would flit across the ship like a cloud. At night also, this could be beautiful. Especially when the rolling waves produced a green, luminous effect, with the repulsed bow-water passing below the lee-side, and the wind playing violin on the taut rigging and the yards tight as strings, and you'd taste the salt water in your mouth.

" . . . With nice weather and a light breeze, under full sail with a favorable wind, the ship would glide almost noiselessly through the water, and all you heard would be the sound of breaking water against the bow. With strong winds and high seas, of course, we had to reduce sail, including on the bow-sprit.

After lowering the stay-sail, which had to be taken in, you'd have to climb over the front of the ship and onto the bow-sprit, to start [reducing sail] clear at the tip. One job that called for paying particularly close attention. You had to time yourself to the pace of the breakers and the rise and fall of the ship's bow, in order to pass the lowest point at the right instant, quick as a whistle, before the front of the ship dove into the oncoming sea and a big chunk of water came across. If you were tardy, you'd have to hold on tight, and at times you'd be submerged up to your waist.

Once you continued on to the tip you were past that point, and because usually at that time they would heave-to a couple of compass-points, the ship would ride a bit more quietly for a spell, which you needed to fasten the sail. At such times also it was a beautiful sight to look back, especially on the larger ships on which I served later on. The sails standing round and tight in the wind, the ship tilting while regularly catching the oncoming waves ... Especially by the light of the moon, that was a beautiful sight." [1]

One of Jan's first ships after the barge was the Dairy Maid, a British coastal schooner. Because the ship's cook quit in Belfast, Jan was given that job, in addition to his other duties:

"The daily menu was rather on the fatty side, because they often had mutton. Plates and silverware were so greasy, and since soda or soap were out of the question, dishwashing was a slippery job which, once at sea, had to be done with sea water besides. The dishtowel used to be as greasy as a freshly-caught eel. The potatoes were boiled in sea water also, because the supply of fresh water was never large." (p. 33)

In 1905, with his father's written permission, co-signed by the mayor of Terneuzen, Jan signed up for *de grote vaart*, or "the big sail", the Dutch term for ocean-going, deep-water shipping. His first transatlantic voyage was to Baltimore, where "... it was obvious from everything that living standards were higher than in Europe, opportunities for making a living greater, and the people more independent in their ways." (p. 77) Next, during the final days of 1905, Jan left Rotterdam on an iron four-masted bark called the Galgate, home-ported in Liverpool, and bound

---

[1] *Jan Geensen, een Jongen van de 'Westkant'*, edited and collated by Ad Willems and Boudewijn Verstraeten, Heemkundige Vereniging Terneuzen. Terneuzen: W. H. Broekhuysen, Postbus 1180, 4530 GD, pp. 29-30. (If my English translation is not always grammatically perfect, that's because Jan's Dutch was not either, and I meant to follow him as close as possible.) For the other quotes I have added page numbers at the end of each one.

for Portland, Oregon. It's hard to imagine today's sailors putting up with conditions of those days. For the first three weeks the Galgate fought fierce southwestern and western storms, advancing only 250 miles. Although the crew wore hip boots and oil skins whenever on deck, they lived in wet clothes all that time. Except for the stove in the galley, the ship had no source of heat, and due to the heaving and swinging the cook was not always able to prepare anything hot, anyway. This experience would repeat itself during the trip around Cape Horn.

"Among deep-water sailors it was common knowledge that on board British sailing vessels the food was nothing to rave about. In the morning we usually got a thick oat porridge boiled in water (burgoo), occasionally rice with curry. After leaving port we got fresh meat at noon as well as in the evening for a few more days, and since refrigerators didn't exist yet in that era, after that they would switch to salted meat, alternating between beef and pork. The latter was best, since the beef consisted almost exclusively of ribs, lean with lots of gristle and bones.

When the fresh meat was gone we got, until it ran out, soup with some potatoes and vegetables in it which, because it had been made from salted meat, was not very tasty. Also we regularly got a kind of hash, pieces of diced potato mixed with meat, as long as the potatoes on board held out. But after a month or so we'd run out already.

During lunch they also supplied [butter, margarine or lard], jam, marmalade, sugar and milk, which were rationed. . . .

Tea or coffee were not provided during the night. When the cook was done with dinner the galley was locked up until the next morning, and it took until six-thirty the next morning before the watch on deck got anything hot to drink. Making coffee was something in which the English did not excel . . .

Between meals we had to report to the rear deck around eleven-thirty and a ration of lime juice was handed out, which had to be consumed in the presence of the steward, in order to prevent scurvy. On English ships this was required by law . ..

Griping usually was more about the skimpy nourishment received on board than about the lime juice ration. In those days ships from Liverpool had the worst reputation. Because of the advance of steam-shipping, ship owners were trying to stay in business by skimping on the food, among other things. The majority of the captains, mostly Welshmen who were known for being thrifty, used all possible means to enrich themselves."   (p. 87)

For some time, while heading into the Southern hemisphere, the weather improved greatly but then it got much worse again, during the three weeks it took to round Cape Horn:

> "It continually got colder, with snow- and hail-storms. The crew's quarters had no heat. Cold and damp outer garments didn't get a chance to dry, and oilskins and boots were soaked. Besides, not every day was it possible to cook in the galley which was located behind the crew's quarters, because a lot of water came across that spot. Instead of a piece of corned beef, hard tack with marmalade and some weak tea or coffee twice a day, we were now being served this three times a day, by necessity.
> The mood among the crew did not improve ..." (p. 94)

Besides the food and living conditions, the monotony of a very long trip must have caused some of the crew's discontent. From Rotterdam it took the Galgate 139 days to reach Portland, Oregon, on May 18, 1906. After arrival the crew's dissatisfaction, particularly with the food, induced the majority to jump ship and seek their fortunes in America's West. Jan writes that he never heard another word from fellow-sailors about the Galgate, but the record says that ten years later, during World War I, it was torpedoed by a German U-Boot off the British coast.

For a fee of one dollar, a Portland employment agency arranged a job for Jan at a sawmill near Astoria, near the mouth of the Columbia. He took the night boat, a three-decked sternwheeler, downriver. Most of the passengers were single, taciturn men of many nationalities, including many Scandinavians who worked in the woods or in the salmon industry. During the trip most of them dozed in a deck chair with their ticket tucked in their hat band, for the conductor. At around 6 AM the boat docked at a pier near the mill, where he also found several other buildings from which the sound of voices rose. Entering one of these, he showed proof of employment (a metal token from the employment agency), and was promptly shown a place at a table:

> "Servants with large platters walked around continually to supply the men's needs, which were not modest. It sure was an extensive breakfast, with oat porridge, two kinds of bread, butter, fried bacon and eggs, small biscuits, still warm, and stacks of small pancakes (flapjacks) eaten warm with beautiful yellow syrup, and your choice of tea or coffee. I did complete justice to the meal and had never before had such an extensive breakfast, so the beginning of my adventure was encouraging in every way." (p. 102)

After this he was shown the way to the mill. Wages were 2 dollars a day, with $2.50 deducted for room and board weekly, which he thought was quite reasonable:

"Back for mid-day food in the cookhouse another extensive meal was served, during which I first got acquainted with sweet potatoes. I got a big one and also a regular potato, both roasted brown, served with fried meat and various vegetables. All of this preceded by a good soup and at the end a dessert and fruit, of which everyone could have as much as he wanted." (p. 104)

In April of that year, perhaps not far from the Galgate's position in the Pacific just then, the San Francisco earthquake and fire had destroyed much of that city, so the sawmills in the forested Pacific Northwest were putting on extra shifts to meet the exploding demand for lumber. On weekends the men often went to Astoria, where the saloons provided free food, and rather good food at that. They only charged for the beer. Eventually a Captain Larsen, the Danish master of the Echo, a 4-mast barkentine, got wind that Jan was a qualified seaman, and asked him to sign on for a trip hauling lumber to Sydney, Australia. So Jan joined the crew of the Echo, his first American sailing ship. Once again, he was surprised by American standards of food service:

The Echo, a 4-mast barkentine built at the Simpson shipyard in North Bend in 1896. Back then most or all local sawmills had adjacent shipyards.

"The meals aboard were plentiful and of about the same quality as in the sawmill's cookhouses. They were prepared by a cook who knew his business, since along the entire American west coast no cooks could sign on unless they were qualified, and members of the union. For the night crews after dinner, the cook would always push a couple of well-prepared dishes through the galley's pass-through, which could be used at any time.

Many of them were Negroes, and the cook we had possessed all the airs and manners of a real hotel chef, a man who knew his worth." (p. 112) . . .

"The food on board remained excellent and full of variety. At mealtimes there were always hot and well-prepared dishes on the menu. However, due to the large quantities sometimes more was tossed overboard than was eaten.

Unlike on board English vessels, here no lime juice was provided but each evening we got canned fruit of the highest Californian quality. As prescribed by law, when a ship was in port fresh fruit must be supplied instead of canned. We also were allowed to use water much more freely. This way everyone was able to keep himself and his clothes as clean as he wanted."   (p. 114)

January/February of 1907 finds the Echo, back from Australia by way of the Hawaiian Islands, at a sawmill on Coos Bay (actually at the town of North Bend, which is a couple of miles north of the present city of Coos Bay, but also located on the body of water that's called Coos Bay) to load lumber for California. Not surprisingly for that time of year, the

The Simpson sawmill and shipyard in North Bend in 1899. Most likely this was the second mill where the Echo loaded lumber for California, the first being the Simpson-owned Porter mill south of this one.

Coos Bay area impressed Jan as a dull and rainy place. One Saturday Jan and his friend William Borland, a Scotsman who ran the ship's donkey engine, went ashore to go drinking with the Finnish crew of a steam schooner. After some time Jan returned to the Echo. Borland stayed behind, but never showed up. After several more days of loading lumber the ship was moved to a different mill with more water depth, to be topped off. It was after that when Borland's body was found floating on the surface.

The Coos County coroner decided that, inebriated, he had fallen off the gangplank, drowned, and had been pressed into the mud by the ship until it was moved. The captain wrote to Borland's mother, notifying her of her son's passing. His wages due were insufficient to cover funeral expenses, so his clothing and personal effects had to be sold among the crew. Jan ended up buying his shaving gear, which he kept for many years as *een aandenken* – a memory.

Jan Geensen with the international crew of the Edward R. West, a four-masted U.S.-owned schooner on which he sailed from Aberdeen, Washington. Rear, from left to right: the Japanese cook, Swedish First Mate, Danish captain (with bowler hat); and Jan Geensen. Front row, l. to r.: Tom, also called Frenchy, a Breton; Nike from Latvia, Christian, a Dane, and Nils Andersson, from Sweden.

Before Jan headed back across the Pacific to Australia, from where he eventually returned to the Netherlands, he made one trip from the American northwest coast down to Chile, leaving from Aberdeen, on Grays Harbor bay in the state of Washington, on board the Edward R. West:

> "The cook, a young Japanese, was a nice guy who came from coastal shipping. He knew his business very well, since cooks, being union members, had to have the required qualifications.
> The food therefore was excellent, ample and of first quality. Margarine was not used. Instead we got pickled blocks of butter, wrapped in cloth, from kegs. We got three plentiful meals a day. The food was handed out through a pass-through from the galley, which was located behind the crew's quarters.
> In the evening, before the cook finished his day, a few more platters were prepared, so all night through the table was set with food for the incoming and outgoing watch. If fresh fruit was not available, canned fruit was provided."
>
> (p. 134)

Later on, now back on a British ship headed for Sydney, Jan recalled wistfully:

> "I have never come across better ship's cooks than on ships sailing along the (U.S.) Pacific Coast, each and every one, whether white or colored, were real professionals, not just in preparing food but also in serving it. Most of them could hold their own not only on board ship but equally well in all sorts of onshore dining establishments, also with regard to conversation and behavior."
>
> (p. 148)

In short, anybody who thinks he can convert this country to the worship of anorexia may end up flattened by the full weight of American culinary history. Not many people try, as shown by the bank across from my restaurant that puts out bowls of free candy. Another local bank offers free cookies and coffee every day. The hardware store keeps a popcorn machine going. They pop about 30 pounds a week: help yourself. A people used to free munchies everywhere is unlikely to favor lean cuisine.

I told my friend and German sausage maker Gary Saks about Jan's observations. Gary had an older friend who had served on a German U-Boot that had been disabled by a US Navy ship. The American ship picked up the surviving crew. Even though food for German U-Boot crews was good (for wartime Germany), Gary's friend thought he'd died and gone to heaven when he was put to work in the galley. The cook had just finished breakfast, and he was going to chuck the leftover fried eggs overboard. His new galley-mate couldn't believe his eyes and intervened, lining them up on his arm and eating every single egg, one after another.

And just the other day, I learned that during all these years, Jan's drowned friend Bill Borland has lain buried in Coos Bay's old, neglected Pioneer cemetery, the way the crow flies perhaps a quarter mile from my house. His grave is in a section that had been purchased by the county back then, for indigent burials. He has no stone, but with the aid of the cemetery map and a measuring tape you can tell where it is. On the map it's grave number 13, located in section 13. How is that for a sailor's luck?

IN A NEW ENGLAND CHURCHYARD

Full rising moon at twilight,
look on these cold, grey stones;
review these granite sentinels
who guard these ancient bones.

They've lichen on their tunics,
and weather-beaten mien;
the chiseled record indicates
the service they have seen.

In different shapes and sizes,
aligned in ragged rows,
they've braved the suns of countless days,
and centuries of snows.

O yes, they stand obliquely –
a motley troop are they –
but stood two hundred years, and more,
and never missed a day!

C. L. Grove

IS IT CONVENIENT?

It's 6 AM local time, which means it's 9 PM the night before, back home in Coos Bay. My mother is still in bed and I wouldn't have minded staying in mine longer, but I couldn't. Jet lag is one of the twin demons of overseas travel, the other being cooped up in a sticky, vaguely polluted, overcrowded airplane for what seems a life sentence. The animal rights people clamor mightily for free-range chickens; how about some room to roam for us long-distance flying fowl? As to the jet lag, last night around 6:30 local time, having lost all hope of being able to keep my eyes open I stumbled off to bed, slept till 11:30, then sat up downstairs with a glass of wine reading the local news until drowsiness crept back. Then I slept a second installment, all the way till five this morning. That comes to more than eight hours of sleep. Not bad, I suppose, considering the almost complete night-and-day switch I inflicted on myself.

Sitting up in the middle of their night, not mine, reading the local news, became my involuntary immersion into local culture, and my re-acquaintance with local values. For instance, the lead headline in the local section of the *Provinciale Zeeuwse Courant* (Provincial Zealand Courant, or PZC) announces the formation of a local visual artists' lobby – charitably called a foundation – to promote sales of their works. To better serve its clientele of impecunious *artistes*, the foundation's governing board will include several local politicians – a *sine qua non*, since in the Netherlands all interest groups, from chess clubs to shady mosques, count on getting subsidies from the public trough. And the *artistes* can cite an important precedent. Decades ago already, a subsidy program for artists devised by the national government in The Hague was experiencing runaway success. By dint of bureaucratic logic, every graduate of a Dutch arts academy was a deemed an *artiste* and therefore entitled to a guaranteed income, as long as he gave the Ministry of Arts and Sciences a small number of his works each year. It sounded sensible, but after a few years, something had to give. Ministerial art warehouses were stuffed with stuff that no sane person wanted to see all day. Here was a crisis like the bursting grain silos of the American farm surplus program, with one key difference: no human beings anywhere interested in consuming it. Last I remember, Art Ministry officials were considering peddling their excess art on EBay, a tactic that held some promise as long as the opening bids were kept below one guilder (this was before the Euro's entry.) Maybe the overlooked solution lay in the

Dutch obsession with recycling, which seems to copy Germany's. Glass here, plastic there, grass clippings in the next bin, and 'art' in number 4.

Another issue of the PZC carries a big picture of the skipper of a freight barge moored in a local canal, touching up the paint on his vessel's stern. To do this he is sitting on a flimsy-looking board that rests (1) on the edge of the dock, (2) on the ship's twin rudders, and (3) on a floating rowboat midway. I suppose he has experience with this kind of seating. There must be hundreds of thousands of inland barges like his in northwestern Europe; there always seem to have been. Often the skipper/owner and his family live on board, although the children may be at a special boarding school. For shore-side excursions, many vessels today carry a small car, traditionally surrounded by the wife's potted plants. According to the paper, waterborne freight hauling is starting to pick up, but the painting skipper is still waiting for a load.

And there is more: a contest for the best local mussel-restaurant has already attracted over two hundred entries. Since time immemorial mussels have been a cheap, popular food around here, with towns in past ages coming to blows over the best mussel-picking waters.

I also learn that at an intersection not far from where I'm sitting a car ended up in the *sloot* – the ditch, pronounced 'Slote' or 'Sloat.' That, by the way, is the meaning of the last name of that creepy killer of party girls, Joran van der Sloot. The Creature from the Black Ditch. This ubiquitous, essential part of the Dutch landscape – not him but the ditch – features in many popular expressions. Bringing up old disputes is derided as "dragging old cows out of the *sloot*." Instead of sliding from the frying pan into the fire, the Dutch slip from the bank into the *sloot*. As to the 22-year-old driver of the *sloot*-car, he claimed that it was all the fault of his 23-year-old passenger's yanking on his steering wheel. But his own powers of observation were diminished by a blood-alcohol level 3.5 times the legal limit, so his license was seized. Perhaps because of their alcoholically relaxed state, the *sloot*-pair suffered no physical harm; their hometown is Wachtebeke, just across the border in Belgian Flanders, a region long infamous for its heroic levels of imbibery.

This trip of mine came up rather suddenly. It had been four years since I visited my mother, and back then she was fine, as fine as a ninety-year-old with seven children, sixty-four years as a shopkeeper and two hip replacements could be. For over thirty years she's lived alone in a charming little house in a small village called Spui, taking care of herself and enjoying visits from children, grandchildren and lately great-grandchildren. But she will be 95 this December, and in recent phone calls my elder brother, the only one who lives nearby, mentioned some changes in her: memory loss and odd behavior. I didn't like the sound of that, but I thought he might be exaggerating. So I called her to chat, and to ask for a local person's address, Kees den Hamer. We had a good talk, she rummaged around and read me his address from one of the stack of notebooks she keeps by the phone. During the conversation she repeated herself a bit, but don't we all? Ten minutes later the phone rang; it was her. "Say", she announced, rather pleased with herself, "I just found Kees den Hamer's address for you."

Instead of flying to Amsterdam, this time I booked a flight to Frankfurt. My plan was to drive a rental car from there, but I cancelled that part shortly before I left. I should have known better than to risk a road trip after a long flight through all those time zones. Weird things will happen. My vision will seem off, and I have trouble focusing. My reaction time expands. So I cancelled the car in favor of a train trip.

During the flight from Portland to Chicago I sat next to a fellow I figured was from China, but I didn't find out because he never spoke a word. Not even a syllable. But in his non-verbal way he seemed kind. On the Lufthansa flight to Frankfurt I sat in the very back row, with a German from a village in the Rhineland for my neighbor. He was very talkative, although that was a mixed blessing due to his abysmally bad breath. He was returning from a research trip about a distant ancestor by the name of Franz Sigel who had fled to America after the 1848 revolt against the Baden government. In Europe 1848 is still known as a famous revolutionary year, when aroused mobs everywhere made petty rulers tremble. As usual the revolt against the established order started in France, from where it quickly spread to the German principalities. In those places, German revolutionaries fought for two goals: civil rights and the unification of Germany, because they were tired of the thirty-odd petty princes lording it over the lands, and they expected a unified Germany to bring them a parliamentary system and the civil rights that other European nations enjoyed. In Baden the revolutionaries were put down with the aid of Prussian troops, and of course the irony was that within about twenty years Prussian troops would be the ones to unify Germany. But in the meantime tens of thousands of Germans who had fought on the wrong side, including Sigel, emigrated to America where they became known as 48-ers. (As opposed to Germans like John Sutter who sparked the California gold rush, making himself the first forty-niner.) Franz Sigel lived in New York and in St. Louis, Missouri, a slave-owning state that did not join the Confederacy, and he served with some distinction as a Union army general during the Civil War, leading troops of German immigrants like himself who supposedly sang: *Ya! Das ist drue, I shpeaks mit you, I'm going to fight mit Sigel.* It was all quite interesting, but I didn't have the heart to suggest that my companion invest in some dental care.

The opportunity to see some German scenery while avoiding the obnoxiously congested roads in the Amsterdam-Rotterdam area had been my reasons for renting a car in Frankfurt. Having canceled the car I headed for the train ticket window, but the reaction of the clerk to my request for a ticket to Goes should have tipped me off that I had made a bad trade. For starters, he had no idea where Goes was. And once he found out, it turned out that I had to change trains half a dozen times, which usually involved lugging my bags up and down staircases to and from underground passages, because walking across the tracks to get to a different platform is as *verboten* in Germany as it is *verboden* in the Netherlands. The only good part was that this kept me from dozing off.

Venlo, the first Dutch train station and the fourth train change, provided me with my first cultural *déjà vu:* airborne cow pollution. The entire depot was redolent with manure! By the way, the same olfactory outpouring greets you while exiting the terminal at Amsterdam airport. It's the inevitable by-product of the massive Dutch dairy industry. But there was some compensation. The Dutch girls on the trains were still blonde, good-looking and svelte; I never saw any 250-pounders like the ones at the Coos Bay WalMart. Moreover they cared for their

The Ghetto reborn: Camel-sponsored smokers' refuge at the Frankfurt airport.

appearance, but not by mutilating themselves with tattoos and jewelry in odd places. Dutch girls today seem to go around in one of two get-ups: many wear jeans that very tightly fit the buns, plus boots, often with very high heels, while the rest favor black tights barely covered with very short and flimsy skirts that look like they might be lost with a minimum of encouragement. All this tantalizing titillation did make me wonder why the Dutch are one of many European nations that have slid into a demographic death spiral: they are not producing enough babies to maintain their native population. Instead, their most prodigious procreators are the pudgy Muslim women that shuffle down the streets wrapped in yards of heavy dark fabrics, never making eye contact.

From Goes (pronounced *Ghoos*) I took a bus through the new tunnel running south under the Schelde, built by miners from now-closed mines in former East Germany. The bus dropped me off a mile or so from my goal, a hamlet called Spui (related to our word *spew*; in Holland *spui* marks a place where excess water is run out of a tide gate at low tide). If I had waited another hour I could have caught a bus that went all the way there, but I figured a brisk walk would do me good. Too much sitting around, and besides, it was a dry day. Pulling my wheeled suitcase and my carry-on I marched down the bicycle path, passed off and on by groups of high school kids biking home, all of whom were very polite. Bicycle paths are one of the pillars of Dutch society. About nine feet wide outside the cities, most are protected not by mere white stripes on the road but by extremely car-unfriendly Siegfried lines: rows of trees, thick brush, concrete blocks, and sometimes all of those together in one stretch of no-man's land. So here I am trudging along the bicycle path, switching over to a sidewalk while entering the hamlet. I figure that since 1980 I've stayed at my mother's place eleven times. This time my brother and I agreed not to tell her ahead of time, because she's taken to worrying so much. He described what sounded like anxiety attacks. Entering Spui I pass the small farm where they breed the handsome Frisian black horses; a few more houses; the contractor who is unloading bricks at his establishment – *Goeiendag* - and I briefly consider ducking behind my mother's new hedge, to preserve the surprise. But it's too awkward to do that, with my rolling bags, and she's not in the habit of gazing out the window. I push open the iron gate, walk up to the front door and ring the bell. No sounds of life inside. A second ring. This time I hear something. The door opens:

"Is it convenient for me to drop in?"

She looks at me uncomprehendingly, then lets me in and gives me a stern look. "Why of course it's convenient. Why do you ask?"

I meant to stump her, but now I'm the one stumped. I'm irreverent enough to think of that superb scene towards the end of the Gospel of John, when a distraught Mary Magdalene, having found Jesus' tomb empty, through her tears asks a dimly perceived gardener where his body has been taken; and the presumed gardener says: "Mary - ", stopping her in her tracks. I hope the reader doesn't conclude that I think I'm Jesus.

"Uh, mother ..."

An interminable second or two, and then the cloud lifts: "Why Wim! What are you doing here? Are you really here? Let me look at you! Oof – I have to sit down! What a surprise! Come, come!" Gingerly with her artificial hips she hobbles down the steps – the old cottage is slightly lower than the street, which is built on an old dike – and she sinks into the red-upholstered tallboy chair where she's been doing her puzzles. We hold hands, we talk, and she keeps asking questions to adjust to this new reality.

I tell her I decided that after four years it was time for a visit, which is only part of the truth. All excited, she calls my brother and his wife, and they announce they'll be over with some food. While bustling around the kitchen, rustling up some food I don't want and a glass of wine I do want, she suddenly stops and turns to ask:

"Have you ever been in my house before?"

CARROT POLICIES

It's eight in the morning. My mother is still in bed, so the window blinds are not open yet. Just outside the house an animated babble of young Dutch voices quickly gains volume, and equally quickly fades away. Next another group of cheery chatterers turns up, only to vanish in a second or two. These are unseen convoys of teenagers, pedaling to school on the bike path in front of the house. Most of these kids, if they are from Axel, the nearest town, travel 10 kilometers (6 to 7 miles) every morning and afternoon. If they are from Hulst or Sas-van-Gent, as some were in my day, they pedal twice that far. They never race; they just keep a steady pace that's set by a *kopligger* or *windbreker* – a lead rider who breaks the wind for the convoy. No, not THAT kind of wind.

School buses are rare in this country, which I think is a good thing, by and large. Most Dutch kids are expected to get themselves to school, even if it takes an hour of bicycling each way, and regardless of the weather. This daily, hearty exercise gives them a life-long upper leg strength rarely seen among American kids, despite the far greater emphasis on sports in U.S. high schools. But one American custom they have copied in recent years is the ingestion of soda-pop while riding, leaving trails of empty cans in their wake. The American remedy would have been authoritarian, consisting of menacing road signs: "FINE FOR LITTERING $2,000. FINES TRIPLE FOR USED CONDOMS."

Something like that. Ours is the stick-approach, while the Dutch wave a carrot. Along the ubiquitous inter-city bike paths, devices that look like slanted basketball nets have been placed. They are called *blikvangers* – a play on words, since the word *blik* means a can but also a glance, a look. And a *vanger* is a catcher. Hence a *blikvanger* is an eye-catcher as well as a can-catcher. After a mile or two from their high school, the home-biking kids compete in making baskets with their empty soda cans and other consumption clutter. They don't all succeed, because when it comes to throwing things nobody can hit the target like an American. The Dutch are soccer-players, which makes them much better at kicking stuff. Still, the *blikvangers* work well enough. If nothing else they concentrate the clutter, greatly reducing clean-up time.

You could say that in spirit, the *blikvangers* are close cousins of the fly-urinals at Schiphol airport, near Amsterdam, because the thinking is the same: to achieve your social goal, which is to minimize cleanup, you offer an inducement. Embedded in the porcelain of each urinal is a ceramic fly. Every guy has an irresistible urge to use his outflow to propel something. If it can't be a million KW turbine, a fly will do, so it gets a lot of concentrated attention, though it never moves. Result: less mopping for the restroom attendants. From Schiphol, fly-urinals have now spread to other public facilities, like restaurants. And more recently someone invented what they call a *vliegsticker;* a fly-sticker. Instead of being embedded in the porcelain, this fly is stuck inside a non-fly urinal and changes color when hit with urine. So the guy gets a real, visible reward for his drain. To get it he may even strain.

This preference for the carrot also manifests itself in the way the Dutch control speeding. In recent years every town has gotten serious about slowing down motorized traffic – but not with speed signs and sneaky radar cops behind trees. Every community, even the little hamlet of Spui where my mother lives, now has *drempels* (thresholds), very long speed bumps that can cause cars to become airborne if their drivers don't slow down. The road to Spui, which used to be a main road before the proliferation of freeways, has lost its stripe in the middle even though it's wide enough for two cars. But on each side it has a dotted white line that seems to remove 4 feet from the driving surface. When when two opposing cars meet they move into those 4-feet margins to pass; then they return to the single lane. Notice that this arrangement keeps drivers away from the shoulders while paying attention to each other. But then, at the entrance to a village or a hamlet like Spui those 4-feet side-strips become inaccessible, having been covered with

The single-lane *drempel* for traffic entering Spui. A second *drempel* awaits cars a couple of hundred yards down the road. Notice the absence of speed signs. The bicycle path is behind the hedge on the left.

concrete-and-brick contrivances that leave only enough roadbed for one car. Thus opposing drivers cannot avoid taking turns coming through. As if this is not enough, the road leading into this arrangement may have acquired artificial curves, and the part inside the restriction is raised by a very long *drempel*. Drempels, because they leave drivers in suspense longer, are far more effective than our speed bumps. Depending on the size of the community, the motorist may encounter many more such obstacles, often without signs indicating who may come through first.

But that uncertainty-inducing vagueness is deliberate too. *Drempels* are the progeny of an un-American traffic philosophy, one that relies on drivers rather than on signs that may produce more fines than safety. (Perhaps to make up for that, parking tickets here are ridiculously expensive.) One Dutch traffic engineer, Hans Monderman, has gained fame for his experiments with removing *all* road signs. At crossings and intersections he favors roundabouts, which have no "signs or signals telling drivers how fast to go, who has the right-of-way, or how to behave. There are no lane markers or curbs separating street and sidewalk, so it's unclear exactly where the car zone ends and the pedestrian zone begins. To an approaching driver, the intersection is utterly ambiguous - and that's the point."

The point being that when confronted with an ambiguous situation, people will pay attention:

> "Pedestrians and cyclists used to avoid this place, but now, as you see, the cars look out for the cyclists, the cyclists look out for the pedestrians, and everyone looks out for each other. You can't

expect traffic signs and street markings to encourage that sort of behavior. You have to build it into the design of the road." [1])

For a long time the Dutch way of dealing with illegal drugs has drawn international attention, not all of it favorable. But law enforcement customs have long been different here. The Anglo-Saxon attitude towards laws is that they should be enforced as long as they are on the books (I know; in some American cities police may refuse to spend expensive time investigating minor crimes such as car thefts and shoplifting. But enforcement may revive at any time, when resources increase.) Anyhow, the prevailing attitude in America is that if you don't like an existing law you should still enforce it until it's repealed. A historical ancestor of this view may be the reaction to King James II of England's decision in 1685 to quit enforcing the Test Act, a law which discriminated against all who did not belong to the Church of England. The Test Act denied protestant dissenters (Methodists, Baptists, Quakers) as well as Catholics certain civil rights, such as being eligible for a government job. James' not-so-secret purpose in *de facto* repealing the Test Act was to favor Catholics, because he himself had converted to Catholicism. But even many protestant dissenters, whom one might expect to favor civil rights for themselves, disapproved of his action. If the law was not to be enforced, they argued, it was up to Parliament to repeal it first. Because of this and other mistakes made by James, who was a rather stupid politician, he lost his crown to William of Orange during the Glorious Revolution of 1688, and all this strife (in the view of the famous historian Macaulay) contributed to English Catholics not gaining full civil rights until the 19th century.

The Dutch attitude is less formalistic, in part due to native skepticism about laws that seek to change human behavior. For an example, take alcohol abuse. My grandfather Opa Vriend was known for frequenting the local taverns on paydays, to try and persuade the drinkers to go back to their wives, with some money. But Prohibition would never have been enacted here. Or if it had, enforcement would have been spotty because authorities routinely decide that if it's awkward to enforce a law, it's better to do so in the breach, a method known as *gedoogbeleid* (tolerance policy). Off and on through the centuries, for

---

[1]) Tom McNichol: "Roads Gone Wild. No street signs. No crosswalks. No accidents. Surprise: Making driving seem more dangerous could make it safer." *Wired*, December 2004.

example, prostitution has been made illegal, but even in such prudish times many local governments chose to ignore the law so they could regulate the hookers, confining them to parts of town where they would give no offense. Hence Amsterdam's red-light district which, as long as anyone remembers, has been located along a few narrow canals east of Dam square. Other towns had similar arrangements. Finally, in 2000 prostitution was legalized nationwide, but this may not be the last word either because a lot of politicians now feel that legalization has caused it to get out of hand, with international gangs running the industry, selling and exploiting the 'sex workers'. In other words, they think having an unenforced law on the books, just to curb excesses, might be best.

The Dutch policy on 'soft drugs' (marijuana and hashish) reflects a similar ambivalence, a pragmatic mix of tolerance and suppression. Less charitably, their drug-policy may be called muddled. For instance, private possession of up to 5 grams of cannabis (here called *wiet*) is not prosecuted, but it will be confiscated if discovered. And private people can have five *wiet* plants without punishment – except that, if found, those will be confiscated too. On the other hand, dealing in drugs, *wiet* or anything else, is illegal and punishable. Possession of more than 5 grams of *wiet* can get you a fine plus jail time, with the size of both depending on your stash. Importing or exporting any illegal drugs merits up to 4 years plus a serious fine. Still, drug-penalties don't come close to what's routinely meted out in American courts.

On this mushy legal foundation has risen the uniquely Dutch institution called "*coffeeshop*". (Like the Germans, the Dutch string related words together into one, which is mainly why they have some very long words). A *coffeeshop* is no Denny's or Starbucks. It's a legalized drug-dealing-den, allowed by local authorities to sell up to 5 grams of *wiet* per day per customer, and it also sells the stronger version called *hasj*. *Coffeeshops* are allowed to stock no more than 500 grams of these substances, a little over one American pound, which in practice would mean that if every customer bought the maximum 5 grams allowed, one shop couldn't serve more than 100 people a day. The theory behind the toleration of *coffeeshops* was that it would keep customers away from hard drugs like heroin and cocaine, and they are not allowed to sell those.

But the arrangement poses awkward, unanswered questions. If wholesale drug-dealing is illegal, how do the *coffeeshops* obtain their inventory, often of several different grades of *wiet*? Silence. And is it really practical to limit sales to 5 grams per person? More silence, and snickers. And here's the $10,000 question: even if the 5-gram-limit is rigorously enforced, how do *coffeeshops* manage to serve far more than 100 customers a day, with only 500 grams on hand?

A few years ago my brother drove me through an old part of Terneuzen where the city had approved the establishment of a *coffeeshop*, called 'Checkpoint'. I could not believe the congestion. Checkpoint had its own parking lot, and the city had constructed an underground parking garage nearby. Yet cars were parked everywhere, some clearly illegally, many with foreign license plates. It was plain as day that 90% of Checkpoint's *wiet* and *hasj* buyers were wholesalers from nearby Belgium and northern France. On prime real estate, the *coffeeshop* owner had built himself an empire which included a pub, a restaurant, with a payroll of about 100, and annual receipts of 26 million Euro, although we may doubt if that was the full extent of his sales. No matter; because *wiet* was illegal in the rest of the European Union, Checkpoint was exempt from paying the EU's Value Added Tax (a type of sales tax) on its gross sales. Even more bizarre, the *coffeeshop*, with 5 cash registers the largest one in the country and maybe in the world, was serving an average of 2900 customers a day, and on some days as many as 5000. So, if you can sell only 5 grams per customer, from an inventory of no more than 500 grams, and wholesaling *wiet* is illegal, how do you satisfy 5000 potheads a day? Finally enough people in power seem to have decided that Checkpoint had become a nuisance, so in 2007 it was raided, and over 200 pounds of *wiet* and *hasj* were confiscated. But the place stayed open. The following year another raid produced closer to 400 pounds, which finally caused the city to close Checkpoint, and prosecute its owner. In March 2010 the judge delivered his sentence. The prosecutor had demanded a jail term of 18 months and a fine of 27 million Euros. The judge gave him only 4 months and a €10 million fine, reasoning that the city had aided and abetted his enterprise.

Besides building the parking garage, the city had placed signs all over town that directed traffic to Checkpoint, despite a national prohibition on advertising for *coffeeshops*. And Checkpoint's owner had never made a secret of his prosperity, so the city could have intervened much sooner.

Today Checkpoint remains closed. But south of town an odd, slanted structure rises out of the damp farmland. It's an expensive indoor ski slope that Checkpoint's owner built with his ill-gotten gains.

While Checkpoint was still open, there were persistent reports of the increasingly high potency of its *wiet*. One illustration of what the Dutch "soft-drugs" policy has wrought may be the provincial court's recent conviction of a 24-year old local who had tried to extort *hasj*-money from his mother, at knifepoint. Fleeing her dopey but cutting-edge son she had climbed across her fence and then, according to the paper, collapsed in the neighbors' back yard. In court 'behavior specialists' blamed the son's conduct on "poorly recognized ADHD and drug use." Unless he was treated promptly his chances of re-offending were great, they warned, and the prosecution agreed. If 'treatment' means he'll be kept out of circulation for a while that would be good, since he already has priors for 'various forms of domestic violence'. But the Dutch don't put much stock in prison terms. The judge gave him jail equal to time served in pre-trial custody (bail is uncommon here), plus *t.b.s.*, which means "to be made available" for 'treatment' by the afore-mentioned behavior specialists. Clearly they are the winners here, although I doubt that their work comes with a guarantee. Meanwhile, with Checkpoint gone, a former police chief now on the Terneuzen city council is promoting the idea of the city itself going into the *wiet* growing business. Why not? That might prevent a repeat of accusations that the mayor was in cahoots with Europe's biggest *wiet* retailer.

A PILL FOR HER WAR

This morning I took mother for a drive through the countryside. We were looking for a place to have coffee but didn't find one open in the little villages. Every one of them had an old hotel/restaurant all right, sometimes more than one, but every such establishment looked stuck in a coma, dark and lifeless. At one time these places must have served a lot of commercial travelers, back when roads were bad, cars were scarce and ferries slow. Today, with everything moving so much faster (The ferries have been replaced by the tunnel I traveled through from Goes), they may only open in the summer months. We ended up driving to the ancient city of Hulst where we had coffee and apple cake in a *brown café*, as they call them here, a very old establishment with walls and ceilings of a unique shade of sepia. This was achieved by centuries of tobacco smoke plus an equally long postponement of painting. People dig the atmosphere of brown cafés, but I wonder if they shouldn't be listed as an endangered species. Tobacco smoke has recently been outlawed here too, following the example of the Land of the Free.

This brown café is on the marketplace near Hulst's medieval basilica. During the fighting in fall 1944 the top of the basilica's tower was shot off, because in this flat country towers were used as military observation platforms. After the war it was replaced with an indescribable concrete thing. With our coffee we toasted the architectural trade, for having foisted another self-promoting eyesore on mankind.

My mother enjoyed the ride, but when we came home we both rested, she in her bed and I on the living room sofa since I'd only slept about four hours last night. After an hour or so the phone awoke me, so I grabbed it but she picked up her bedroom phone at the very same time. Soon afterwards she came in to confide that it was her doctor

who had returned her call because she was so worried about going crazy. But of course I already knew that. It was pitiful. She nearly cried. "Doctor, I'm so afraid that I'm going crazy! Can't you give me a pill for that?" He

soothed her and promised to have some pills dropped off. More anxiety pills, I suppose; and I'm not at all sure that they do her more good than harm.

Now over a year ago, my brother was already telling me about her telephone habit, as bad as a valley girl's or worse. He is the eldest of her seven children, and the only one who lives nearby, so he and his wife have carried the lion's share of the care burden. But it's only in the last one or two years that it became heavy. By the spring of last year she seemed to think nothing of calling him at four or five in the morning when she had an upset stomach. Food and her digestion seem to have taken on endless importance. Even while I'm here she will call during the day to have him pick up this or that grocery item, and when I help her put it away I find that she already has several. I've had the same experience with the shopping I've done on her behalf. So there is a lot of waste, at least of fresh foods and dairy, and Lord knows if she'll ever use up her expanding stock of non-perishable items.

Her need for most of this stuff is put in doubt, anyway, by the services of a local meals-on-wheels outfit, here called *Tafeltje Dekje*, or 'Table Set!' aftere a well-known fairy tale. Its food is actually quite good, but because I had planned to cook several meals during my stay, and my brother wanted us to come to dinner, he had arranged to suspend *Tafeltje Dekje* for a week or so. But then, while nobody is paying attention, she gets on the phone to have meals dropped off anyway, which is another

waste. But she says she doesn't care, and into the garbage it goes. This is not how she used to be, exhibiting telephonitis and wasting food left and right. It may well be part of whatever else is afflicting her, particularly her heightened state of anxiety.

But when I want to discuss her health and her medicines I bump into her hopelessly naïve faith in pills and doctors. What makes it worse is that, in my experience, doctors here are much less frank with their patients than they are in America. It has to do with the socialized medical system, or with a general reluctance to challenge authority, or both. The doctor likes to play God and not be questioned; that way he can charge the third-party payer for call after call, without second-guessing by the patient. Having had experience with both medical systems, I prefer the American one, or what's left of it.

Another novel aspect of living in her house is the tropical temperature generated by her unprecedented craving for heat. Her house, built of brick with a stone floor, used to be on the cool side, which she never seemed to mind; during most of her life warm temperatures exhausted her. When I was growing up we were comfortable in homes that only had a working source of heat during the winter, and only in one room at that. When I was a teenager my bedroom upstairs had a wash basin with cold water only, which my father would shut off during cold spells, so the pipe wouldn't freeze. I'm talking about the pipe *inside* my room. But now, with her central heat going full blast, she sits in her chair flanked by two red-hot electric heaters directed at her feet. It's oppressive enough to drive me outside. As with the wasted food she is nonchalant about the expense, telling me more than once to open the garden doors wide if I need to, but what's the point of heating the rest of Spui? Why these drastic changes in her personal habits? In two months she will be 95. My guess is that her circulation is not what it used to be, so her extremities get cold, causing her to crave heat. It might help if she dressed a little warmer, but she won't, because she still has her vanity. But the real point is that, if less blood is reaching her feet and her hands, less blood must be reaching her brain, and this may well be the cause of her forgetfulness and confusion and panicky behavior. Those things can be caused by problems other than Alzheimer's, I've read. And I can't believe that the medication she takes to reduce her blood pressure improves that at all. I would think a higher blood pressure makes it more likely the blood will reach her brain. But I'm no doctor.

When she turned 90 in 2005 I came over for her birthday party, and she was just fine. When we visited the following year she was perfectly fine too; she even joined us on a lengthy visit to a local sheep farm, in pretty rough weather. The year after that, at

October 27, 2006, visiting the sheep farm.

age 92, she was able to renew her driver's license. This December she will turn 95, but some time earlier this year she quit driving, so when I arrived the car had been sitting in her garage for months. During my first evening, when my brother and sister-in-law dropped in, he had it jump-started, drove a bit, then found he needed the garage-man to come back because it still wouldn't start. He ended up getting the battery replaced.

Half an hour after he returned and reported all those events she suddenly said: "O Wim, if you want to use my car we will need to get it checked. It won't start."

"No mother, it's all been taken care of. It has a new battery now."

She said the same thing again, a bit later. You could blame some of that on poor listening skills, but it happens too often.

"Do you want some tea?" she asks. She still has that old habit, part of the mothering instinct.

"No mother, I'm making myself some coffee." Making coffee with the Douwe Egberts Senseo machine is a snap, and it's great coffee. Compared to the U.S., the Senseo coffee "pads", which everyone here calls *pets*, are a bargain. I want to be sure to pick up a bunch before I

leave, doubly useful as padding in my suitcase. I bring my coffee to the table and start drinking it. Ten seconds later she brings me a cup of tea.

"Here, drink your tea before it gets cold."

Some sort of eraser seems to have swished across her long-term memory too. Through the years many, many were the times when she related how they had bought their business property back in 1936, a house with a small florist's shop in front, and a greenhouse in the back yard. She had pushed for the purchase because she had grown up in a bakery, and liked being a shopkeeper. They took down the greenhouse, and turned the florist's shop into a tobacco shop. At first my dad, who had a job with the Belgian-owned local railroad, wanted nothing to do with it. But when business slowed down again in the late thirties, he was one of the Protestants laid-off by the line's Catholic owners. (I'm saying that, knowing full well that the reverse was common too.) Next, during the pre-war mobilization he was recalled to the navy in September 1939, the Dutch lost the war in May 1940, and when he came back, unemployed again, he risked being sent to work in Germany. As a shopkeeper he would be exempt from that, so that's what he became, and he applied a lot of his typical drive to his new trade, expanding the shop in stages into a grocery store that at one time was the largest in town. But just as in America, independent grocers eventually lost ground to the big chains, and in 2000 the property was sold. It's a pet store now, and the new owners filled and paved the back yard to create parking. The back yard that, back in 1936, had the greenhouse that I never saw. It was gone before my time.

Inevitably the conversation turns to how the new owners of her old place of business are doing. "Those folks got the greenhouse in the back yard into the bargain," she comments, apparently pleased. "That will come in handy for their plant business."

I had brought a laptop to share old family photos that I had scanned during our 2006 visit. Most of those were originally hers, and I had labeled many with the stories she had told me about them. She didn't watch the show very long, but told me not to throw away those pictures, because they seemed nice. A lot of the stories seemed new to her also.

An acquaintance of ours in Coos Bay got Alzheimer's when he was only in his fifties, and what struck me most in the first stage of his horrible affliction was his loss of vocabulary. Ralph had been a contractor and a developer, but while we were having a conversation early in his decline he was struggling to remember one particular word, and just couldn't. He ended up calling a 'thing' what turned out to be a 'building,' which is like a composer forgetting what a key is. She shows no such loss of verbal abilities, but she no longer has her confident, mischievous sense of humor, either. We always did a lot of laughing together, poking fun at this and that and ourselves and mimicking this stuck-up person and that weird character – but not this time. At best, with a little encouragement she may repeat one of her standard wisecracks from the past, but without gusto.

And she used to have lots of gusto. Great deadpan deliveries too. Sister #1 did not want to breastfeed her babies; she had neither the time nor the patience. But she had a father-in-law who not only was a tax collector, a profession for which my parents had New-Testament-grade contempt, but who also turned out to be a militant breastfeeding activist. Out of the blue, in mixed company, Mister tax collector used to loudly remark: "This child is not being breastfed!"

When Sister #1 related how much this bothered her, my mother's advice was: "*Och kind,* tell him to do it himself."

Once after she had bought a new little car she got a speeding ticket. "Do you enjoy making a pest of yourself?" she asked the young cop. " 'I'm doing my duty,' is what he said," she smirked.

Many years ago, she and I were returning from a trip down to California. Darkness set in when we were approaching Brookings, the southernmost town on the Oregon coast and a mere two hours from Coos Bay. Along the road she spotted a small nursery with an OPEN sign, advertising flowers for sale. This meant we HAD to stop and buy flowers for my wife who had held down the homestead. I argued against it, but couldn't win. Thanks to a centuries of brainwashing by their flower industry, every Dutchman and Dutchwoman considers it bad manners to arrive at someone else's door without flowers. It's like Germans coming to visit long-lost relatives without bringing schnapps:

utterly unthinkable. So I made a U-turn and drove back to the place, which turned out to be a rather low-effort operation. After mother finally found something good enough, she asked me to ask if she could use the lady's restroom. With a semi-disdainful smirk the flower woman said no.

At that point I revived my campaign against the purchase, but she insisted on going through with it, gave me the money to pay the woman, and briefly disappeared. Driving away from the place, I started carping again: "Why did you have to do that? She wouldn't even let you use her bathroom! And you can get better flowers tomorrow, in Coos Bay!"

"O drop it, I got even," she finally said.

"Even? How?"

"I *lekker* tinkled on her flowers."

July 4, 1970

Although she never knew much English, I was always impressed with her ability to talk to people when she visited us in Coos Bay, which happened about a dozen times. She never worried about wording things just right, or about pronouncing them perfectly – things I worried about too much, probably. And whomever she talked to in America, she impressed as upbeat and likable. This time, since she doesn't read English well, I had translated a few of the funnier stories from my book to read to her. She sat and listened, but that's all I got for my trouble. It ran like rain off a duck's back, even though my story was a lot like the funny customer incidents from her store that she used to relate. What's the difference? In order to have a sense of humor you must have a sense of the absurd. As I see it, to recognize absurdity you need to be well-grounded in reality. Her decline has diminished that, while destroying her self-confidence in the bargain. She must feel terribly lost and adrift; and Lord, if I could have just one wish, it would be to restore her sense of humor. She sure could use it. But this may have to be the way she goes. There are worse ones.

Since books tended to put her to sleep she was never much of a reader. Still, I credit her for my way with words, and also for my talent for mimicry, which has caused most Americans never to notice my accent. Even though the Netherlands is a very small country, two Dutchmen from opposite ends may be unable to understand each other when each one speaks his local tongue. The speech in our area was a mixture of two dialects: West-Flemish to the south, and the Zealand dialect to the north. They sound very different, so we were always mimicking the expressions and the speech patterns of the Belgians to the south, of the Zealanders from the northern bank of the Schelde, and other people's too. I now realize how much all that tomfoolery helped me when I was studying languages. In French, German and English, I delighted in discovering odd idioms, figures of speech, and pronunciations. After a couple of years in school I was able to impress my parents by making a hotel reservation for them in Luxemburg by phone, alternating between German and French. Sadly, when they came back from an *ouderavond* – 'elder evening,' a parents-teachers' conference – I remember my mother saying that she felt so stupid, being around all those

December 1980

learned teachers. At my graduation ceremony she cried, which bothered me. I'm sorry she didn't know it, but she had supplied the raw material.

My brother told me that not long ago she announced that she was ready to move out of her house and into an institution, so he took her at her word and made the arrangements, which included a short stay on a waiting list. But when her name reached the top, she backed out – twice. Being given to making sweeping decisions, he announced that this had been his last and final effort to get her to move, and he made a sullen withdrawal. Even so, he is still at her beck and call, day and night. But when I happen to stop at their house without mother, his wife goes into an relentless, hateful rant about her while he sits there, without a word. Twice I threaten to walk out, and finally I get up to do so when she shuts up. But in their defense, they are in their seventies too, and not in perfect health. Also, they never had children, and the self-centeredness my mother displays these days is what you'd expect of someone very young. She claims mother has always been that way, but I don't buy that. During all the years I've known her my mother was a competent woman with an upbeat outlook, and extremely loath to impose on others.

Better yet, I could always count on her to find my stuff. Her usual comment after she discovered something I had given up hopes of ever retrieving: *Dao was is een boer, die zocht nao z'n peerd, en die zat er op.* "There once was a farmer who was looking for his horse, and he sat on it." In other words, how simple could it be? But these days she's lost that ability. She's misplaced her keys several times, and was extremely distraught over that. Finally I had to be the one to find them, stuck in the keyhole of the back door. Not having her as my expert tracker of lost objects is inconvenient, but I'm coping. Fortunately back home Trudi has taken on the job. What is it about women that they can find things so well? I don't know, but it sure is handy while they have it.

In sequence, her seven children consist of my elder brother, myself, sisters #1, #2, #3, and #4, plus one more brother who used to be called, to his disgust, *den kleinen* – the little one. Adding an extra layer of weirdness to my stay, the morning after my arrival sisters #4 and #2 in quick succession telephone to read me the riot act, hurling accusations that I've given my mother anxiety-attacks by dropping in out of the blue. I told sister #4, who has some manic qualities herself, that she was all wet, and left it at that. Then I told #2 that my mother had been having unfounded anxiety attacks well before I got here.

"How do you know that?"

"It's all in her *zorgdossier*, her care file, that I've been reading."

"What care file?"

"It's right here, on a table in the entry. In a blue plastic binder, if you care to see it."

"O." And she immediately returned to her charge that I was causing my mother untold trouble with my unexpected visit.

"Sister #2, I've heard you, and you are wrong. Now, if you don't change the subject, I'm going to put an end to this conversation."

But she continued yammering without taking a breath. She's not the first female who believes that rapidity and repetition are the keys to persuasion, so I did what I promised, and hung up. I've never done that to members of my family, but all my four sisters have control issues, albeit in different ways. And some have gotten worse. That may sound as if I'm including my mother, but I'm not. She always had a pretty easy-going temper, which was a good thing for the spouse of a man who was the opposite. A real A-type personality, a sharp mind and a sharp tongue, and yet at the same time far too concerned about what people thought of him. That's a lot of pressures to put on yourself, and he didn't even live to be sixty. While my sisters are all different, each and every one picked a husband who was not at all like my dad. And after he died in 1970 my mother herself never remarried although, as she confided once, she turned down more than one respectable proposal.

And one not so respectable too. There was an uncle – I'm not going to say his name – who had told me, when I was still a teenager, that he thought my mother was quite a dish. He even carried on about her in the presence of his own, long-suffering wife. But she had died, so he invited himself to stay at my mother's place. She knew what he was up to, but didn't let him get to first base. When she retired for the night, for lack of a better weapon she took her big soup ladle to keep on the night stand. Fortunately he didn't press his luck.

During her first of four decades of widowhood she moved into this little house that she chose herself, where she was happy. All that time she kept working in the family store, accumulating 64 years behind the cash register, until my brother sold it in 2000. All during that time too, she enjoyed her music, her church, her children and her grandchildren. I well remember when I was there for her 80th birthday, in 1995. One afternoon she told me that I'd have to fend for myself, because she was off to play the piano ". . . for the old ladies in the home." That was my mother. But re-marriage: no. She never told me why, but I think that if she could have met the famous 18th century British wit Samuel Johnson, she might have agreed with his views on serial marriage.

When we sat down for dinner today I said:

"Mother, I told you that I came because I had not seen you for four years. But I also came because I got a little worried about you."

> "The subject of his father's second marriage was much on [Boswell's] mind, and in order to draw Johnson he 'censured a gentleman of my acquaintance for marrying a second time, as it shewed a disregard of his first wife.' But Johnson thought otherwise: 'Not at all, Sir. On the contrary, were he not to marry again, it might be concluded that his first wife had given him a disgust to marriage; but by taking a second wife he pays the highest compliment to the first, by shewing that she made him so happy as a married man that he wishes to be so a second time.'
>
> That this was his considered opinion is shown by his remark, on hearing of a man who had promptly married again after a wretched time with his first wife: '**It was the triumph of hope over experience.'** "
>
> Hesketh Pearson: *Johnson and Boswell—The story of their lives.* London: Cassell, 1987, p. 183.

"Y-yes?

"You're not going crazy but you don't remember things as well as you did. And you worry too much. You get anxious at the drop of a hat. Why do you worry like that? Remember the lilies in the field. You've got everything you need. The help comes in the morning and in the evening, and not a day goes by without visits and calls from the children. And still you get all worried and you get on the phone in a panic, as if you're all alone with nobody willing to help. It seems to me you need a different home, where you have people around you all the time, so you'll get over feeling lonesome. Don't misunderstand me, I'd love to see you stay here forever. But nothing can last. And wouldn't it be better to make the change while you still can, instead of waiting until things get real bad? *Hou de eer aan jezelf.*"

"Keep the honor to yourself." It's an old Dutch expression, meaning that it's better to take credit for an unavoidable decision than having it made for you. She looks at me, unresponsive.

"Remember, some years ago, your old girl friend in Axel. The mayor's daughter, from when you were girls. You discovered that she'd totally gone off her rocker, living by herself in a house with plumbing that didn't work.

"I don't want to take the decision for you, whether you should move to a different place. Nobody should force you to do that. But look, you always made us say our prayers and you made us go to Sunday school and to church and trust God. Now when you get worried, what you crave most is a pill. Pills and doctors can't perform miracles. You need to ask the Lord for help. You need to ask him to help you make the right decision."

I didn't add the stock formula in my evangelical church: "Turn your life over to Jesus, accept Him as your Lord and Savior." I don't know how many people besides the Saints practice that rule 24/7, and this is not the time to introduce novel terms to a life-long Dutch-Reformed woman. We say a short prayer for help from above, and she volunteers that she thinks she really should leave her house. And then she starts fretting about having lost her spot on the waiting list.

The next morning my brother drops in, joining us during a visit by a woman called Ilse, who carries the title of geriatric assistant. She is a sort of elder-care coordinator, apparently a liaison to my mother's doctor. Mother is still looking for magic pills:

"I feel a little unsure, sister. Can you do anything for that?"

From what I've learned by reading her care file in the middle of the night, her confidence in pills is not just misplaced, it may be making things worse. For anxiety and sleeplessness she has been prescribed Diazepam, which is called Valium in America, and she's been taking it for quite some time. When you look it up, the product information warns that it should not be taken for long, and no alcohol. The many possible side-effects include confusion, depression, agitation and itching with a possible rash. She shows all of the first three symptoms, and according to the care file she gets regular treatments with Vaseline and Cetomacrogol cream to combat itching on her back. When I ask her about the itching, she talks as if it's news to her.

Omeprazole and Domperidone are medicines she's been taking for digestive problems. Omeprazole reduces stomach acid. Driving and drinking alcohol are not recommended, but not being able to drive must have intensified her feelings of isolation. Possible side-effects of Omeprazole include stomach upsets, diarrhea, rash, itching, confusion and depression. The other pill, Domperidone, is to combat nausea by speeding up digestion. Like the other two, it may occasionally cause a rash and itching. Common horse sense suggests that when somebody takes different pills with the same possible side-effects, the combination makes them more likely to occur – but again, I'n not a medical man.

I've noticed that she's developed a habit of eating shortly before going to bed. That is not a good way to avoid gastric distress, nor does it promote a good night's sleep. Besides, sleeplessness is extremely common among the elderly, and she may make it worse by taking naps during the day.

The other day I noticed a bottle of wine on her nightstand. She confided that when she can't sleep, she takes a sip. The problem is not that she's ever been a drinker, but the instructions for all her pills advise against it. In the case of Diazepam, alcohol may intensify its negative effects, and it may counteract the benefits of Omeprazole and Domperidone, which are intended to remedy stomach irritation. But when I try to convince my brother to question her pill-regime, he tells me I'm not a doctor. It's the Dutch habit of authority-worship.

To Ilse the geriatric assistant she confirms what she told me the night before: "I do think it would be better if I went to a rest home. Can you arrange that?" She repeats her wish to leave her home, twice.

This is encouraging, but it doesn't last. I'll bet that an ancient memory still looms large in her mind, that of the old folks' home where *her* parents lived out their lives. Her older sister, now gone, had talked them into moving into that place, a dingy, depressing dump that smelled like chewing tobacco and worse, offered the residents tiny rooms without private bathrooms, and the type of supervision you might find in an orphans' home from a Dickens novel. It was torn down long ago, but for decades she has beseeched her children not to force her out of her home and into something like that. But unless she's forgotten about her old girl friend, she should know what can happen to old people who live alone. One little daily step towards self-neglect, and pretty soon they are living in a filth-filled hovel, invisible to the world. Because many people look in on her it won't get that far, but still it would be better to save her the indignity of being forced out.

The Friday before I leave, a local pastor drops in. Like many Dutch-Reformed ministers, *Dominee* Hovinga is a Frisian; his special assignment in the parish is elder-care, and he came to the ministry late, after having been a farmer. I consider that a positive thing. Most Dutch-reformed ministers' life-experience is limited to long academic studies immediately followed by the ministry, which seems to turn many into namby-pamby characters. I prefer clerics who've lived in the real world, like the pastor of our local church who was a professional boxer and a fireman before he became a Christian.

The subject of mother's anxiety comes up, I observe to the *dominee* that a lot of people say they look forward to going to Heaven, but when push comes to shove nobody seems to be in a big hurry to get there. The Dutch-Reformed church is big on Old Testament stories, so after reading from Genesis 32 he talks about Jacob crossing the Jordan to the Promised Land, and about the Israelites doing the same later on, and he closes with a prayer. He leaves me with mixed feelings. Is this the right message for an anxious woman who does not have much longer, evoking dark prospects of a dangerous journey, like the dead Greeks crossing the River Styx to the Underworld?

He is barely gone when Ad Willems shows up. He is my sister-in-law's step-brother, and it was only in the last twenty years when he started exploring his ancestry. I never knew it; most likely nobody was supposed to know it when memories of the war were still fresh, but Willems was his mother's name, and he was the product of her affair with a soldier of the German occupation force.

Oberfeldwebel Rudolf Reinhart

Oberfeldwebel (first sergeant) Rudolf Reinhart, whom Ad strongly resembles, served in the 15th Army, which guarded the coast from Breskens south to the Pas de Calais, in France. In the summer of 1944 his unit was summoned south to fight the allied forces that had broken out of Normandy, and he was killed down there. My sister-in-law's mother had died very young, and after the war her dad married Ad's mother, getting Ad into the bargain. Adding some mystery is the fact that her dad was a strong patriot, and had served in the Dutch liberation forces. But in the nineties Ad made considerable efforts to discover his "roots," which included tracking down relatives of the German father he never knew. Some welcomed him; some wanted nothing to do with him. But like me, his experiences have given him a lifelong fascination with the war. He's collected a mass of pictures of our area's German occupation and its liberation by Canadian and Polish troops, which he let me copy. Half a dozen show Field Marshal Erwin Rommel, inspecting coastal defenses in the Breskens area. After Hitler abandoned Rommel's gallant Afrika Korps, unable and unmotivated to supply it, he gave Rommel the job of reinforcing his so-called Atlantic Wall, a line of coastal bunkers, guns, mines and obstacles that was supposed to make "Fortress Europe" safe from allied invasions. With his typical drive and initiative the field al threw himself into the job; my father was among many local men required to plant "Rommel asparagus" in the farm fields. Those were logs planted straight in the ground, often connected with wires at the top, and at times equipped with mines. They were intended to prevent glider landings, since both sides used gliders during invasions.

Despite giving it his best shot, Rommel knew very well that the odds were against him. And of course, his personal odds were even worse because in the aftermath of the failed July 20,

April 18, 1944: Field Marshal Erwin Rommel arrives for a third inspection of the defenses at the port of Breskens. In the background is a recently-built bunker for a 47 mm cannon.

1944, attempt on Hitler's life it was discovered that Rommel had some peripheral involvement, even though he didn't approve of the assassination plan. In any case, he had not passed on his knowledge of the plot, and that was enough. Since he was Germany's most popular general the Nazis thought it inadvisable to put

April 19, 1944: Field Marshal Erwin Rommel arriving in Breskens for an inspection of the defenses. On his left is a German Navy captain, on his right Werner-Albrecht Freiherr (Baron) von und zu Gilsa, the much-decorated commander of a German infantry corps that was part of the Schelde defenses. A year later Gilsa, then defense commander of devastated Dresden, died in what is now part of the Czech Republic, either in a firefight or at his own hand to escape imprisonment by the Russians.

him on trial and hang him with the other conspirators, so on October 14, 1944 two officers came to see him at his house with an offer he couldn't refuse. The Nazis had revived the ancient custom of taking out their wrath on an opponent's entire family (the Communists in Russia did the same thing), but they offered to leave Rommel's family unmolested and to make sure his wife had a pension, if he would take the poison that the officers had brought. Publicly, his death would be blamed on injuries received that summer in Normandy. Within minutes Rommel took the poison. He received a big state funeral, with a military honor-guard and a gigantic wreath from Hitler himself. Barely 53 years old, he had earned the respect of friends and enemies alike.

Rommel's wife and his 15-year old son Manfred knew full well how he had died, but they had been sworn to secrecy. During that winter Manfred deserted from the German army to surrender to the approaching French forces under General de Lattre de Tassigny, whom he served as an interpreter. The truth about his father's death would not emerge until after the war, during the Nuremberg trials.

In 1987 Manfred Rommel, then mayor of Stuttgart, came to Israel on behalf of his late father to receive the honorary title of "Protector of

Jerusalem" from North African Jews, who credited him with having saved their lives. During his North African campaign the field marshal had ignored Hitler's order to wipe out the local Jews, the type of order that was being carried out all too well in eastern Europe, where Rommel had never served in battle.

Below is the text of 'Ich hatt' einen Kameraden', which was played at Rommel's funeral, as it had been for over a century at military funerals. The song has been translated into many other languages, and used by many other militaries; the translation below is mine.

ICH HATT' EINEN KAMERADEN	I ONCE HAD A BEST BUDDY
Ich hatt' einen Kameraden, einen bessern findst du nit. Die Trommel schlug zum Streite, er ging an meiner Seite *In gleichem Schritt und Tritt, in gleichem Schritt und Tritt.*	I once had a best buddy, our friendship was complete. The battle drums were sounding, the cannons, they were pounding; *We'd march to the same beat, We'd march to the same beat.*
Eine Kugel kam geflogen: Gilt's mir oder gilt es dir? Ihn hat es weggerissen, er liegt vor meinen Füßen *als wär's ein Stück von mir, als wär's ein Stück von mir.*	A bullet came a-flying: One for you or one for me? He is lying at my feet now, we no longer are complete now, *'cause he was a piece of me, 'cause he was a piece of me.*
Will mir die Hand noch reichen, derweil ich eben lad'. "Kann dir die Hand nicht geben, bleib du im ew'gen Leben *Mein guter Kamerad! Mein guter Kamerad!"*	Please do me one last favor, for a second hold my hand. "No, I can't shake hands, dear buddy, I'm on earth, you're in eternity, *My best buddy and my friend! My best buddy and my friend!"*

MY WAR ON HOW-ARE-YOU-?

"Well, good afternoon, folks!" I greet the family entering the restaurant:
"Four for lunch? Would you like a booth or a table?"

A booth it is, and mom, pop and two cell-phone-addicted daughters
fit it snugly. While I bring menus and ice water – with an "Excuse me,
please," for the girls whose frantic tapping on tiny buttons makes them
dangerously oblivious to my water glasses – the mother rears up, peers
at me sharply over her reading glasses and bitingly enunciates:

"AND - HOW - ARE - YOU - TODAY?"

"Ah – it could be worse, and you?"

"JUST – WONDERFUL – !!!" she states with a gusto as shrill as it
sounds fake. This must be her passive-aggressive way of denouncing
my failure to ask how SHE is. Which I compounded by failing to
describe my own condition as 'JUST WONDERFUL !!!!'

I'm going to ignore this culture-clash, and simply try to be nice. But
I have to come clean: I'm increasingly irritated by that American urge to
mutter: "How are you?" at everybody, all the time. Even terminal
patients in their death throes are expected to moan back: "Just fine, and
you?" Neither side ever means it. And if the dying victim has lost
enough self-control to dwell on his symptoms and prospects, he can see
his inquisitor think: "O crap, I'm sorry I asked."

Even so, NOT asking may cause people like this matron to think you
are rude. In actuality the American *How are you?* is much more ambitious
than *Buenos Dias* or *Guten Abend* or *Bonjour messieurs-dames* in other lands.
A Frenchman entering a public place may even skip the *bonjour*, and just
say *Messieurs-dames*. All those utterances are the equivalents of dogs
engaged in mutual butt-sniffings. They acknowledge the other's
presence. Only in America *Good afternoon* is judged inadequate, and even
impolite. Lord, protect me from pompous, self-righteous matrons.

We're starting to get busy, and between customers I try to help
Adam in the kitchen. The kitchen phone rings. "You need to get rid of
that thing," Adam reminds me. "Get a cell phone like mine. They don't
call you on those." He's talking about the telephone sales calls we get
every day. And he is right; they are a bigger nuisance than the AND-
HOW-ARE-YOU-TODAY? - activists.

I pick up the phone, but for about two seconds I hear nothing.
Experience has taught us that this is a sure sign of a boiler-room
operation with the sales pitch about to be launched, either by a live

person or a recording. And I don't know which is more annoying. I'm about to hang up when a live, youngish woman's voice comes on:

"Hi, how are you?"

O great, this character has decided to apply the latest wisdom about making successful sales calls. I read it the other day, in a piece by some self-anointed cold-call-expert:

> "When we start our cold calls with a mini-pitch about who we are and what we have to offer, we've introduced sales pressure right away. . . . So instead, start your conversation by focusing on a need or issue you know the other person is likely facing. Step into their world and invite them to share whether they're open to exploring possible solutions with you."

I knew it, I knew it! I knew I would see the day when good old American salesmanship would interbreed with touchy-feely encounter-group mush. I think I'll waste a minute to find out if this cold-caller is 'open to exploring possible solutions' for the HOW-ARE-YOU issue I am likely facing. I'm holding my fingers over the mouthpiece:

"Huh? What was that? This connection is BAD! Can you speak up?"

"HOW ARE YOU?"

"What? LOUDER!"

"HOW ARE YOU TODAY?"

"Why do you want to know?"

"I'm just asking."

"But why? Are you selling health insurance? Or life insurance? Graveyard plots, maybe?"

"I'm not selling anything." Ha-ha, I'd like to get a nickel for every salesman who's told me that.

"We have a policy against giving out that kind of information. Do I know you?"

"My name is Sue, and how are you?"

"Well, Sue, you're being kind of fresh, aren't you? Calling perfect strangers on the phone to find out how they are? It's a good thing my wife doesn't know about this, or you'd be in trouble, young lady!"

CLICK, and the line goes dead. Well, that worked.

A few days later I'm sitting in the waiting room of the Coos Bay eye clinic. After I discovered a hazy spot in the middle of my right eye, more than 20 years ago, that eye turned out to have a leaky macula. It was not exactly part of today's macular degeneration epidemic, but it came to the same thing: too much fluid flowing into that part of the eye, distorting my central vision. I can't prove this, but I think it was the delayed effect of youthful trauma. We'd had snow, a partial thaw and then a freeze. I was 15 or 16, watching from the side of a soccer field where masses of kids were pelting each other with snowballs, when out of the blue I got one on my right eye, hard. The impact left no doubt that it was an ice ball, not snow. After several hours the pain went away, and at my high school's annual charity fair I kept winning the air rifle for marksmanship. But after I was drafted into the Dutch army at age 21, I could no longer hit the target. I wondered why, but blamed it on the recoil. And that army's physical screening was not very thorough.

"Uh . . . Bill?"

"Uh, no." I would not have responded except that nobody else did.

"William?" the nurse tries again.

"Close enough." I proceed to the counter behind which she emits these puzzling ejaculations, as they were commonly described a hundred years ago, before linguistic sexualization. "How are you?" she says, relieved. "We need a copy of your photo I.D. and insurance card."

She makes copies of my paperwork, and I sit down again. But within a minute I hear, from a different direction: "Willem?"

"Yes?"

"Will you follow me, please?" asks the second nurse. And as I follow her she adds: "How are you?"

I try to think of a thoughtful response – it's imprudent to alienate medical personnel – but before I can say anything she responds: "Good." Obviously her patient interaction runs on auto-pilot.

She brings me to an examination room with the usual eye doctor equipment, plus a reclining chair that won't recline. "I'm giving you some numbing drops," she says while making me tilt my head back as well as I can, ". . . and dilating drops next. Is your birthday 11-5-41?"

"I don't believe it has changed."

"Just making sure," she says. It's a good point, really, when you read the horror stories of surgeons cutting limbs off the wrong patients. But what if two patients happen to have the same birthdays? Fresh material for another medical horror story? She makes me read the usual letter chart, and puffs air into both eyes for a pressure test. Then she leaves, while explaining that full dilation will take some time. I try to recline into the chair that won't recline, wishing I had brought one of the magazines from the lobby. So I'm almost asleep when another cheery voice says: "Hi, I'm Emily, and how are you doing today?"

"Uh – I'm here to find out."

"Goood," she coos, regurgitating her imprinted script. And next, while pulling up my chart: "Is your birthday still 11-5-41?"

"O yes, been that way for years."

She tells me to focus on the blue light, takes pictures of my eyes' insides, and then asks me to wait in the hallway. I pick up an issue of the Saturday Evening Post. The weekly SEP, once read by millions, died around 1970, and this nostalgia issue see s to appear every two months. But it has articles worthy of the old Post, like this one about our obsession with the weather, which today is fed by the Weather Channel, an army of TV weathermen, and of course the Global Warming crowd. Through an increasingly bright fog I learn that a lot of weathermen are skeptical of the global warming fever, and of claims that it's making our weather more extreme. They blame the damage from hurricane Katrina and others on more intense news coverage, and on more people living in vulnerable areas, like low-lying beaches. Sounds plausible to me.

"Willem? Hi, how are you?"

Two more nurses, and finally one doctor, approach me with that inescapable question. As soon as I've mumbled my sixth or seventh fuzzy response, the doctor pokes a shot of shot of Avastin into my right eye and sends me on my way, warning that my eye may feel like it has sand in it. I tuck plastic dark glasses behind my regular ones and gingerly make my way out of the parking lot, driving slowly toward the restaurant. Still plagued by a shimmering fog, I stop to do a bank deposit across from the restaurant. While entering the bank I can see well enough to observe only two tellers working, and some fifteen people waiting in line. Leaving and coming back seems like too much trouble, so I join the line, which shrinks very slowly. In fact, it doesn't shrink at all because more people are joining. That I'm no longer the very last one is no consolation because there are still ten people ahead of me, and the few customers who finally reach one of the tellers' windows seem excessively chatty.

But behold, here comes a third teller. I can tell because she wears a purple t-shirt with the bank logo, just like the other two. But instead of jumping into the ring where the action is, she stays in the customer area, apparently to solicit some information from the elderly lady now first in line. I strain to find out what could be so important, but it turns out to be no more than pointless chit-chat, preceded by: "Hi, how are you?"

"Just fine," lies the ancient woman with the walker, who then goes beyond the call of duty by moaning: "And how are you?"

"Just grrreat!" Of course; she's found a novel way of loafing while getting paid. Chit-chat completed, she chants: "Have a good one!"

Another vapid slogan hatched by our slack culture. What's wrong with a good day or a good afternoon? The word 'one' epitomizes the emptiness of this pathetic exchange. Far worse, why doesn't the purple t-shirted woman move behind the counter to do some real work and speed things up? But no – she moves on to the second person in line.

"Hi, how are you?"

"Uh, fair to middlin'," grumbles the rather unkempt fisherman, for this is what I derive from a few words drifting my way. Their conversation concluded with no apparent dispatch, she moves on to number 3, still in a very insouciant way.

"Hi, how are you?" she coos at #3.

"Just grrreat!" gushes the overly-perfumed matron who sounds like a cheerleader in the Soroptimist movement. It seems that Soroptimists work for peace, and for international goodwill toward women. But even if she is part of that crowd, my stock of goodwill is shrinking, due to hostile feelings rising inside me. Why in tarnation is this bank woman not doing something useful? Has she just returned from an overpriced retreat where some human relations guru told the assembled bankers that this kind of dilly-dallying will smooth their way into their customers' hearts, not to mention up the corporate ladder?

"Hi, how are you?" She has reached #4. I'm clenching my teeth and curling my toes, to keep from exploding. Another serene, pointless exchange. Out of the corner of my eye I can see her moving on to #5. By now, this means a mere two customers separate me from being her next victim. Hmm – maybe she won't butt in if I'm talking to someone. Turning, I engage the man behind me in a conversation about the weather, plagiarizing a couple of talking points from the article in the Post. Soon we discover that both of us are 'climate deniers', the kind of heresy that frantic climate activists equate with Holocaust denial. Actually, I don't deny that the climate may be changing; it's been doing that for thousands of years, and the feared rising of the oceans is another piece of old news. I just think that we humans overestimate our powers, both in causing the problems, if they are problems, and in trying to fix them. I'm in the midst of making a marvelously incisive point along these lines when I feel a tug at my sleeve:

"Hi, how are you?"

THE WHITE CRANES OF WAR

It's Spring Break, a welcome sign that there is life after our slow winters of recent years. Spring Break brings the first tourists. And so it has done this year, although our daytime business remains quiet. But we should be grateful for what we get, since the national economy has not yet crawled out of the hole it fell in a few years ago. It may even be slipping back. Besides, for traveling families the weather has been lousy, with driving rains and nasty-cold temperatures that could make it a challenge to get the kids out of the car, even at the beach.

This afternoon I served a Russian family of four, with a couple of very cute teenage daughters. The dad was the only one who looked a bit rough, with about a week's worth of beard stubble. Maybe that's the Russian way of hanging loose on vacation. The women ordered an Oktoberfest dinner, a sauerbraten, and our salmon with mango chutney; the dad had oyster stew, and they had some trouble finishing it all. Turns out this fellow has a bartending business, for he gave me his business card: Vladimir Zhuravlev, BARTENDER BROTHERS, Moscow, Russia. I can see how an American vacation by a Russian bartender might have made big news before the USSR's totalitarian shackles finally broke, now more than two decades ago. I remember watching the Berlin wall come down, the Romanian dictator and his greedy wife shot against the wall, the Kremlin deciding NOT to send in the tanks this time. Are we better off? Well, today this Russian obviously makes a good living, teaching and training Russian bartenders. He even bought my book. But it must be his first time in the USA; he is still on the European tip system, meaning he assumes it is included on his bill, so he left nothing for the waiter, me. It doesn't bother me, but I'm afraid that as they make their way down to San Francisco they will alienate quite a few American servers. But they were very nice people.

Their reason for stopping, Vladimir confided before they left, was our neon Blue Heron sign. His last name, Zhuravlev, means "crane", just like some Americans have the family name Crane. The way he told me this suggested that there was more to it, so after I got home I checked the word zhuravli (Журавли in Russian) on the internet. It turns out that Zhuravli is also the name of an incredibly beautiful Russian song about World War II, possibly the most popular one in the Russian-speaking world. The original inspiration came from a Dagestani poet who saw a memorial to the victims of Hiroshima, featuring white cranes made of paper by a Japanese girl. The memory haunted him for months, inspiring him to write a poem: "It seems to me sometimes that our soldiers who did not return from fields of gore, did not lie down in our land, but turned into a triangle of white cranes…"

The poem was translated into Russian by the poet Naum Grebnyov, and published in 1968 in the prominent Russian journal *Novy Mir* which, for some years already, had been running articles that could be described as "dissident". Notable examples were parts of Aleksandr Solzhenetzyn's "One day in the life of Ivan Denisovich", the groundbreaking novel about the freezing, starving slaves in the Soviet Gulag system, the kind of book that stays with you. "One day in the Life" was one of the first books given to the defected MIG Pilot Viktor Belenko, who stayed up all night reading it, recognizing many things that had puzzled him.

Naum Grebnyov's poem in *Novy Mir* caught the eye of the famous singer and actor Mark Bernes (originally Mark Naumovitch Bernes, because his father, a Jew from Odessa, had the name Naumann). Bernes asked Yan Frenkel, a Jew from Kiev, to set it to music. When Bernes first heard Frenkel's composition, he cried because it seemed to be about his own fate. He himself was ill with lung cancer, and he died that same year, a week after he first sang and recorded Zhuravli. But reflect on this: here were Naum Grebnyov, Mark Bernes and Yan Frenkel, three Russian artists of Jewish descent whose combined talents increased even more the many blessings the Jewish people have bestowed on mankind.

In the Russian-speaking world, the song was a total smash hit. But according to Wikipedia, the "… Soviet ruling bureaucracy orchestrated a campaign against 'The Cranes', citing the song's religious undertones." The case was finally put before doddering old Soviet dictator Leonid Brezhnev, who decreed it "acceptable to perform, but not too often." Those 'religious undertones' seem a bit overstated to me; all that Zhuravli's lyrics do is associate hope for eternal life with a vague suggestion of reincarnation. But then, any religious sentiments irritated the Kremlin, which for seventy years tried to replace God's Gospel with Marx's Manual.

You can listen to Bernes's original version of Zhuravli on YouTube, but his rendition has been overshadowed by that of the glorious Russian baritone Dmitri Khovorostovsky, or Hovorostovsky. But no matter which version of *Zhuravli* I hear, I find it hard not to lose a couple of tears.

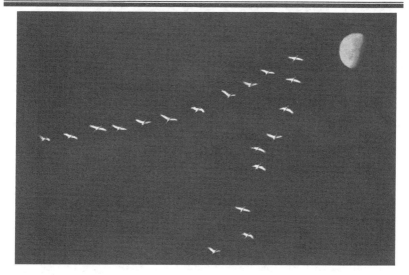

White Cranes

It seems to me, sometimes, that soldiers
who didn't return from the bloody fields,
didn't lie dead in our soil a single moment,
but turned into white cranes.
All along, from time immemorial,
they fly, calling to us from afar.
Maybe that's why, often ruefully,
We fall silent, gazing up into the air.
The crane formation is flying warily in the sky,
flying in the fog, till dusk.
And in this formation is left a tiny gap,
this may be a place made for me.
A day will come, when together with the cranes,
I will soar into the same blue skies,
calling from the air, in bird language,
to all whom I left on earth.

Let us hope that the Russian soldiers who never returned from the bloody fields found peace with the millions of Germans who shared their fate. Like the father of my friend Gary Saks, who lies somewhere in a mass grave in the Crimea. Gary himself, now in his seventies, still has trouble with it. "Pray!" he once shouted at me, angrily. "Prayer? What good does that do? My mother made us pray every night for my father to come back from Russia!"

"It doesn't work that way, Gary. God is not Santa Claus." But, looking back, maybe I should have cited this, by a prominent rabbi:

> "The purpose of religion is to make us aware that we live in the presence of G-d, to help us become better people, to increase our sensitivity, and to amaze us through the miracles that surround us every moment. These are the real rewards. The goal is *not* that G-d change His behavior towards us, but that we change our behavior towards Him and our fellow human beings."

In contradiction, the German soldiers' belt buckles said *Gott mit uns* -- 'God with us'. And almost all European wars of the last millennium were between Christian nations. The idea that Christians would not go and kill each other *en masse* proved as illusory as the Marxists' expectation that the solidarity of the international proletariat would make the common soldiers put down their arms and embrace.

If we have been created in God's image, then His face, though so many times more handsome than ours, must have carried many a wry smile while hearing our wartime prayers. As a boy during the American Civil War, Teddy Roosevelt was made to pray for the North, while young Woodrow Wilson had to pray for the South. And in both North and South, eloquent preachers assured their flocks of the justice of their side's cause, and of God's blessing on it.

I've never shared the worshipful attitude of so many Americans toward that war's creator, President Lincoln; my feelings have been mixed at best. But he and I got off to a bad start; I was still a foreigner

when I first saw the Lincoln Memorial in D. C., and found it appalling. Here was a heathen temple housing the enormous statue of someone who, like the Roman emperors, had been raised to divine status – for obvious propaganda purposes. And when we look at the Great Emancipator's written record, we find that he didn't really care about slavery, anyway. His priority was the preservation of a large and powerful political entity, the United States. That made him no different from any other 19th century politician who worshipped the state. And perhaps it made him worse because for this cause, out of a population of only 31 million, he sacrificed between 600,000 and a million lives, more than died in all other U.S. wars combined.

Having got that off my chest, I grant that Lincoln was a remarkable writer and speaker. Religiously he was an outlier too. Neither a regular churchgoer nor a zealous believer, as the war progressed he said he felt a spirit guiding his most critical decisions. Before making them he waited for a communication, however it came, from something that more religious people might have called the Holy Spirit. And when asked once whether he thought God was on the side of the Union, he replied: "I am not at all concerned about that, for I know the Lord is always on the side of the right. But it is my constant anxiety and prayer that I and this nation should be on the Lord's side." [1]

But when God is seen as Santa Claus, people will be disappointed. The same will happen when politicians are seen as God. Politicians like Hitler, whose portrait had to be in every German home – or else. "And then finally," Gary added, "came two officers to our door, to tell my mother that my father got killed over there. And when she heard that, she yanked the picture of Hitler off the wall and stomped on it. And one of the officers said: 'What you just did is against the law, but I'm not going to do anything about it. You just lost your husband.' "

Gary Saks (on the left) and I in front of the lodge at his RV park, the Honey Bear Campground in Ophir, Oregon.

[1] Paul Johnson: *A History of the American People*, NY: Harper, 1999, p. 471.

> Sun Valley, May 21st 2012.
>
> Dear Winn,
>
> Please send the book, "Odd Customers" to my address in Sun Valley. Enclosed final check for $18.— Carl
>
> I came to the U.S. in Nov. 1951 from Flensburg on the Danish border. On March 14, 1920 people voted for Germany (remain). We had been Danish till 1864 when the united Prussians and Austrians freed us from the Kingdom Denmark through making war with a newly invented rifle! Now, since I was born German citizen, I was "entitled" to join the H.J. and the Arbeitsdienst and then the Wehrmacht and Go in 1942 to fight the Russians, what they didn't like and I felt it. But I survived.
>
> My mother died in 1977, 84 yrs old and my wife said: Let's go to Oregon. So we went through Coos Bay with 3 Dalmations in our Dodge Van along the coast, along the Columbia to 395 and back home. We have a niece in Oregon and visit almost Oregon every year. Now we're old and can't do it anymore!

KURT FREDERICKSEN'S WAR

The note signed "Kurt Fredericksen" came with a check for a copy of my book "Odd Customers". A mixture of customer incidents at my restaurant and short WWII-stories, "Odd Customers" had been running in installments in the *Staats-Zeitung*, a weekly for German-Americans.

Being in the *Staats-Zeitung* had not sold a lot of books – a few dozen, maybe – and besides positive responses like Kurt's I had received a few huffy ones. One reader was offended at my impression of Germans as being noisy, and the editor, Jes Rau, told me that a couple of such cranks had canceled their subscriptions, perhaps proving my point. I felt bad, but whenever you write something with a point of view, a few people will get steamed up, especially if they lack a sense of humor. Oddly enough, Jes Rau suggested once that I take over his job as editor of the *Zeitung*, but I couldn't see how that would work. I can pass as a German for a minute or two, but only in simple conversations. That's because my knowledge of the language is incomplete (I still have trouble conjugating German nouns and adjectives), and I lack the easy familiarity with German culture that comes from having grown up there. *Staats-Zeitung* readers were bound to notice such things, and might have objected to a Dutch interloper. But maybe I shouldn't have worried so much, since most of that paper consists of articles copied from German media, along with memoirs of German immigrants. So it might have worked, and it might have improved my German besides. "I came to the U.S. in 1951," wrote Kurt Fredericksen, ". . . from Flensburg on the Danish border. On March 14 1920, people voted for Germany

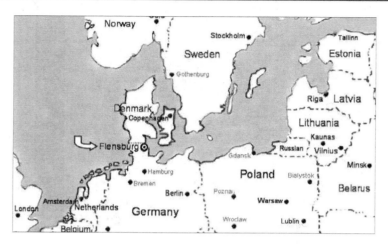

(remain). We had been Danish till 1864 when the united Prussians and Austrians freed us from the Kingdom of Denmark through making war with a newly invented rifle! Now, since I was born German citizen, I was "entitelt" to join the *H.J.* and the *Arbeitsdienst* and then the *Wehrmacht* and to go in 1942 to fight the Russians, what they didn't like and I felt it. But I survived."

The 1864 rifle was the Dreyse needle-gun, a breech-loading weapon that a soldier could load lying down. Gravity forced the Danish soldiers to load their older muzzle-loading rifles while standing, so they made better targets. That's why, although the unopposed Danish navy shelled the Prussians, Danish casualties were triple the Prussian number, and the Danes lost the battle plus the lands of Schleswig and Holstein. All that Denmark achieved was to inspire the Prussians to fight more wars and to get their own navy. After a few more short wars, the Prussian king became Kaiser Wilhelm I of a united Germany, which rapidly became the continent's leading power, industrially and militarily.

But then his grandson, Kaiser Wilhelm II, lost World War I. After that defeat the residents of the northern lost land, Schleswig, were finally allowed to decide if they wanted to stay in Germany or to re-join Denmark. (The southerly territory, Holstein, didn't get to vote because it was obvious that most Holsteiners wanted to stay German.) The results of the two Schleswig plebiscites were mixed. Northern Schleswig, which had a big Danish majority, voted 3 to 1 to re-join Denmark. Southern Schleswig, where Germans were the majority, voted the other way. And this is why today Flensburg is located right below the German-Danish border (see arrow on the map).

May 23 1945: Admiral Dönitz (in black Navy uniform) being led to his arrest by British troops in Flensburg. Following him are two members of his government, General Jodl (left) and Albert Speer, Hitler's architect and armaments production manager.
At the Nuremberg trials Dönitz got ten years, Speer twenty, and Jodl, who had been one of Hitler's military yes-men, the death penalty.

The *H.J.* that Kurt was 'entitelt' to join was the Hitler Youth, which became compulsory for boys 10 to 18. The *Reichsarbeitsdienst* or RAD was a depression-era make-work scheme which the Nazis had also made compulsory. Besides putting young men to work for six months, from harvesting crops to heavy construction, the RAD prepared them for military service. Men (and later on women) were given a uniform, a spade and a bicycle, were divided into companies and battalions, and performed drills with their spades and their bikes. They also served as auxiliary troops in military campaigns, moving supplies and building bunkers. To sum up, the Nazi régime militarized millions of children, from age ten until they were killed in action, most on the eastern front.

At the very end of World War II Flensburg gained a moment of dubious fame as the last capital of Nazi Germany. Before Hitler killed himself in his Berlin bunker, in late April 1945, he had appointed Admiral Dönitz Reich President (he had abolished the position of Führer, thereby restoring the pre-Nazi dual leadership of a Reich President and a Chancellor, both of which he had taken on.) At that late point in the war, one of the few German-held areas not in imminent danger of being overrun by allied forces was Flensburg, so that port city became Dönitz's headquarters. For about three weeks the Flensburg government, as it was known, issued orders to what was left of Germany until the allies arrested Dönitz and abolished his government.

Between the lines of Kurt's note ran his perplexity at the bizarre effects of national frontiers. If a boy happened to be born on one side of a nation's border, that might obligate him to shoot at his cousin who was born fifty feet away. Not many years before, they might have been comrades-in-arms instead of enemies. It all depended on kings and politicians and generals – and the quality of rifles, not so long ago.

As it turned out, Kurt didn't have to fight his cousins, but he did his duty fighting on Germany's eastern front. In January 1943 his parents in Flensburg received a letter he had written at a hospital in Voronezh in southern Russia, northeast of the Black Sea. He apologized for his handwriting, but that was not just because he wrote in the old German chicken-scratch script that untrained people like me need help reading. During the Nazi era it had been taught in German schools as more "Germanic". But in 1941 Hitler had made a u-turn and prohibited its teaching, substituting a cursive script that was similar to the writing styles in other west-European countries. Frieda Kunkel's letter (page 25) is a good example of the new style. Hitler claimed the old style must be abolished because it had been invented by Jews, but more likely he quashed it because it obstructed communications in the occupied countries, where nobody could read the old 'Germanic' script.

The other factor making Kurt's letter hard to read was that the previous evening, while on guard duty, he stood out against the freshly-fallen snow. And this was helpful to whom German soldiers called 'Iwan': "Suddenly flared a flash and at the same time a beam of light goes through my right shoulder and the hit knocks me down." Besides an injured shoulder he suffered lung damage. But he was in great spirits, because he would be going home while his comrades were being ordered back from leave early. I believe this was because the 5-month battle for Stalingrad, 300 miles to the southeast, was in its final stage.

When the Allies landed in Normandy in June 1944, Kurt was home on leave. Lucky for him he was not ordered to go there, but in August of that year he took a bullet in the back, in Prague. Kurt received the wound badge, the infantry assault badge, and the Iron Cross.

In 1951 he arrived in America on board the Gripsholm, a Swedish ship. He spent his retirement years in Palm Springs, a far cry from Russia, but when he wrote me a second time he had just gone through rehabilitation for a stroke in his left arm. It had occurred while he was trimming ice plant along his sidewalk on Memorial Day, 2012.

Ice plant – it sounds like something that should grow in Russia, but it prefers warmer places, as Kurt Fredericksen did.

A BIG FAN OF THE THIRD REICH

Early this morning I was checking our reviews on Tripadvisor.com, one of several Internet sites that invite customer-comments about travel-related businesses, including restaurants. I found some good ones about us. And I also found this one, by 'justjane1' from Coos Bay:

> My friends and I visited the Blue Heron Bistro . . . after one of my friends read glowing reviews about the restaurant online. We were horribly disappointed.
> I don't know what was more shocking -- the clam chowder that tasted nothing like clam chowder and was inedible after two bites (according to my two friends, both of whom have eaten hundreds of bowls of clam chowder from across the United States in their lifetimes) or the GIANT NAZI POSTER on the wall when you first walk in to this establishment (it's directly opposite the cash register area). No, I'm not kidding: this poster clearly contained multiple swastikas and seemed an homage to the Third Reich. Upon entering the restaurant, one friend stood in front of it so I wouldn't see it because he knew I'd be offended by it. We had been traveling all day along the Oregon Coast, it was late and we were hungry. Once I saw the poster as we were leaving the restaurant, I threw my leftovers in the nearest outdoor trash receptacle.
> (. . .)
> Unless you're a big fan of the Third Reich, swastikas, suspect "clam chowder" and poor service, find another place to eat.

Printed in 1932, the year before Hitler came to power, what she called a "GIANT NAZI POSTER" was one of a stack of *anti-Nazi* election posters I purchased several years ago, from a lady in England. They had belonged to her father, who served with the British army in Germany after the war. He must have bought them from a German who had kept them hidden in his attic all through the Nazi years: what the Germans call '*ein Dachbodenfund*', an attic-find. That they came from a hiding-place seems a reasonable assumption about an era when merely cracking a joke about Hitler could get you the death penalty. Several of the anti-Nazi posters were in poor shape, so I had them professionally restored. The next page shows the poster that gave 'justjane1' hyperventilations. It's reproduced in black & white, but the original had yellow and red added. The two flags at the bottom, one communist and the other Nazi, were both red, and you can see Adolf on the bottom far right with his brownshirted brawlers, the flat-hatted S.A., or storm troopers.

To assist people who don't know German, I had hung a letter-sized, framed translation with some historical background right next to the poster (see above and below). But clearly I made a mistake, assuming that people who saw the poster would have the self-control to read it.

The nearby German poster is very rare. It dates from one of the last elections (1932) before Hitler came to power. (Soon after he became Chancellor, he outlawed all other political parties.) The poster, from the Catholic Center party, says:

> # Vote CENTER List #4
> ## Brüning
> ### Last Bulwark of Freedom and Order
> # TRUTH * LIBERTY * JUSTICE

The bottom of the poster accurately depicts the violent nature of German politics of the time, shortly before the Nazi takeover. Competing bands of German Communists and Nazis try to storm Chancellor Brüning's "bulwark", the so-called Weimar Republic. In fact, both groups wanted to overthrow the government. At times "gentlemen's agreements" were made between Communist and Nazi street fighters. They would refrain from attacking each other during a jointly planned, violent disruption of a social-democrat political meeting.

Contributing to the Nazi takeover of 1933 was the fact that Chancellor Heinrich Brüning was a well-meaning but somewhat inept politician. To fight the Great Depression he raised taxes and reduced unemployment compensation. By 1932 Germany's unemployed numbered 6 million, and he had to resign. After Hitler's takeover the following year Brüning emigrated to the United States and taught political science at Harvard. He died in Norwich, Vermont, in 1970.

In response to Brüning's campaign, the 1932 Nazi election theme was simple but effective (right): *"Our last hope [for the unemployed] - Hitler"*, without further details. Hitler himself made great speeches that said very little.

After he came to power, Hitler ordered that former German Communists should be given priority if they applied for membership of the Nazi party.

Communists and Nazis can thus fairly be described as competitors rather than diametrically opposed antagonists. As to their methods, radical utopians who want to overthrow the existing order have always relied on violence, from the French revolution to today's animal rights activists.

So why have this poster in my restaurant at all? I suppose one reason was the pride of the collector. Since I don't get many opportunities to travel, I collect historical memorabilia. Authentic German election posters from the pre-Hitler era are very rare, so as an amateur historian I thought it worthwhile to display it. With an explanation, for those who don't know German but can read English.

American journalists, who tend to be glib and uninformed in equal measure, are always writing about 'Nazi armies' during World War II.

But the German armed forces had a long-standing custom of staying out of politics, exemplified by a requirement that new recruits must cancel their memberships in the Nazis party. And one fact this poster proves is that not all Germans were Nazi supporters. As a matter of fact, Hitler's Nazi party never received a majority of the German vote. It was only through the peculiarities of the European parliamentary system, the effects of the Depression, and Nazi intrigue and intimidation, that Hitler gained dictatorial powers in 1933/34.

One factor that puts tyrants in power is the common human tendency to act on emotions without ascertaining facts. This explains why many who claim to abhor Nazis and fascists end up behaving just like them, throwing fits and yelling 'Nazi' at the drop of a hat; and 'justjane1' made herself a prime example. The phenomenon has led to a prediction that "the fascists of the future will be called the 'anti-fascists'." It's ascribed to Winston Churchill, but whoever said it, it contains plenty of truth. And it was coined well before the masked 'Antifa' urban hoodlums showed up.

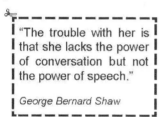

"The trouble with her is that she lacks the power of conversation but not the power of speech."

George Bernard Shaw

Still gloomy about bloviating blowhards ruining restaurants' reputations, my lunch shift on this rainy day in February starts with a woman in a poncho, soaking wet, asking if we accept résumés.

"I'm real sorry," I tell her. "But the people I have want more hours, so we won't be hiring for some time. You'd be wasting your résumé."

And when she smiles and turns to go back into the rain: "I'm sorry. I know it's hard to find work out there. Good luck to you." It's the least I can do.

Next to walk in is a single fellow in his mid-twenties who is looking for a bar with hard liquor. We have hard liquor, and he orders a Jack and Coke. I always wonder what induces people to numb the brain at such an early hour. It's not that I'm a neo-prohibitionist, but it's not even noon yet. Maybe he just needs sympathy. I pour the Jack – 1-2-3-4-, rather slowly, and offer him a warm slice of my German rye bread and butter for free. He reveals that he just got laid off from a job driving log trucks. "Only worked 11 shifts," he adds. "And we just moved here for the job."

He pauses and adds: "And we got a new baby."

"So where did you move from?"

"From Sweet Home. Hey, the first day I was here, though, I won seven hundred bucks at the casino."

"O? Did they win it back yet?"

"They won back more than that," he admits, his mood obviously not improving.

A couple comes in for two bowls of clam chowder. As soon as they have taken their first bite I anxiously inquire if the chowders are to their liking. O yes, the chowders are wonderful; and when I mention the terrible review on Tripadvisor.com they suggest that those people may only ever have eaten the ready-made chowder that a lot of places serve straight from the can or the freezer. Instead of fretting over one weird comment, I need to remember what Tom Land, my former boss, told me many years ago, when I worked for his market research agency. Tom took the time to explain that every consumer products survey will produce a small percentage of nonsense replies. Ask people how they like Brand X beer, and sooner or later somebody will say he is glad the Mets won the game, or he thinks we're going to have snow. "Think of it as static on the radio," Tom warned me. "It makes noise but it doesn't mean anything. Ignore it."

Unfortunately, back then senseless prattle was not being multiplied a billion times all across the Internet. There was no Internet, which must be inconceivable to many people today. The chowder man reminds me that we've talked before, when I stopped to leave some flyers at his motel in North Bend. That must have been at least a year ago.

"So how has the motel business been this winter?" Maybe I shouldn't ask. He was not too enthused when I talked to him last.

"We'd like to sell it," says the wife. "It's not that great, living at your job, you know."

Arguing that it avoids commuting may not help. "I've got an idea," I offer. "What if you placed an ad in a newspaper for people from India? They seem to LOVE the motel business. I'll bet there are several papers for Indians in this country. Place an ad that says your place would make an ideal Patel Motel."

He is not enthused about that, either. "Before we bought the place it had an Indian owner," he explains. "But they didn't make it."

"And you know, not everybody wants to sleep at motels run by Indians," the wife adds.

"Really?" It makes no difference to me, as long as my room doesn't smell like curry. But the husband elaborates:

"I've had several people come in who say: 'O good, you're not wearing a turban. I won't stay at a motel where the owner wears a turban.' "

"Actually, most people from India don't wear turbans, I don't think."

"Well, that's what they say. They don't want to see any turbans."

Hmm. The anti-turban crowd seems to have the same pernicious proclivity that vocal anti-Nazi customers have: proclaiming harsh judgments based on absent evidence.

In come two regular customers who are in the lumber business. They always have clam chowder, with or without something else. This time it's two bowls and a couple of salads. Then a single fellow comes in who is looking for work as a bartender. I give him the same answer as the lady earlier on, as nicely as I can. Next is an older couple with a girl whose appearance suggests a history of overdosing on both food and the manifold dark sides of contemporary culture. Her hair is dyed shades of black and red that cry out: "Look! One-hundred-twenty percent artificial!" Her eye shadow is of prodigious proportions. A cheap jewel pierces her nose (some time ago, I quit inquiring if such hardware creates booger-dams inside my female customers' noses); her wrists are tattooed with a semblance of barbed-wire bracelets, and each finger with one letter of the word L-O-V-E. Now, it is true that because of the direction L-O-V-E was etched on her fingers, the word may look illegible to her, but there can be no such confusion among the people she meets – if they can read. So this may function as an availability signal, like the South-American monkeys whose butts change color, and it may explain the presence of a healthy-looking baby.

"We have heard good things about this place," reveals the dad, or more likely the baby's common-law grandfather. "And we love German food." They are visiting the girl, who lives in the residential Tioga hotel, just down the block. The grandma orders Sauerbraten, the grandpa and the girl order the Oktoberfest, which is our traditional combination of German sausages. And they want cups of chowder first. They love the chowder, so we're off to a good start. As I pass through the bar the laid-off truck driver compliments me on the drink; "When you get a chance, can you get me another one like this?"

After getting another I bring him one of our local papers. An Australian-owned company is getting ready to dig Coos county ore, chromite, that will need to be trucked to a processing facility in town. Their trucking contractor may be looking for drivers. Apparently he knows nothing about this, so he spends some time absorbed in the paper. Meanwhile two of the three generations are eating their German food, and gushing over it. The Jack & Coke man finally gets up to leave. I have charged the poor bugger five instead of 6 dollars for each drink, although he probably didn't notice.

"I think I'm goin' to apply for a job," he announces, putting a three-dollar tip on the bar.

I can't accept this. "No no, keep it, you need this more than I do. And look, I don't mean any offense," I say. "But I have some experience with people applying for jobs, and you don't want to come in smelling of alcohol."

"No problem. I was goin' home to shave first, anyway."

"Good man. And good luck to you." I pat him on the shoulder. He does have about a 4-day beard.

After I've served several more small tables, here comes Gary, or should I say Gerhard Saks, out of my kitchen; he's brought a load of sausages in through the back. Gary came from eastern Germany, from an area called the Uckermark north of Berlin which today borders Poland. When he was a butcher's apprentice shortly after the war, his family survived on the leftovers he brought home. He arrived in America without knowing a word of English, shortened his name from Sakschewski to Saks, did well in the meat business in Chicago and in Los Angeles, and then moved up to Oregon to develop his RV park near Gold Beach where he still makes German meats. He showed me his *Prüfungszeugnis* for the *Fleischer-Handwerk* recently, his diploma for the meat craft. This very official-looking document from 1958 not only listed his qualifications but provided room for every one of his employers to make entries attesting to his performance and behavior, sort of like a sailor's personal log. To prove himself worthy of his *Prüfungszeugnis* Gary had to perform the entire process of butchering an animal and processing it, while identifying any diseases it might have. In those days this kind of über-qualification for a craft was common in Germany, as it was in Holland. But it's much less common now. The European Union has done away with a lot of professional requirements, as anti-competitive barriers to trade. I'm sure they were, but on the other hand a lot of craftsmanship is being lost. According to Gary, today most German meat shops get their sausages ready-made from big meat processors, and German butchers are only required to take a four-month course. I have bought Gary's sausages for over twenty-five years now; he's the one who got me started with German food. His Bratwurst, Knackwurst, Wieners, Kasseler Ripp and other meats all have the right flavors, the ones you taste in Germany. And yet, now and then some know-nothing blowhard complains that our sausages are not the real German thing. It's absurd, just as absurd as the sporadic complaints about our clam chowder.

Gary is meeting a German delegation from Eugene today. They are led by Monika, a sunny, beautiful German lady who imports German wines from the Pfalz, or what the British call the Palatinate, an area on the upper Rhine. You have to hand it to the Germans. Until recently I didn't know that they make excellent Chardonnays, and some very respectable reds, too. They've advanced considerably since the era of sugary-sweet *Liebfraumilch*. Or maybe we're finally getting the good stuff they've been keeping for themselves.

On her way out, the girl with the excessive bodily embellishment stops to ask if we have any openings. I tell her the same as the other would-be applicants. Not at this time – sorry – good luck. A good thing there is no federal anti-discrimination law protecting Goths – yet.

Pretty soon Monika and her party come in; she's bringing a case of wine and picking up some meats from Gary. And, they came to have lunch. Every time I see her she deplores the absence of a German restaurant in Eugene: "You would be so busy over there! There are lots of Germans in Eugene! We would have a *Stammtisch!*" But starting a new restaurant is an incredible amount of work, the desire for which declines with age. Not to mention the huge bother of moving to a different town. Monika's party sits down with Gary, and I bring them warm slices of my German sourdough rye bread. One lady, Brigitte, exclaims she absolutely has to buy a loaf, and they engage in animated German *Stammtisch* chatter. I'm sorry I don't have time to join in. Last time they told me Gary still has a real Berlin accent, which is something I can't really discern. On the other hand, I can tell the geographic origin of most Dutch people I meet from their speech, within fifty miles or less.

Last time they were here, the *Stammtisch* bunch immediately started trading memories of the human consequences of the Nazis' 1945 defeat, particularly the widespread robbing and raping by the Russians. Hoping to avoid such brutal treatment a lot of Germans back then made an effort to surrender to American and British troops rather than to the Russians, but of course not all could make it to western Germany. Some, particularly the women, just hid. Some killed themselves. And then there were the millions of ethnic Germans who were forcibly driven from eastern European lands where they had lived for centuries.

Yes, I know: the Nazi régime's crimes had provoked those outrages, but they had been approved by British and American leaders who were far too eager to please Stalin, a monster as bad as Hitler or worse.

Monika's party of 5 orders Kassler Rippchen, Goulash, regular- and Jäger-Schnitzels, and they are vocal in their appreciation. When they are about done I show them the GIANT NAZI POSTER. And I tell them about justjane1's hissy-fit.

"That's a very valuable poster," says one of them, Peter. "But you shouldn't count on people's intelligence so much."

FOOD BLOGGER JAILED. WAY TO GO !

Next I started thinking of suing 'justjane1' or, to be honest, of merely threatening to do so. Threats are much cheaper. Then I asked an acquaintance, an attorney by the name of Muenchrath, for advice. In reply to my story he responded in sympathetic attorney language:

> "Ladies may have a fit upstairs."
>
> Sign on Hong Kong tailor shop

> "Interesting, but I must confess that mostly it just made me want to come to your restaurant to eat. The review [shows] ignorance and bad taste. . . . [Approaching] Tripadvisor.com . . . would be my initial advice as normally you should allow the party "in the wrong" to rectify the behavior prior to taking legal action. . . . Besides, with an attorney last name like "Muenchrath" on the letter regarding this topic, they may go way off the inappropriate scale by thinking this is just a big Northern European plot . . . just kidding."

Apparently, Political Correctness has now turned 'Northern European' into a euphemism for 'Nazi'. But when I approach Tripadvisor.com for a retraction, all I get is this canned response from their 'Review Team':

> "We have looked at the review in question and determined that it does meet our guidelines. . . . It is our policy to allow any review that meets our criteria to be posted to our site. We are very sorry to hear about the situation you experienced with your guest. However, we are not in a position to make judgments about the character or intentions of reviewers."

So what might Tripadvisor's undisclosed 'guidelines' say? Rule #1: "Rant all you want; we don't care if you're insane, incompetent, or a vengeful windbag."? Rule #2: "We don't give a rip whether anything you say is true or not; it's not our Department."?

> *Don't say that he's hypocritical, say rather that he's apolitical. "Once the rockets are up, who cares where they come down? That is not my department," says Wernher von Braun.*
>
> Tom Lehrer: "Wernher von Braun" *(the father of the post-WW II American missile program)*

Obviously Tripadvisor's "Review Team" is populated by zombies, desperate for more 'reviews'. My only recourse now was to contact 'justjane1' herself, an action which Tripadvisor – fortunately – does enable:

> *"Dear Justjane1:*
> *I recently became aware of your review. . . . I'm not objecting to your comments about our clam chowder. Plenty of other people love it.*
> *What is very disturbing, however, is your description of our restaurant as some sort of neo-Nazi place. You based that conclusion on a very incomplete glance at a 1932 ANTI-NAZI poster by the German Center Party, which was the Catholic party of Chancellor Bruening.*

[Here I repeated my explanation of the poster, how I acquired it, and why I had put it on display.]

> *. . . In legal terms, since your comments on the poster are untruthful, they amount to libel and tortious business interference. I would appreciate it if you would remove them. Should you want more information about these matters, I am at your service."*

Although I did not get a reply, her silent reaction spoke loud enough. Within a week her 'review' was gone from Tripadvisor.com. Matt Muenchrath sent congratulations, while adding sage advice: ". . . the best practice of law is the litigation that never occurs." Having been taken to the legal cleaners before, I could only agree.

About a century ago the British author W. Somerset Maugham wrote a self-described autobiographical novel, called "Of Human Bondage", which contains the story of a young man taking a few wrong turns until he finds his true calling in life, as a physician. Like Maugham, who had studied medicine himself, he spent time as an unpaid intern in a London charity hospital, what in America is called a residency. Wrote Maugham, undoubtedly drawing on his own experiences *(Emphasis added)*:

"He was pleasant, encouraging, and friendly. Like everyone connected with **hospitals** he found that male **patients** were more easy to get on with than female. The women were often querulous and ill-tempered. They complained bitterly of the hard-worked **nurses**, who did not show them the attention they thought their right; and they were troublesome, ungrateful, and rude." [1])

Take out *hospitals*, *patients* and *nurses*, and substitute *restaurants*, *customers* and *waitresses* – and you can keep the rest of the story as is, verbatim. The majority of restaurant complaints are spouted by females, and that's without including those mouthed by males forced to do the bidding of some petulant, controlling female, lurking in the background. The occasional complaint we do get from independent men is more on the order of a power game, an attempt to assert control over a helpless restaurant worker. Sometimes what they say is correct, and we take it seriously. But very often the guy is just showing off for his companion, usually a female, trying to impress her with his vast expertise in international fine cuisine.

But the female complainants – people like 'justjane1' – can get me ranting like Henry Higgins in '*A Hymn to Him*': "They're nothing but exasperating, irritating, vacillating, agitating, calculating, maddening and infuriating hags!"

There are exceptions, of course; I'm happily married to one. But when I complain about my female customers' habit of complaining, she always argues that, as humanity's housekeepers, cooks and shoppers since time immemorial, they earned the right – and the competence – to carp about restaurant food. I have just two little problems with that. One, it's past history. Thanks to radical feminism, the abolition of 'home economics' in schools, plus affirmative action, Title IX, and several more self-destructive societal manias, today's crop of American females is virtually bereft of domestic skills. This includes, but is not limited to, the crucial areas of child-

> "Now that virtually every career is an option for ambitious girls, it can no longer be considered regressive or reactionary to reintroduce discussion of marriage and motherhood to primary education."
>
> *Camille Paglia*

---

[1]) W. Somerset Maugham: *Of Human Bondage*. New York: Doubleday, 1936, p. 390.

raising, housekeeping, and cooking. As to the cooking, bear in mind too that the great majority of famous chefs are still men.

Do I need to supply more evidence? When somebody wants their fried oysters well-done, it's always a woman. Sorry girlie, no can do. An oyster is an oyster, not a steak. When somebody wants their sauerbraten gravy 'on the side', it's always a woman; and we won't do it because that dish, basically a well-done beef roast, is great with the gravy but no good without; too dry. Same story when somebody wants the cream sauce for her shrimp pasta 'on the side'. For crying out loud, this is a restaurant, not a friggin' grocery store. We don't say those things, of course; we just think 'em. If these women insist on knowing why we won't go along with their idiotic requests, we just tell them it's technically impossible. We know that will shut them up, since we also know they lack the expertise to contradict us. So – does the fact that it's mostly women who make these inane demands prove they know something about cooking? *Au contraire, madame.*

I often wonder if it the food isn't a pretext, anyway. Partly because women talk more than men – twice as much, is the lowest estimate I've seen – they seem to have a much greater proclivity towards complaining. But it must also be in their genes, because since time immemorial they have gotten their way by playing the victim – and still do.

> If women are as likely — perhaps more likely — to complain about being oppressed today when they aren't oppressed ... simple logic suggests two choices: Either women remain as oppressed as in the past, or women tend to be malcontents.
>
> Given that the reality is that American women — especially the ones who do the most complaining — are not oppressed, we are left to conclude that the female of the human species may tend toward being malcontents. The simple-minded will respond to this exactly as they were indoctrinated to respond — not by asking, "Is it true?" but by accusing the person who offers this suggestion of sexism and misogyny. [1])

> *"Gib, dass ich meine Johanna wiedersehe."*
>
> "Give that I see my Johanna again."
>
> Last words of Otto von Bismarck, former German chancellor, before he died on July 30, 1898. His beloved wife Johanna had preceded him in death four years earlier.

It's a very safe bet that one of our major political parties would not exist if it wasn't

---

[1]) Dennis Prager: "Are Women Malcontents?" April 9, 2019.

for the female vote, along with that of several other victim-groups that together fill one gigantic seething cauldron of whiners. Many years ago that party realized that the secret to political prosperity consisted of doling out public recognition and money to every group that blamed its misfortunes on somebody else. Those groups were persuaded that government would be their sugar daddy who would set everything right. In the process that party got the support of another big bloc of voters, i.e. the professionals who make their living catering to victims: race- and gender-baiting politicians and bureaucrats, union bosses, diversity consultants, outreach coordinators, sustainability facilitators, queer theory professors, abortion providers, women's shelter counselors, mental health quacks, and so on.

In a way, there is nothing new under the sun. Feckless females have always looked to sugar daddies for a meal ticket, but since modern feminism's rabidly anti-male attitudes made that recourse unfashionable, the GBNEAWFIW (Great But Not Entirely Altruistic White Father In

Washington) happily took on the part. Similarly, for the perennial victims 'of color' the Great White Father replaced the plantation owner, doling out scraps of sustenance while ignoring immoral and lawless behavior, in a hugely expanded version of Harry Truman's overlooking the petty thefts committed by his family's 'nigger-cook.' His words, not mine.

That same political party regularly launches campaigns to give the vote back to another griping victim-group, even phonier than the rest: convicted criminals. On that subject, American history goes back a long way. Most people know that for quite some time Great Britain used to got rid of its criminals by shipping them to Australia, a social experiment that worked out tolerably well except for the funny accent of the descendants of the 165,000 felons hauled down under between 1787 and 1867. But there was a reason why the shipping of British criminals to Australia did not commence until 1787. It's because at first they were taken on a shorter trip, merely across the Atlantic. From 1717 to 1776, the year when the 13 American colonies elected to forego its mixed blessings, the British Empire shipped 60,000 felons over here, mostly to southern states. As the historian Paul Johnson describes it,

> 10,000 serious criminals were dumped on Maryland alone. . . . In 1755 in Baltimore, one adult male worker in ten was a convict from Britain. They were much more troublesome than non-criminal indentured labor, always complaining of abuses and demanding 'rights.' . . . From Virginia, William Byrd II wrote loftily to an English friend: 'I wish you would be so kind as to hang all your felons at home.' [1])

But there you are, you see! We have found America's oldest political constituency! Criminals who, just having escaped the hangman, are still itching to scream about unfairness and to demand their rights!

By now this historical digression, brilliant as it may be, must have lost me the affection of every reader of a certain political persuasion that will remain unmentioned. That could be a lot of readers, so I will make up for it by inspiring one if that party's core constituencies, trial lawyers. I am about to reveal a new area of legal endeavor. This consists of suing volunteer restaurant reviewers for slander and business interference, two causes of legal action that deserve to be revived, Internet or no Internet. And since some of our Supreme Court judges are enamored of International Law, I recommend adopting the legal standards of the Taiwanese, successful pioneers in this field:

FOOD BLOGGER JAILED FOR CALLING NOODLES "TOO SALTY"

TAIPEI -- A woman was jailed for 30 days by a Taiwanese court for writing on her food blog that a restaurant's noodles were too salty.

The blogger, named only as Liu, visited a Taichung beef noodle restaurant in 2008 and wrote on her blog that the cuisine there was "too salty," . . . The restaurant's owner, known as Yang, learned about the review from a regular customer and sued Liu for defamation.

The Taichung District Court . . . ruled that her criticism of the restaurant exceeded reasonable bounds because she only tried the noodles and two side dishes.

She was sentenced to 30 days in detention, two years of probation and was ordered . . . to pay $6,900 in compensation to the restaurant . . .

Liu, who apologized to the restaurant, was told by the judge that she could not appeal against the decision.

> "She looks as if butter wouldn't melt in her mouth."
>
> Jonathan Swift

---

[1]) Paul Johnson: *A History of the American People*. New York: HarperCollins, 1997 (softcover), pp. 95/96.

Yang said that he hoped the case would teach her a lesson.

Huang Cheng-lee, a lawyer in Taichung, said that bloggers who post restaurant reviews should remember to be "truthful, objective and fair" and should post photographs to support their comments. [1])

Father's Day this year was rather wasted on me. Trudi and Maarten wanted to take me out to dinner, but the restaurant that sounded most interesting to me turned out to be closed. For a fallback plan they proposed to drive 25 miles down the coast to Bandon, and eat at a place that sounded vaguely familiar. When we drove up I recognized it as an establishment that had not impressed me in the past, but I didn't want to play the "Father Knows Best" card.

The place did have a nice view of the Bandon boat basin. But during the drive back I started silently composing a description of my experience. Later that evening I filed it, in the form of a review on Tripadvisor.com:

> ". . . one can no longer read a news report online without one hundred bilious and moronic comments following it. Everyone today has become a commentator, parading his or her idiotic and illiterate musings for the world to see and read."
>
> *Taki*

"The salad they served was pathetic; a bit of chopped Romaine or iceberg, it was hard to tell which, with a "house" raspberry dressing that was sweeter than ant-bait. I like rock shrimp, so I ordered the rock shrimp pasta dish. It turned out to be a big oval plate with a lot of noodles and Parmesan cheese, but not much else. I couldn't find the basil and sun-dried tomatoes it was supposed to have, nor the cilantro which I had asked them to add. But the worst part was the rock shrimp; the few that were hiding under the noodles were shrunk, rubbery and tasteless. For all I could tell, they could have been just overcooked bay shrimp. Overcooked, or freezer-burned.

The waitress was one of those who constantly talk Valley Girl: "I'm like …," "O my god," and "You guys". She did perfunctorily ask if the food was OK, but didn't really listen. But then, I did not want to make a big stink about my food in front of my dinner-mates, who were more tolerant. To make up for the absence of vegetables on my own plate I stole some of theirs and found to my horror that they were limp and soaked in soy sauce or in Teriyaki sauce. Nasty. And overpriced."

[1]) http://www.foxnews.com/leisure/2011/06/24/food-blogger-jailed-for-calling-noodles-too-salty/#ixzz1RBkVVJMQ

Pretty soon I realized that publishing this tirade was not going to make me feel any better, but worse. How was this any different from the rants about my own restaurant? I hate it when customers

> "The world rings with praise . . . Praise of weather, wine, dishes, actors, motors, horses, colleges, countries . . . I had not noticed how the humblest, and at the same time most balanced and [accomplished], praised most, while the cranks, misfits and malcontents praised least. The good critics found something to praise in many imperfect works . . The healthy and unaffected man, even if luxuriously brought up and widely experienced in good cookery, could praise a very modest meal; the dyspeptic and the snob found fault with all."
>
> C. S. Lewis, *A Word about Praising*

never complain about their meals but then carp afterwards, on the Internet. So why do it myself? Besides, my own piece sounded as narcissistic and as petulant as the worst found on Tripadvisor.com. I didn't have a good night's sleep.

Early next morning I found that Tripadvisor had not posted my review yet. Apparently it was still at their Review Committee, and they had been too busy inking their rubber-stamps. So I logged on and retracted it. When it comes to restaurant reviews, the Golden Rule is not a bad one to follow.

Postscript

A couple of years ago I received a parcel that the mail*person* had delivered at the restaurant, but was addressed to me personally, so I was asked to pick it up. It contained a copy of this book. For some time Adam, the Blue Heron's new owner, has sold it at the restaurant, and that is how the woman, who lived in Eugene, home of my alma mater the University of Oregon, had acquired it.

Her handwritten note accused me of having Nazi sympathies, and of making 'misogynistic' statements in this very chapter; and she demanded a refund. Speaking for myself, through the years I have acquired many books, and I have disagreed with some of their contents, but it never occurred to me to march back to the bookstore, demanding a refund for hurt feelings. So I mailed the book back to her, with a note:

> *... you had ample opportunity to peruse 'Everybody's War' before deciding to buy it. And by now, the book shows visible wear.*

Since I have not had complaints like yours before, I wondered if you're connected to the U of O, one of many contemporary refuges for ideological snowflakes. People who require trigger warnings and a room full of teddy bears and play-do and blankets if there's the slightest chance of hearing or seeing anything they may disagree with.

> "There is a well-established rule among serious people: If you compare anybody to Hitler, you lose the argument. Comparing Trump to a man who systemically slaughtered six million Jews and millions of others he also thought were sub-human, is hate speech - the very hate speech that liberals who are now making Hitler comparisons routinely decry."
>
> *Bernard Goldberg*

What you call "misogynistic nonsense" ... happens to be true, and based on many decades of observations. If you had finished the chapter instead of throwing a hysterical fit, you would have found even more proof.

And then you have the nerve to accuse me of imitating the Nazis. You want Nazis? ... a gang of people like you laid siege to my restaurant and almost succeeded in bankrupting me, in retaliation for a simple expression of opinion. You sound as if you would have fit right in with those totalitarians ... provoked by someone just like you who ignorantly accused me – just like you – of being a Nazi. May the two of you find bliss.

> " . . . recent struggles for freedom and equality within Western societies have been intimately bound up with freedom of speech. The demand for their voices to be heard has proved central to the struggles for women's emancipation, gay liberation and racial equality in the UK and US. There is a grim irony in the fashion for feminist, trans or anti-racist activists today to demand restrictions on free speech as a means of protecting the rights of the identity groups they claim to represent. Without the efforts of those who fought for more free speech in the past, these illiberal activists would not be free to stand up and call for less of it in the present."
>
> *Mick Hume*

WOOFTER'S WAR

His official name, the one we gave him when he first came to us as a puppy, was Bertie Woofter, but from then on he pretty much went by Woofter. It's more British to use the surname and ignore the Christian name, as they call it, and besides, Woofter was a prime specimen of a great British breed, the Jack Russell terrier.

Woofter was not a lap dog but he came to do a job, the kind of job a Jack Russell loves: chasing critters, mostly non-human ones, that dare trespass on his master's homestead, which must be ferociously defended. Coons, possums and herons had discovered our recently-dug fish pond, and had become interested in the nutritional value of our ornamental koi, so something had to be done. Trudi had had dogs most of her life, and after spending days reading up on the characteristics of

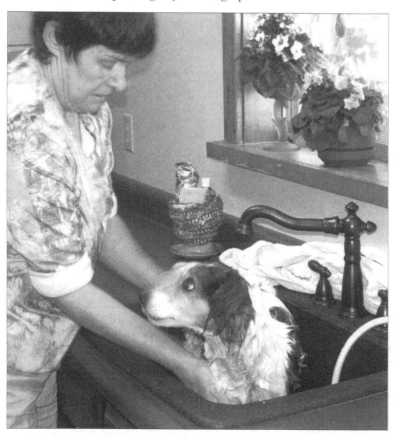

numerous dog breeds, she decided that a Jack Russell would provide near-perfect critter-control. Jacks have not yet acquired the degeneracy that plagues dogs bred mostly for their looks. Dachshunds are notorious for having weak hips; Dalmatians may be deaf as well as dumb, as in stupid. And toy poodles are – well, what ARE they good for? In looks, Jacks vary a great deal more than these highly standardized breeds, but they make up for that by being strong, hardy, enterprising, curious, intelligent, and sociable. To all of those Jacksian qualities I would add that they are fearless. Except for thunderstorms and baths, from both of which he used to hide, our Woofter was afraid of nothing. On the negative side, Jacks are not the best indoor dogs because when left alone too long they may get bored and damage your belongings, and some may bark endlessly. Also most Jacks don't like cats, and they may become competitive with small children, if not downright jealous. And finicky gardeners may not like Jacks because they are dirt-diggers, originally bred by the Reverend Jack Russell to go after burrowing animals such as foxes and badgers. Our Woofter was considerate, though. Trudi would show him some place away from her flowers where he was free to dig, and he happily made the dirt fly.

Unlike the Jack Russell terriers made popular by the movies, with long legs and short, wiry hair, Woofter was a country Jack with short legs and hair that was long and soft. Not that his country-looks mattered to him. From the outset Woofter understood that he was to be our anti-varmint defense system. Fortunately, while giving us years of service, Woofie had the good fortune of never running into a cougar or a bear, both of whom inhabit the woods that border our back yard. And he never ran into any elk, one kick of whom could have finished him. A herd of elk has wandered from those same woods into local backyards. They ate the recently-planted orchard of Ryan, our neighbor up the hill, to the very last sprout.

During the early part of Woofter's career I was often aroused by noisy commotions in the darkest of nights. A gusher of barking, growling and snarling had erupted from the near-impenetrable brush between our house and Ryan's. So I would get up, arm myself with flashlight and Colt .25, and make my way into my tolerant neighbor's backyard to settle the dispute. Despite the incessant barking and snarling, this was no simple matter; thickets are so thick in this country that you can't see what may be growling furiously just one foot away. Gingerly moving the brush aside I would finally locate the spot where two enraged animals, without paying any attention to me, were having a conflict that neither intended to run away from. Careful not to injure Woofie, I dispatched the coon or possum with my Colt .25. This always took more than one shot, I suppose because of the stratospheric adrenalin level. After some of these incidents Woofter would be left with a scratch or a bite-mark, which didn't seem to hurt his pride at all. And sometimes he would drag his opponent's carcass onto the deck behind the house, where he spent hours basking in his glory. Until I disposed of it.

After a few seasons word must have got around in the possum-&-coon world that our place was something to avoid, and the nightly critter-commotions became less frequent. Woofter spent lazy days on the deck, occupying himself by chasing chipmunks, which we deplored, and rats, which we encouraged. I mean, the chasing.

Even though he longed to do so, Woofter never figured out how to climb trees. This was unfortunate because the rats were roof rats, a

breed native to southeast Asia that had originally come to harbors like Coos Bay as stowaways. Roof rats look a lot like Norway rats, a little slimmer maybe, and they are black or grey instead of brown. The two breeds, Norway rats and roof rats, don't mix. Roof rats are very comfortable with heights and they live in trees, not sewers, but for greater comfort in our climate they prefer people's attics. When we first heard them run around above our heads, we put it down to harmless excursions on the roof. When they kept scurrying to and fro I sometimes went outside to see if I could spot them up there, but never saw anything. Finally it dawned on me that they must be inside, running between the roof rafters. Somehow they had gained access and set up housekeeping. And since no breed of rats is particularly fond of same-sex marriage, this always means more rats, and soon. Worse, not only did our old-fashioned home offer low-cost housing for these prolific illegal immigrants, but the framing allowed them to go almost anywhere, traveling unseen up and down walls, between floors, and through ceilings. Most of our house dates from 1903, when wooden houses were built with balloon-framing, a method that was out of use by the 1920s, and for good reason. Balloon framing meant that walls had no upper plates or lower plates or fire stops, hence no rat-travel impediments. Once a rat got inside he might turn up anywhere, in the attic, in the basement, sometimes even in the living room. And not just rats, either. We've had squirrels and weasels take advantage of our unintended hospitality.

Knowing a Jack Russell's fondness of varmint-control, I took Woofter to a few of the hidden cubbyholes, dead spaces and other voids in the old house, but I soon realized that would do no good. The smells and the thrill of the hunt were heavenly to Woofter, but most of these places had insulation, which he would tear apart without achieving anything; the rats had moved on. Until we figured out where this plague entered the house we would have to use traps, and I would have to construct the internal travel impediments that the carpenters of 1903 had omitted. I still think with horror of the hours I spent in small, hot spaces reeking of rat piss, blocking connections to other small spaces and leaving poison and traps behind. These efforts never met with more than partial success, for years on end.

The compensation we allowed ourselves for this incessant grief may outrage PETA (People for the Ethical Treatment of Animals). Once I had succeeded in restricting inside travel, we no longer saw rats in the basement or the ground floor, but hardly a day went by when we didn't catch one in the attic. Most were stuck on glue traps, so they were still alive. On one occasion we found four rats stuck on one glue trap; they must have been on a family outing. Rat Spring Break, maybe. At first we would finish them off with a 2 x 4 that we kept handy, but then I decided they might have entertainment value. I would carry the trap downstairs, rat and all. Once outside I would peel it from the trap and dangle it towards Woofter who was gazing upwards as if in a religious trance, slobbering with rodent rapacity. I dropped the rat, Woofter caught it, but only for a second or so before he tossed it up in the air again. "Squeek!" said the rat, before landing back in Woofter's mouth. Another toss, and another squeak. Repeat. After several tosses the squeaker no longer worked, and neither did the rest of the rat. But, as a consolation prize, he'd become Woofter's trophy of the day

After several seasons of rat-catching in the attic, I set up ladders against the house and promised Maarten a reward if he could find the rats' entrance hole, which must be somewhere on the roof, though I could not spot it myself. Praise to his sharp eyes! He found it in

no time, between the roofing overhang and the gutter. The fascia-board must have had a small piece of rot, which the roof-rats had enlarged into an entrance. No wonder we kept catching so many in the attic. I replaced the fascia board with a treated one, and that was the end of our roof-rat-nightmare. Except for a week or so of dead rat stench in the house, on account of the ones who'd been caught in the act, immured, and starved. O yes, and the rat flies. Big fat black ones that buzz all over. But they do useful work. While still maggots, they eat the rat.

Woofter's physical decline may have set in with the arrival of Jazzie, our second Jack Russell. Jazzie, a female, came from a Jack Russell rescue place in northern California. A lot of people who buy Jack Russells have no business owning this kind of dog. It's how a fair number of Jacks end up in dog pounds or in rescue outfits, the latter set up by people who love them and know what they need. Jazzie's former owner lived in an apartment, and a bored young Jack in an apartment may turn into an all-day barker, which she was, although when first she joined us she only croaked. Evidently her failed master had kept one of those electric collars on her, the kind that give a dog a shock in the throat when she barks. Jazzie had been neutered but Woofter never had, so we had him fixed – too late, as it turned out. Wet spots appeared in the house. Because of his age or because of the fix, he had lost some bladder control, so since he was spending more time in the house, Trudi manufactured a dog diaper. Oddly enough he still looked for chances to slip outside in order to mark his territory, so when we weren't paying attention we were treated to the sight of a diapered dog going through the motions of spraying a shrub, without visible results. But lifting his leg seemed to lift his morale.

Next came the day when we realized Woofter had lost much of his hearing, and the day when his eyes looked opaque and dim. Next came unmistakable signs of arthritis, since he was now even having trouble jumping an eight-inch stair step. Trudi fed him Chondroitin pills in his soft food, which seemed to do some good. He now was an indoor dog although he still spent a couple of hours outside, warming his old bones in the sun or slowly patrolling the outside perimeter. There was no chance he would get lost, because he no longer strayed far.

Then came that fall day when Jazzie wanted to go outside and Woofter did not. But the weather was fine and Trudi thought he should join her, anyway. She took off his diaper and opened the door to let him answer nature's call, if nature was so inclined. But nature seemed to have a different call, a worrying one that brought an indignant growl from deep inside Woofter. And then he was off, on an unstoppable rush into the brush that had been the site of so many historic, heroic deeds. Arthritis? What arthritis? This was Woofter's Charge of the Light Brigade.

He didn't come back that evening, or that night. The next day Maarten and I searched a short distance into the woods, but found no Woofter. That doesn't mean he was not there; it's exceedingly difficult to find anything in our tangled Oregon jungle, as I've explained. But if he was there, he was not alive. We will never know if it was a heart attack that finished him, or a hostile varmint. He did not know it, but in his condition he would have been no match for the enemies he used to persecute with so much zest.

When can their glory fade?
O the wild charge they made !
All the world wondered.
Honor the charge they made,
honor the Light Brigade,
noble six hundred.

THE WAGES OF SIN ARE ARTISTS

"Many of the insights of the saints," the famous longshoreman-philosopher Eric Hoffer wrote, "stem from their experience as sinners."

Hoffer was embroidering on St. Augustine's alleged prayer, thirteen centuries ago, when that holy man was still a skirt-chasing youth: "Give me chastity and continence, but not quite yet. Amen." But once Augustine was a serious Christian, he was eminently qualified to preach against sin. He knew that it is luridly enticing.

One of those lurid lures, though perhaps a minor one in the Almighty's catalog of sins, is the promise of public subsidies. That's because, as in the devil's attempts to seduce Jesus (Matthew 4 & Luke 4) there's always a string attached. Jesus spotted it of course, but we tend to overlook that the officials who are so generously spending our money on us obtain a license to mess with us as well. And when we object, they will smirk and point out that who pays the piper plays the tune.

In the city of Coos Bay, subsidies have long come as Urban Renewal grants. For reasons that would take too long to explain, Urban Renewal is a fancy name for property-tax money that has been inexplicably diverted by a City Council of people whose main reason for running for office was the chance to spend it. And boy, do they spend it.

Before I got snared in their trap, I had enviously watched gushers of Urban Renewal money burble up all over, but never quite reaching me. Usually that was because my business was located just outside the UR District. In the 1990s, when the City Council was using UR money to tear down the canopies of the failed downtown mall which they had built in the 1970s, also with UR money, they decided to buy new awnings for the downtown businesses to make up for it – also with UR money. As usual, their reasoning was suspect. The mall canopies were being trashed because they were counterproductive, besides being rotten from neglect. Situated east-west in a windy, cool climate, they had made a dark, dank wind tunnel, so by tearing them down the City Council was merely removing a mistake. But the Council's downtown businessmen never pass up a chance to spend public funds on themselves, so to make up for the 'loss' of the canopies, they promised free awnings to covere theh sidewalks in front of any business inside the downtown UR District. The rules they set were not terribly practical, though they acted as if they were. UR money would pay for "the lesser of the bid to build and install the awnings or $150 per lineal foot of awning." But, the City warned, "Property owners are responsible for future maintenance of the awnings." But enforcement was unspecified.

> "Nobody spends somebody else's money as carefully as he spends his own. Nobody uses somebody else's resources as carefully as he uses his own. So if you want efficiency and effectiveness, if you want knowledge to be properly utilized, you have to do it through the means of private property."
>
> Milton Friedman

The awning program created a nice windfall for people in the awning business who managed, through some miracle of awning economics, to make every bid come out at $150 a lineal foot. On a typical downtown corner building of 100 x 100 feet, that came to $30,000 worth of awnings. Not everybody had that kind of paying footage of course, but by 1997 the City had spent $330,000 to festoon 22 buildings with brand-new awnings. As to the requirement that the property owners must maintain them – that was a laugh, and a sad one. Within a few years some were already falling apart, and nothing was ever done.

In 2006 we took a European trip, which included a week in the Alsace. Although Eric Hoffer was born in the Bronx, he spoke with a heavy German accent because both his parents had come from there. In the 17th century King Louis XIV, exclaiming: *"Quel beau jardin!"* (What a beautiful garden!!) stole the Alsace for France. The Alsatians still spoke German when, in 1871, Germany stole the Alsace back after beating the French during the Franco-Prussian war. Thanks to the American intervention in World War I the French recovered it in 1918, after which they required the Alsatians to start speaking French, but they couldn't finish the job because in 1940 Hitler beat them again, thereby incorporating the territory back into his third Reich, where it was going

to stay a thousand years. Despite that prediction, five years later Hitler lost the war, though not so much due to the French, who took the Alsace back anyway. Today everyone there speaks French, although some

Alsatians must still be bi-lingual.

And since World War II all the half-timbered little villages in the Alsace have been restored, which has caused an economic boom. Everything is as quaint and

picturesque as the backdrop in Walt Disney's "Pinocchio," and packed with tourists as a result. It does seem a bit perplexing, being surrounded by French-speaking people, French street signs and French shop signs, while many of the ancient *Fachwerk* buildings still carry German inscriptions.

Here's one I liked: in the local German dialect the owner of a house in Riquewihr had chiseled an inscription on his gable-stone, boasting that with God's help he had built his own home, ending as follows:

ER·IST·GEMACHT·NACH·MEINES·SINS·GESTALT·
ICH·WEIS·DAS·ER·NIT·IEDEM·GEFALT·
· 5 · 5 · 7 · 4 ·

IT'S DONE THE WAY IT PLEASES ME
I KNOW IT WON'T PLEASE EVERYBODY
1574

A man after my heart. If you got a problem with that, go eat worms.

Ever since we started specializing in German food at the Blue Heron I had pondered giving the place a Germanic look, one that would instantly communicate what we were about. And I came home from that trip very inspired, carrying gigabytes of pictures. Then I learned that the City Council had not only expanded the downtown UR-District to include my place, but it was promising grants up to $25,000 to help businesspeople spruce up the outside of their buildings. This was called the Façade Improvement Program, and here, I thought, was my chance

at a facelift. I mean, for my building. Armed with pictures from the Alsace and a rough sketch I went to see Butch Schroeder, a local designer, not a full-fledged architect, but a man with more creativity and good sense than is usually found in that trade. Butch produced a design that met all my expectations: the half-timbered look, roof tiles, mansard windows, plus a corner tower. The tower came out on the big side, but that way it was centered over the entrance. I submitted Butch's design to the City Council. They welcomed it, but to my surprise they mentioned that Frank Hanson, the owner of the office supply store across the street, had also recently applied for a facelift with a tower, albeit a tiny one. As a next step, I was told to submit Butch's design to the city's Design Committee.

The last time I had heard of the Design Committee was when the avaricious owner of several decrepit downtown buildings headed it. To no one's surprise this slumlord had loudly defended the principle that the awnings that the city was buying with UR money should only be given to owners of downtown buildings. It turned out that he'd been dethroned, and the city had re-constituted the Design Committee *without* downtown business owners. But to my great surprise, that change had not improved it. To serve on the committee, people were now required to have degrees in architecture or in art. And this time it was chaired by a skinny Albert Einstein lookalike by the name of Stroganoff. He was a big-shot retired professor of architecture and "community planning," a craft that has done this world, including Coos Bay, precious little good. Under his eagle-eye, the re-constituted Design Committee demanded that my building's facelift must "harmonize" with Frank's, but especially the tower. Mine was big, but his was puny, as seen nearby. →

It may be a waste of good railroad track, but it's art: the sculpture on the waterfront. The patterns visible on the legs are woolies knit by elderly ladies who thought the Daddy Longlegs looked awfully cold.

Although I wasn't sure how we could harmonize the two, I promised to try. But the most strenuous demands came from Mike Vaughn, a lifelong artistic dilettante whose most recent (and most gigantic) work has disgraced the rundown Coos Bay waterfront for years. Labeled "ART – For Sale," it consists of several lengths of railroad track, weirdly bent and welded together. On account of its legs sticking up in the air it reminds me of a prehistoric Daddy Longlegs: very big and very dead – but also very rusty. Claiming that my neon sign, the one with the blue heron, would "clash with the building's architecture," Vaughn demanded that I get rid of it. The sign would be out of harmony.

In battles like this, where artists can smell the victories that elude them in the real world, their ammunition consists of words like "balance," "blend," and "harmony," which they fire at random from their cultured cannons, and at will. But when the gun smoke clears, those are mere code words for "Do it my way." Still, in the end the armistice conditions seemed reasonable. I would keep my neon sign but remove the reader-board that was part of it. That would reduce its overall size, to minimize clashing with the precious architecture. In hindsight, I know I was being stupid. My sign was a landmark, designed to communicate something to the occupants of 15,000 to 20,000 cars a day, moving at 30 miles an hour. Getting rid of the reader board would rob me of that opportunity. But I was so enchanted by the idea of the city paying for part of my project that I gave in, oblivious of what all this balancing and blending and harmonizing would cost me.

Next, to try and harmonize the two towers, I went to see Frank with a rough concept of how he might get more bang for his buck. He looked at my sketch, copied it and, as is his wont, didn't say much. He didn't do much about it either, but I can't blame him because he was already spending more for his facelift than I was for mine, which ended up costing $80,000. The City was going to give each of us the maximum possible UR-grant, $25,000; the owner paid the rest. And this, I will admit, made the façade program the first UR scheme that showed some consideration for the taxpayers. When property owners are paying for a project with their own money, even with a partial contribution from the public purse, they will be motivated to do it right, and once it's done they are more likely to take care of it. People who have the entire job paid for by the taxpayers won't, and the city's Free Awning

Program had proved it. That's just human nature.

Alas, when the bills came in I realized that the city's $25,000 was much less than what the numbers said. It was not just the annoyance of having to deal with the artistic busybodies. Removing the reader-board from the neon sign had not been a simple matter. It required rebuilding it, and that cost $6,000. Since then I have spent thousands more to have banners made to advertise outside. I don't think they "harmonize" with the architecture, but I need to communicate. On top of that, since the maximum façade grant of $25,000 was calculated by the lineal feet of the improvements, I had the builders, two superb craftsmen by the names of Tom and John Stiegeler, do some things that were superfluous but increased the footage to the max. And as soon as the five year "keep-it-the-way-it-is" period mandated by the City expired and I could find the money, I planned to install an electronic message board outside, an expense made necessary by the Design Committee's wish to harmonize and blend me out of my reader-board. After taking all those things into account, I figured most of the URD's $25,000 grant was lost to the blenders and the harmonizers, and with the superfluous aggravation added, it had not been worth it.

But it took me a while to reach those conclusions, and the old rule "Once burned, twice shy" had not yet sunk in when I considered applying for a second Façade Program grant. To be frank, I figured that this project, a simple front door replacement, would receive no more attention from the Design Committee than motorists entering California get from the fruit fly inspectors.

But after thirty years of being yanked open by hungry humans and stiff southwesters, my twin entry doors must be replaced, this time with a handsome single door, with a stained glass window and matching sidelights. That would enhance the building's traditional German look, which the old, aluminum-framed glass doors had never done. Surely the Design Committee could find nothing wrong with that.

Instead, they came down on it – and on me – like a ton of bricks. First they wanted twin doors, as more 'in scale' with the tower above. No way did I want twin doors. A dozen winters ago, one particularly vicious storm had blown one of the old twin glass doors clear out of its frame, with understandably shattering results.

On the committee was a woman by the name of Hillary, the proud owner of an architecture degree from Liverpool. Like many architects she had mostly done local government work, but her portfolio also included Frank's façade design, which seemed to have given her an ownership interest in mine. She was probably put out that her work was left in the dust by Butch Schroeder's, who had not even studied in Liverpool. Hillary's lengthy take on my new front door was larded with the words 'balance' and 'blend', spoken with a British accent. First she argued that the door should not have a window. When I objected that this could cause collisions between leaving and entering customers, she switched to advocating a full-length window, in order to "create something more solid, with more mass under the tower." When I characterized a full-length window as another safety hazard she changed tack again, now arguing that I could only have a half-

> "The aesthete aims at harmony rather than beauty. If his hair does not match the mauve sunset against which he is standing, he hurriedly dyes his hair another shade of mauve. If his wife does not go with the wall-paper, he gets a divorce."
>
> G.K. Chesterton – *ILN*, 12/25/09

window in the door if the side-lights were also half-length. I still don't understand why. But it was clear that not just Hillary but the entire Design Committee thought that their job was to take over this very minor project and re-design it from scratch.

Next, Stroganoff got into high dudgeon about the new door's medium-brown color. He thought a darker paint, identical to the very dark brown of the building's trim, "would give a stronger base for the tower" – whatever that meant. I think the entry to a business should not blend too much with the rest of the building. It needs to stand out, or some people won't be able to find it; and I speak from experience.

Then Stroganoff started grousing that my building had three different kinds of windows – something impossible to avoid since it had grown in stages, during three decades. Besides, except for this assembly of addlebrained *artistes*, my windows had never offended anybody. And then, virtually in the same breath, he started accusing me of bad faith, for having slimed out of my obligation to 'harmonize' my tower with Frank's, back in 2007. At that point I forcefully lowered my fist on the table, almost causing Stroganoff to wet his pants. Drowning his indignant sputters that fist-slamming was not allowed at his meeting, I bellowed that I had made an attempt to 'harmonize' the two towers but had gotten nowhere, and besides, the City Council had agreed that it was unnecessary. He continued grousing, supported by his wife who was also on the committee, albeit by a different last name. Maybe it was Borscht. Vaughn was quiet this time around, but now Hillary moved on from the window-issue to join Stroganoff's jeremiad about the color of the door. In the end the micro-managing meeting voted to approve my new front door *only* if *both* the door *and* the side-lights had half-size windows, *and* if the whole thing was painted an extremely dark brown to *blend* with the *mass* of the tower. To achieve the latter they would pick the paint themselves, from a color sample.

And to my surprise – I was still naïve enough to expect common sense from small-town politicians – the City Council supported the Committee, without reservations. Why was I so insistent on doing it my way? "Because it's my property," I replied, "and besides, I don't think your committee knows what they're talking about."

"Ah, but you're wrong," the mayor smirked. "These people are highly qualified, and if you want our money, you gotta play along."

"I don't think he should get Urban Renewal money more than once, anyway," mused Mark Daily, a council member whose use of UR money for radio advertising of his downtown business had recently come to light.

"It's not going to happen," I said as I walked out.

What a waste of time. Since then I have learned that half a dozen businessmen who were considering taking advantage of Coos Bay's façade program have changed their minds, on account of the Design Committee's artsy bully-boys. One was going to spend a million dollars, but he gave up when told he had to do the whole thing in an expensive Victorian style.

And when I spent 4 grand, all of it my own money, for a new front door last summer, I got the windows I wanted, and the full-length sidelights I wanted, and I personally painted the whole thing a bright blue. I think it looks pretty good, and so do a lot of people. And when members of the Design Committee drive by, I hope it gives them severe heartburn.

IT'S DONE THE WAY IT PLEASES ME
I KNOW IT WON'T PLEASE EVERYBODY
1574

CHESTER KAUFFMAN'S WAR

It's Sunday morning, and we're in church. The edifying part (the sermon) just ended, but the previous item, the 'contemporary worship songs', was like slogging through a swamp of mawkish monotony. Worship songs seem to be obligatory in today's evangelical churches, like suits and ties were once. But they remind me of my experience, never repeated since, of a Wagner opera: seriously short of good tunes, and as endless as winter in Antarctica. Just last week I had an exchange about this with Adam, when he mentioned he had taken his girlfriend to church, but didn't care for the music. Same objection: worship songs.

"It kinda sucked."

As a rule our tastes in food and drink and cars and quite a few other things are far apart. But here was common ground, albeit on a minor devotional point.

"I'm on your side there, Adam. I like the old hymns, the rousing kind. *The old rugged cross, A mighty fortress, Amazing grace* … But these worship songs – lyrics without poetry, and tunes without music. Insipid, really. And repetitive – repetitive – when you think we're finally done, here we start again, all the way from the beginning. You'd think we're Buddhists, chanting a mantra."

"That's right," Adam says.

"And you know, Adam, to me some of those songs sound like recycled pop tunes that didn't catch on, so let's peddle them to the Christians. One line stuck in my mind – I can't get rid of it. *Jesus I am so in love with you.*' I'll bet some music agent just substituted 'Jesus' for 'honey' or 'sweetheart' to make the sale."

This fills him with so much elation, it's practically squirting out of his ears. "That's awesome! That's awesome! Did you see that on South Park?"

"See what on South Park?" It's been many years since we've watched TV. And I didn't think we had missed much.

"On South Park, a couple years ago, they had this episode where one of 'em is trying to figure out how to make a lot of money, and they discover a stack of pop music that didn't sell, and they put the name of Jesus on it, and they make a killing. That was awesome. You can see it on YouTube!"

I always had mixed feelings about the old saw that truth is stranger than fiction; after all, there's some awfully weird fiction out there. But voilà: a smidgen of evidence. Still, I need to keep in my snooty mind that religious music has always been related to popular music styles of the day, so I should not be down on my fellow-Christians for liking the music style *they* are used to. Some even listen to this stuff all day on the radio, something I couldn't do if I got paid for it. But when organ music was first introduced into churches, centuries ago, it was resisted by stuck-in-the-mud traditionalists too. People like me, I suppose. So I put on my best moralist's disguise:

"But Adam, we should remember that the idea with singing in church is to praise God, not to please me or you."

"I guess."

He is not wrong to take that with a grain of salt. Another function of church music is to raise the spirits of the congregation. It seems to work for some, though I'll be -----d if I know how.

"Still, I can't help thinking while we're singing, Adam, that God must have better taste in music than this."

"Yeah, yeah, right. Awesome!"

"I mean, God inspired Händel and Schubert and Beethoven and Valerius and Gounod … and Luther… "

My voice trails off, partly because Adam may not have heard of all those guys, and partly because the Lord may not approve of cultural snobbery among the unsteadily faithful. Anyway, as I head toward the church exit I spot Chester Kauffman, who promised last Sunday he'd bring photos of his time flying B-17 "Flying Fortress" bombers during

Chester Kauffman in 1944 with B-17, and in 2010.

World War II. Because an old war injury has given him bad neck
vertebrae, Chester sits toward the back of the church so he won't have
to raise his head to see the projection screen in front, the one that shows
the indispensable worship song lyrics. As always, he is spiffily dressed in
suit and tie, the way churchgoers used to be. And he has a big brown
envelope.

"Chester! How *are* yah today?"

He gives me the biggest hug that his bony, slightly bent frame allows,
and hands me the envelope. The first pictures are of Italian landscapes:
a powerful eruption of Mount Vesuvius, taken during a fly-by in March
1944; a village built on a lava flow down the mountain's slope; the entire
Isle of Capri from the air

"We were there on R & R," he explains, adding proudly: "The
Roman emperors had a villa there, too."

"Where were you stationed, Chester?"

"In North Africa at first, but mostly in Italy." From an airfield near
Foggia, just below the "spur" on the Italian boot, they made bombing
raids on the Romanian oil fields and refineries, about 600 miles to the
east. The name of that area was Ploesti or Ploiesti; it seems to be

spelled both ways. He spelled it Polesti on the back of one photo. Ploesti supplied over a third of the oil for the German war machine. You can't make war without oil, so they defended it tenaciously. Chester's Ploesti picture shows a group of B-17s flying through flak bursts so thick, it looks like you could walk on them. Another shows a B-17 with its two right engines on fire. "A photographer flew with us to take those," Chester explains.

"Was this over Ploesti too?"

"No, that was over east Germany." You can see a big railway yard down below. He explains that was the target.

"Did that crew manage to bail out?"

"O no, that plane just banked and it was gone. They never got out."

"Good grief." You wonder how the military, any military, manages to get people to do those jobs. The illusory immortality common to that age group, I suppose. When he signed up in 1942, Chester was 19. The next photo shows a B-17 with most of its tail blown off.

"Where was this, Chester?"

"That was over Italy. Northern Italy."

"Did they make it back to base?"

"They had lost the tail gunner. It was a rocket-firing Me-109 did it. But they made it back."

"But how do you steer a plane without a rudder?"

"You can regulate the engines to turn," he explains.

Then he tells me about his own plane returning from Ploesti with only two engines, one shot out and the other gone. "We couldn't gain enough altitude, and there were these mountains in Yugoslavia, about 8,000 feet high. We just couldn't make it. Then we found a pass. Everybody thanked the Lord."

On the way east to Ploesti they would climb to 37,500 feet. At that altitude the temperature would get down to 52 below, and the B-17 was neither pressurized nor heated.

"I thought you guys had heated flight jackets, Chester. Jackets you could plug in to keep warm? I read about those."

"O, they didn't work very well," he says. "They would short out, and guys would get burned by the wires. The wires would break in your elbow, you see. Besides, I was the flight engineer, I couldn't stay plugged in. I had to get around in the plane. But the worst part was your legs and your feet. You couldn't feel them any more. When we got out of that plane, we'd fall down. We couldn't stand."

He points at his feet. "It's one reason I got trouble getting around these days," he explains. He always carries a cane.

Chester has a mechanic's mind, and his job on the bomber was to be the in-flight fix-it-man, monitoring the equipment and improvising quick repairs. He starts telling me about the time when enemy fire hit one of his B-17's engines and the 35-gallon oil reservoir behind it, and he needed to "feather" the propeller. Feathering meant turning the prop blades parallel to the wind speed, so they would stop turning. And the oil was needed as hydraulic fluid for changing the blades' pitch. Once it was gone you could do nothing. So they feathered the prop real quick, with what was left in the reservoir.

"What would happen if the propeller didn't stop?" I'm the kind of guy who is not usually interested in what's under the hood, and it shows. I just expect things to run.

"If it was not stopped it would start to windmill," he explains. "Without oil the engine would freeze up, but if you didn't feather the props while you still had the oil, they kept turning."

"Was that – did that slow down the plane?"

"O yes, a prop that turns without engine power slows down the plane. Increases drag, you see, and you can't afford that when you've already lost one or two engines."

"So that's why you kept an eye on the oil pressure?"

"There were oil pressure gauges for each engine. That was part of my job, checking those."

Then he adds: "If those props kept turning on a dead engine they would break loose from the engine crankshaft. They would spin and windmill and slow down the plane but they'd stay on all right, until you landed. Then they'd fly off."

"Because of the plane suddenly slowing down?"

"Yes, and if that prop was on one of the left engines it might plow right into the pilots' compartment."

Those boys had to improvise, and the B-17 was a tough bird, tougher than the B-24. On the internet you can find photo galleries of B-17s with enormous holes in their fuselages from .88 anti-aircraft shells, even from rockets that exploded inside. All those planes made it back to base, or we would not have had the pictures to awe us. But for the crews, going through all that must have been pure hell.

Pure hell, compared to which my suffering through the worship music sounds downright petty. Maybe the Lord is still trying to teach me humility. He's been at it for some time.

THE LOST AIR FORCE

This Monday morning while driving out to Chester's place I can't get one of yesterday's worship songs out of my head:

> *"There is no one else for me,*
> *crucified to set me free."*

Sticking my pinkie in my ear doesn't help, nor does the thought that singing this pop-trash inspires some of my fellow-churchgoers to rise up and raise their right hands, in an uncomfortably close revival of the infamous Nazi salute. And as I try to think of a different song, any catchy old jingle to counteract this Jesus-is-my-girlfriend earworm, it suddenly comes to me: that tune was ripped off from a thirty-year-old hit by Charlie Rich:

> *And when we get behind closed doors,*
> *then she lets her hair hang down -*

Maybe God, who works in mysterious ways, got someone to write this ditty to give me a foretaste of hell. Or maybe the one in charge down there, the one that scoffers depict with red horns and pitchfork, did it as part of a despicable plan to make people of good taste lose their faith. But wait!! The other day I found that I have a prominent theologian on my side. A.W. Tozer (1897-1963) moved like a bulldozer against 'songs without theological content set to music without beauty':

> "Many of our popular songs and choruses in praise of Christ are hollow and unconvincing. Some are even shocking in their amorous endearments and strike a reverent soul as being a kind of flattery offered to One with whom neither composer nor singer is acquainted. The whole thing is in the mood of a love ditty, the only difference being the substitution of the name of Christ for that of the earthly lover."

But enough about Tozer the 'dozer. I'm picking up Chester to take him to lunch, partly for selfish reasons, because I find his World War II stories interesting, and partly, I suppose, for altruistic ones. I've come to feel a great urgency to record the oral memories of the World War II veterans who are still with us, and in a month or so Chester will be 88.

> "We are now friends with England and with all mankind. May we never see another war! For in my opinion there never was a good war or a bad peace."
>
> Benjamin Franklin, *letter to Josiah Quincy, September 1783*

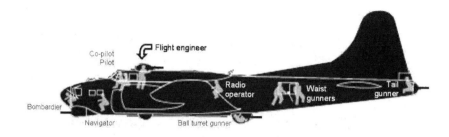

Co-pilot
Pilot
Flight engineer
Radio operator
Waist gunners
Tail gunner
Bombardier
Navigator
Ball turret gunner

Before we met again I looked up what exactly his World War II job entailed. A flight engineer on B-17s had multiple duties. One was to man the top gun turret in combat, a very important position because it gave him a 360-degree view of the top of the plane, and enemy fighters usually attacked from above. The flight engineer controlled that gun turret by means of two hand grips. The left one was the trigger for the twin 50 caliber machine guns. Both hand grips also worked as joysticks. Pushing them up or down raised or lowered the guns, while pressure to the left or to the right rotated the turret. An interrupter prevented the guns from firing at the tail or the propellers.

Since the top turret was located right behind the pilot and co-pilot seats, the flight engineer was also expected to monitor the airplane's power systems, especially the engines, by checking all the various gauges facing the pilots, who had no time for that. Besides all that, he was a jack-of-all-trades, with the rank of tech-sergeant, which gave him five stripes on his sleeve. The pilot, the co-pilot, the navigator and the bombardier were officers; the various gunners were enlisted men. As it happened, in his teens Chester had practiced hobbies that pre-qualified him as an aircraft-handyman. He built and raced cars, and he prided himself on his ability to modify farm equipment.

Looking up into a B-17's top gun turret, Chester's position in combat. Notice the two 50 cal machine guns.

During his extensive training the flight engineer gained a lot of knowledge of the bomber and its equipment, more than any crew member including the pilots. This enabled him to service the aircraft if it landed away from its home base, including jobs a ground crew would normally do. And as a handyman with detailed knowledge of the bomber's engines, power systems, guns and bomb racks, he was a key figure during in-flight emergencies.

At engine start and during pre-flight procedures the flight engineer stood behind the pilots on the flight deck, checking the fuel and engine gauges. Next, during take-off he would call out the airspeed so the pilots could concentrate on running straight down the runway. Once the plane was airborne he would keep watch on engine performance and fuel consumption throughout the flight. Flight engineers had become necessary during the run-up to World War II, when planes quickly became larger and more complex. Later, as technology advanced, the flight engineer's monitoring tasks were taken over by computer chips so that by 1976, when Viktor Belenko, the defected Soviet MIG-25 pilot, was being flown to the U.S. on a Boeing 747, he had trouble believing that such a big aircraft was being flown by a crew of two. He thought his hosts might be playing a Potemkin-village trick on him.

One of the first things I wanted to know was how it happened that Chester had been trained to serve on B-24s but flew all his bombing missions on B-17s. "Fifty missions," he said, but then he corrected himself: "Fifty-one." He also mentioned that his daughter thought he shouldn't drive any more, so I'm picking him up at his home, located on a rise along Ross Slough, one of the seasonally-flooded valleys outside Coos Bay. Chester lives with his daughter and son-in-law in a good-looking pre-fab house, set on a few acres they bought from his grandson, who still lives next door. His grandson is a civil engineer who works on wastewater projects; so he must have inherited some of Chester's

Chester Kauffman with his 1935 Harley-Davidson 74 cu inch bike

technical skills. While I run up the driveway, a few minutes early, Chester comes walking out the front door, using his cane.

"Your place looks nice," he says as we drive up to the restaurant. A couple of weeks ago we put up the German-style window-boxes with the new crop of vine-geraniums. This year's blooms are bright red, a better choice than last year's pink.

"They should look a lot better yet, in a few weeks," I agree. "They started blooming late this year. It's been awfully cold. What did you think of my other story, Chester?" I had given him a draft of the Al Kampen story to read. He chuckles.

"That guy who claimed he jumped out of that B-24 at 1000 feet and hit the ground right away – it only takes 300 feet for the chute to open, and that slows you down to about 25 miles an hour," he scoffs. "At least, that's what they told us."

We go in, I grab some blank sheets of paper and a pen, and we sit down. Chester's observation reminded me of a question I've been meaning to ask.

"Did you ever have to jump out of a plane, Chester?"

"No, but we all had parachutes. Everybody wore a harness, and if you had to jump out you just hooked the chute to the front of the harness."

He chuckles again. "We had this new crew member once who was sent to the parachute shack to pick up a chute and harness, so they showed him how to put on the harness and how the heavy snaps are hooked into the two rings on the chute. And when they asked him if he understood the instructions he said he did. But then, walking out, he turned around and he asked: 'What if it doesn't open?' " He looks at me.

"What did they say to that?"

"No problem, just bring it back and we'll give you a new one."

Then he starts his story, without any prompting from me. It feels as if he's been looking forward to this. In 1942 he was a farm boy living near Fresno, in California's central valley, and he volunteered to join what was then the Army Air Corps, later to become the US Air Force. But at first the service would not take him on account of his 'sunken chest', a birth defect that had not kept him from playing football, or from working long days doing farm work since he was nine. But finally he was accepted, entering the service in December 1942 in San Pedro.

"First we went to gunnery school in Laredo, Texas," he starts, explaining that most of that gunnery training took place on platforms and trucks, or inside stationary planes.

Ground training for gunnery, at Laredo

"But near the end of training we did some flying and shooting at tow-targets. Those targets were pulled by another plane, and the gunners dipped their bullets in paint, a different color for each gunner. That's how they could count the number of hits, from the color of the holes in the target."

"And then we went to this air field near Biloxi, Mississippi. It was called Keisler – no, Keesler Air Field. That was the flight-engineering school. Normally that training took a lot longer, but they shortened it, and classes went on twenty-four hours a day, in three shifts. We took five different classes, and we spent four weeks in each building. We finished in August, and we had a sergeant's rating after that."

That would have been August of 1943. "Did you get to fly yet, Chester?"

"O no, not yet. From Biloxi we went on a train up the East Coast and through Pennsylvania, and by way of Chicago and Wyoming we ended up in a sub-depot in Salt Lake. That's where we got all our flying equipment, our suits and stuff. And from there we went to Clovis, New Mexico, to do our first real flying."

"Um – that seems like a long way around. I mean, circling the country like that, on trains. Going west by way of the East Coast and Chicago."

"Yes, well, you have to understand, there were some train routes that were only for military use. Just certain ones. So you had to go on those, but – we still spent a lot of time waiting for other trains to pass, along the way. It took a long time . . ."

"Then from Salt Lake we went to Clovis, New Mexico, for the first one of three phases in real flight training. In Clovis we got used to the plane for a month. There were 44 crews in the group, and we'd fly at different times of the day. At night we'd fly to places in the desert that were marked with smoke pots.

"Well, we finished that, I can't tell you what month, and then we got sent down to Alamogordo, also in New Mexico, for more training. This time we flew higher, used oxygen, and we trained for more navigation in the desert. Flew to different places – landmarks in the desert. And night-flying was part of that. This one night we were the last plane to take off. We pulled onto the runway and we ran the engines up for a power check, and then a control check, rudder, elevator and ailerons. Then the pilot did a second check on the ailerons and he said there was something wrong, that the ailerons were too hard to operate, that they should move more freely. So he called the control tower and was told to bring the plane back to the engineering hangar to have it checked out. Well, the officer in charge was there to meet us and he was quite angry with us for bringing one of his planes back with a supposedly serious problem. We told him what happened, and he said 'You find the problem then, that plane has been flying fine every day.' So we got some ladders and some screwdrivers, and we went to work. I set a ladder under the leading edge of the left wing, and removed all the screws holding an inspection plate in place, removed it, and with a flashlight looked inside. Now, the B-24 wing ribs are pressed out of a sheet of aluminum, and they have several holes in them, like this, the largest in front and smaller to the back." He gives me a little drawing he has made. "Well, the control cable is supposed to run through this big hole at the front of the rib, but it ran through the second hole, and it had cut almost all the  way through it, causing the drag on the controls. So we went and told the engineering officer what we found but he wouldn't go and look for himself, he sent a maintenance man who could not believe his eyes and grounded the plane."

That was not the last time they had a defective plane, either. Without belittling America's enormous war production efforts, it may be said that quantity must at times have trumped quality. Besides, when you produce 18,500 B-24s and 12,700 B-17s within a few years, not to mention all the other war equipment, there are bound to be some lemons. The Germans were bigger sticklers for quality, and they built excellent war equipment. But when all was said and done they didn't have enough of it. And they didn't have a bomber force like the allies'.

"And then, one month later we left there by train, for Charleston, South Carolina. That was to fly different places over water."

"So – was that in preparation for flying across the Atlantic?"

"And other seas too, I suppose. So we flew to Cuba, and we flew to Bermuda. That was some 600 miles. We did bombing too, and more gunnery training. And formation flying."

He looks at me quizzically, and asks: "Have you heard of that – triangle near Bermuda?"

"Well, yes, but I don't think it's for real."

"Well, we'd fly over there, to Bermuda, in a group, and come back at night, single plane. We'd take off every ten minutes. And this one time we were the last plane to take off. I forgot how many planes there were, a good number ahead of us, and it was dark when we finally took off. We had a navigator-instructor, and also a pilot-instructor who rode in the co-pilot seat. I didn't think we needed a pilot-instructor, but I suppose he just wanted to see Bermuda. He was a heavy-set man, and before we started back I saw some clouds coming on. I figured the wind was gonna bring them in, so I asked about the weather at the briefing, but I was told, no problem. Well, those clouds did come in, and more, and it got so thick that we decided to go over them, to 12,000 feet. But we had no oxygen."

"Do you need oxygen at 12,000 feet?"

"No, not really, but then all of a sudden the navigator-instructor starts moaning: 'I can't breathe!' And he kept it up. Now I had an oxygen canister with me, I carried one as flight engineer. I knew it was empty, but I didn't know what else to do so I took it off and I gave it to him, and he quit gasping and he perked right up – he said he was OK!

"Then we got up to 14,000 feet, and the other guy, the pilot-instructor, he starts complaining too. I don't think we had another empty canister, but maybe they traded. Anyway, they survived. But about that Bermuda triangle – then suddenly our instruments started spinning, our compasses and this and that, and we didn't know where we were at. So I got up into the top turret, and I spotted a beacon light they had set out there for these flights. So I told them – keep on course."

"So you made it back all right. Despite the Bermuda Triangle."

"Yes, but when we landed there was not a plane there. Not one of all the ones that took off before us. That seemed weird too, but it turned out the next day that they had flown to an airfield in Virginia. They flew around the storm."

"Do you like clam chowder, Chester?"

He does, I order two cups, and he continues:

"We did other training too, out there. We did target shooting, where short-winged B-26s would tow a target. And sometimes we'd fly down the coast looking for subs.

"And we got interrogation training. About what to say and what not to say if you're caught.

"And then, by train again, we went up to New York, to Mitchel Field. We were supposed to get our new planes there and then fly them overseas. So get this: On the crew we got a gunner from New Jersey, a tail gunner from Brooklyn, a radio man from Brooklyn, and a bombardier for the nose turret from Tennessee."

"Could you understand them all right?"

"I got used to it. But our bombardier just got out of Bombardier School, and he had not got his furlough yet. So we had to wait for him. And we were the 44th crew, the last one of the group. I remember saying that our plane looked like a wounded bird, all sagging. But I couldn't put my finger on why. Well, we checked the engines, and we used an air compressor to pump up the shock strut for the landing gear, and off we went for our shakedown flight. We taxied up to the end of the runway. We called the tower for clearance. They OK'd us for take-

Looking up from a position on the floor: the crew member on the left stands between the two pilots during take-off, part of a WWII Flight Engineer's job. On the right you look into the top gun turret, with one of the machine guns visible.

off. I was calling out our air speed: 90 – 100 – 110 – 130 – by now we should be flying, have lift-off, but there was no lift at all. At the last moment I called for a stop, and we came to a stop, just before a chain-link fence, and behind the fence was a highway and behind the highway were fuel tanks . . . The tower said we made a good decision. There were tire marks all over that runway, our landing gear was all twisted from the braking . . . We left it there, and we told them, don't tell us to come back and get it. So we had to wait again, for a new plane.

"The new plane came in, I believe from the Ford plant in Detroit. We made a one-hour shakedown flight, and the next morning we loaded all our baggage on that plane and flew off to Florida, to Miami. O, they had a good-sized airport there, with lots of mechanics to fix things."

"Was it normal for new planes to have mechanical problems?"

"O yes, but everything was fixed by the book. They had a book for the plane and a book for the passengers, and they were still working on it at 9 PM. And the next day we flew to Porto Rico. They had mechanics there too. The nose wheel door wouldn't stay closed, and the wind from that blew all through the flight deck, making our papers fly everywhere, so I tied it up with some wire."

"I suppose you remembered to take that wire off before landing."

He ignores that wisecrack, or maybe he didn't hear it, despite his twin hearing aids. We get our lunches, and I try not to ask more questions. But he continues.

B-24s at Ford's Willow Run plant

"And next we flew to Trinidad. On these B-24s they have an electrical system powered by an A.P.U. – "

"What does that stand for?"

"A.P.U. – Auxiliary Power Unit. It sat under the flight deck, and it runs electrical to the hydraulic system while the plane is on the ground; and our A.P.U. quit working. Our ground brakes quit when we took off. So we reported that, and got a new unit. Next morning we took off for Belem, Brazil. You fly over a lot of dense forest that way, but it's best to fly short hops, before you get the downpour every afternoon. The B-24s bound for Dakar, in North Africa, left from Fortaleza, and the B-17s from Natal."

"About how far is it to Dakar from there?"

"O, about 2,000 miles."

So – you flew about 300 miles an hour?"

"O no, closer to – 200."

"So that was about a 10-hour trip. Tell me, did the gunners sit in their turrets?"

"O no, there was no need for that. They just laid down and slept somewhere. So the next night we were supposed to take off for Dakar. We were ready to go, we started up the engines – and all the power went out. The electrical had failed again, I guess. Anyway, we called the tower, though we had to rev the engines to do that, and they said they'd tug us to a hangar, so the electricians could look for the problem. And while our plane was still on the runway, no other planes could leave. So this tractor tugged the plane to a hangar by its front wheel axle. And without electricity we could only crawl out through this hatch in the ceiling of the flight deck, and onto the wing, so that's where we laid down and went to sleep, on the wing. About 2:30 in the morning they woke us up, because they'd found the problem."

"So what was the problem?"

"I don't know, but they fixed it. So we took off. On the way we met two different storms, but this time we went under 'em, and we got there late in the afternoon. They had guards there, for all those parked planes, because we always left the bomb doors open, and the natives – they would get in and steal whatever they could, over there. You never knew."

"Did you *have* to leave the bomb doors open?"

"When the plane sat for a while it always filled with gas fumes. I guess it was from the gas lines inside, all the joints and all those valves, so we left the bomb doors open. Well, the tail gunner and a waist gunner, they spent the night in the plane, just to be sure nobody got into it. Well, the next morning – you see, the B-24s were all lined up on one side of the strip there, and this long line of C-47s on the other side. Dakar has a seaport, and the cargoes that came in there were loaded on the C-47s, and they took it to Tunis and as far as India. O, they overloaded them – they probably carried about twice the allowable load. Well, the runway – it was really just a gravel strip, and this C-47 was gonna take off but it hit a chuckhole, and it bounced off the runway and broke the linkage between the upper and lower parts of the landing gear and that broke the brake line, causing the plane to veer to the left and into our B-24. Well, it bumped into our B-24's nose and busted it, tipped the plane and broke the hydraulic lines and there it sat on its tail, broken nose in the air."

"Were they able to fix it?"

"O no, there was too much damage. We had carried two bins with spare parts in the bomb bay, so they took those out, and that was it: we didn't have a plane again. I think we stayed there some time before they had a C-47 with extra room. So this C-47 took us up to Marrakech, overnight, with everything blacked out, though they stopped at several towns to drop off mail. So that's how we got to Tunisia. Our group

A C-47 in North-Africa, 1943.

A B-17F Flying Fortress from the "Diamondbacks" (the 99th bomb group; see diamond on tail) flying past a ruined Roman aqueduct to land at Oudna Field, Tunisia, 1943.

was leaving from there for Italy, but of course we were not part of it. In the end we were given a B-17, so that's what we flew, as part of the 99th bomb group, 348th squadron."

"Did your B-17 have a name? A cartoon character or something, on the nose?"

"O no, that was mostly just the 8th Air Force. They got all the publicity up there in England, and that's where all the newscasters went, and Ronald Reagan made a film there, and Clark Gable. We were known as the 'lost air force', the 15th."

Until now it had not sunk in with me that all those movies about the American bombing war on Germany were about 8th Air Force bombers flying from England. That applied to wartime propaganda films like *Memphis Belle* as well as regular Hollywood fare, the best-known of which may be *Twelve O'clock High*, with Gregory Peck. No movies at all were made about the 15th Air Force, the boys who hit the Germans from the south; and they certainly did their share, because 8th Air Force bombers were often idle due to the British weather. No wonder the 15th felt a little neglected.

Following the conquest of Sicily the allies had invaded the Italian mainland on September 3, 1943, with the Germans retreating to the north, to more defensible positions. By the end of that month the allied forces had captured the vast complex of airfields at Foggia, just below the "spur" on the east side of the

> "May I give you a word of advice? Next time you invade Italy, do not start at the bottom."
>
> Fridolin von Senger und Etterlin, former Wehrmacht general during World War II in Italy, when being introduced in 1960 to the historian Michael Howard, who had fought in Italy himself.

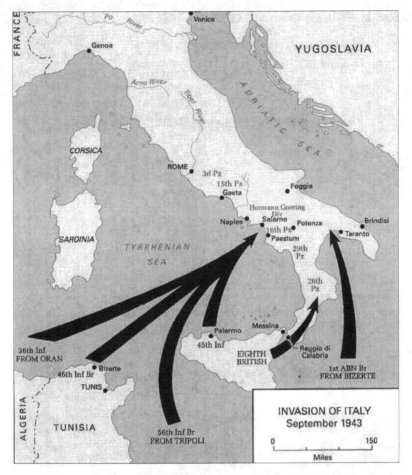

Invasion of Italy
September 1943

0   150
Miles

Italian boot. Those airfields would enable allied bombers to hit targets in the Balkans, in southern Germany, in Austria and in France, jobs that distance or weather had prevented the 8th Air Force from doing. In early December 1943 the B-17 and B-24 bomb groups that made up the 15th Air Force moved to Foggia; Chester's 99th group was based at a Foggia-area field called Tortorella. As an unofficial history of the 99th relates: "Living conditions at Tortorella were very harsh. The summers were hot and dusty, the winters cold and wet. Buildings were few, and airplane maintenance crews worked out in the open. The men lived in tents using homemade gasoline stoves for heat. The men constantly had to struggle through mud and water, snow and ice, or choking dust, depending on the season."

FIFTY-ONE MISSIONS

Lunch with Chester is becoming a weekly event, due to my wish to get all the technical stuff straight and understandable to a layman, which describes me well. And Chester, bless him, has been patiently correcting my drafts. On this occasion I show him some pictures of the Tortorella air field, copied from the 99th bomber group's website. The first one shows an airman sloshing through a vast field of mud, tents in the background. Using his magnifying glass, he identifies him as a ground crew chief.

"That place had been a great big grain farm," he explains. "So it was pretty flat, but the runways were not paved, so they used those perforated steel strips – Marsden mats, they called 'em. They were interlocking and they worked well enough, but then they also brought in crushed limestone, from a limestone mine near Mafronia, near the lower bend of the spur.[1]) That helped smooth things out too, after they compacted it. But about those tents -- we slept in those 6-men tents. But we added pup tents on the outside, to get more room. And all they

---

[1]) Manfredonia.

had for light in there was one bulb, in the center of the tent, not enough
to read by. But it was on 110 power, and from some of our planes that
were under repair I swiped some light bulbs, and there was also a
crashed Ju-88 there that had been strafed and burned, but it still had
some good electrical wire in it. The Germans were using plastic wire
before we did. I used it to string up the 24-volt bulbs I had found, but
we strung up 6 of them in series, stripping the insulation and poking one
lead through the bottom of the bulb, the other taped on the side. Our
waist gunner manufactured a switch, and that worked pretty good.

But oh, the cold over there, in the winter; we had to do something.
There were plenty of 10-gallon drums, so we made a stove out of one.
Cut a hole in it for a door, and holes near the bottom for air. We set it
on top of a bomb fin crate, which was metal, and then we put rocks in
the bottom."

"What were the rocks for?"

"To hold the heat." I should have known that.

"What did you use for fuel? I don't see any wood there."

He smirks: "Airplane fuel. There was plenty, it came in to Mafronia,
this little seaport where the tanker ships pumped it into the pipeline. To
use airplane fuel we set up a jerry can outside the tent, and we ran a
piece of copper tubing out of it, into the stove. One end was the
burner. I crimped the end of the tubing to close it, and then I used a
hacksaw – you shouldn't cut too hard with it, just a few nicks, barely
through the tubing – and that was the burner."

"Yankee ingenuity, Chester. What about the stovepipe?"

"By the railroad track that ran by our field there was a station house,
and on the north side of that the Germans had left a building, and there
was some corrugated metal roofing lying around. So we got a piece of
that, and with everybody helping we rolled it up until we had a pipe, a
kind of pipe, and we tied a wire around it."

"Did it work?"

"O yes, but one morning we woke up to go on a mission to
Germany – they would wake us up at 2:30, to have time to shave and
have breakfast and all, and this time it was so cold, COLD, you couldn't
believe it. Well, the stove had gone out. So one of our guys – I think he
was a waist gunner – before I could stop him he opened the stove and
threw a lighted match in it, and – BOOM, a great big loud roar up the
chimney. Holy Mackerel, but that was not the worst of it, soot and
embers flew up that chimney and the embers came down on the tent,
and they were burning holes in our tent. Well, the firemen, they helped

us put it out, but we were out of a tent. So they promised us a new one, we got cleaned up and went on our mission to Germany, we got back, and guess what – our old tent is still sitting there, and the new tent beside it, all folded up into a package. So we had to do all that, take down the old tent and then set up the new one."

The next picture shows a very primitive-looking control tower.

"That's the Sand-fly control tower at the Tortorella airfield," he says. "It had the same name in Tunisia. So we just kept it on."

The picture after that shows a ground crew turning propellers by hand. "We often did that ourselves," he explains. "When the plane sat, all the oil drained to the bottom, and you risked having a hydraulic lock."

"What's a hydraulic lock?"

"Well, see, these bombers had round engines, radial engines, with the cylinders arranged in a circle, nine cylinders. There's oil in every cylinder, but it would drain from the upper cylinders and collect in the bottom ones. You don't have that problem with a car engine, or a fighter engine like the P-51 or the Spitfire – they had the same straight engine. The B-24 also had a radial engine but with fourteen cylinders – two rows of seven cylinders each. You had the same problem there. Oil doesn't compress, so if you didn't move it out of the bottom before you started the engine, the piston would come down, the oil wouldn't give, of course, and you would break the piston or bend the piston rod.

So, before starting the engine of the B-17 or the B-24 or the P-47, you had to rotate the propeller. Seven blades made two revolutions, and that was enough to clear the oil out of the bottom of the cylinders."

"By the way," he says, still studying the picture, "these are some small bombs lying around, and you can see the bomb fins that are already atttached. Those came in the bomb fin crates like the one we set our stove on. Those crates were made of metal so the fins wouldn't get damaged and the bombs come down wrong."

"I read somewhere that the B-17s were easier to fly."

"They were. The B-24 had a longer wing span but a shorter body, and they zigzagged. It wasn't so noticeable if you were by yourself, but when you were flying in formation."

"I've heard, too, that B-17s were better at surviving a belly-landing."

"O yes, if a B-24 made a belly-landing that would be the end of it. Why, it was done for. That high wing gave no protection to that boxy fuselage. But with the B-17 – you showed me that photo from Foggia with all four engines off, being worked on. The only reason would be if

it bellied in, bending all the props. Usually then they'd have to replace the props, and they'd have to change the engines, replace the ball turret, and of course check the landing gear, do whatever's to be done there. But usually it could still be fixed. With the B-24, if it bellied, forget it."

"You told me you flew bombing raids on the Rumanian oil fields."

"That's right; our first flights there were from Italy. Seven of my missions were to those oil fields, and on four we came back badly damaged. But the first big raid happened in August 1943, from North Africa, from Tunisia. That's before we got there. They had five bomb groups, and they were going to attack at a low altitude, to evade German radar, and by day too, because they thought the place was not well-defended. O, and no fighter escorts of course, at that time. But the Germans knew they were coming, and they had lots of AA, and fighters too. Two groups got lost on the way, I believe, and then they came back to the target anyway, but there was a lot of confusion, and they lost about one third of the planes and hundreds of men killed . . . some of these things are hard to tell." He swallows.

"Those oil fields were about 600 miles away, over the roughest terrain you ever saw. And after we started raiding them from Italy, until April 1944 we had fighter escorts only part of the way, P-47s and P-38s. It was not a good feeling when they turned back to base, because of the range, 600 miles. And then finally in April of '44 we got P-51s to fly with us all the way to the target. The 8th in England had got them back in the fall of 1943 already, because of their heavy losses."

"Didn't the P-51s carry extra wing fuel tanks?"

"O yes, and they had another 85-gallon fuel tank in back of the pilot's seat. The new wing on those P-51s was thicker in the center, to

have more room for the six guns and ammo, besides the wing tanks.

"We also flew raids on southern Germany, to Munich and Regensburg. Aircraft manufacturing plants. And to Vienna, and Wiener Neustadt. A lot of AA there, too. That was about 500 miles. But to get to some of those places you had to skirt around Switzerland, that was neutral. Or else you might get shot down. The highest we flew was over the Austrian Alps, over 30,000 feet. The highest we could go was 37,500."

"I know the Swiss shot down some German planes too, that strayed over their territory. That made Hitler mad."

"And we bombed southern France, Toulon and Marseille."

"What did you bomb there?"

"Submarine pens, railroad bridges … on the day of the Mediterranean landings in France we were there at 7 AM to drop bombs behind the beach. The landing craft were to come in about 7:15.

I show him a picture of a briefing at the 99th. "When we took off on a mission," he explains, "we didn't know where we were going. They

kept the information quiet, to avoid leaks. Only the officers went to the briefings, and then they would tell us at take-off. But we could always guess, because the night before they posted the bomb loads and the fuel for the next day. 2,700 gallons of fuel is a lot of weight. If it was a short trip you wouldn't get as much fuel, so you could carry more bombs. And you could tell something by the type of bombs. The size, and the type. For bombing air fields we took anti-personnel bombs that were small and caused a lot of damage on the ground. So anyway, this one day we took off on a mission to southern France, Toulon or Marseille, I don't remember which. Well, at the briefing the officers had been told to fly due west first, and after Naples switch to a north-westerly heading, over the sea."

By this time the allies had taken Naples, but Rome, further north, was still in German hands.

"We were not flying very high," he says, "and some of us were dozing fifteen minutes after we left the base. Then all of a sudden AA shells come up, hitting every one of our 24 planes. What's going on? Well, come to find out, instead of flying due west, the navigator on the lead plane flew northwest right away, the second heading. And we had flown across a railroad to Rome, right over a German train that was running north as fast as it could, but with a lot of flat cars carrying AA guns. And they used them. Nobody was shot down, but every plane was damaged, so bad we couldn't go on with the mission, so we circled back towards Naples and that lead plane had smoke coming out of its wing, had fire coming

Fly-by of an eruption of Mount Vesuvius, March 1944.

out of a big hole in it. Well, we all came back to base that day except the lead plane, he pulled out of formation and landed on an air strip south of Naples. He had to be very careful of course, with a full load of bombs and gas. He called for help, but when the firemen got there the pilot was out on the wing already, putting it out with his fire extinguisher."

"Did the navigator on that lead plane get blamed for all that?"

"No, it was not really one person's fault – all the officers were there at the briefing, and all the planes had compasses. And on that air strip near Naples they had a lot of planes already that had been damaged by that volcano they have over there. That eruption had damaged a lot of moving parts that were fabric-covered, their ailerons, their rudders and such."

"I didn't know parts of those planes were just fabric."

"O yes, they were. It was to save weight, you see. Of course, they were painted so they looked like metal, but they were just fabric. Anyway, it took two days before we could leave again, that's how much patching they had to do."

"Did you just leave the bombs on the planes during that time?"

"O yes, they were not armed yet – that was not done until shortly before the drop, when the bombardier pulled the cotter pins out of the fuses."

"And one day we got a call for a new kind of mission; they had discovered the headquarters of Albert Kesselring."

2000-pound bombs being loaded at Foggia

Luftwaffe general Kesselring had been made commander of all German forces in Italy, and he was a crafty one who made the Americans pay for whatever ground they gained.

"From photographs they had figured out that his hide-out was on the coast southwest of Rome, buried in a mountain. So we loaded these 2,000-pound bombs on the planes –."

"How many planes?"

"Twenty-four planes, and we bombed real close – no altitude. We just-about pulverized that mountain. You could tell their communications had been destroyed, because the Germans retreated for several days after that."

"Did you drop 2,000-pound bombs on any other targets?"

"O yes, because the Germans had more and more hardened targets. They'd been moving their aircraft factories underground. But we could only carry four of those bombs. That was 8,000 pounds, and then we had the fuel, 2,700 gallons on a long mission. Plus, each engine had a 35-gallon oil reservoir. So that's all one plane could carry. Unless you carried less fuel."

"You must not have got Kesselring."

"No. I don't know why – I think he was away talking to Hitler. But you know," he adds thoughtfully, "when Clark's group had their victory parade in Rome, they all had these nice clean uniforms, and nice shiny equipment. Why didn't they show the stuff that was all battle-scarred? That would have meant more. Or why didn't they let the Japanese group march in that parade – they deserved it."

He glances at a picture of the waist gunners checking their guns, pointing out the cables strung inside the fuselage: "These govern the rudder and the elevator and the trim tabs," he explains.

"What's a trim tab?" If I'm going to be an aviation expert, I've got a long way to go.

He makes me another drawing: "It's a horizontal piece only about 18 by 4 inches. On the back of the elevator. They've got them other places too. It controls the plane's altitude, and over the Romanian oil

fields some shrapnel came
through and cut that cable,
the one for the trim tabs. So
the plane's nose went up and
the plane went up into the air
until it stalled. You see,
there's weight in the tail too,

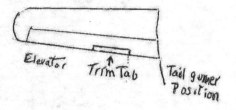

Elevator   Trim Tab   Tail gunner Position

with the tail gunner and his ammo, and that didn't help. And then after
it stalled it fell about 10,000 feet, from 37,000 down to 27,000. We were
still over the target, and there's AA fire all around. So I figured I'd
better fix that cable, by hand."

"Didn't you have any tools on board?"

"No, no tools; I guess they'd been losing too many."

This astonishes me; how can you expect a flight engineer to do
repairs without tools? But he explains that without any air pressure to
fight, you could easily pull the cables: "Do you know what a turnbuckle
is?"

"Yes." At least I know that.

"Well, every line had several turnbuckles in it, and they were secured
with copper safety wires, so they wouldn't turn and loosen the cable."
He explains that to gain length for the cable splice he twisted the
turnbuckles, after removing their safety wires, and then he braided the
cut ends together, using the safety wires to secure the joint again:

"And while I was doing that, all of a sudden the plane went up again,

The American General Mark Clark received much criticism for
disobeying orders to pursue the retreating German 10th Army, instead
taking Rome, so he could hold a victory parade there on June 5, 1944.
The "Japanese group" was the highly-decorated 100th infantry battalion
made up of Nisei (American-born soldiers of Japanese ancestry), who
fought bravely in Italy and elsewhere in the European theater. The sad
irony was that at that time many of those boys' families were
imprisoned in American internment camps, as suspect aliens (See
"Toyoka Oka's war"). Besides ignoring the contributions of the
"Japanese group," Clark also refused to include the remnant of a Polish
unit that had been sacrificed at Monte Casino. I heard TV talker Chris
Matthews pontificate once that the U.S. entered World War II "to fight
racism." The U.S. fought Germany because Hitler foolishly declared
war on it, but the purpose of that American fight was to prevent
German domination of Europe, and the U.S. fought it with segregated
armed forces. President Harry S. Truman, who would order their
integration in 1948, told the Nisei battalion in July 1946: "You fought
not only the enemy, but you fought prejudice—and you have won."

stalled again, and we lost another 10,000 feet. Now we were down to 17,000. So I called on the intercom: 'What's going on?'"

" 'O', they said, 'we tried turning on the autopilot.' Well, that didn't work because the autopilot couldn't compensate for the trim tab, but we got the tail gunner and his ammo out of the tail to lose that weight, and my joint on that cable held long enough, almost till we got back to base.

"And after we landed two or three guys, officers, came into our tent about the incident. They wouldn't believe my story, even when I showed them the piece of cable. 'No way that could ever work,' they said."

"So what did you tell them?"

" 'Well, it sure got us back', is what I said." He smirks.

"What kinds of targets did you bomb in Germany, Chester?"

"We bombed aircraft factories in Munich and in Regensburg. And anything having to do with oil or with transportation. One time, on a mission to Munich flying over the Alps, all you could see was clouds. We knew we were over Munich, but there was no way we could see the target. Well, our target of opportunity was Regensburg. But Regensburg was all covered with a heavy cloud cover too. So, flying northeast at 30,000 feet, we're getting close to Germany's eastern border, we keep on looking for an opening. Then the navigator comes on the line and says, 'There should be a railroad yard somewhere around here!' That navigator, his name was O'Rourke, and he was a great navigator, he'd been studying the maps. He was a Catholic of course, but he attended church services with us. So I get in the top turret to take a look, and there was an opening just ahead, and through it you could see the biggest railroad marshaling yard I've ever seen. So we lined up on that hole and the marshaling yard, opened the bomb doors and 'Bombs Away!' shouts the bombardier over the intercom. That marshaling yard was full of tank cars. O, there must have been a thousand, and to the east a big warehouse."

"Were you by yourselves that time?"

"O no, we were 24 planes, and when we dropped our bombs – you never saw such fireworks. They must have carried airplane fuel and everything else, flames shooting up high. We made a 360-degree, and by that time the clouds were covering that railroad yard again."

"Did you get any AA fire?"

"O no, I guess they didn't have any, or it was a total surprise. The Lord must have had a hand in this. It was not long before my 50th mission."

"I meant to ask – I thought you only had to fly 30 missions."

"That was the 8ᵗʰ again. We had to fly 50."

Then, adding without much gusto: "Actually, I flew 51."

"How did you happen to do that?"

"O, that was on account of one of those 'Extra Maximum Effort' campaigns by the brass."

And he confesses: "We didn't really want to. It got so you'd go into the operations room to check the plans for the next day, and somebody said: 'O boy, we get to do it all over again tomorrow.' That's how it was. You'd try not to think about it, but – I probably won't sleep several days now, and toss and turn."

"I'm sorry about that, Chester – I didn't mean to – do you know Dr. Crane, in our church?" He doesn't seem to.

"Well, Dr. Crane, he worked in a V.A. hospital for years before he came back to Coos Bay, and he told me one of his patients there was the bombardier of the Enola Gay, you know, the B-29 that dropped the bomb on Hiroshima. And he said this guy had gone totally crazy."

He purses his lips. "We do these things because we have to," he says matter-of-factly. "You know it's not right, but if you don't do it, it's going to be worse – and I did the best I could – maybe too good. When there was a captain or a major on the lead plane, they could pick their own crew, and I got picked too many times to be their engineer. It's best not to break up crews. You get tuned in to each other. And I was on a lot of cat crews too."

"Uh – what's a cat crew?"

"They called 'em that because the cat always comes back. The cat crews flew planes that had been repaired, which often took days, and they took them out for a trial run, and I often went along as flight engineer, because the pilots didn't know enough about the mechanics of the plane."

"Did you ever have to take over from the pilot?"

"O yes, it was up in Germany one time, over Regensburg or over Munich, and I had not flown many missions yet, only maybe ten or fifteen – and we had a new pilot as our co-pilot, and the pilot, he was good, but he got a piece of flak under his left kneecap. It came up through the plane and into his knee, so he couldn't use his leg. You have to use your leg, being the pilot. But the co-pilot, he was brand-new, it was his first mission, and he was scared. So I slipped into the pilot's seat, which was odd, because he was a big guy, over six feet, and I'm pretty small. But I brought in the plane, firing red flares, the sign of injuries, so they took him to the hospital as soon as we were on the ground."

"You know, Chester, I had not thought about this, but those planes had no armor, did they?"

"Armor?"

"Thick metal plates on the bottom, for protection."

"O no, no, no. None of that. You know, I still remember my grandpa, when they were building these planes when the war started, he was all excited: 'O boy, they're making them out of metal now! Now they can't hit you!' But they could. Those shells would come up right through the floor, a foot away from you. There was no armor on the belly of that plane.

"And twice, a shell came through and we got our hydraulic system shot out. During the flight the hydraulic pump creates pressure inside what was called the 'accumulator', for our brakes on the ground. Well, this 88 shell tore right through the plane, about this far from me" – he indicates a distance of about a foot-and-a-half – "and took out the pump. That still left the pressure already in the tank, but it would be good for only one application of the brakes, no more. But we made it OK.

"But the second time it took out the whole works, and we had nothing, no brakes at all when we landed.

"Well, we told the tower, but they didn't tell us there was a 30-mile an hour crosswind that day. We landed, I cut the engines so it would stop, but that crosswind got our tail so we turned west towards the wheat field. So I started the #1 engine to keep from running off the runway and into that wheat patch. Well, the engineers were working on the runways with big equipment, and we were headed straight for a great big ole tractor, and no way to stop. This looked real bad, but then – POP! – we heard an explosion. Seems that a piece of the steel mat was bent up, the tire hit it, and it blew out – and that swung us back around the other way again. The engineers had run off but they came back out,

and here comes a command car down the runway, with the officer looking out the window: "What's the matter, can't you control it?" But we didn't mind – we figured the Lord had a hand in popping that tire."

"So the plane was basically a frame that held the fuel and the bombs and the crew, but it was just covered with thin sheet metal. Or fabric."

"Yes. And the top of the plane, it would get all dented up too, from the shells fired above you, I mean from the empty cartridges dropping from the gun turrets above you. Not all cartridges were lost, though. The waist gunners, and the top turret, and the radio operator, they had a fireproof canvas bag that caught the spent cartridges, and then they'd dump those into the old ammo box. But the tail gunner and the ball turret gunner, they just lost 'em."

"Did they re-use those cartridges? The ones in the bags?" After all, ours is the era of recycling.

"O yes, they got sent back to the ammo factory."

Come to think of it, during World War II recycling was a real need. Paper drives, scrap metal drives, collections of all kinds.

"When I watch video of strafing in World War II, I see flashes of light. Were those explosive shells?"

Chester's B-17 group in thick flak at 37,500 feet over the Ploesti oil fields.

"No no, they were regular shells. But every fifth one had a little bit of phosphorus on it, and the phosphorus lights up when you fire it. That's how you can see where you're shooting."

"How well did it work, to re-cycle the cartridges?"

"They must have crimped them somehow where the bullet sat – cartridges expand, so they might have re-sized them. I don't know. But on one mission, when I was firing on another plane coming in out of the sun, the way the Germans always did, my left gun quit firing. So I kept firing my right gun, but it was not long before that gun stopped too. Well, there was nothing else for it, I kept on moving those guns so they'd think I was tracking them, and it worked out. But those guns jamming, it must have been that a shell came apart in the barrel, that they re-used a cartridge that was cracked. It was carelessness on their part, back in the factory, that they re-used shells that were cracked. They should have been discarded. Or it could have been sabotage. Because those cartridges all came from the same ammo box."

"Sabotage would have been more likely on the German side. I know of Dutchmen who were hauled off to work in German ammunition factories, they sabotaged the product whenever they could."

I change the subject to his hearing, specifically his dual hearing aids. "Do you have your service to thank for those, Chester?"

"Ah," he says, "When you meet a fellow my age who's hard of hearing, they probably were on a bomber. The worst plane was the B-25. Pilots and flight engineers of B-25s are all hard of hearing. They had very loud engines, and the exhaust ports were wide open. On the B-25s the flight deck was the loudest, with engines nearby and guns in turrets right near you."

Coming back to the B-24: "Didn't the B-24 have a bigger bomb load than the B-17?"

"That's a mistake everybody makes," he scoffs, "because the B-24 had two bomb bays, one in front of the other. "But on that raid on the oil fields in 1943 they needed to carry fuel tanks in that bomb bay. So carrying more bombs, no. That plane didn't have the lift.

"Did you ever keep a list of your missions, Chester?"

"Some people wrote down their missions – I didn't – I figured I wouldn't get home anyway. Now I think I should have, but back then I didn't think I'd make it.

"It's awful distressing, seeing other crews go down. Once when we were over the oil fields two planes came too close together, and one cut off the tail of the other B-17. Everybody dead except the tail gunner.

He came down inside the tail section, and survived."

"Did he come down in the trees, or something?"

"No, I think the tail section came down slower. It's not that heavy. And at the base once,

The B-17 tail gunner's position, under the rudder.

coming in for a landing, one plane got too close to another one and cut off its tail also. Dead. And they were a good crew. They cleaned up their plane and the gun barrels, when other crews didn't bother. But people relax once the mission is done."

In my trivial way, I'm reminded of what can happen after a big rush at the restaurant. When it's all over people relax, and when new customers come in, they may ignore them. Unintentionally, but still. Chester sits there, his thoughts

> "Do not neglect the principles of foresight and know that often, puffed up with success, armies have lost the fruit of their heroism through a feeling of false security."
>
> *Frederick the Great*

backed up to a time nearly seventy years ago. Then he sums up:

"All these things – they are hard to forget. They're burned in your mind."

"What happened after your 51st mission, Chester?"

"There was this fairground about 10 miles north of Naples – Cazerta I think it was called – that was the gathering place for the troops to go home. There were thousands of men there, and a dozen ships in the harbor. Some had been Grace Line ships in peacetime. So this major got up on a platform. Everybody gathered, and he starts calling out names. Mine was the first one called out, and I was made C.Q."

"C.Q.?"

"Charge of Quarters – to supervise the men on the ships. I was told to choose a couple of guys to help me, so I picked a couple of flight engineers. And it wasn't just all men, on the ship. There was a WAC Captain, and she had sixteen pregnant WACs.

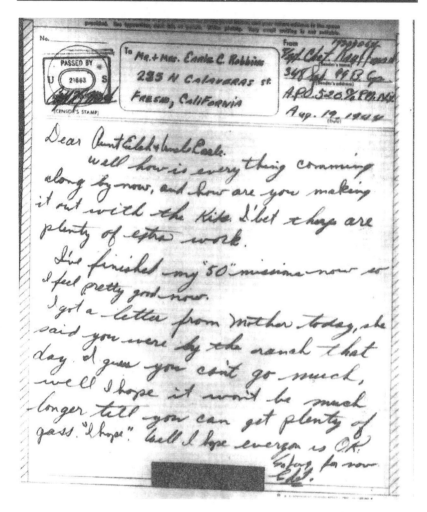

"It was a slow trip – took two weeks. We carried 600 men above deck and down below we had 600 prisoners. We ate good Navy food – oh, Navy food is the best – but the prisoners got C-rations. Well, the Captain said those were not fit for human consumption, but we'd eaten them all along, in the Air Force, and they were OK. But he saw to it that everybody got regular Navy meals, so we had to share our food with the prisoners. I don't know what they did with all those C-rations. Throw them overboard, maybe. But we used to eat them. We'd open the cans and throw it all together in a big pot, and that's what we ate on the base, a lot of the time."

The Kauffman family farm in Fowler, near Fresno, around 1950. The stakes all around the place are grape vines, for raisin production.

"I'll bet those Germans had never had it so good."

"O yes, I was watching the military channel on TV, and they were interviewing this one German prisoner, and he said: 'If we ever have another war with America, I want to be captured right away and live over there, in luxury!'"

After leaving the service Chester came back to the family farm in the Fresno area, in California's central valley. Evidently farming ran in his blood:

"My first ancestor who came over was an Amish farmer," he says. "He came in 1717, and the Amish and the Mennonites were against all warfare. And they'd been chased from one part of Europe to another. Lived in – in a part of France – "

"In the Alsace, maybe?"

"That's right, in the Alsace. And the French king, he didn't want them there, so they had to move again, I think to an area on the Rhine, and finally my first ancestor came over to America on a ship – I believe it sailed from Antwerp – called the Harle. And a few years later his wife came over, on a ship called the Charming Nancy."

Not long ago I visited with a local by the name of Claude Coffman. When I wondered if his name might have started out as Kauffman, he enthusiastically confirmed it, and showed me a genealogy book about the Kauffman family. He was not sure why Kauffman had become

Coffman, but my guess is that it happened during World War I, when hateful government propaganda incited widespread hostility against people of German descent who had been loyal Americans for generations. Many changed their names; many changed their family histories. Not long ago Delpha, my former mother in law, talked about a relative who had been researching the family tree. Delpha's mother was a Bohnett, and the story had always been that the Bohnetts had come from Alsace. But it turned out they had come from Baden-Württemberg, on the eastern side of the Rhine. There was also a family branch by the name of Ross, a common British name. But a family genealogist discovered that it had started out as Roess or Röss. And there is more: my second wife Trudi's maiden name was Ahlgrim. Her story too was that the Ahlgrims had come from the Alsace. So when we traveled in the Alsace, I checked the phone books for Ahlgrims. None were to be found. Afterwards an internet search showed that the name Ahlgrimm was common in Prussian territory.

Chester was one of five children; his older brother served in the combat engineers, so during the war his parents had kept a sign with two silver stars in the window. "My brother, he dropped out of the eighth grade," Chester explains. "But he was good with equipment. His unit invaded France and they rebuilt bridges and stuff."

"Really? In the town where I lived, we had a Bailey-bridge for many years after the war. In the war somebody was always blowing up bridges."

"Yes. And in early December he was working ahead of the tanks, clearing snow off the road towards Remagen. But he backed up over a land mine, it blew up the rear of the bulldozer, and a piece of shrapnel tore through his arm above the wrist, so he wound up in Paris, in a hospital. Later on when the fighting was over he hauled tanks back from the front, two at a time on a trailer, to France. I don't know if they shipped them all the way back here, or they scrapped them over there, or what. He ran his truck so hard doing that, the engine gave out. He didn't make it home for Christmas that year, 1945. Too much to do, cleaning up all those messes.

"And when he finally came back, he was living in Arcata, he was asked if he'd like to do some driving, hauling trailer-homes. So that's what he did. He could drive all the way to southern California in one day, 800 miles, and bring back a trailer. Then later on half a trailer-home at a time, when it took two to make one. And later yet it took three, like the one we live in. O, he could drive and haul things, and he

Chester Kauffman, Anna Mae, LouAnn and Jeanette

loved it. He's gone now, he died three years ago. He was eighty-eight, my older brother. His wife died at eighty-eight too. And my sister also, at eighty-eight. All three within a year."

And, looking at me sideways: "There were five kids. I was the middle child. And I'll be eighty-eight next month."

I put in my five cents' worth: "My dad died when he was fifty-eight. So when I turned fifty-eight, I had a funny feeling too. But I got over it. Well – sort of."

A couple of years after the war Chester got married, and they had two daughters. But then, in the early 'seventies, his wife developed mysterious health problems.

"We went to this doctor, and that doctor, and nobody knew what was wrong with her. 'Course, all they had in those days was X-rays ... Then finally we got sent to this specialist. He did tests and he'd figured it out, he said, but it was bad news. She had a brain tumor, and it was incurable, and it was gonna get worse, and she would get Ole – Ole – Ole Geezer's Disease."

"So here we were – no health insurance, you know – and after a while she needed to go into a nursing home. That was very expensive – I worked all the time to pay the bills, running half a dozen ranches at the same time, as much as ten miles apart. She needed care all those years, from 1972 to 1992, when she died."

"How many acres did you manage, between all those ranches?'

"O, about 600 acres in grapes. Plus about sixty acres of orchards. Plums and peaches."

Fifty-one missions, and half a dozen ranches. Maybe one was preparation for the other. He's a grand old man, Chester, a true

American, the way they used to make 'em. Do your duty, take care of your family, work hard, pay your bills, honor the Lord.

And this year I took him to watch the annual Memorial Day parade, from the restaurant's patio. I had a table and chair out for him, but he stood all that time, ready to salute the marchers, in his 15th Air Force uniform. Some people stopped by to thank him for his service. And that same week I was able to bring him copies of a local weekly, The Sentinel, that had started printing his story in installments, with his picture on the front page.

"How can I ever thank you?" he mumbles when he sees it.

Chester's grandparents, Eugene and Sally Kauffman

"How can I ever thank YOU, Chester? If it hadn't been for you and your buddies, my whole family would be speaking German today."

"My grandparents spoke German," he muses.

"Well, you know what I mean," I add as I leave. Why am I in a hurry to leave? Because I haven't quite sorted this one out, so while driving back I analyze it.

Our problem in the Netherlands was not with German, or even with the Germans. Prior to World War II, the Dutch admired and often copied German culture. And for centuries Dutch people moved to Germany while Germans settled in the Netherlands, without problems. Through the ages millions of people everywhere have changed their mother tongue without ill effects, and usually to their benefit. Besides, German is not difficult for Dutch people to learn, and the Dutch royal family, the House of Orange, is of at least 90% German origin. Queen Beatrix's late husband, Claus von Amsberg, was a lovely man who spoke perfect Dutch. A bunch of anarchists tried to ruin their wedding in 1966, because he had been in the Hitler Youth. But he was born in 1926, and teenagers in the Nazi era had no choice in the matter.

No, our problem was not with German or with the Germans, even if a lot of people thought so. Our problem was the evil régime whose bidding they were doing, the one that Chester helped wipe off the earth.

A Special Note—

We landed and Taxied up to our revetment with everyone staring at us, they couldn't believe what they were seeing. There was a new B-17 in our place. The crew chief had gotten word that we we went down over the Oil Fields of Polsti Romania, we walked back to our squadron and found out we were missing in action and our crew mission chart had been removed from the wall. We still had a few missons to finish our tour; we wound up flying 51 missions three of us with Purple Harts and The crew with many Metals and oak leaf clusters.

STRANGE WAR ENCOUNTERS

We pick at what's left of our lunch. I can tell something puzzling is on Chester's mind.

"Several times, coming back from Ploesti, we were a single plane because we'd got shot out of formation. O, it was worrisome, all by yourself up there. And then we saw another B-17 out there at some distance from us, but an old model, without the nose guns. It was at our speed and altitude, and we figured it was the Germans flying it. They were probably calling in our speed and altitude and calling in AA. Sure enough, we got some right away but we didn't get hit."

"What markings did that B-17 have?"

"We couldn't see them, just the black shape. It was flying south of us, same as the fighters did. You had to look into the sun, so you couldn't make them out.

"Another time, coming back from the oil fields I said to the tail gunner, 'Isn't that a plane back there?' 'Yes,' he said, 'and it's coming closer. It's a P-38.' Well, it was coming right behind us, the way a German fighter would. 'Tom,' I said, 'give him a burst over his head.' I had never seen a P-38 painted like that. It was a real dark green and very bright red, different shades from anything I'd seen. Well, Tom, he fired, and that P-38 peeled off and was gone. I still don't know what it was. But we sure looked into the sun a lot, for German fighters. I've still got a problem with my eye on account of it. My macula. And when we'd finally got out of that plane – you couldn't feel your feet any more, and your knees collapsed. It's part of why I always use a cane now.

"And another time, coming back from those oil fields with a long way to go, out of the blue we got a streak of fire across the windshield, and the last 20 mm shell hit the windshield post to the left and in front of the pilot. Of course it exploded, it hit the radio control cable, that you turn for different frequencies, and tore it up, and pieces hit the pilot's throat. So he was bleeding, but he said he'd be all right. He was a wonderful pilot. So I went back to the waist gunners, to find out why they didn't spot that plane, it was a Ju-88. But the gunner had been fiddling with an unplugged cable, so he didn't see or hear anything."

German-captured B-17.

"Did you have any more trouble from the Junkers plane?"

"O no, he didn't come back. He knew he'd snuck up on us, but he wasn't gonna get a second chance."

"And, you know, by the time I was finishing my missions the Russians were closing in, on the oil fields too, and we had a case one day where a German plane came skimming into Bari. Those Germans figured they'd rather be prisoners of the Americans than fall into Russian hands."

"And, I got another story. One time during a bombing raid over Germany this plane from a different bomb group lowered its landing gear and its flaps. That's the international sign of surrender. So the German fighters approached them, and this plane opens fire and shoots one down. And – I'm not making this up – from that time on that bomb group was the unluckiest of the bunch. The Germans always seemed to pick on them." He adds, pensively: "You're the first one I told my whole story to."

And then, by way of a post script: "You know, losing our B-24 in Dakar may have been a good thing. Because if that had not happened we would have been part of that bomb group."

In the midst of World War II's monstrous, murderous mayhem, did the two sides ever practice chivalry? Chester's story suggests they did, but woe betide those who took unfair advantage.

In my research I've come across some inexplicably chivalrous acts that showed kindness, consideration, even compassion; acts that could have cost the chivalrous warrior's own life. That they were exceptional stories should not be surprising. It's a truism that exceptional people are rare, as are exceptional deeds.

All the same, in writing about exceptional people and stories in wartime, a writer is taking a risk. That risk is that his readers will assume they were common rather than the exception. I've seen this kind of objection made against popular WWII movies like *Schindler's List* and *The Pianist.*

During a raid by B-17s of the 15th Air Force's 97th bomb group, in late March 1944, pilot Ped Magness witnessed an unusual event:

"A B-17 was hit and on fire and the crew was baling out. One of the airmen pulled his ripcord too fast and his parachute opened and caught in the bomb-bay. The man was hanging and the wind was whipping him against the aircraft. The war, and time, seemed to hesitate, and everyone stopped shooting. An Me 109 then flew into the middle of the B-17s. The gunners were amazed at the guts the German displayed, as he must have known that all our . . . guns were pointed at him. The fighter pilot eased up to that boy and shot him. Not a shot was fired back. He peeled off and came out of there, our gunners letting him go, and then the war started again.

The boy was doomed to a horrible death. We didn't want to shoot him. Indeed, we were trying to get away from him because we knew that his B-17 was going to blow up, and the resulting fragments would have struck a lot of us. It was the humane thing to do, and that was why no one shot the German down." [1])

Many Luftwaffe pilots had great respect for their opponents, and when given the chance they treated them well. Generalleutnant Günther Rall, who died in 2009 at age 91, was the third-highest-scoring fighter ace of all time with 275 aerial victories. (Many of Rall's early 'kills' were very inferior Russian aircraft, and unlike allied fighter pilots, Germans served for the duration of the war.) Rall always spoke highly of the British, calling the RAF pilot "the most aggressive and capable fighter pilot during the Second World War." Other famous aces held the same view. They included Adolf Galland and Johannes Steinhoff, the latter of whom said: "The Americans and British treated us as gentlemen, as we did our enemy pilots when they were captured."

On August 21, 2011, British Air Commodore "Dim" Strong died at age 97. In September 1941 he was a flight commander on a Wellington bomber, part of a 76-aircraft force sent to bomb the Fiat factory in Turin. On the way back his plane was struck by lightning, which damaged, among other things, the compass and the radio. They were

---

[1]) William N. Hess: *B-17 Flying Fortress Units of the MTO*. Oxford, UK: Osprey publ., 2003, pp. 54-55. The writer, a gunner in the 97th bomb group, flew 16 missions until his B-17 was shot down and he became a POW. Sticklers for spelling may have noticed that in the UK, airmen bale out of planes while in the US they bail out.

more or less flying blind. Finally, almost out of fuel, Strong ditched his plane in the North Sea. The crew was picked up by a Danish fishing boat, which landed them at the port of Esbjerg. There they were met by Hauptmann (Captain) Hans-Kurt Graf von Sponeck, adjutant of the Von Richthofen Staffel, a famous Luftwaffe unit. As Strong's obituary in The Telegraph reported:

> "Two Mercedes staff cars brought Strong and his crew to the officers' mess, where all the Luftwaffe airmen gathered to greet their RAF visitors. An all-night party ensued, with food, Danish beer, brandy and musical entertainment.
>
> The following morning Strong was told by a German officer: "We are front-line chaps – you won't be treated like this in the rear." After bidding their hosts farewell, Strong and his crew were taken by train to the POW reception centre at Frankfurt. Strong and von Sponeck kept up a regular correspondence after the war."

During his years as a POW Strong made himself notorious as an inveterate plotter of mass-escapes from the German camps. But at Stalag III at Sagan, he was appointed representative of a large part of the POWs, and he developed such a good working relationship with the German camp authorities that it was decided he would not be part of the 'Great Escape' planned by the men for March 1944. This was the tunnel-digging plot immortalized in the movie with Steve McQueen which, in typical Hollywood fashion, grossly falsified history by turning the Great Escape into an American enterprise. No Americans were at the camp. What *was* true was that of the 76 prisoners who got away and were caught, fifty were shot on Hitler's personal order, so Strong's exclusion from the escape probably saved his life. The Luftwaffe officer who told Strong that his men wouldn't be treated quite so well away from the front line probably had no idea how right he was.

Staff Sergeant Sam N. Fain, ball-turret gunner in a B-17 belonging to the 452nd bomb group (8th Air Force) relates a ferocious mid-air battle:

> "I picked a FW 190 up in my sight track for one second and opened fire. I followed him. He was going by off our left waist . . . I got him. He exploded in a ball of fire. I swung my turret to 6 o'clock and could see five of our Forts going down in fire and exploding, throwing flames around the sky. I saw seven men bale out of a Fortress. An enemy plane circled them once and came in firing at the 'chutes. They all

caught fire and I could see the men falling to earth. I fired at the enemy ship for eight seconds. I saw smoke trailing from his engine and hoped that I got the rat. . . " [1])

Shooting defenseless men was considered dirty pool by both sides, but that didn't mean it never happened; combat left a lot of scope for individual initiative, clean or dirty. Richard Wynn, a B-17 navigator in the 8th Air Force's 100th bomb group was returning from a raid on German oil targets:

"We were hit in the No. 3 engine and lost oil pressure before the prop could be feathered. . . . with a windmilling prop and all of the drag it created, we were unable to keep up with the formation and became a single straggler on the way home with heavy fuel consumption on a very deep penetration. I did a fuel consumption problem after a while and had us running out of fuel about the time we would reach the Channel. Hollywood not withstanding, a single B-17 is mismatched against a flurry of fighters usually. Six Me 109s hit us from the rear. They plastered us good, knocking out the controls and who knows what else. We baled out and got out OK, were buzzed, but not fired upon in our 'chutes by the remaining 109s. We were captured immediately." [2])

In J-27, a famous German fighter wing stationed in north Africa during Rommel's desert campaign, new pilots were asked by their commanding officer, Lt. Gustav Roedel, what they would do if they spotted their enemy floating down in a parachute. If the questioned airman was at a loss or said he'd shoot, Roedel told him: "If I ever see or hear of you shooting at a man in a parachute, I will shoot you down myself." Roedel often explained that the rules of war were observed for the pilot's own benefit, to preserve his humanity. And he hated the use of the word 'kill'. The correct expression was *'victories'*, which were achieved by shooting at a machine, not a man.

[1]) Martin Bowman: *B-17 Combat Missions*. New York: Metro Books, 2007, p. 122.

[2]) Bowman op.cit., p. 51.

February 1942: Hans-Joachim Marseille in the desert with one of his victories, a downed RAF Hawker Hurricane.

Of course, there may have been other considerations. If enemy soldiers were treated well by one nation, the enemy was more likely to reciprocate. And it is clear that not everyone in the Luftwaffe held Roedel's views. Neither did every allied pilot. In early 1945, some American pilots strafed pilots of downed Me-292 jet fighters, figuring they must be really good since they had survived as long as they had. [1]

But apparently Roedel's views were held by the pilots of J-27, some of whom applied them at serious risk to themselves. One of those was Hans-Joachim Marseille, who during his brief career scored 158 victories against British Commonwealth fighters. (He was killed in a flying accident in September 1942.) Marseille was a risk-taker, who had pulled some outrageous stunts that had caused the destruction of more than one of his planes. A year before his death he shot down an Australian pilot by the name of Pat Byers, who had been captured. Byers had been badly burned and Marseille, having learned his opponent's name and unit, took the trouble to overfly Byers' airfield, where he dropped a note saying Byers had been captured and wounded, but was being cared for. Even though Marseille had done this at great risk from enemy AA batteries, he repeated his stunt two weeks later, this time dropping a note saying that Byers had died of his injuries, and expressing his regrets. When Luftwaffe commander Hermann Göring heard of it he issued an edict forbidding such risky initiatives.

---

[1] Adam Makos: *A Higher Call*, p. 54, 70, 301. More particulars about this book will follow.

Another of JG-27's famous aces, Johannes Steinhoff (176 victories), rose after the war to four-star general in the West German air force. Of his 176 'kills', Steinhoff had made 152 on the eastern front. One of those was a Russian Yak fighter that continued to fly, but was on fire. The pilot was desperately trying to get out, banging against his canopy glass. It was clearly jammed, and he was about to be burned alive. Steinhoff, who had pulled up to the side of the

Johannes Steinhoff (right)
at post-war NATO event

plane, saw the pilot's panic. He looked at the Russian, and the Russian looked at him in terror, from a cockpit filling with grey smoke. Then the Russian nodded. Steinhoff dropped back behind the fiercely burning fighter and blew it out of the air with a burst of cannon fire. Afterwards a fellow-ace who had witnessed the incident found him standing behind his own fighter, crying. He never spoke of the incident, but asked his friend: "If I am ever in that situation, please do the same." As it turned out, while taking off in the world's first jet fighter, the Me-262, on 18 April 1945, Steinhoff had a tire blowout and crashed, sustaining serious burns himself. His recovery took two years; his eyelids were rebuilt by a British reconstructive surgeon.

On 20 December 1943, Lt. Charles L. Brown of the 8th U.S. Army Air Force, barely 21 years old, was a B-17 pilot on his second mission over Germany, a bombing raid on a Focke-Wulf aircraft plant in Bremen. During Brown's final approach, German flak blew away his plane's Plexiglas nose cone and killed his #2 engine; his #4 engine had already been running erratically. After dropping his bombs Brown turned his B-17 northwest to leave Germany and return across the North Sea to England, but his reduced engine power and the drag of his damaged nose slowed him down too much. Soon his bomber was under attack by German fighters, which always picked on stragglers that couldn't keep up with their formation.

Now Brown's crew found that most of their 11 guns were frozen and useless, because of a maintenance error. All they could do was threaten the German fighters by turning their turrets and mock-aiming guns. As it turned out many of the fighters attacked from the front to strafe the cockpit and kill the pilots, but Brown repeatedly minimized that by turning into them, finally even turning his plane upside down. He had not intended to bank that far, but the destruction of his oxygen system at over 22,000 feet had temporarily blacked him out. In the end his opponents failed to shoot down the B-17 but they did inflict further, near-fatal damage. In addition to shooting big holes in the fuselage and destroying the oxygen system, they had destroyed many other controls, along with its hydraulic, electrical and communication systems. The B-17 had also lost its left stabilizer and part of its tail, and was flying on only one fully functional engine and two partial ones. The tail gunner had been killed, and five other crewmen including Brown himself were wounded, with one near-dead waist gunner writhing in agony.

After Brown had unintentionally flipped his plane, it had gone into a steep dive during which he woke up, apparently thanks to increased oxygen. After coming to, halfway to oblivion, he got the B-17 out of its plunge at around 3,000 feet. His report contains hints of disbelief that such a thing was possible with only one stabilizer. When the plane finally leveled off over the town of Oldenburg it was at roof level, "blowing leaves from trees and shingles from homes" while the locals gazed up in awe at the bomber thundering away. But the B-17 and most of its crew had survived. Better yet, its plunge down to earth had convinced the attacking fighters that it was done for, because they were all gone. In fact, one of them had claimed the bomber as a kill. [1]

Next, continuing on a northwestern course out of Germany, Brown overflew a Luftwaffe airfield near the village of Jever, west of Wilhelmshaven – to his own great discomfort. Serving as bait for more German fighters had not been his plan. As it turned out, a highly proficient and decorated fighter pilot by the name of Franz Stigler had just landed his Messerschmitt-109 at this field. His home base was Wiesbaden, but he needed to refuel and re-arm.

---

[1] Adam Makos & Larry Alexander: *A Higher Call*, New York: Penguin Group, 2012. According to a footnote on page 195, Lt. Ernst Süss had claimed Brown's B-17 as a kill. But he had to bail out of his own plane, his parachute failed to open and his body was found in a field. Other quotes or references to "A Higher Call" in this section will be followed by a page number.

Just as the ground crew at Jever had finished servicing his Me-109 they heard the engine noise of the approaching B-17, followed by its slow, very low overflight. Shooting down a bomber was worth three points to a Luftwaffe pilot, and Stigler already had 27.

Side by side: Me-109 pilot Franz Stigler and B-17 pilot Charlie Brown

Thirty points would entitle him to the Knight's Cross of the Iron Cross, at that time a much-desired, neck-worn decoration that expired with World War II. Despite his plane's damaged radiator, and without waiting for clearance, Franz Stigler took off after his new prey.

Catching up with the laboring B-17 was no problem since it was only moving at about 135 miles an hour, just above stall speed. But when Stigler reached it he had trouble believing his eyes. As he said much later, he 'had never seen a plane in such a bad state'. About the only positive aspect was that it was still flying, proof of its rugged construction. Approaching it from the rear Stigler had first aimed at the tail gunner, only to realize that he was already dead. Curious to see what else was amiss with this plane with half its tail shot away, he cautiously moved to the right, flying about even with it, barely higher than its right wing tip. This put him out of reach of the ball turret gunner, but enabled him to inspect the rest of the plane, since he'd noticed that the right waist gun had been blasted away, and there was no one in the top turret. Then he saw, through a huge hole in the fuselage near the radio room, crew members huddled together, trying to care for their wounded comrades.

At this point Charlie Brown, struggling to gain altitude for his flight back to England, looked out his window and saw the Me-109 alongside, Flying alongside meant the German was not attacking the B-17, and as if to confirm that, he waved at Brown. Then he motioned for him to land the bomber in Germany. Brown did not respond, but stared straight ahead. Along with everyone else on the plane he was convinced the Me-109 was going to shoot him down, and he did not understand the fighter pilot's gestures. As he related much later, "I look out and there's the

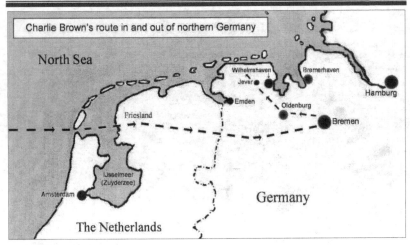

Charlie Brown's route in and out of northern Germany

North Sea

Wilhelmshaven
Bremerhaven
Jever
Hamburg
Emden
Oldenburg
Friesland
Bremen

IJsselmeer
(Zuyderzee)

Amsterdam

Germany

The Netherlands

world's worst nightmare sitting on my wing. That little sucker looked like he owned me and belonged there." (Makos, p. 203). After all the other mishaps, the fear generated by a new, confident enemy on his wing had closed Charlie Brown's already-troubled mind.

Franz Stigler was an excellent fighter pilot, but also a good Bavarian Catholic. At the most basic level he had every right to shoot down this enemy, since the war had already cost him his brother August, also a pilot. But he now knew that the B-17 was defenseless. Franz Stigler was fingering his rosary, and decided he did not want to have the deaths of all those defenseless people on his conscience.

But there was a serious danger, getting closer by the second: the flak batteries that defended the German coast. There were no gaps in that chain of guns, and on its course northwest the bomber had to cross it, at a low altitude at that. German AA operators were the best in the world (They actually shot down more enemy planes during the war than all the German fighters put together). Stigler moved a few feet away from the B-17, and continued flying parallel to it, as a sort of protecting angel. He gambled that the flak operators on the ground would not shoot at either plane as long as they flew together, in formation. And this is what happened. After identifying the fighter as one of their own, the battery commander on the ground ordered his crew to hold their fire. He did not want to shoot down a Me-109, and reasoned there must be an explanation for the two planes flying as a pair. It was well known that the Luftwaffe possessed captured B-17s that had been patched up and were being used for various operations including aerial combat practice for fighter pilots: B-17s like the one Chester saw over Yugoslavia.

Thanks to Stigler's gamble, Charlie Brown had crossed the hazardous coastal flak zone and the North Sea beach before he realized it, and left Germany behind. For his part Stigler had very little confidence that the B-17 could reach England in the state it was in, so he gestured to point the way to Sweden, a neutral country where quite a few allied crews landed planes damaged over Germany, to be interned by the Swedes for the duration of the war. Flying to Sweden would take less time than it would take to reach England. But Sweden was on the Baltic, not on the North Sea, so Stigler pointed east. No response from Brown. Stigler mouthed "Sweden!" and gesticulated. Still no response; the B-17 headed west, not east. As far as Brown was concerned, Stigler might as well have been speaking Greek, and he told someone to get into the top turret and aim the guns at him. But Stigler could see what was going on, and decided it was time to quit. He saluted Brown, rolled over, and disappeared. All told, the two pilots had flown together for about ten minutes. (pp. 205-209)

Stigler had broken off the encounter without any confidence that the B-17 would make it back, and he was almost right. Despite the crew's jettisoning all superfluous weight – radio, guns, ammo, anything they could find – Brown's bomber kept losing altitude, slipping below 1,000 feet halfway to England. Three-quarters there they were down to 500 feet. But then they got an unexpected escort home: two American P-47 Thunderbolts that guided them to Seething, one of the most easterly air fields in England, which had been inaugurated as an American B-24 base just three weeks earlier. Ten or twelve miles after crossing the Norfolk coast Brown landed there – barely, since his diminished engine power had reduced his elevation to between 200 and 250 feet. His B-17 would never fly another bombing mission.

After his debriefing Brown and his crew were promised medals for their performance, but then the promise was withdrawn and they were ordered to keep their strange encounter with the German fighter a secret, clearly because painting the enemy as human softens wartime morale. Brown stayed in the Air Force, retiring as a lieutenant colonel in 1972 before starting a second career. But during all those years he wondered: 'Why did he not shoot us down?' It took him 46 years to find out. Official records, American or German, were no help. Finally, in late 1989, thanks to the intervention of Adolf Galland, the most famous German ace of World War II, Brown was able to place an ad in a newsletter for former Luftwaffe pilots, and got a response from his angel of mercy. Franz Stigler, it turned out, had left Germany for Canada after the war and was living in the Vancouver area.

In his ad Charlie had mentioned the time and place of the encounter, in which "a single Bf-109 made a non-firing gun camera run on the B-17 and ended up flying formation on the right wing." [1] But he purposely had not included damage details such as the loss of his left stabilizer and his tail gunner. If his ad elicited a response, he would carefully question the respondent. Charlie did not want to be victimized by phony opportunists – people like Douglas Fairbanks.

But he had included his name and mailing address in the ad, and remarkably soon a letter arrived from Franz Stigler. That letter contained no details about the incident either, but Stigler related what he'd done immediately after the incident, and that he himself had tried to find Brown through associations of former American airmen. His letter opened: "All these years, I wondered what happened to the B-17, did she make it or not?"

Franz Stigler had not included a telephone number, but Brown could not wait to speak to him, so he found it and called. During that conversation, awkward at first, he asked Stigler to describe the B-17's battle damage. Stigler knew it all – the damaged tail and missing stabilizer, the tail gunner. Finally Stigler said: "When I let you go over the sea, I thought you'd never make it across."

That settled it: Charlie Brown's ad had only mentioned flying over land, not over the North Sea, and he broke down. They had an emotional reunion in Seattle, and went on to make many joint appearances before enthusiastic WWII aviation fans.

The internet is an odd place, sort of like an old-fashioned market where everybody peddles information, much of it worthless gossip and much that, even though it may have started as truth, has been re-hashed until the original author would barely recognize it.

Something like that happened to the Charlie Brown/Franz Stigler tale, which since 1990 has spread to many sites for World War II aviation enthusiasts. Some say that Stigler had been ordered to shoot down Brown's B-17, and that afterwards he lied to his superiors about what he'd done. Stigler's own story does not support that, but it is a fact

---

[1] The fighter's official name was Messerschmitt Bf 109, with BF standing for Bayerische Flugzeugwerke (Bavarian Aircraft Works). The Germans usually referred to the plane as Bf 109, while most allied pilots called it Me-109. Either way, it was a match for any allied fighter throughout the war.

that he never said a word to anyone about his peaceful escort flight with the injured B-17 and, of course, it could have been very bad for him if he had done so.

I've also read claims that Brown's damaged compass caused him to be flying east instead of west towards England, and that Stigler showed him the way, but this is

(L-R) German Ace Franz Stigler, artist Ernie Boyett, and B-17 pilot Charlie Brown.

not supported by the pilots' stories either. It's unlikely anyhow because even without a compass, an airman would know his approximate direction by the position of the sun at that time of day. Time was critical to any mission, and everybody was aware of it.

According to yet other reports, Stigler saw pieces of the dead top gunner spread all over the top of the B-17, but that could not have been true either. The plane's flight engineer who, as was customary, doubled as top gunner, went by the name of Frenchy, and he was not seriously injured. Instead the tail gunner, Ecky, had been killed by fighter cannon fire, but his remains were still in the tail gunner's compartment. A poignant detail of Ecky's story is that he had been looking forward to a Christmas party planned for local English kids that evening. To provide treats, Ecky had been scrupulously saving his own chocolate rations.

In short, many of the details you may find published about the Brown/Stigler story are untrue. Still, its essence is true. And finally, 22 years after the two former enemies' tearful reunion a well-documented book was published that contains the most reliable version. *A Higher Call* by Adam Makos is based on extensive interviews with both Brown and Stigler, plus a great deal of research.

"I didn't have the heart to finish off those brave men," Stigler said. "It would have been the same as shooting at a man in a parachute."

"I was too stupid to surrender," explained Charlie Brown. "And Franz Stigler was too much of a gentleman to destroy us." (364)

After being great friends for eighteen years and speaking together at many military gatherings, Brown and Stigler both passed away in 2008.

During the German *Reich's* Kaiser Era, Jews were able to rise in civilian government as well as in the military. Anne Frank's father, Otto Frank, served as an officer in World War I and greatly respected the German military's strict code of behavior. Shortly before that war's end Otto Frank's unit in Belgium needed some horses. As was customary they went to a local farmer to requisition them, but this poor man was quite beside himself; in those days a farmer's horses made all the difference between a living and starvation. So Otto Frank promised, on his honor as a German officer, that he would bring them back. The Armistice came in November 1918, but Frank didn't make it back home to Frankfurt until January 1919. First he had returned the horses to the Belgian farmer, who 'received them with amazed gratitude.' But by this time Frank's unit had left, so he ended up walking all the way back, which took him three weeks. And when, after he had paid this price for his honor, he finally staggered into the family home and explained what had taken him so long, his mother was so outraged at his silly priorities that she threw a dinner plate at him. [1]

In recent decades many books have been published in areas occupied by the Germans in World War II that actually give them credit for good behavior, something that would have been unthinkable during the first decade or so following the war. Here is a story from the area where my family lived, south of the Schelde estuary, about the German 15th Army's retreat in the fall of 1944:

Commotion over a lost razor in the Front Line

Until the very last, discipline in the German army . . . was maintained. One striking example: a small group of Germans is billeted on a small farm in the front-region. The farmer has just finished shaving. A German soldier asks to borrow the razor. The farmer doesn't get it back.

When he makes a complaint with a German officer, this man's reaction is typical of German discipline. Who would bother about a lost razor, a few kilometers from the front? But the officer immediately summons his soldiers for a roll-call. The razor is as yet tracked down. [2]

---

[1] Carol Ann Lee: *The Hidden Life of Otto Frank*. New York: HarperCollins, 2002, pp 19/20.
[2] Jacques Cats: *Volk in de Vuurlinie*. Vlissingen, Den Boer/De Ruiter, 1991: p. 45; my translation.

The "BRESKENS POCKET"
October 1944
〰 Dutch-Belgian border

Walcheren · Zuid-Beveland · Vlissingen · Breskens · Schelde · Schelde · North Sea · Zeebrugge · Cadzand · Terneuzen · Belgium · Braakman · Sluis · Belgium · Leopold Canal · Damme · Belgium · Canal Brugge-Ghent · Brugge · Maldegem · Selzate

Operation SWITCHBACK was a two-pronged assault to clear the "Breskens Pocket", mostly Dutch territory still held by the German 15th Army, between Zeebrugge in the west and the Braakman inlet. On October 6 it was launched by a flamethrower-attack by Canadian troops across the two canals near Maldegem, followed by an amphibious landing from the Terneuzen area, which had been cleared by Polish troops by September 20. The Germans quickly recovered from their surprise. The allied campaign took about a month, causing many hundreds of civilian deaths and the virtual destruction of the local towns.

And here is another one from those same days, the story of *Max de Blaffer* (Max the Barker, or Barking Max), a moniker given by the locals to a 15 cm (6 inch) cannon belonging to unit #203 of the German Navy Artillery, because of the sound it made. The Germans had set Barking Max on top of a dune near Cadzand, west of the town of Breskens, to slow down the allied forces approaching the 'Breskens pocket' from the south. From where this gun sat it could hit targets over 25 kilometers (about 15.5 miles) away. Repeated bombing raids by the allies had failed to destroy it – not very surprising, given the typical accuracy of bombing in those days.

As I mentioned before, in that flat country any kind of tower was considered a potential enemy-observation point, hence a military target.

Immo Hopman, commander of the German artillery unit, was ordered to aim Barking Max at the Belfort tower in the center of the ancient city of Brugge, in Belgium.

Called Bruges by the French and the English, Brugge, meaning 'bridge' in Flemish, had already been taken by allied forces and was only 22 kilometers away. In the Middle Ages Brugge had become very wealthy because of the cloth trade, and military adventurers bent on plunder were plentiful then, which was why in the mid-13th century the Belfort tower, 272 feet high, had been built as a lookout spot to give the city early warning of enemy troops or other impending calamities. The Belfort also housed

The Belfort tower in Brugge (above) and the sidewalk cafés on the adjacent Grote Markt.

the city treasury. If you climb the tower you can still see this very elaborate chest, which took several keys to open. Later on, after its access to the North Sea silted up and centuries before powered dredges were invented, Brugge stagnated and its population shrank from 200,000 to 50,000, but that stagnation achieved its preservation. Today it's a huge tourist attraction.

Because he was aware of Brugge's cultural and historical importance, Captain Hopman argued against carrying out the order, because he thought it irresponsible. His objections could have cost him his life, or at least a court-martial. But in the end he persuaded his commanding general to go along. About what went on during that highly-charged dispute we can only guess. Perhaps Hopman and his commander were painfully aware of the destruction that Belgian Flanders had already suffered during World War I, when medieval towns similar to Brugge – Ieper or Ypres being one tragic case – had been completely leveled by artillery fire. It's also possible that Hopman benefited from his father's reputation. He was the eldest son of Albert Hopman, a highly decorated admiral in Kaiser Wilhelm's navy.

Brugge survived intact, as did Immo Hopman, whose artillery unit was entirely destroyed during the fighting. In the 1960s he came back to Brugge for a visit, and related:

> "On the *Grote Markt* [Grand Market] I sat down at a sidewalk café. Great inner joy rose inside me when I saw this wonderful square, with its gorgeous buildings, again. Besides all that, it gave me special satisfaction to know that once upon a time I had been able to make a contribution to the preservation of so much beauty."

Reading this reminded me of how during my own visits to Brugge I wondered how it had managed to preserve all of its ancient glory while every town in the "Breskens pocket" just north of it had been leveled to the ground. But – it needs to be said – the lion's share of that devastation had been caused by allied bombing and by the attacking Canadian troops, not by the Germans.

In northern Bavaria, the 1000-year old fortress-town of Rothenburg ob der Tauber is a prime tourist attraction, the crown jewel of Germany's medieval cities. Much like Brugge it flourished during the Middle Ages thanks to commerce, but the disastrous Thirty Years' War (1618–1648) reduced the city to poverty, and it never recovered. But in the late 19th century tourists discovered Rothenburg's ancient splendor, and its fame grew.

During the final months of World War II German troops were stationed in Rothenburg with Hitler's standard orders to defend the town to the last man, which also would have meant to the last ancient stone. Part of the town, including much of the old city wall, had already been destroyed by allied bombing.

U.S Assistant Secretary of War John J. McCloy, then in the field with approaching American forces, knew of the ancient city's beauty. In his parents' New York home hung a picture of Rothenburg, brought back by his mother. He ordered commanding General Jacob L. Devers, an artillery specialist, not to use his guns to take it. This was the kind of order that the beleaguered Dutch people in the contested Breskens

ROTHENBURG OB DER TAUBER

pocket would have loved but didn't get, but it could also have meant a costly campaign of hand-to-hand fighting. In this case, a combination of American initiative and enemy cooperation solved the dilemma. Devers drove up to the city gate and asked to see the German commander, Major Thömmes, to negotiate a surrender. Thömmes agreed to ignore Hitler's order. He told his soldiers to stay out of the way of the Americans, who on April 17, 1945, peacefully occupied Rothenburg.

After the war, the residents of the city quickly repaired the bombing damage. Donations for the rebuilding were received from all over the world. The reconstructed city walls feature commemorative bricks with donor names. In November 1948 McCloy was honored with the title of Rothenburg's honorary protector. During the post-war years he also served as U.S. High Commissioner of Germany, during which time he oversaw the creation of the German Federal Republic.

Even though stories like these tend to give the credit to one side, it usually took two to tango. The German pilot's mercy-killing of the trapped American airman was enabled by the gunners on the other American bombers. The same could be said of Franz Stigler's sparing of Charlie Brown's B-17, unless Stigler knew Brown had no effective guns left, which was not the case. And Rothenburg might still have been destroyed if it hadn't been for the German commander's cooperation.

Jumping back to the battle for the Schelde in the fall of 1944, after the conclusion of operation Switchback the allies' remaining task was to clear the estuary's northern bank, so ship traffic to the sorely needed port of Antwerp could finally solve their logistical problem. That task had become harder because of Montgomery's disastrous action at Arnhem, operation Market Garden. The largest airborne operation of the entire war, Market Garden had wasted forces that could have easily taken both banks of the Schelde, while the distracted allies had allowed the Germans to reinforce their positions on the two islands north of the estuary, Zuid [South]-Beveland and Walcheren.

Finally, on October 24 Canadian troops, after proceeding north from Antwerp, pushed west into Zuid-Beveland, but they were stymied by strong German defenses including flooded polders, a defensive tactic they had copied from the Dutch. But amphibious landings by British troops from the southern bank of the Schelde outflanked them, and the island was taken one week later. It took another week of fighting and another amphibious operation, this one originating from the Belgian coast, to take the island further west, Walcheren. These were bloody campaigns, but the water and the mud may have been the worst parts.

While the Germans had flooded parts of Zuid-Beveland to obstruct the allies, the Allies had flooded almost the entire island of Walcheren to handicap the German occupying troops. And they had done so by bombing its dikes, killing a lot of civilians.

In a book of personal memories of those days, one poignant story shows up the hazards that chivalry posed for both sides. It was written by the son of a local minister by the name of Boersma, like many Dutch-Reformed ministers a Frisian. [1] On a certain Friday morning in October 1944, *dominee* Boersma's son was a teenager. It was still dark when the doorbell rang at the manse in Kloetinge, east of Zuid-Beveland's main city of Goes:

Ist dein Vater da? "Is your father here?" asked the German soldier. He was soaked through-and-through, without helmet, without rifle, and he seemed catatonic. The boy recognized him as one of a platoon of "stomach patients", a mix of soldiers with digestive ailments and others who had been wounded on the eastern front. Some had been billeted at his family's home. Most were sick of the war:

"Monday morning the orders had come in. For days the front had been around the dam that connects South-Beveland with Brabant. Now it was their turn. The *Feldwebel* [sergeant] was barking as always, but now he used even bigger words. It was all about the decisive battle, the honor of the fatherland, about until the last bullet, *Heil Hitler*, and more stuff like that. Then he marched off for further instructions.

This was the moment my father had been waiting for. Until then he had only talked to the Germans when there was no other way. 'It's because you and I are at war,' he would explain each time in a friendly but determined manner. Now he did speak. They were standing there, all twelve of them. 'If they still want to do something for Germany,' he said, 'they should remember that Germany has more use

---

[1] Curious cultural note: most Catholic priests in Holland came from the opposite side of the country, the southern provinces of Brabant and Limburg that were strongly Catholic, and the different accents of the Reformed and Catholic clergymen were frequent sources of jokes.

for a living German than a dead one.' He made me get the handbill I had found on Long Dike, and read it to them: 'Message from General Eisenhower, Supreme Commander of the Allied forces, to the German soldiers! You are guaranteed to be treated well if you surrender!' He closed with a prayer. *'Danke, Herr Pfarrer!'* "Thank you, Pastor!' said one of the men. 'I hope we make it . . .'"

"Ist dein Vater da?" the man had said. When the doorbell rang so early in the morning his father had fled into the garden. So he went to get him:

"At first the man only shouted: *Alles Panzer! Alles Panzer!* Then he began his story. About how they had wanted to surrender, the way my father had told them to. About how they had waded forward through the water, hands up. And how the Canadians had machine-gunned them. 'This one is dead and that one is dead,' and one after another he mentioned six names. 'The *Feldwebel* too?' 'Yes, he also, but that happened earlier . . . And I pulled Helmut out of the water, but I had to leave him . . .' And that was all. He cried. As if in a coma he had walked back to our house, his last home. None of us said anything.
After quite some time he started again, told of his life. Of Duisburg, where he was from. Of the war that he had always hated. . . ."

Since the family needed to abandon their home because of the encroaching war violence, they couldn't do much for the desperate German soldier. But in a day or so they found themselves back home, hiding in the cellar with two other desperate German soldiers.

The next soldiers to reach the manse were Canadians from Quebec who refused to speak English with the family. Finally an English-speaking Canadian major arrived, and his father

Guarded by Canadian soldiers, and apparently not too unhappy with their situation, German POWs in Zeeland are marched off to imprisonment.

asked him about how they dealt with prisoners of war. Standard procedure, the major told him, called for assembling groups of German POWs and taking them to internment sites. Then the father told him of the massacre. The major was astonished that he already knew of it. Then he showed him, on a map, where it had occurred. Right before the German platoon from the manse arrived, another stray German soldier had approached the Canadians with his hands up, but it turned out he was carrying hand grenades:

". . . and he dropped them when our men came walking towards him. Then things got out of hand." He showed the father his report about the incident.

"The reason I asked is because I have a couple more in my cellar," father said."

In almost every one of history's wars, more people died of famine and diseases than died of injuries. The proportions changed in World War II but still, the disruption of transportation and utilities and food supplies and sanitation took a frightful toll. Shortly after the lone German survivor had come to their door, and after the father had conducted joint Thanksgiving services with a British chaplain, the entire family contracted typhus. One week before Christmas the father died:

During his final hours he was delirious. He talked a mish-mash of German, English, French too. It was obvious he was dealing with soldiers. Was he negotiating? Then, quieting down a bit, we heard him say: *'Wat is de mens? – What is man?'* And we completed it: *'. . . dat Gij zijner gedenkt – that thou art mindful of him?'* A little later he switched to Frisian, his birth-tongue. We had recognized Psalm 8: *'For thou hast made him only a little lower than the angels, and hast crowned him with glory and honour.'*

That's why it says on his grave at the cemetery near the windmill along the road to Kapelle: *Psalm 8:5.* But sometimes I wonder if, considering the bitter story I have just related, he may not have been thinking of a different text, the one in *Job 7:17*:

"What is man, that thou shouldest magnify him? and that thou shouldest set thine heart upon him? And that thou shouldest visit him every morning, and try him every moment?" [1])

---

[1]) J. Boersma: "Ist dein Vater da?" in: Redactie Provinciale Zeeuwse Courant: *Chocolade, witbrood en tranen – Zeeuwse verhalen over de bevrijding.* Vlissingen; Den Boer/De Ruiter, 1994; pp. 57-60

THE PEOPLE ARE HUNGRY ! ELECT HITLER !

Today when I drive up to the restaurant after lunch I notice a bike parked against the wall, a bike with a six-foot 1 x 6 board tied to it, with the front of the board raised high enough so it won't get in the way of the turning front wheel. Back in the Netherlands this would be nothing out of the ordinary, but around here it sure is. When I come in there's a fellow about my age, with a white beard and thinning white hair in a pony-tail, sitting at the bar drinking coffee. The smiley way he looks at me suggests that we're acquainted, but if I have any memory of that, it's vanishingly vague. Besides, regardless of whether he is an aging hippie or a Deadhead or a biker, I find a pony tail on an old guy pretentious. Like a ship sailing under a false flag. Not that I'm jealous, of course. So I walk past him to go behind the bar, with a nod and a "How ya doin'?" But since the last lunch customers are leaving, he's hard to avoid.

"Say," he says, "didn't this used to be the Hurry-Back Café? Gino's place?"

"Gino? The Hurry-Back? Why yes, but that's a long time ago."

"I used to come into Gino's when I lived here," he reveals. By Golly, now I do recognize him, if ever so vaguely, as a sometime-patron from long ago, back in the late seventies, no less. Aged considerably. Like me. Gino's Hurry-Back Café was a hippie-founded, big-city-style-deli-sandwich place that did a good business back then but it was tiny, seating no more than a dozen people. A lot of the clientele practiced the all-natural lifestyles of the seventies, like the tie-dyed girl with too much hair who thought nothing of changing her baby's diaper on the eating counter. The Hurry-Back Café was located three blocks down Commercial Avenue from our present location. We bought it in 1976, ran it for three years, and then built the present restaurant. But in business, timing is at least 90% of success. Soon after we opened the doors of our new place, the economy dove into the notorious recession of the early 'eighties, which was even worse locally. On the heels of this, the fast-food and sandwich scene in Coos Bay suddenly became very crowded, with McDonald's and Burger King and Subway and Arby's moving in, plus multiple pizza and Mexican places. To give people new reasons to come to our place we started diversifying and expanding our menu, while continually cutting back on the sandwiches. After many abandoned experiments, that evolution created the Blue Heron, specializing in German food and seafood. To get there we took the

A grave from pre-revolutionary America, in the church yard of the Dutch-Reformed church at Fishkill (formerly Viskil), NY. The inscription suggests creeping integration into the larger English-speaking society: the Dutch woman buried had an English husband, and the Dutch spelling is a bit shaky.

Anno 1771. Den 22 September Is In Den Heere Gerust Carhanna Lawrence Huys Vrouw van Lawrence Lawrence Oude Zynde 42 Jaaren 9 Maanden En 4 Dagen. Hier Leght het Overschot Van Een Godvrugte Vrouw Haar Deugdt Wordt in Geen Steen nog Diamant Gedreeven.Maar Eeuwig Zal Haar Ziel By Godt in Vreude *[sic: Vreugde]* Leeven Al wie Haar Voor Beeld Volght Heeft maar Eem *[sic: een]* korte Rouw.	Anno 1771. The 22 September Rested In The Lord Carhanna Lawrence Housewife of Lawrence Lawrence Being Aged 42 Years 9 Months And 4 Days. Here lie the Remains Of A Godly Woman Her Virtue is in No Stone Nor Diamond Embossed. But Eternally Will Her Soul Live in Joy With God All who Follow Her Example Have only A short Mourning.

example of some doctors, trying new remedies on their patients. But not as many of our customers died.

"You'll have to excuse me," he says, but I have a poor memory. I don't remember your name."

"My name is Wim, and I have a very poor memory for names myself. Don't feel bad. I think it's common."

"I'm Jerry Ouderkirk," he says. "Originally it was spelled different."

"With an e instead of an i, I suppose."

"That's right," he confirms, "and some branches of the family made other changes. Ouderkerk is a town just outside Amsterdam."

"O, I believe I've been there. When I lived in Amsterdam, in the 'sixties, I used to go running along the river Amstel, and that's where it is, right on the water."

"The first Ouderkirk arrived in this country in the sixteen-hundreds, in New York."

"Hey, that's interesting too. I happened to come through a town up the river from New York City once, that was called Fishkill. And there, in plain sight, was this Dutch-Reformed church from the seventeen-hundreds, built in the correct style, complete with a churchyard from the era, with all the grave inscriptions in Dutch. Obviously that had been a Dutch-speaking town for a long time. Its original name had been *Viskil*, because *kil* is a common Dutch word for a body of water. One of many Dutch words for bodies of water. You know, like the Eskimos have all these words for snow. To me it was like time-travel."

"I had your sauerbraten the other day," he says. "The flavors were perfect, just like I remember them."

"Well, thank you." And because that's the most common reason for such food nostalgia: "So, did you spend time in Germany, with the American military?"

This turns out to be a wrong guess, because he went over there to work as a carpenter. Then, as a sideline he started working for Deutsche Welle, because he had studied journalism although he never got a degree. He also worked for Reuters, the originally-German news syndicate. And now he's back in Coos Bay. Riding a bicycle with a sideboard.

"I've got something for you," he says. "When I lived in Cologne I found this stack of old stuff in my landlady's basement. She didn't care about it, so I took it with me. And this is one piece I still have, but nobody is interested."

The piece he brought is a handbill measuring a mere 5 ½ by 8 ½", kept in a small frame. In old-document-expert-jargon, the paper has "foxed", or browned with age. We translate it together,

> ### 6 Million Unemployed
> **That is the result of 14 years of black/red parliamentary arts!**
> **Where are the much-praised achievements of the "glorious" revolution?**
> **Bitter plight and profound misery reign today in Germany!**
>
> ### The People are Starving!
> **A tired, dull despair has seized the great masses.**
>
> ### How much longer?
> **Millions have lost faith and are disillusioned. For years they have longed for work and bread.**
> **In vain!**
>
> ### Put an end to it, you unemployed!
> **Get rid of the system of mass-misery!**
>
> # Elect Adolf Hitler!

and I notice his German is not bad at all, certainly not for an American. "Six million unemployed …"

"The black/red was a shortcut to describe a parliamentary coalition," I explain, ever the teacher. "I'm guessing that it was a temporary combination of the Catholic Center Party and the Socialists. Black for the Catholics, red for the Social Democrat Party. In Germany of the early 1930s."

"Right," he says.

"And all this stuff, six million unemployed, and all – that was true. Trouble is, the facts were true, but the solution was a disaster. And it's an old, really old political gimmick. Today still, every two-bit politician around here that's looking for votes promises to 'create jobs'. It's the same racket. They're all up to no good. Just look at this headline about our local county commissioners' election. County-commissioners can't create jobs. Government can't create jobs. The only helpful thing it can do is get out of the way, and remove obstacles."

"Ah yes," he says and then he quotes: *"Mit der Dummheit kämpfen Götter selbst vergebens* – Schiller said that." I can only agree: Against stupidity the gods themselves struggle in vain.

I give Jerry something for his little pamphlet, which I will add to my collection of political documents. But my gratuitous sermon about the lure of the 'job- creation' scam was based on decades of studies. Studies of reality.

Hitler's seizure of power in 1933 was followed by much breathless press on how he singlehandedly turned the German economy from depression into boom, giving everybody a job. In reality he was lucky enough to have an economy that was beginning to recover. Still, making three-

Can they create jobs?
Position 3 hopefuls disagree on ways to solicit business

quarters ofGermany's 6 million unemployed vanish within a few years looked impressive. But much of that was achieved by make-work programs that didn't benefit the German consumer. Re-armament was one. It provided paychecks, but guns and bombs did not improve the life of the average German. Another one was Germany's Autobahn-system. The first Autobahn-segment had been promoted by Konrad Adenauer, the then-mayor of Cologne who wanted a better road between his city and Bonn. That made sense, because that part of Germany is very densely populated.

SPEED ALONG GERMAN REICHSAUTOBAHNEN

Adenauer dedicated it 1932. In 1933 Hitler came to power, promptly claiming the program as his own *Arbeitsbeschaffungsmassnahme* (job-creation-program) one of those long, barky German words that delight Americans. During the Nazi-era, Autobahn-construction employed some 125,000 people, maybe twice that many if you include the suppliers' personnel. Clearly the siren-song of JOBS *über alles* dominated the project, and its usefulness was dubious. Pick-and-shovel substituted for heavy equipment, working conditions were poor and pay was low. And the Autobahns' strategic value (their alleged ability to move military forces quickly from one end of the country to another) never materialized. All during Hitler's reign the scattered segments were never joined into one Autobahn network, and the German army's tracked vehicles and heavy trucks would have torn them up anyway, so they were hauled by railroad. The Autobahns' economic value did not materialize until the post-war era, when former Nazi concentration camp inmate Konrad Adenauer became West-German Chancellor.

The Hitler economy was known as the *Zwangswirtschaft*, which literally translates as the forcible economy, or "command-economy." Workers were recruited – or pressed into service – for many unproductive purposes besides making guns and bombs and Autobahns. And they were told by ever-growing Nazi-bureaucracies which trades to enter and which trades to leave. Those were not the only ways in which the Nazi economy resembled the Soviet system. The régime controlled prices as well as wages; to facilitate the latter the Nazis had outlawed labor unions. It's true enough that all private enterprises were never taken over by the Nazi state as they had been by the communists in Russia, but government meddling was so extensive that there was no practical difference. Enterprises were told what to produce and how much, and their raw materials were rationed. Prices and allowable profit margins were set by the state, dividends sharply limited, and the larger industries were required to invest their retained profits in government bonds that were never repaid.

And what did all this achieve for the German consumer who – in the American view of things – should have been their beneficiary? A set of economically foolish policies – the command-economy, armaments production, and the régime's Autarky-policy (its effort to achieve economic self-sufficiency for Germany) yielded pathetic benefits.

Clothing, for instance, was expensive and of poor quality. Much of it was being made of *Zellwolle*, "cell wool," or rayon, which was very poor protection against the frigid German winters. Textiles were in such short supply that some authorities prohibited burying the dead in real clothes, which some people couldn't afford to do, anyway. [1] Gary recalls how upset he was when his grandma died: "How can Oma go to heaven in a paper dress?" Food was so expensive that the average German spent 45% of his income on it. (The comparable figure for Great Britain at the time was 41%, for the United States 24%; today it's less than 10%.) Germany didn't have enough arable land to feed its population but it tried anyway, thus driving up domestic food prices. The autarky policy also limited imports of feed for livestock, thus reducing both quantity and quality of meat and dairy products. When Göring announced that guns would come before butter, he wasn't kidding. Many of the German boys who invaded the Netherlands in May 1940 had never tasted it, but Hitler's conquests filled such gaps. After the annexation of Austria in 1938 already, "locust-like swarms of German tourists" had mobbed Austrian coffee-houses and bakeries to wolf down whipped-cream pastries. [2] Next, after the Blitzkrieg in the west, the occupied countries made up for the German economy's

---

[1] Richard Grunberger: *The 12-Year Reich – A social History of Nazi German 1933-1945*. New York: Holt, Rinehart and Winston, 1971, p. 211.
[2] Grunberger, p. 207

inefficiency by supplying vast quantities of other luxuries: Norwegian furs, Dutch butter and cheese, Belgian coffee, French silks. For the occupiers "most of the continent rapidly became a buyers' market in which the power of the purse spoke out of the mouth of a gun. After the fall of France so much perfume found its way into Berlin that the German capital 'smelt like a gigantic hairdresser's'." [1]

When an economy is forced into a straitjacket, people will try to get around the rules, not necessarily out of greed,

A Saturday Evening Post cover from August 1940, when the U.S. economy was still officially in a Depression. The designers of the German Zwangswirtschaft had neither the intention nor the imagination to create an economy that served the consumer.

as those who condemn black markets always charge, but for sheer survival. During the Nazi peacetime years of the 1930s already, German butchers, bakers and grocers surreptitiously started charging higher prices than the régime allowed. Or if they feared to do so they would offer their customers package deals: you can buy this item, which is price-controlled and unprofitable for me, as long as you buy this other one which is uncontrolled. It was a classic example of how, even under price controls, inflation develops when government pumps too much money into an economy in which consumer goods production is not increasing. Because price controls usually lead to shortages, as they did in the Nazi economy, the next step was rationing. It was imposed by 1937/1938, well before war broke out in September 1939. But the régime feared consumer discontent, so throughout the war, even when Germany was clearly losing, the Nazis kept stripping the occupied countries of their resources. "Late 1944 saw a vast upswing in German

---

[1] Grunberger, p. 31.

19 October 1944: *"Are these animals being protected from war violence?"* asks the caption added after the war to this photo of German troops driving a herd of cows through a town in the southern Netherlands.

meat consumption because in its retreat the Wehrmacht drove large herds of cattle back into the Reich for slaughter, and thus left countries like Holland in the grip of famine."

Hitler and Stalin had many, many things in common, and the perennial leftist propaganda that they were at opposite ends of the political spectrum grossly contradicts the facts on the ground. Each dictator ran his country with a one-party system, a vast, authoritarian bureaucracy, secret police, and terror. Each one had mandatory youth organizations, constant political rallies, government-controlled media, and slave-labor camps. And they both believed that economic progress could be achieved by a command-economy, which included forcible industrialization that made no economic sense and paid no heed to the consumer. But both did it 'for the People'.

Even more ruinous for the people, each dictator also believed that economic progress could be made by robbery. To Stalin, whose economy was woefully unproductive despite the presence of vast natural resources, that meant confiscation from his own people. He sent out his armies to seize the harvests of obstinate farmers, millions of whom starved. Another aspect of that method was the stripping by Russian troops of everything stealable in the German territories they overran in 1945. Even while the assault was still in progress, a solid line of trucks, loaded with every imaginable kind of loot of the Russian soldiers, was driving back to Russia. The Russian government was no different, dismantling entire German industries to take them home.

Similarly, Hitler thought economic progress required stealing Stalin's farm land and oil, since Germany didn't have enough of either to be self-sufficient in food and fuel. And we all know how that worked out.

For three years after the war, Germany was in terrible economic shape. All the basics were in short supply, money was worthless, and the *Zwangswirtschaft* was being continued by the occupation authorities: the military mind always favors control. But in the summer of 1948 the economist Ludwig Erhard, an adviser to the Americans, announced currency reform, which meant the introduction of the new Deutsche Mark. Without American approval, Erhard also abolished price controls and dramatically lowered income taxes.

The immediate effects were breathtaking. A U.S. economist with the occupation forces wrote that the "spirit of the country changed overnight. The gray, hungry, dead-looking figures wandering about the streets in their everlasting search for food came to life." On Monday, June 21, the day after the announcement of the new Deutsche Mark, shop windows filled with goods as the shopkeepers realized that their money would now have value. Almost overnight the barter economy vanished. Millions of people who – in a repeat of wartime practices in the occupied countries – had roamed the countryside to swap goods for food were back doing real work. They could see that a living could now be made, and with good old-fashioned German vigor they pursued it.

During the second half of that year, Germany's industrial output rose by more than 50 percent. By 1958, ten years later, production per capita had tripled. This became known as the German *Wirtschaftswunder* – the economic miracle. Erhard himself was not surprised. As a free-market economist he was well aware of the effects that ending inflation, removing price controls, and slashing high tax rates could have on productivity. Now the German people's formidable energy was producing real progress for the common man, not conquest, destruction and ultimately a disastrous defeat.

Not Dying – Living for the Fatherland!
Post-war election poster for the German Socialist Party

THE FÜHRER PRINCIPLE

"All we need is the right man," sighed my bar customer, in a semi-confident wrap-up of his side of the conversation. "The right man, who has the connections and who knows how to bring in new businesses !" His rigid posture while getting up to leave seemed to put an **A-men!** behind the idea that 'the right man' would pull Coos Bay out if its economic doldrums. Not until he walked out did he produce a semblance of reflection: "I don't know why they haven't found him yet. He has to be out there." And then he was gone.

During our chat I had objected that Coos Bay had been down that road before, hiring one Right Man after another Right Man, always at greater cost than his predecessor. And none of those costly Right Men, though always welvomed with great expectations, had brought in the hoped-for new industries that would bring new paychecks and prosperity. But as I talked his eyes glazed over, in a sort of trance that seemed to include his ears. And after all, what do I know? I've only written a book on the subject of government-directed economic development. And that book, "The JOB Messiahs," covering forty disastrous years of local history, was over twenty years in the making.

My customer is not a stupid man, but not many years have passed since he came here after a successful business career in California, a state whose economy seems to convince its businessmen that they are the cleverest in the world. During my years in Coos Bay I've met several. Since they had done well in the Golden State, they decided to come up to Coos Bay to show the aborigines how it was done. What they forgot was not just that a rising tide lifts all boats, but hopes and dreams go out with the tide as well. Building a subdivision has an excellent chance of paying off if done in an environment of rising property values – like California. But they thought they'd been so smart. And when such people come here and their new ventures don't prosper very fast, what do they fall back on? They want to hire the Right Man. They demand an economic savior, someone who will bring them prosperity like Hitler promised to bring the Germans, and did – well, sort of.

I've called such worldly saviors JOB Messiahs; hence the title of my book. In hindsight, I suppose I could have picked better ones. 'Waiting for Superman' came to mind, as did 'Boondoggle Bay'. And although suggesting that Coos Bay has a Nazi mentality could get me run out of town, 'The Führer Principle' could have fit too. That would be a semi-translation of the German term Das Führerprinzip. In English that could have been *'The Leader (or the Guide) Principle'*. But somehow that doesn't seem to have much of a punch.

Back in the Hitler days, *Das Führerprinzip* gave tyranny a thoughtful gloss of respectability, thereby making living in a dictatorship palatable to some Germans. According to *Das Führerprinzip*, the Führer's word and the Führer's wish were above all written law, so regardless of what that law said, all government officials were obligated to work toward realizing the Führer's grand plans, because he was the closest thing to divine wisdom in all Germany. Not surprisingly, Wikipedia compares *Das Führerprinzip* to military organizations, since "unquestioning obedience to a superior supposedly produced order and prosperity . . ."

All through that bar conversation I had felt an odd sensation of re-living history, but not just the history of 1930s Germany. I recalled a heated meeting almost forty years ago, when a band of noisy 'economic development' activists was pushing the then-stodgy Port of Coos Bay to hire its first Great Man to direct our economic future. Now, the local government agency known as 'The Port of Coos Bay' had never been a working port. Instead, its main job had been to lobby the federal government from time to time to dredge and deepen it, due to the lack of local funds to cope with the increasing draft of ocean vessels arriving to load lumber products. The Port had also managed some small-boat docks near the harbor entrance, where the fishermen could tie up. That was all that the port management had ever done. It ran no shipping docks or railroads or towboats or trucks or pilot services. All those things were provided by private enterprise, and it was private enterprise that called for a deeper harbor so it could ship more lumber, logs, plywood and wood chips. Without those things there was no reason for the harbor to exist.

But to poorly informed people it seemed that the Port possessed magical powers. Back in the 1970s and 1980s the Coos Bay harbor was still full of ships and log rafts, and the highway choked with trucks, while the railroad ran day and night. Many people thought that the Port was behind all those activities, so it must possess the secret to our future prosperity. That is why during that heated public meeting in 1974, a noisy gang of local activists insisted that the Port must hire a man who 'knows all the angles.' Even more worrisome, they wanted a bellicose character who would 'declare war on the Port of Portland.' Although Portland is by no means one of the nation's busiest ports, Coos Bay has always seen it as its nemesis.

The previous Port manager, whose title 'Harbor Master' truthfully conveyed that he knew something about shipping, was a retired Coast Guard officer by the name of Ernie Payne. Coos Bay, Payne kept pointing out, was simply too isolated to ever attract big new industries except for lumber, its main asset. Payne was right, and the activists who wanted to replace him with a Great Man who would go and recruit new industries and find new cargo for the ships were wrong. The ships calling at Coos Bay always arrived empty. To the activists that was a crazy situation that cried out for change: Coos Bay must become an importing harbor. But that made no sense because Coos Bay was too far off the beaten track and had no suitable inland connections. Wherever in this world major harbors have developed, they always did so thanks to good connections that could rapidly and cheaply forward the cargo brought into port to other destinations. Given the ancient principle that water is by far the cheapest mode of transportation, ocean harbors at the mouths of navigable rivers had that advantage. This is one big reason why northwestern Europe developed such a thriving economy. Besides having a large number of navigable rivers, the flat northern European coastal plain allowed connecting canals to be dug without major problems. It also allowed easy construction of railroads, the next cheapest transportation mode after ships. Hence Europe has the world's largest concentration of economical transportation modes. America's heartland has a similar advantage in the Mississippi-Missouri river system, but when it comes to navigable rivers the American west coast is seriously handicapped, more or less as Mediterranean countries are. From Spain to Turkey and beyond, there are almost no usable natural waterways, and the coasts are too mountainous to create them – just like here.

Making things worse is that Coos Bay's only inland connection is U.S. 101, the coastal highway, which runs north-south, not east-west. The main local waterway, Coos River, is only a few miles long and very shallow, which is why no sizable ships have ever ventured into it. And the rugged coast range mountains preclude building an eastbound highway, not to mention canals and efficient railroads.

But the 'economic development' crowd was oblivious to all that. Ernie Payne was retiring in 1974, and hopefully his opinions with him, so the Port of Coos Bay caved and hired a brash character by the name of Steve Felkins to take Payne's place with the title of Port Manager, at twice his salary.

It's an odd fact of public administration that the salaries promised to supposed miracle workers are never commensurate with the new man's qualifications, but with the hopes of his new employers – which usually turn out to have been vain. That the Port had bought a pig in a poke soon became clear as Felkins turned out to be more of a preacher than an economic genius. To him, 'economic development' was not a matter of dollars and cents but a leap of faith, so he hit the revival circuit, haranguing Chambers of Commerce and Rotary Clubs and similar hubs of conventional credulity. His basic approach was to exhort them to close their eyes, take a deep breath and throw lots of money – usually taxpayers' money – at risky business ventures, usually proposed by itinerant stock swindlers and other shifty promoters. And that's how the Port of Coos Bay ended up with a herd of expensive boondoggles including a ferry boat, fish plants, a dock, a barge slip, an ancient railroad and more, all idle and useless, and acquired with failed loans and government grants. On the heels of those flops Port Manager Felkins was advocating that the local airport must be expanded AT ALL COST. For what purpose? Well . . . "even if nobody landed at the damn airport, it would demonstrate that we are willing to work together for something."

If some readers consider that a reasonable statement, they favor the religious-revival-method of economic development.

Government can do a great deal to foster business development, but mainly by improving infrastructure (like deepening a harbor) and by clearing obstacles such as burdensome regulations and confiscatory taxes. Beyond that, business investments should not be made with public dollars, but private. That is not because private investors are exceptionally clever; some are as dumb as a doorpost. But government officials are even dumber, and/or more careless, because they are not spending their own money.

If government creates the right conditions, entrepreneurs will spot profit-making opportunities and create 'development.' And why haven't more entrepreneurs done so? One reason, already mentioned, is that Coos Bay is unsuitable for the kinds of industrial projects favored by the local establishment. Another is that our 'economic development' experts are too myopic to see the real economic strengths of this beautiful part of the Oregon coast. Yet another reason consists of the obstacles they have erected, obstacles intended to preserve the *development dignitaries'* jobs while discouraging people from settling or investing here. That is why entrepreneurs who could have done Coos Bay a world of good have gone to other coastal towns instead. While we lost population, all those towns saw healthy growth.

How did stupidity and ignorance gain such lasting power? I have to conclude that our leaders never looked closely at the Right Men they hired. Once, back in the 'eighties one of the Port's managers was asked what would happen if the Port ceased to exist. His reply: ". . . there would be no agency to supply jobs." And nobody laughed.

Neither did Coos Bay's 'leaders' chuckle at the nonsense put out by the most disastrous Port Manager ever, an Irish con man from Chicago by the name of Frank Martin who made it on my book's cover. All through his tenure, from 1983 to 1988, the pillars of our community never wavered in their support of this corrupt blowhard, bully and swindler who verbalized his understanding of his own job as follows:

"Public agencies should be innovators, creators and financiers for the private sector, and should then move on to something else."

So it would seem that in this blowhard's world, all promising new products, from the Model-T to Microsoft Windows, were invented by Port Managers and other publicly-paid Right Men. Those Right Men then gave money to people like Henry Ford and Bill Gates and Steven Jobs, so they could market the Right Men's brain children, making undeserved gazillions for themselves.

Totalitarianism will always have advocates, not only among the unemployed in a depressed town but also in academe and in the press. It's well known that the most fervent supporters of the Nazi program included German university chancellors who eagerly participated in the infamous book burnings. Just as eagerly today, American university faculties embrace totalitarianism as long as it pushes leftist causes. For many years, when newspapers were still influential, Coos Bay's daily paper was run by a man whose economic philosophy was just as despotic. His final solution consisted of forcibly 'relocating urban industry, business and populations' from inland areas to Coos Bay. This has not been tried since the Soviet Union fell apart – for good reasons.

Here is a piece from that paper by a reporter who later on was appointed Public Relations flack by the very Coos Bay Port Manager she described. In 2005 Manager Jeff Bishop promoted an LNG (Liquefied Natural Gas) import terminal (since then, like so many grand industrial plans for Coos Bay, made unviable by market forces):

> "Bishop's presence is hard to miss. He's a tall man with a big handshake.
> As Thursday night wore on, his smooth forehead was flushed. Somewhat out of character, he didn't quote the words of any great thinkers. . . . . No one said a word. . . . "It's a large moment," Port Commissioner Caddy McKeown said letting out a big breath. "I thank you for the effort that's come forth here. It's a long time coming."
> And then there was a long silence. . . ."
> Longshoremen who had come to the meeting to complain about a lack of jobs "were shocked and humbled. And very pleased. 'Wow,' one ILWU delegate whispered . . . after the meeting. . . . (Bishop) walked out into the dark, down the steps of City Hall, seeming confident he has begun to push down the barriers that have long prevented the port from prospering.
> "That's what they hired me to do," Bishop said. Then he headed off alone, down toward the port's offices overlooking Coos Bay."

Great Men are not only expensive, but they have pernicious effects on the people's money, on their liberties, and on openness in government. This is because of the old error that the goal sanctifies the means. The history of 'economic development' in Coos Bay includes many, many episodes of Great Men intimidating critics, conducting business in secret, and committing financial and electoral fraud.

The worship of (and the wish for) Great Men must be part of human nature. John Dalberg-Acton, also known as Lord Acton (1834-1902), was the historian who formulated the famous quote "Power tends to corrupt, and absolute power corrupts absolutely." Not many people know that Lord Acton, a devout Catholic, wrote this in a letter criticizing the assumption of infallibility which the Catholic Church of the time wanted to give the Pope – and did. Acton explained: "Great men are almost always bad men."

Regardless of Acton's warnings, people in Coos Bay keep looking for Great Men, which places them in the awkward position of advocating fascism, and with corresponding results.

In World War II the Germans had invaded Holland for reasons obvious to themselves, but not so much to the Dutch, and for many years after the war many Dutchmen had a lingering resentment against their eastern neighbors. What didn't help much was that in the 1950s, as a result of their near-miraculous post-war economic recovery, the Germans started new invasions of the Low Countries, mostly on weekends and holidays, on inadequate highways choked with miles-long lines of Volkswagens, BMWs and Mercedeses. The usual objective of those peacetime incursions was some Dutch beach where the new occupants would dig foxholes to protect themselves, this time from North Sea breezes instead of an allied invasion fleet. While it's neither true nor fair to say that those Germans behaved like the conquerors of World War II, it was reported that a few, upon returning to their foxhole the next day and finding it occupied by another family, sternly demanded it be surrendered on the grounds of adverse possession.

> "It is a great advantage to a president, and a major source of safety to the country, for him to know that he is not a great man."
>
> Calvin Coolidge, *after choosing not to run for another term as president.*

But one day a group of Germans was strolling along the canals of Amsterdam when they were approached by an enterprising university student. During the tourist season many Dutch students, all of whom spoke several languages, made some money by acting as tour guides. Now, as I already mentioned the German word *Führer* means 'leader' but also 'guide.' So this eager-beaver student walks up to the wandering Germans, asking: *"Brauchen Sie einen Führer?"* Do you need a guide?

"Nah," one of the older Germans said. "A *Führer*? We already tried that. Didn't work out *so gut*."

April 2011

THE REST OF TWO STORIES

These pictures show my mother enjoying the springtime sun in front of her cottage. She looks happy, one reason being that in her later years the long, dark, northern European winters depressed her. We got her a therapeutic UV light once, but she was too impatient to set it up every day. But here she sits, blinking at the reborn sun, likely looking forward to the riders on the bike path passing by.

But that was to be her last spring. That summer the children moved her into a care home, where she died in September, three months shy of 96. I did not really want to come all that way just to attend the funeral, but I didn't need to say so because my brother had discovered that the undertakers had set up a camera for remote viewing by computer. That worked fine, although it occurred to me that I could have improved the mood at the service. I've grown to value American funerals, where anyone can get up and say something good, something remarkable, even something funny, about the departed. It encourages those left behind to remember his or her life in a positive way, and my mother deserved that.

But unlike a lot of other American customs, like Halloween and McDonald's, joyful funerals don't seem to have made it across the Atlantic. The service we watched was dour. Three of the grandchildren did relate a few things about Oma, but that was about it. It was clear that to the assembly, being dutiful children meant going through the motions in a downhearted way because that's what dutiful children are supposed to do. And it's not impossible that if I had tried to add some levity, my siblings would have been indignant.

As I write this, my mother's cottage has been standing empty for a couple of years. Just like around here, the Dutch housing market is still depressed, and especially so in that corner of the country, which does not have a growing population. It's a shame; the place would make a great home for a retired couple or for an artist. It would be less suitable for a family with children, although the Dutch are not as demanding about bathrooms and privacy as Americans are. And it's in a lovely spot, in farming country with a creek in the back, and through the front window a view of the local windmill, which is still operational.

And on a cold February day in 2013 Chester Kauffman, that gentle warrior who didn't expect to survive World War II, was buried with military honors in the veterans' section of the Sunset cemetery south of Coos Bay, with an honor guard and taps and the flag presented to his daughters. Chester got to be 89, but I doubt he's bragging about it to his already-departed siblings who were only 88. Chester was not a braggart. During our visits he never even mentioned his war injuries.

Since last summer Chester, already gaunt, had been losing weight. After a minor operation it was found that he'd had a defective heart valve all his life, and it was no longer up to the job. That's why the last three times I saw him he used an oxygen tank, something he never would have bothered with at 12,000 feet in a non-pressurized plane, way back when. But such is life. Even so, during every one of our last visits he kept up a lively conversation during which I learned more about his post-war life as a farmer. A born tinkerer, he derived a lot of pleasure from building and modifying farm equipment, and as a farmer he was well-respected in the Fresno area of central California. After his long-suffering wife died in 1992 a neighboring farmer gave him a plane ticket to Australia, where his sister and her husband had started a huge produce farm. He showed me pictures of that venture, which enabled him to build more farm equipment. A new tradition had developed: one year he would come to Australia to help out; the next year his sister and her family would come over for a visit, and so on.

Chester's military service helped pull off the greatest victory in human history, and I don't doubt for a second that humanity would have been very much worse off without it. But it's high time we asked ourselves: where would we be without farmers like Chester, without their dogged resolve, without their skill and their incredible productivity? Without them 98% of us would barely make it, as subsistence peasants.

My final visit with Chester was just a few days before he passed away. He'd been moved to a small, home-like nursing facility, he had lost more weight, and his weakness was now affecting his speech. It was hard to understand him, except for one thing:

"I'm waiting," he said.

I thought of saying: "Chester, they're waiting for YOU." But I didn't, even though he'd been a Christian all his life, trusting the Lord, grateful for His favors, expecting to see Him. I suppose I should have said it. What do you say to a dying man? We held hands.

I have visited his grave, and in June, 5 months after his funeral, I made a pilgrimage of sorts. The Collings Foundation, a 'transportation museum,' brought three of its World War II planes to our local airport, including a B-17. It was a B-17g, the same model Chester flew, and I took a half-hour flight in it. During take-off and landing the ten of us had to sit on the floor, but I didn't mind; I sat right behind the cockpit, propped against the slightly raised round platform where the top gunner would have stood – where Chester would have stood.

The B-17 was a large plane for its time, but inside it's very cramped. Americans have gotten so big, I don't see how many of today's generation could have gotten around in that bomber. The catwalk that runs through the middle of the bomb bay is only 8 or 10 inches wide; and while standing there the crew had to activate the bombs, and in case of trouble manually drop them, with the doors wide open underneath.

I knew I was flying, but all that time I was on hallowed ground.

And in October 2019, the same B-17 developed engine trouble and crashed on takeoff in Connecticut. The plane was totally destroyed and Mac McCauley, who had piloted my flight, lost his life with 6 others.

LILLI KIRSCHBAUM'S WAR

This afternoon I'm talking to Lilli Clausen at the Clausens' oyster farm on Haynes Inlet, a northern branch of Coos Bay. Lilli's ancestors, by the name of Kirschbaum (on her dad's side) and Meisel (her mom's), were among numerous German farm-families who during the 19th century had migrated into a part of eastern Europe called Volhynia, or Wolhynien in German, and that's where Lilli was born, in 1936. Back then Volhynia was part of Poland, but toway it's part of Ukraine.

That she didn't stay there long was due to the politics of those days. The infamous deal between Hitler and Stalin that had facilitated Hitler's invasion of Poland, in September 1939, required the Volhynian Germans to abandon their homesteads and leave. But as compensation Hitler's government would give them farms in recently-conquered western Poland, now annexed to the German *Reich*.

Unfortunately, Adolf's arrangement had built-in problems. First, the reason why the Nazis were able to instantly provide the Volhynians with replacement-farms was legally dubious: they had simply kicked out their Polish owners, without compensation. True, the new German owners had been forced to leave their own farms, and without compensation, so they were hardly in a position to object. Still, in order for their ownership to become legally unchallengeable the Nazi eagle would have to spread its protective wings over it for a long time. That this was not going to happen became clear five years later when, threatened by vengeful, unstoppable Russian armies, the former Volhynians had to abandon their new farms and flee west as part of a tsunami of "ethnic" German refugees from all over eastern Europe, 12 million in all. Homeless and destitute, they would land in ravaged post-war Germany as so-called DPs, or Displaced Persons. It's estimated that during that mass-migration, much of it during the bitter winter of 1944/45, some ten percent of the DPs died, or well over a million.

In its doomed campaign to achieve independence in food production, Nazi Germany not only invaded other countries to take their land but also glorified its farmers in a near-religious way. This poster advertises the fifth annual farmers' meeting in the ancient town of Goslar, using the standard slogan: BLUT UND BODEN – Blood and soil.

Through the ages, countries in that part of the world have risen, grown, shrunk, grown again, moved, disappeared, and re-appeared to start all over. It can be bewildering, but to make sense of Lilli's story we need to digress briefly into those changing borders, and the reasons behind them. To avoid turning this into a lengthy lecture, I'll do my best to limit it to Poland, Germany, Austria, Russia, and Ukraine.

For centuries Volhynia had been part of the Polish Empire which once controlled huge territories including Lithuania on the Baltic, Belarus (White Russia) to the east, and the Ukraine in the south. Like Germany later on, Poland was quite capable of winning wars, but not against several enemies at once. As a result it vanished in the late 18th century when three powers, Prussia, Austria and Russia, ganged up on it, defeated it, and divided Poland's lands among them. By far the largest part, including Volhynia, went to Russia, which kept it for well over a century until losing it to Germany during World War I.

Next, Germany's defeat on the western front in World War I enabled the victorious allies to re-draw the map of Europe, a disastrous feat of cartography since it set a lot of the fuses that ignited World War II, two decades later. First, a large number of unviable states were created. Some were internally incompatible – think of Yugoslavia and Czechoslovakia, neither one of which exists today – and almost all were far too small to resist a re-armed, aggressive Germany. One of the newly-created states was Poland, which the allies had cobbled together by joining pieces chopped off several other states including Germany. Resurrected Poland also included Volhynia which had been Polish once, now over a century ago. So when Lilli was born in Volhynia in 1936 that made her a Polish citizen, but only for a few years. After World War II Volhynia became part of the USSR, and since that evil empire's dissolution in 1991 it's been part of the Ukraine.

For close to a millennium a migration had been happening that in time and scope went far beyond the 19th century German farmers' trek to Volhynia. Starting back in the 12th century, and perhaps earlier, Germans (and Dutch and Flemish people) had migrated to eastern Europe in search of land and/or a better life, and those movements had continued. Some had a military nature, but many of the migrants were traders, religious refugees and land-hungry farmers. In many ways they were like the land-hungry settlers moving onto America's Great Plains during the 19th century, but they moved more slowly, and they seem to have been easier on the local Indians. Much like the 19th century U.S. Congress too, rulers like the Russian Czars had actively encouraged the Germanic pioneers to come and farm in their vast and fertile, but underexploited territories. Since the migrants were more knowledgeable and ambitious than the local peasants, the Czars saw their arrival as a way to improve the Russian economy, and they promised them special rights including freedom of religion, exemption from military service and taxes, and the right to maintain their German language and customs. By the onset of World War I there were German-speaking settlements all over central and eastern Europe. Besides Volhynian Germans there were Baltic Germans and Volga Germans and Black Sea Germans, not to mention Germans in Hungary, Romania and the Balkans.

Outside today's backsliding Middle East, the idea that a viable state needs all its

"Lord, we cleared this land. We plowed it, sowed it, and harvested it. We cooked the harvest. It wouldn't be here and we wouldn't be eating it if we hadn't done it all ourselves. We worked dog-bone hard for every crumb and morsel, but we thank you Lord just the same for the food we are about to eat, Amen."

Jimmy Stewart as farmer Charlie Anderson in "Shenandoah".

citizens to confess the same religion seems absurd even though a few centuries ago politicians believed it, and fought bloody wars to enforce it. On the other hand, in our day it is commonly believed that everyone inside a state should speak the same language. But in much of the past the language factor was not given much attention in politics, and there are plenty of examples of empires that combined very different native tongues. For centuries the Austro-Hungarian Empire was a functioning, multi-lingual political system. Switzerland still is. In North America during much of the 19th and part of the 20th century you could find rural communities where all sorts of languages other than English were spoken, written and taught, and this was true of parts of major American cities as well. But not many residents of such communities would have considered themselves loyal to their foreign country of origin: the idea that language determines loyalty would have seemed odd. With exceptions that confirm the rule, for a long time this was true of the Germanic farmers living outside their native lands. They saw themselves as farmers first, citizens of their host countries second, and not necessarily bound to do the bidding of the potentate who ruled their German land of origin – if they even knew who he was or had seen his realm. Nor would they have felt more fondness towards the Prussian government in Berlin than to any of the thirty-odd petty rulers of the other German lands. Their loyalties mainly depended on their local ruler's attitude, as it influenced their freedom to make a living and to practice their religion. And for many of the migrants, especially the Mennonites, religion was supremely important because in their German lands of origin they had suffered oppression because of it. Thanks to some east-European rulers' promises of toleration they were loyal to them. And the arrangement worked not only for German-speaking settlements. The same general area might contain villages where everyone spoke Polish or Czech or Yiddish. The arrangement worked, and the homogenizing influence of intrusive, centralized government had not yet reached today's strength.

But this could not last, due to the ideas of 19th century philosophers which ambitious 20th century politicians couldn't wait to put into practice. One of those ideas was the worship of an all-powerful state. Another was nationalism which, by conflating language with nationhood, assumed that the scattered German-speaking communities in the east nurtured a profound loyalty to the newly-united German nation, whose strength was growing fast. It was a situation ripe for exploitation by politicians who dreamed of a future when all German speakers abroad could be called upon to do Germany's bidding. But as history shows, one dictator's dream can become a lot of regular folks' nightmare. Aware of Germany's potential to become a major power, eastern European rulers needed little encouragement to start distrusting their German 'colonies' as potential fifth columns for the Kaiser's ambitions. During World War I already, German colonists living in Russian lands were being banished to faraway parts of the Russian empire, while others fled for their lives to Kaiser Wilhelm's *Reich*. And during World War II, thanks to the Nazis, things got far worse yet.

When Hitler's régime gained power in 1933, it described the centuries-long settlement process of the dispersed Germanic colonists as *die Ostsiedlung*, 'the settlement of the east', a term that hinted at the long-planned creation of a far-flung German empire even if the original migrants nurtured no such plans. And it wasn't until 1938 when the Nazi-concocted term *Volksdeutsche* or "people-Germans" popped up, to describe the settlers and their descendants. This served to distinguish them from *Reichsdeutsche*, or Germans living inside the German *Reich*. Clearly both terms, *Volks-* and *Reichsdeutsche*, assumed loyalty to German state interests. Combined with the Nazi-invented slogan *Heim ins Reich* (Homecoming to the Reich) all these terms served Nazi expansionism well. By spreading the questionable idea that people who speak the same language should all live in the same country, the Nazis aimed to annex all foreign lands that contained substantial numbers of *Volksdeutsche*. Where this was not possible, they sought to 'repatriate' the *Volksdeutsche* to newly German-controlled lands, where they could serve the state by developing and/or Germanizing them.

Even if many of the assumptions behind those policies were questionable, they generated awareness and some enthusiasm abroad, with Hitler's constant harangues about the oppression of the *Volksdeutsche* by their host countries resonating far and wide. And of course, the Nazis' consciousness-raising campaign was bound to make distrustful local rulers even more distrustful, enough to make them want to get rid of their Germanic guests.

When, after Russia's seizure of Volhynia from Poland in the late 18th century, German farmers started settling on Volhynian land, much of it was still covered with primeval forest. After a slow start, the migration had accelerated so by 1900 some 200,000 ethnic Germans were living and farming in Volhynia. Many were Lutherans, and many others were Mennonites who besides good farmland valued their religious freedom very highly. Alas, even as their numbers and their fortunes grew, it became clear that they had bet on the wrong horse, because they started losing their privileges. The Mennonites, who have a strong pacifist tradition, particularly objected to being drafted into the Russian army, and by 1870 groups of Volhynian Germans started leaving for greener pastures. Today sizable colonies are found in widely scattered parts of the world. When I lived in Mexico in 1970, the only decent cheese you could buy there was *Queso de Chihuahua*, which was made by German

Queso Chihuahua, also called "Menonita"

Mennonite farmers who in 1921 had migrated to that Mexican state from Manitoba and Saskatchewan. Once again they had left for religious reasons, since those Canadian provinces had made attendance in secular public schools mandatory for Mennonite children.

I mentioned that after World War I Poland had been re-created by combining pieces carved off other countries including Germany and Russia. The losses of such lands were greatly irritating to dictators like Hitler and Stalin, regardless of whether at some earlier time their own predecessors might have stolen them in the first place. Adding fuel to the fire, during the interwar years central Europe was brimming with irritable dictators. By the time Hitler had been made Germany's Führer, most countries in that part of the world seemed to have put a so-called strong man in charge. None was opposed to grabbing another one's lands when given a chance, and that included Poland's dictator too.

But dictators come in various grades, from tolerable to horrible. In August of 1939, when resurrected Poland was barely twenty years old, dictator Hitler was determined to wipe it off the map again. Right before attacking Poland, he signed a "non-aggression pact" with dictator Josef Stalin of the Soviet Union. Despite its peaceful-sounding title, that deal between two tyrants was the spark that would set off World War II because it cleared the way for Hitler's attack, which in turn caused England and France, which had promised to defend Poland, to declare war on Germany. But the pact had removed Hitler's biggest worry, Russia, which had a traditional interest in Poland, as an obstacle to his

A column of Polish residents of the Warthegau, being escorted to evacuation trains by German troops. As part of the Nazi ethnic cleansing following the 1939 invasion and defeat of Poland, they were being expelled to areas further east.

conquest. Stalin agreed not to interfere with the German attack, because Hitler promised him a bribe. The Nazis would strike the first blow by invading and occupying Poland's western half. Next the Russians would invade and take the eastern half for themselves, along with some territories further east where Germany had an interest. But Stalin was a paranoid character who distrusted everybody, foreigners above all. Hence the pact also provided for the resettlement on German-owned soil of the ethnic Germans who had lived on Polish soil but now suddenly found themselves inside Russia. Those included Lilli's family along with all the other Germans living in Volhynia, which was Polish when the Hitler-Stalin pact was signed but would soon – thanks to Stalin's part in the conquest – become part of the USSR. The Volhynian Germans were to be moved to land in former western Poland that was to become part of Germany, and given new farms there.

After Hitler launched his attack on September 1, it took five weeks for the two warlords to defeat and divide Poland. Next, in December 1939 and January 1940 more than 100,000 ethnic Germans left their homes in Volhynia and in Galicia, which was located just south of Volhynia. Most would be resettled in a Polish area recently-annexed to Germany, which the Nazis called the Warthegau or Wartheland. The

November 1939: *Volksdeutsche* from the Baltic republics (Estonia, Latvia, Lithuania), which the August non-aggression pact between Hitler and Stalin had also given Stalin the green light to invade, are being shown their new farm in recently German-conquered Poland.

Warthe (or Warta) was the name of a local river, and the last part, *Gau*, was an old Germanic word revived by the Nazis that in the Middle Ages denoted a province or a county. By 1943/44 the number of ethnic Germans from Soviet-Russian territories re-settled in the Warthegau had risen to 350,000. To make this mass-migration possible the Nazi régime had expelled an equal number of Poles and Jews to a different part of conquered Poland, seizing their lands and homes and businesses to hand them over to the new arrivals, whose own properties had been taken by the Russians and Ukrainians. The exhortation below, taken from a Nazi propaganda poster, is a good illustration of the totalitarian megalomania of that era. People were no more than pawns, to be uprooted and moved all over the map to realize their dictator's fevered dreams:

*Nach dem Feldzug der 18 Tage begann die bisher **großzügigste Umsiedlungsaktion** der Weltgeschichte. Alle Volksgruppen, die Draußen ihre Aufgaben erfüllt haben, rief der Führer zurück in die Heimat ihrer Väter. Sie helfen jetzt mit beim Ausbau und der Fertigung des großdeutschen Reiches. In besonderem Maße werden beim Aufbau des Warthegaues ihre kolonisatorischen Fähigkeiten wirksam werden.*

> After the 18-day campaign [to conquer Poland] started the **largest-scale resettlement operation** in the history of the world. The Führer has re-called to their ancestral land all population groups that have fulfilled their assignments outside. They are now assisting with the enlargement and completion of the Greater German Reich. Their skills as colonists will be especially effective during the development of the Warthegau.

I pull up to the Clausens' building and walk into Lilli's office, to the right of the retail shop. Lilli is at her desk, which overlooks the oyster-processing room; Max, her husband, sits by the door, checking his blood sugar. Max has long had type-1 diabetes. You'd never know it from the pictures of when they were starting out, everyone working like beavers in the oyster flats, but lately its effects have become more serious, and he needs a walker to get around. And Lilli herself has bad knees.

"So, Lilli, you mentioned that your family came from the Ukraine, in 1939. Was that the western Ukraine?"

"Yes," she says. "We lived in a small village in an area called Luzk, after the local city."

"Do you remember the name of the village?"

"O yes, it was Ludwikow." She spells it for me. "And the name of the local parish was Torczyn." She spells that too. "Ludwikow had mostly German people. There were other villages in the area that were all-Polish, or all-Jewish. It was only in the town, in Luzk, where the population was more mixed."

"I know you were little, but do you remember anything

at all from your time in Volhynia?"

"O yes, I remember aunt Hannchen's house, all surrounded by green rye fields. And there were lots of oak trees. And I remember my grandfather's house, with the big *Kachelofen*."

Wherever Germans had to endure cold winters they would build a *Kachelofen* in their homes. Made of stone and cement and covered with tiles, which the Germans call *Kachel*, it held the heat for a long time. You don't see them in Holland much, but the Dutch supplied a lot of the decorative tiles for those stoves. Now the teacher comes out in me:

"It's interesting how words change meaning, Lilli. In Dutch the word for a tile is *tegel*. But their word for a stove is *kachel*. So the word changed meaning, and you can see why. And here's another example. In German the word for an angle or a corner is *Winkel*. But in Dutch that same word means 'shop'. I'm guessing that happened because shops used to be located on street corners."

"It is interesting how words change," she agrees with a smile. Lilli used to be a German teacher.

"Do you know if your family had any trouble during the famine that Stalin engineered in the Ukraine, around 1931?"

"I don't remember that, but they had other troubles," she says, while it dawns on me that despite my research I got my history mixed up. When Stalin set out to starve the peasants of the Ukraine in the early 'thirties, Volhynia was still in Polish territory, so he couldn't touch the Volhynian Germans. Not at that time, anyway. Blame those ever-changing east-European borders.

"But during World War I, when Germany was fighting Russia, a lot of German families had to leave the area, and they fled to different places. My mother's family fled east, and that's why she was born in Tashkent, in 1917."

Historically that makes sense, because until the Germans defeated the Russians during World War I, Volhynia had been Russian, and Russia was not the only country that persecuted aliens suspected of favoring the enemy. America did the same thing to its Germans. Tashkent is in Uzbekistan, one of several central-Asian 'stans' located north of Afghanistan and well east of the Caspian Sea – a long way from Volhynia.

"And my mother was born with a heart condition, because of poor nutrition where they were." Her mom was a slight looking woman, even more so in the company of her brawny-looking brothers.

"And my father's family went to Germany, to Stettin." Through the ages then-German Stettin, an important port-city on the Baltic, had changed hands between Danes, Swedes, Poles and Germans. Under the name of Szczecin, it's now part of Poland.

"And when they came back to Ludwikow after the war, the whole village was destroyed, burned by the Russians. So they had to rebuild the farm."

Lilli has given me a little notebook to read. It contains the written memories of a friend, Erna Wysock, who was godmother to Lilli's brother Siegfried. If parts of my translation of Erna's story seem grammatically flawed, it's because I tried to stay true to Erna's original,

Lilli's mother, Adele Meisel, sits in front with her brother Julius. Brother Gustav and sister Reile stand behind them. The Meisels were German Baptists but Adele's husband's family, the Kirschbaums, were Lutherans.

which is in the form of a long letter to Lilli that contains her memories "as they came to her" while writing. About fourteen years older than Lilli, Erna spent most of her youth in Volhynia, followed by a few years on a formerly-Polish farm. Next, toward the end of the war Erna and Lilli's mom, with two children each and no husbands, joined the mass-flight to Germany, sharing many experiences. Now in her late eighties, Erna lives in Concord, California.

Erna had married in 1938, the year before the Volhynians' unexpected, ill-fated trek to the Polish Promised Land. Her first husband Friedrich became one of the millions of German soldiers killed in World War II. Unlike Lilli's family, Erna's had not lived in Volhynia very long. Initially her parents had been looking for a farm in East

Erna Wysock and her family

Prussia but when that didn't work out they had chosen a *Hof* (a farmstead) in Volhynia, not a huge distance to the southeast. In 1930, when Erna was just seven, they had settled in a village called Adamov, where Lilli's mom's family also lived. It was not far from Ludwikov, Lilli's birthplace. Lilli's father Edmund used to do a lot of work at Erna's parents' farm, so she remembered him well. Winters were quiet in Volhynia, but:

"In the summer there was plenty to do outside, and we the children had to help out in what way we could, I for example had to watch my brother Erwin, who always wanted to play by the water, for we had a brook next to the farm that we children would also get into, in the summer. The neighbor girls would also come there in the evening, of course the young boys were soon there and would hide their things when they were bathing in the brook and having fun in the water the boys quickly would sneak up on them to surprise them. When the girls wanted to get dressed they couldn't find their things. Whether your mom was part of that I don't know. . . . People had to work hard but there must have been fun too. . . . Adele your mom also sang in the choir, the Church choir. She was always doing things. When we children went home after school we often talked while your mom was working in the garden or was taking down laundry, the Meisels' land was adjacent to the school. Adele spent more time with the young folks of the Baptist congregation, but your father's family belonged to the Evangelical Lutheran. . . . I believe your mom also played guitar and mandolin that she must have lost during the flight, and we would often come and listen at Baptist events, because there was not a lot of entertainment, like going to church on Sunday.

I was still attending school. Then I heard my parents and Heinrich chatting, about Edmund your father too, that he was going with Adele, your father, and she should marry one of the Baptist boys and her brothers were squabbling with her, she has told me that. That she loved Edmund, and she said I can't help it."

On the farms the kids had to pitch in as soon as possible; Erna recalls that by the time she was ten she had to help out with the milking. Lilli's mom, Adele, had lost her mother when she was 14 or 15, which gave her even more work, or – reading between the lines – motivation to marry early, at 17 or 18. Erna remembers seeing Lilli as a little baby:

"Your mom always dressed you up as nice as possible. You had a sister who was two years younger and died when she was a baby. Afterwards your mom was very ill, and weak for a long time."

"So, Lilli, in 1939, how did it work for the local German people to go to Poland? Did you *have* to go?"

"The Russians gave us a choice. Either become Russian or go to Germany."

"Were you able to sell the farm?"

"O no, we couldn't sell the farm. But we would be given land in Poland, where the Polish people had left. First we were in a camp, and then we arrived at the Polish farm in the summer of 1940. We had four horses, seven cows, and we had sheep and geese."

"Did you also grow crops there?

"We grew rye, wheat, potatoes. And we grew *Gerste*, for *Gerstengrütze*. (barley-groats). And sugar beets, and yellow beets to feed the cows."

"So – were the horses big draft horses?"

"No, they were not heavy horses, no. They had slender ankles, almost like race horses."

"How much land did you have?"

"Twenty-one hectares."

"That would be a little more than fifty acres." In Germany of those days that gave them a medium-sized farm. Even though the Nazi régime put farmers on a pedestal with its slogans about *Blut und Boden* (blood and soil), German farm productivity was not very high. Compared to American farms there was little mechanization, and in their obsession with economic independence the Nazis frowned on importing things that might have boosted farm production, like fodder for livestock.

When they got their farms in the Warthegau, Erna's and Lilli's families met again. "Of course, they didn't tell us that the Polish people had to leave," Erna wrote, adding as an afterthought: *und wir auch* – "As did we. They had deported the Poles, and now it was supposed to become German territory. We were put into their houses."

It was a beautiful day in July 1940 when Erna's family and Lilli's family moved into their new homes. The *Treuhand* (trust) that handled the moves and property transfers for the Nazis' massive resettlement program had allowed some young Poles to stay on at the farms, as laborers. Obviously, by the time many of the settlers arrived they had missed most of the growing season. But for Lilli, the best part of their new home was the opportunity to go to school:

"I started school in 1942. I loved school. There were eight grades in one class, and *Fräulein* Ebert, from Austria, was our teacher. I sat in the front seat, where I could study this huge map. O, I loved school, and my dad said I would be a teacher. But he got drafted in 1941, when my brother was only six weeks old. He had to leave on the first of August."

So her dad never even completed one entire growing season on his new farm. Ignoring the non-aggression pact signed less than two years earlier, Hitler had launched a surprise-attack on Russia on June 22, 1941. With 3.9 million troops it was the largest invasion in the history of warfare. If he had not invaded he might well have been left sole master of the west European continent, but he had the grand vision of a new Germany that could feed itself – an economically independent Germany. To achieve that he needed (besides foodstuffs and other products from the countries Germany had already overrun) the raw materials and the vast stretches of fertile farmland in Russia and the Ukraine. As it turned out, of course, Hitler's attack on the USSR was the beginning of the end for his régime. The eastern front would account for 80% of Germany's 4 million military dead in World War II, while the Soviet total of 10 million accounted for two thirds of all allied casualties. And that's without counting the USSR's estimated 20 million civilian war deaths. It's no wonder that to this day the Russians play down the allied war effort, claiming that they were

The Kirschbaum family, probably during Edmund Kirschbaum's first home leave during the winter of 1941/42, when Siegfried was a half year old. The other picture shows Edmund with his unit in Russia, his back to the camera.

the real victors of World War II – in the European theatre, anyway. But of course while making that claim they overlook the fact that Stalin was woefully unprepared for the German attack, and they minimize the importance of America's gifts of tanks, planes and other war materials for his counter-offensive.

"That must have been hard, running the farm without your dad."

"Yes, he had been on the new farm only a year, and when he left he told my mother to take care of the farm, and to let Siegfried have it. We had four Polish people helping us – they were nice people, and we treated them as family." According to Richard Grunberger, that was actually against Nazi rules:

German farmers were commanded – on pain of dire punishment – to [segregate] eastern workers . . . . Their accommodation was to be kept well apart from the other living quarters, and under no circumstances were they to eat at the same table as the farmer's family. The latter prohibition was often honoured only in the breach, since its observance, which was difficult to supervise anyway, would have entailed additional domestic chores. But labour-saving motives were not the only ones behind the evasion of race-hygienic quarantine measures on the farmstead. It seemed illogical to some famers, whose eastern workers were pulling their weight, not to consider them as part of the farm family.[1])

Obviously talking about her father brings back a lot of emotions to Lilli; she wipes away tears.

"Was your dad drafted into the army or the air force, Lilli?"

"He was with the *Luftabwehrwaffe* – air-defense service – on the Russian front, as an *Obergefreiter.* I'm not sure what rank that is."

"Not a sergeant but something like a corporal, I believe. But I suppose he didn't have much choice, about being drafted."

"No, there

was no such thing as a conscientious objector, you know. If you didn't go, you were shot. And in September 1944 he was reported missing in action, near Lublin. We didn't know until much later that he'd been sent to a Russian POW camp in Siberia, and he died there after the war, in 1946, when we were in Czechoslovakia, in a DP camp." She wipes away another tear.

He must not have been very old when he died; I hate to think of the cold, the brutality and the starvation in those Russian camps. "When was he born, Lilli?"

"He was born in 1911, on the fifteenth of September. And my mother was born in 1917, on the tenth of May."

"So he was about 35." Lilli reminds me of my mother who knew everyone's birthday, along with the day they died, if applicable. In the Netherlands it's long been a family value, supported by the tradition of

---

[1]) Grunberger, p. 165.

During the Kirschbaums' stay in the Warthegau Lilli's great-grandfather died. Lilli is the little girl standing at the coffin, her mother behind her.

keeping a *verjaardagskalender* – a marked birthday calendar – on the wall by the toilet, to give the seated inmate something to ponder and plan.

"When was your brother born?"

"Siegfried was born on June 15, 1941."

"You know, we have more in common than I thought. My dad was also born in September of 1911, like yours. And I was born on June 12, 1941. Three days before your brother."

"We went back in 1976," Lilli says, "to visit with the Polish people who were still living on the farm. They were very nice, and they had helped my mother a lot. She couldn't do the hard work on the farm because of her heart condition, from the bad times of World War I. And she was already gone by then."

"So where was this farm, exactly?"

"Krummbach, in *Kreis* (district) – in the area – of Wielun, not far from Posen. It's southeast of Berlin."

What accounts for the German names is the fact that prior to Germany's defeat in Word War I this had been German territory for over 120 years, albeit with a Polish majority population. During the Polish partition of 1793 it had been incorporated into Prussia, and later into the Prussian-led German Empire. Today Posen is part of Poland again, and called Poznan. A phone call comes in. During a conversation with someone called Armando, she discusses the best low tide to harvest the oysters for his order. Turning back to me, she mentions the tentative title for the memoirs she was going to write but hasn't yet: "Waiting for the tides, and for the blood sugar readings."

"Do you remember any incidents from your time in the Warthegau, in Krummbach?"

"Yes, I got a spanking once," she says. "From my father. There was this poor Polish man, he was dressed in a linen sheet and riding a bicycle. He must have been mentally ill, you know, but a bunch of kids were running after him, taunting him, and I joined them, like kids do. Well, my dad, he was inside the fence repairing a harrow, and he grabbed me, took off his belt and gave me a good spanking with it. He didn't like that."

One little incident, but one that reveals quite a bit. Then we turn to the next phase of the Kirschbaum family's odyssey. Erna wrote:

> "Lilli, you must still remember the flight. I believe my sister Hilde rode in your wagon and helped your mom with the horses. You must still remember, during the flight it was mostly just the women with the children, men were in the war, where – and I believe your father was already missing, must have ended up a Russian prisoner, it was 1944. My husband at that time was coming from Italy where he'd been most recently to Germany – Wittenberg, I wanted to go there, before I arrived he'd been sent away again, to the Eastern Front with his regiment. In a last letter to Erwin, he wrote that they'd been ordered to the Eastern Front, I got the letter from Erwin before the end of the war in Obernesse [?] near Leipzig where I was, before I found my family in Dauba – Czecho-Slovakia, where all of you ended up. Yes, I was lucky to find my children, mother and sisters again, only Else was absent . . ."

> "When you drove away from Krummbach you were directed towards Breslau – by way of Oels, in a small town that's called Reichtal, where the Russian caught up with you. That's where the Russians took away Else along with some other girls in a Panzer,[1] there must have been five, that's what our mother said. Lotti and Günter went over there in 1980 but couldn't find out anything, it's too long ago already."

Lilli never knew those details, but she did learn afterwards that relatives who had not been able to leave the Warthegau before the Russians' arrival fared very badly. An aunt who was 17 at the time, a strikingly

---

[1] The correct spelling for Reichtal seems to be Reichenthal. The *Panzer*, usually translated as a tank, is more likely to have been some kind of armored car or personnel carrier, perhaps a trivial point in the context of the sexual predation that accompanied the Russian onslaught.

blond and blue-eyed girl, was beaten to death. Another one made it to Germany much later, bringing a little girl who was the product of a rape. But Lilli remembers well the start of her own odyssey:

"On January 18, 1945, I vividly remember it was snowing, the whole village left. That was twenty-four families, most with fathers absent. We tied two horses to the wagon, and we filled the wagon with what we could, and the feather beds too. Siegfried and I were bundled up in the back of the wagon. Stefan, our Polish man, held the reins, our mother sat next to him. There was fighting in the area, and we travelled through the night. The second night the Russians beat the Germans back, and the next morning the Germans beat the Russians back. There was shooting in Reichenthal, and so we turned back into the fields, and we hid – in – what do they call that, in the army, dug in a field – "

"In the trenches?"

"Yes, in the trenches. The Russians were strafing the area, killing all they could. So in the morning we collected everybody, and some families went to Bavaria, and others to the Sudetengau."

Bavaria was to the west, and the Sudetengau (or Sudetenland) was to the south from Reichenthal. For centuries the Sudetenland had been part of Austria-Hungary, but after the post-World War I breakup of that empire it had been included in the newly-created republic of Czechoslovakia. After the *Anschluss*, Nazi Germany's annexation of Austria in early 1938, the Sudetenland looked like a big bite taken out of the German Reich, since it was now bordered on three sides by German territory. Inside the Sudetenland, a majority of the people in the parts bordering on German lands (the white areas) spoke German and had been there for centuries, while the rest of the area also contained many

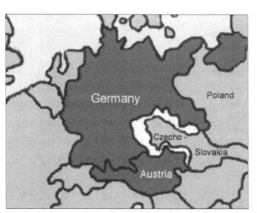

German speakers. Many of these people were highly pro-German and pro-Nazi, which should not have been surprising since prior to the creation of Czechoslovakia they had lived for centuries in a country where German

1938: German residents of the border town of Ash in the Sudetenland welcome the Nazi takeover.

was the language of government, education and literature, with Czech considered a lower-class lingo. And now the tables were turned: the Czechs were in charge.

After Austria's annexation the Sudetenland was next on Hitler's list of lands to grab. Using the same tactics he would use in his run-up to the invasion of Poland the following year, he financed, provoked and publicized incidents inside the Sudetenland that he claimed showed the Sudeten Germans were being oppressed by the Czechs and deserved to be part of the German Reich. The French and British governments had military agreements to defend Czechoslovakia but no desire to honor those, and at the infamous Munich conference on the Sudeten-Crisis in September 1938 they let Hitler have the Sudetenland's majority German-areas, with Prime Minister Chamberlain's plaintive reasoning that Britain had no wish to go to war "because of a quarrel in a faraway country between people of whom we know nothing." A few months later Hitler showed his real hand. His takeover of the Sudetenland had robbed the Czechs of a chain of fortresses that had made effective defenses against a German attack. Freed of that concern, he now took over the rest of the country, which would be subjected to very harsh treatment throughout World War II. In return, after the war the Czechs expelled the Sudeten Germans along with all other ethnic Germans living in Czechoslovakia, some 3 million in all, to Germany, sometimes with a great deal of violence.

Another phone call comes in. From her side of the conversation I conclude that it's a woman looking for organic oysters. With a great deal of patience Lilli assures her that Clausens' Oyster Farm doesn't use chemicals of any kind – I doubt that any oyster growers do – and then she recites her entire price list for shucked oysters, repeatedly answering questions how many of each size are in a pint. When she finally hangs up, she says: "Oof, I hope I didn't sound impatient with her."

"Good grief no, Lilli – I was sitting here admiring your patience."

"She said they would stop in for some oysters."

"Don't be surprised if they never show up. Now, coming back to the Sudetengau – today that's part of the Czech Republic, right?"

"Yes, and we had to travel through the Silesian mountains to get there. We were on the road six weeks. My mom sent our Polish helper, Stefan, home so he wouldn't get killed for helping us. But it was a very foggy place, and once she pulled the wrong rein, the horses speeded up and the cart had no brakes – it was made for flatland farming, you know, and we would have gone off the road. She got help from the others, or we would not have made it. And finally we came to a place in the Sudetenland called Dauba, in a nice little valley. [1] I went to school there for two weeks, and then it got bombed. Then we ended up, we *Flüchtlinge* (refugees) in one room at a *Gutshaus* (an estate)."

According to Erna it was a large farmhouse owned by German people who . . . *später ihre Heimat auch verlassen mussten.* – "who later on had to leave their homeland too."

"On May 8 of 1945," Lilli continues, "the Russians came. I still remember the Cossacks dancing on tabletops in a local restaurant. My mom hid our pictures, so they wouldn't know my dad was in the army.

Dubá today

---

[1] Today called Dubá, in the Czech Republic, it's located in the northern border area of former Bohemia, about 25 miles north of Prague.

In one way it was good they came, because until then we kept fleeing into the woods and hiding under rocks, when the bombers came."

Erna wrote that they all had to work at the farm, and that the Russians, while stealing everything they could, also came and butchered all of the farmer's livestock to feed their troops. Lilli's uncle Adam Schulz helped out with the butchering, and that way the refugees got some leftovers to eat; there even was enough left over for canning.

"But a month later," Lilli adds, "we still had our horses, and they took those. Then trucks came from Czechoslovakia, they took us fugitives to Melnik for two or three months, and then on trucks by way of Prague to Budweis." At this point the area's native Germans were already being chased out. At Melnik, according to Erna, everyone had been put to work until it looked something far worse might happen. The Russians had found out that they had come from Volhynia, which was now Soviet territory, so they wanted to send them back. Apparently this was why they were next taken to an internment camp in Prague. Erna writes:

"There we found a whole lot of our acquaintances from Volhynia and a lot of Black Sea Germans who during the war years had also come to Germany with our army when the retreat began. Now we would all be sent to Siberia. A big scare for us. But no way out. The people were being called alphabetically, to be interrogated.

When we were in line our mother was interrogated first, while we waited with the small children. I had my identification in my hands and was looking at it, and there it says previous citizenship Polish, and it occurs to me – I'm going to say, we were still Polish citizens. When I was called and came in – I asked where they . . . were going to send us. Then the officer said, to Altaiski Krai. I asked if he would show it to me on the map. He was friendly and went with me over to the wall where a map was hung, showed me where Altai is and I said, that's in Siberia and we are from Volhynia and we were still Polish citizens. He looked carefully at the identification and asked if I'd rather go to Poland. I insisted that I wouldn't go to Siberia, with 2 small children who have no more clothes to wear and it's already fall (It was in September). He laughed out loud. You've got courage, he said and another officer joined us and asked What's with her? "O, he said, she must have a friend in Poland that she wants to join. Meanwhile it was very late and he said, if you are still a Polish citizen, you don't need to be written down [on the list]. I thought of mom and Hilda, whose identification they had already kept, and he looked at it and gave everything back to them. When the people who had already been written down heard of it next morning. There they went to the office. All the people from Volhynia got their identification back, and we were transferred to the Czech authorities, and we were very happy about that.

The people who were from the Russian areas – who were called Black Sea Germans had to pack their things and were taken to the railway station, what happened to them we don't know, for sure they ended up in Siberia. Later on in Bavaria I met people who had been sent to Siberia with the Russia Germans and not until 1950 were they allowed to come back to Germany.

The officer felt sorry for us. He saw that our Hilde was wearing a high school uniform. While we were being loaded onto the truck by the Czechs, he asked if Hilde is a student she said yes it was her student uniform, then he told the Czech who was taking charge of us, he should give her light work and he came again in the camp where we were and inquired about us with the Czechs.

He saw that we had good food, it was from the military kitchen, because a lot of Czechs worked there. It was field work. Our Hilde and mother worked in the kitchen. We couldn't complain, the Czechs were OK. It was heavy work in the field, first the grain was threshed, and then came the potato harvest, which is hard work, because you have to gather the potatoes behind the machine. We worked in the potato fields until the night frosts came. Day after day – from sunup until night. One day when we were coming from the field the farm was full of Russian soldiers. They were bringing in the cattle for the winter. Now we had to milk cows in the evening and in the morning. Our mother came to our aid and said we couldn't milk. But the soldiers yelled at us – an da way da way and showed how it's done there was no way out. . . .

Then more cattle were brought in and the Russians had their kitchen, right next to our kitchen, where our mother with another woman had to cook. They were also butchering there and one of the Russian soldiers, an Asian often came in the German kitchen. We were getting very little meat, he saw it then he brought meat for us, which the commander didn't know. He would hide it in straw and bring it over in the evening and we first had to clean it, of the straw that stuck to it. But we had gotten decent meat to eat."

Next Erna's family and Lilli's spent the 1945/46 winter south of Prague in Budweis, the original source of what, through a slow, unstoppable process of enfeeblement, became the top-selling American beer. From there they were sent to the *Ostzone* – the eastern part of occupied Germany that was controlled by the Russians. Lilli remembers travelling by train to Falkenberg in Saxony that summer. "We spent several weeks in a collection center there, in a *Kaserne* – what is that?"

"A barracks."

"There was still very little food. There was this one time when my mom and her friend Erna climbed over the six-foot fence to a potato field, and brought back some potatoes. And from there we went to a little village nearby that was called Kölsa, where we spent the winter of

In the early 1950s, the newly-created Communist-run East-German state (DDR) would create strict border controls, officially to keep people out, unofficially to keep them in. Besides fences, walls, mines, guard towers and border police who shot to kill, these controls included a *Sperrgebiet* – an exclusion zone about 3 miles wide in which all traffic was strictly controlled. **The sign on the left announces: BORDER AREA – exclusion zone – entry only with special permission.** The picture on the right shows the official border crossing near Helmstedt, with guard tower.

1946. We were assigned to live with a family who wanted to adopt Siegfried, but my mother wouldn't consider it. And we kids would go collect mushrooms in the woods, and nuts from *Buchen* – "

"Nuts from beech trees?"

"And we would go collect leftover wheat in the fields, and trade it for bread."

"It's called gleaning in English. I remember when I was little, going with my grandpa, Opa Wissink, to help him pick up leftover wheat stalks in the farm fields, soon after the war. He'd been a baker, and he traded it for bread also."

"Well, we were living one family to a room, and mom and her friend decided they didn't want to live under Communism. They had two kids each. So we took the train to Helmstedt, and we walked all night to get to the English zone."

"So when was that?" Erna wrote that they left in May 1947, and that they got a very kind reception from the military in the British Zone.

"That was in the summer of 1947. Siegfried was barely six. So then we spent weeks in a refugee center in Celle, in Niedersachsen [Lower Saxony]. And from there to a village in the mountains, Langenfeld, *Kreis* Rinteln, on the Weser."

"Do you know where Bodenwerder is?"

"O yes, it's in the same area. On the Weser."

"I spent a week there once, in the 'sixties. It's a nice area, the river reminds me of the Umpqua River here. They have a statue there, in Bodenwerder, of that nobleman who told all those fantastic stories."

"The Baron von Münchausen, yes. In Langenfeld we were supposed to get a room, just ten by ten, in the house of the Beissner family. But they wouldn't let us in; the police had to come so they would take us in."

Erna also had trouble gaining entry to the large house where she and her children were billeted, because it already held several families. It should not have been surprising that some homeowners objected to the arrangement. But with 12 million homeless people flooding shattered West Germany, it's hard to see what else could have been done.

"It was no palace at the Beissners'," Lilli adds, "we ran a stovepipe through the window, but this was 1947. And eventually we got two rooms somewhere else. But I finally got to go to school, I told you I loved school, and I had missed half of third grade, and fourth, and fifth grade. So I attended sixth grade in Langenfeld, and we lived there from May 1947 to May 1954. I attended the *Oberschule* [a six-year high school] in Rinteln but I had to go back to fifth grade to get started in English, because I had missed that. After I finished that school I could have gone on for two years for my *Abitur*, [a school-completion certificate that entitles the student to attend university] but I was impatient to start working and making money. After the change from the Reichsmark to the Deutsche Mark, I believe my mom was getting 150 marks as a war widow, and Siegfried and I each 60 marks *Waisenrente* [orphan allowance] from the government. It was barely enough to buy food, let alone clothes, but I didn't have to pay for my *Oberschule* as long as I got good grades. I had to send those in every year. So then mom moved to Heilbronn so I could get a job there, working for Knorr Soups as a bookkeeper."

"Knorr soups – oh my, we ate a lot of those, back in the 'fifties. I got very tired of them. But we had a big family, and it was a big time-saver for my

Lilli's mom with her involuntary landlady in Langenfeld, in front of the Beissner home.

mother. So how long did you work there?"

"I worked there for four years. I was good at keeping records, and I was in charge of keeping track of two hundred salesmen, how many boxes of soup they sold."

"You said your mother didn't live very long, the poor thing."

"Yes, she was always sick. She had very little food when she was young, and then later on too. She had a heart condition and she

Lilli pretending to be in charge at the boss's desk.

couldn't work, and she was in the hospital a lot. She was able to go to a *Kurort*, to Bad Orb, and that helped."

Germans have always been big on staying at a *Kurort* (literally 'cure place', a healing resort or spa) where they 'take the waters' loaded with minerals that are brought to the surface by residual volcanic activity. Health insurance paid for such therapy.

"That helped her nerves," Lilli says, "and in Heilbronn she was more at ease than she had been for a long time. I had work there, and Siegfried was apprenticed, and that helped. In Langenfeld I used to sleep on the couch in that one room, and she was afraid so much, she would ask me to come lie next to her." Wistfully she adds: "Now I know what she must have gone through."

"And in 1964 she and Siegfried came to visit me in California, in Encinitas. They both went to night school to learn English, but she was bending over to pick up a pencil and fell down, she'd had a stroke and was taken to Oceanside hospital. The doctors were very nice there, but in Germany the government paid her health care, as a war widow, but not here, and we had no insurance, so she went back to Germany, and she died there three years later, in 1967."

"When did you come to America, Lilli?"

"We had relatives in Chicago who were going to sponsor me. But they were not citizens, and only citizens could be sponsors."

Under American immigration law, someone wanting to settle in the United States had to be "sponsored," which meant a U.S. citizen with some means had to vouch for that person's character and financial responsibility, so he or she wouldn't become a burden to the public. Today a sponsor does not need to be an American citizen, just a legal resident. Aside from that, immigrants don't seem to bother much with immigration procedures nowadays. And as to not burdening the public finances – enough said.

Lilli and her mom at Bad Orb

"So then a cousin found the Miller family in Des Plaines, Illinois, and they sponsored me. I left from Munich on December 16, 1958, and by way of Shannon, Ireland, and New York I flew to Chicago. I stayed with family there, and applied for a job with the Chicago Sun-Times. But I flunked their test. They had these rows of words, and you had to indicate if they meant the same or the opposite. I guess my English wasn't good enough yet. So the first few months of 1959 I did light housekeeping and babysitting, and then in April a cousin saw an ad for a clerk-typist at the Welfare Department, and I took a test and passed. That lasted two years, and then the government passed a rule that non-citizens couldn't work for the government. So I worked part-time typing for the Plewke Company, writing letters, and then for Fireman's Fund, the insurance company, typing again. That's where I started learning Navy English – one of the clerks had been in the Navy, and I heard him talk about 'broads', I didn't know what those were, and I'd been hired because 'they were short on hands.' And I learned other expressions, like 'blighted areas', where insurance companies don't like to insure. And during that time I was attending night school, learning to use the Dictaphone. I worked for the Fireman's Fund from 1960 to

1962, and then I went to California. And I married there, but after 17 years of marriage my husband wanted to retire to Arizona. I was looking forward to a teaching career, but living where he wanted to go would have meant driving to work over mountains in the winter. So we divorced, and later I came to Grants Pass, where I worked as a teacher."

"Did you have children?"

"No, I never had children. I couldn't have children. I had a thyroid problem, and I still remember Dr. McKeown telling me that my temperature was too low to have children. But I got along great with my husband's extended family, they taught me what America was all about. And the divorce was stressful, but today we're friends again."

"You mentioned that your brother was with your mom when she fell ill. Did he go back to Germany too?"

"Yes, he went back about a year after she went back. But Siegfried ended up with health problems too. He had been doing well in Germany. He had been an apprentice in engraving and lithography, and he was a journeyman. But after he came back he was in Düsseldorf to see his grandmother, and he must have been in a tavern or something, bragging that he'd been in America, and some people didn't like that and he got attacked and robbed by three men, they even took his car, and on the train going back he tried to jump off. One doctor diagnosed it as schizophrenia without even examining him, another as schizophrenia and depression, and he ended up in a mental hospital, Weinsberg by Heilbronn, where they gave him Thorazine. For a couple of years he was in and out of mental hospitals; he was not even allowed to come to my mother's funeral in 1967. Before she died she wrote me desperate letters about how poorly he was doing, about his mental condition.

"So I did a lot of research at the library in Grants Pass. Mrs. Hill, a very kind research librarian, helped me find articles and books on mental illness and schizophrenia and depression. There I learned of Dr. Hoffman from Tennessee, who said that 147 physical diseases can cause mental illness, and pellagra was one of them. And I found the book by Dr. Abram Hoffer, "Niacin Therapy in Psychiatry". He cured mental patients with niacin but the establishment, the AMA ignored him, and they said niacin doesn't help schizophrenia.

"It turned out, Siegfried had pellagra, and that was the cause of his mental illness. We figured the pellagra was caused by malnutrition when we were in Czechoslovakia, when he was only 4 or 5 years old. It's caused by a niacin deficiency, and the symptoms are the four D's."

"Uh – what are the four D's?"

Pellagra, one of many illnesses caused by poor nutrition, causes physical as well as mental symptoms. Its main cause, a niacin deficiency caused by improper processing of corn, was not identified until the 1930s. In Latin America, corn had traditionally been cooked in lime water before being used; this alkaline process made niacin (vitamin b3) nutritionally available. As corn cultivation spread around the world this cooking method fell into disuse, causing widespread Pellagra, which around 1900 also reached epidemic proportions in the American South. The Pellagra findings led to the U.S. government mandating the addition of niacin to white flour. Pellagra can also be caused by a lack of tryptophan, a substance in soy, meat, poultry, fish and eggs which the body converts into niacin.

"Diarrhea, dermatitis, dementia and death."

"And when I came over for my mother's funeral I got Siegfried out of the hospital and took him back with me, on a tourist visa. He still had symptoms but he wanted to stay. So I went and bought niacin tablets at the health food store. I crushed twelve, that made 3,000 mg of niacin, Dr. Hoffer's recommended dose, even though the normal requirement is only 20 milligrams a day. First I mixed it with a milkshake but he wouldn't drink it, it was all floating on top, and then I put it on a cream cheese and jam sandwich. He like that and ate it. Niacin is also a vasodilator, so he turned beet-red, but the next day he was perfectly normal. It was amazing. And he found regular work and he did fine, just not in what he was trained for, in Grants Pass."

And she adds: "Our friends from the Missionary Alliance Church in Grants Pass said it must have been a miracle, for him to get so well so fast. I didn't care what they called it. But obviously Siegfried's problem was pellagra, not schizophrenia. People with mental illness can't qualify for an immigrant visa and a green card, but with the help of Senator Hatfield he did, so he was not deported and he stayed.

"I imagine somebody trained in lithography and engraving would have to go to a big city like Portland to find work."

"Yes, but in Grants Pass Siegfried worked at an emergency services company. He bought a home and four acres, and he did fine. But he died ten years ago. He was sixty."

"Did you go to college in this country, Lilli?"

"O yes, it was a wonderful thing, being able to go to community college in Grants Pass. The first term at Rogue Community College I took 13 credits, the next 18, and the next 21. And then I attended Oregon State. Between Rogue and Oregon State it took me two and three-quarter years to get my BA in German and in English, and my Master's in Health Education in four summers. But it was difficult to find a job teaching Health Education. Most high schools pair it with P.E., and I didn't have the background. I didn't know most of the American games. So all I did was substitute-teach, even though I had a 3.86 GPA in English, a language that was foreign to me. Ah, but substitute-teaching is a little bit like entering the lions' den. I had to spend the first ten minutes explaining where I was from, and that life in other countries is different. But the worst experience I had in the classroom was not from the kids, it was from the teachers' union. During the strike at the Coos Bay schools, I think it was in 1986, this union boss had warned me not to substitute, and then he hung a poster in my classroom, a poster that showed those terrible pictures from the concentration camps."

"Did you ever feel at home in this country, Lilli?"

"O yes, but I never felt at home in Germany. In Heilbronn I felt like a guest, a foreigner. I never spoke *Schwäbisch* dialect either, in Swabia I only spoke *Hochdeutsch,* High German. My brother, he was younger and he adjusted better. I guess I felt short-changed."

"Tell me how you got into the oyster business."

"Well, when I came to Coos Bay after my divorce I married Max, and he had learned the oyster business at Qualman's oyster farm."

Lilli during her first year in the oyster business with "seed oysters," single shells to which oyster larvae have attached themselves. These were set out on the oyster flats to grow. Today, rather than buying the seed oysters, the Clausens prepare them in specially-built tanks.

Like many early settlers of the Northwest, Max's grandparents were Scandinavians. They had come from a Danish island in the Baltic called Ærø. The Æ part is pronounced somewhat like the <u>a</u> in "ladder," and the <u>ø</u> like the u in "nurse." At age 11 or 12 Max's grandfather had gone to sea as a cabin boy, and by the time he met Max's grandmother in San Francisco he was master of his own sailing ship, hauling coal and lumber from the Northwest to San Francisco.

"My grandma had come over as an indentured servant," Max

explains. "To work for a family in San Francisco that had paid her fare. But they had never met before. After they married she sailed with him for a year or so, but then she wanted to live on shore. They already had a child. So they bought a dairy ranch on the Coquille River, and he built a house there."

"Is the house still there?"

"O no, but they had built it close to the river, and there was a bad flood and their child drowned. So then they moved it further up the hill, quite far up, with horses on rolling logs. But it's gone now.

"And they had six more children," Lilli says.

"There is still a road called Clausen Road, off North Bank Road," Max adds. "And the baby is buried in the Coquille cemetery."

"So how long did you work at Qualman's oysters, Max?"

"I worked there for twelve years."

Qualman's is the oldest oyster farm in the Coos Bay area, and for many years it was the only one. It's located on an arm of Coos Bay that's very close to the ocean entrance, which guarantees clean water.

"It was in the late 'seventies when the EPA gave Coos Bay money for sewage treatment," Lilli explains. "That made it possible to grow oysters further up the bay, because of no more contamination. Max knew everything about the oyster business, so I said, 'Why don't we get into it ourselves?' So I investigated how to lease the mudflats from the Port and from the County, and we're now leasing 635 acres altogether, 120 from the Port. It comes to about $9,000 a year for the leases. At first they cost a bit less, 5 to 7 dollars an acre, but when you start out you don't make any money either, it takes a few years for the oysters to

grow, and you spend a lot of money buying the seed. Eighteen thousand dollars for a thousand bags of seed."

"I suppose that feels a little bit like throwing your money in the water."

"O yes, and besides the cost of seed and the leases you end up paying taxes and royalties too, once you are in production. And some years you don't make any money."

"I suppose that makes it a lot like farming."

"It *IS* farming. And Max, he not only knew the oyster business, he had a degree in agriculture and he was good with the technical stuff. He built the sleds we used for years, to haul the baskets of oysters across the mud."

Among the scans I made of her photo collection is one of Lilli in the early days, in hip boots pushing an oyster sled across the mud with all her might: a real trooper, but a mud-caked one. She's embarrassed by it, and wants me to use a different picture. Vanity, thy name is woman. I really liked that photo. It showed a lot of pluck.

"I joined the AAUW at one time," she confides. The – ah – American Association of University Women. And they asked, 'He makes you work like *THAT?*' "

A few years ago she and Max commissioned the construction of a flat-bottomed oyster boat with a crane on its deck, for lifting the baskets of oysters. It's a huge time-saver compared with the old method.

"You said the oyster business *IS* farming. Does the weather affect the harvest much?"

"Yes, but we've had much bigger disasters," she says. "In 2007 and 2008 we were hit by the Tubiyashi problem, an introduced organism that kills the larvae. That was a major loss. A good year's production can bring you $3 million in sales, but we only got ten percent of the normal return. And then of course there was the New Carissa."

For many decades Coos Bay has exported wood chips, made of ground-up low-grade wood, as raw material for Japanese paper mills. The New Carissa was an empty chip carrier that a careless captain allowed to run aground overnight on the beach, in February 1999. Making things worse was the ineptitude of the government agencies that descended on Coos Bay to direct the salvage operation. Calling themselves the Unified Command, their first priority was keeping the public from watching their activities. (The official term is 'securing the area'.) Their second priority was to prevent oil pollution, and their un-brilliant plan was to burn the beached vessel's fuel oil inside it, with

November 2004: the wrecked stern of the New Carissa in the surf.

napalm. Since both the U.S. Navy and the Coast Guard were involved, this may have been due to the military mind's fondness of fires and explosions. To the cheers of a mass of onlookers on a hilltop miles away, a big bang resounded, a red ball rose from the hulk and then – nothing. The Unified Command had overlooked that burning stuff deep inside a ship may need an oxygen supply. But the short-lived fire had weakened the New Carissa's hull enough so it broke in two, causing the exact problem they had meant to prevent. Copious sheets of oil drifted into Coos Bay with the tide.

Like clams and mussels, oysters are filter-feeders, but they can't eat oil. The Unified Command had promised to protect the Clausens' oysters with a boom across the bay during incoming tides, but the only boom ever installed, Lilli says, was the one that protected South Slough, the federal 'Estuarine Research Reserve' near the harbor entrance. Oil travelled unimpeded to the Clausens' oyster flats, 8 or 10 miles up the bay. "Seventy percent of our oysters died," she says sadly, showing me pictures of dead oysters on the flats, interspersed with shiny oil patches. Adding disaster to disaster, during that same year Max broke his ankle, which made him permanently unable to work the oyster flats. And this at a time when they had started thinking of retiring.

Because the New Carissa case was complicated, the Clausens spent two years in court fighting the shipping company, ending with a favorable verdict which the company appealed. In late October 2003, almost five years after the disaster, they received $1.4 million in damages. But by that time they had exhausted their credit, which meant they had lost the ability to buy oyster seed Between that and their reduced sales, they'd come close to bankruptcy.

That was not Clausen Oyster Farm's only bad experience with government agencies. Out of the blue a couple of years ago, Oregon's Department of Environmental Quality decided to fine them $25,000 for some minor bureaucratic oversights and for not having the right screen on a wastewater discharge pipe. The wastewater had been used to wash harvested oysters, and according to a local DEQ official the pipe had to have two filters in it, each with forty drain holes to the square inch.

"But it must have plugged up right away!" I object. Even I can figure that out. Oyster wastewater must be loaded with shell fragments, grit and seaweed.

"Of course it did. And it flooded the whole building."

"Why would you have to filter the outflow, anyway? Whatever came off the oysters is nothing that isn't in the bay already!"

"That's right, and we used city water, so we weren't polluting anything. We'd been doing it for years with the permit we had, but apparently they had changed the rules and they didn't tell us. And I know that *[other oyster farmer's name withheld]* doesn't even use any filters, just a ten dollar window screen. But they have a different inspector."

In the end, thanks to a local state legislator, the fines were dropped and the case was settled. Government. But – at least this government won't ship the Clausens off to the Warthegau. Or to Siberia.

FIGHTING ANOTHER WAR

I've finished clearing the lunch tables and am settled in for a quiet afternoon of reading Carlo d'Este's biography of Eisenhower. D'Este seems fairly even-handed in his assessment of the famous general: not a brilliant strategist, nor even a great tactician, but a manager-politician with a ready smile, the right one to hold together a gang of prima donna generals of many nationalities. Out of the corner of my eye I notice a very old, rotund man slowly shuffling past my window. Odds are, he will shuffle into my place. Sure enough; somewhat disconcerted by the ringing cowbell on the door he turns and blinks at me: "Still lunchtime?"

"Why certainly. Would you like to sit here?"

He does, and after studying the Early Bird menu he orders the EB Sauerbraten, I deliver it and get back to my book. After he slowly eats his mini-Sauerbraten he wanders to the back of the room to view the Saturday Evening Post posters, each one of which shows an enlarged S.E.P. cover page from World War II. The Post employed a stable of prominent illustrators, many of whom produced grand American images supporting the war effort.

"I've seen all of these!" he proclaims in a shaky voice.

Considering his age, I wouldn't doubt it.

"You know," I say, "the other day a man came in here who used to peddle the Post when he was just a kid. He'd climb the rope ladders onto the ships in the harbor, selling the Post for a nickel, or the Post plus two other magazines, all three for a dime. And one time when he was climbing aboard a British ship the boatswain got all annoyed and started shaking the rope ladder until he fell off and ended up in the water with his magazines. These covers are all from World War II," and, sizing him up: "Were you in the war?"

"O yes, I was in England. I'm from '22, you know."

"Did you go to France with the invasion forces?"

"O no, I was in charge of handling freight. I was a buck sergeant, and together with a corporal I handled the cargo coming into British ports. Southampton, Plymouth, Liverpool. I'll never forget Liverpool. We were moving freight for days in this huge shed that had both ends blown off. I've never been so cold in my life. That wind blowing through there, off the North Sea, that was somethin' else."

"I thought that was the Irish Sea."

"No no, the North Sea."

"Isn't Liverpool on the west coast of England?"

"Yes, on the North Sea."

I'm sure he's wrong about that, but why argue. He's got his memory of World War II – I'm sure he's told many, many people about that Liverpool warehouse, and that's what counts. So I mention that I came from the Netherlands, which does happen to be on the North Sea.

"The Netherlands? Holland? That's where the Germans were shooting the buzz bombs from."

"Well, yes, they shot them from France and Belgium too, and from Holland when they had to pull back."

"Holland, yes. We used to listen for them. When the engine quit, that's when they came down and – boom. Then later on the bigger ones came. They didn't work the same way."

It's interesting – everyone who has been in World War II has one or two stories that sum up its meaning for him – or its absurdity. A few years ago a retired couple with British accents came in who were living in Nevada. Back during the Blitz in 1940 Jack Walton was a teenager in a London suburb, and he related standing in the garden behind his home when a German fighter-bomber came over, very low. It was flying so low that he ducked, and he remembered seeing the streaks of grease running down its belly and smelling its exhaust. The plane carried one bomb which it dropped, about a second later, in the next block, setting off explosions and fires. A mere one second difference between life and death. After the war Jack came to the U.S., where he worked as a maintenance mechanic for United Airlines for many years. One day in United's cafeteria he was telling this very same story when somebody at the next table spoke up: "You know, the fellow in that plane could have been me." When the speaker introduced himself he related how at that time Luftwaffe pilots like him were under orders to drop the single bomb they carried, no matter what. If they returned still carrying that bomb, they'd be shot.

The other day I tried to call Jack to refresh my memory of his story, but his number now belongs to a local garage. He may well be gone from this earth, along with so many of the World War II generation.

Another companion for a brief stroll down memory lane was the father of my friend Dieter Manderscheid. I met him at the restaurant, a year or so before his death. While Dieter mumbled under his breath that talking about the war was such a pointless waste of time, Manderscheid senior enjoyed relating his own World War II story, when he was a driver for a German general. In June of 1944 he was driving his general through a woodsy area of eastern Belgium, close to the Dutch border, when the radio announced that the allies had landed in Normandy, and were establishing beachheads. A little later the general asked him to stop near a small forest. While the general walked off into the trees Mr. Manderscheid waited in the car, and then he heard a shot. When he got out to investigate, he found that the general had killed himself. He may have been the first German general to do so following the Normandy invasion, but by no means the only one.

The former buck sergeant pays and slowly shuffles out, leaving the place empty. Five or ten minutes later an elderly couple walks in. "Will it be a long wait for a table?" the man asks with a grin.

"Uh – no more than half an hour," I smirk, while inviting them into the nearest empty booth. Before long they've made up their minds: Sauerbraten. "Make that two," he says.

"Are you sure you both want the same thing?"

"I was gonna have the Schnitzel," the man says. But it's pork, not veal."

"You'd have trouble telling the difference," I assure him. He is unimpressed.

"It's up to you, of course. But these are sizable meals, so there'll be plenty to share."

"I'll have the Schnitzel," the wife cuts in.

"Excellent choice, ma'am." I head for the kitchen. Pretty soon I serve their meals and they tuck in. When I discreetly look over they are trading food, and he ends up consuming a sizable part of her pork schnitzel.

"Say, I'm glad you suggested that schnitzel," he tells me when I fill their waters. "I used to have one of those every day, in Berlin. With a fried egg on top. Cost me all of sixty cents."

I'm sure no German restaurant is serving schnitzels for sixty cents today, with or without a fried egg. "So – when was that?"

"In 1951. We were stationed in Berlin. Living at Tempelhof airport, actually. And a couple of other places too. We were also at a little place called Lingriesel, in Bavaria. Close to the Austrian border. That was a beautiful area. But then we got to travel halfway around the world. And we made the news: two hundred elite troops had landed in Korea. And of those two hundred only two were left in the end. Wiped out. I was one of the two."

"Good grief."

"Yes," he says, "All those boys. All dead. But it could have been worse. Another company was sent to Vietnam, to reinforce the French. And they ended up at Dien Bien Phu. Totally wiped out, every last one. Do you remember anything about Dien Bien Phu?"

"O sure, that was the French's big defeat. That's when they decided to get out of Vietnam."

"And that's when the Americans decided to get in. Way before Kennedy, and way before Lyndon Johnson." They get up to leave.

"And now we're fighting again," he says. In Afghanistan. What for, I don't understand. But we don't seem to be able to quit going to war."

A WAR ON EARS

This morning I need to unlock the doors for Kevin, Adam's brother. Kevin will be working for Adam, who's planning to ride his new motorcycle up to Florence, with his new girlfriend. Florence is fifty miles north of here, it's a beautiful spring day and the wild rhodies are out all along the road, so that should be nice. Kevin usually gets to work early, so I get there a little before 10:30. No Kevin yet. Well – I'll turn on a few lights and unlock some doors until he gets here. Coming back from opening the backyard gates I run into Adam, who comes walking out the back door.

"What are *you* doing here, Adam?"

"Uh …" he says sheepishly. "We were just getting in the mood, my girlfriend and I, when Tamera texts me, about what time she should be coming in. So I text her back. So then my girlfriend lights into me about always being on the phone and texting and stuff, and she tells me I'm being rude and she gets on her phone to her mother. That always takes a while, and then she goes outside to pout. So in the meantime my dad calls me to see if there's any chance at all that Kevin can work for him today."

Their dad is a contractor, and it does look like an auspicious day for pouring concrete. Or for a roofing job. But not for – ah, other stuff.

"So I tell him OK because I figure, our trip to Florence is off anyway. And I know Kevin will like it, because he'll make twenty dollars an hour."

"Yeah, but it sort of ruins your day," I commiserate. We walk through the kitchen to the front, and there's a 20-dollar bill on the bar.

"She must 'a come in a minute ago, when we were outside," Adam says. "I had lent it to her, and (looking at his phone) here's a nasty text message about here's your money back."

I'm tempted to share my lifelong observation that the best-looking girls can be the meanest ones, but I save that for later and leave.

When I come back towards 2 o'clock, Adam is all leathered-up to mount his motorcycle. "She's been texting me constantly," he says, and then he points at a table for two: "That's the only one today."

"Good grief." We've had some decent days this week, but this is the second lunch that didn't happen.

"They're both having a bratwurst and a side of potato salad," he says.

"Why didn't you suggest bratwurst sandwiches? They'd get more food for less money."

"I would have, but – ah, they were being assholes."

"What happened?"

"They sit down, I look, and their menus are closed. Actually, I guess they never opened them. So I go see if they're ready to order, but the guy is going to the bathroom and she snaps no, wait for him. So the next thing I know, he is at the bar, yelling at me that they're ready to order. Two bratwurst appetizers, and two sides of potato salad."

I peer at the couple. He is the animated one, talking and eating in a busybody way, and he has that Adolf-look, with the same tiny black mustache veiling the same great mystery: where does the nostril hair taper off, and the mustache start? Better not to dwell on such things. This may be a good time to work on one of my chapters, so I set up my laptop in the empty, adjacent booth. But I barely get started when the bratwurst fellow emits the sort of satisfied grunt I've heard from people who just finished some very urgent business in the restroom. You know: "Aaaah!! Haaah! Snorrrt!!" This is followed by: "Check, please!" And Mystery Mustache snaps his fingers. We love that, in the restaurant business. On our ranking of favorite customer communications it's right up there, with coffee drinkers waving empty cups above their heads.

A few more tables show up, and finally around 2 PM a couple shuffle in who more than deserve the title "elderly." The white-haired lady pushes a walker, but she still looks better than her husband, who is gravely bent over and has oxygen tubes running up his nose. They are followed by a woman about one generation younger.

"Table for three, please," says the younger lady, who must be the couple's daughter. I conduct them to a booth against the back wall, which offers a bit more than average room between seat and table. Even so, getting settled takes time, what with parking the walker, the oxygen tank, and stiffened extremities. When I bring them water, the younger lady announces she will have the vegetarian submarine, with a green salad. I've been thinking of getting rid of the veggie sub; such a boring sandwich. So I try to discourage her.

"Don't you think that might be overkill?"

"What do you mean?"

"We'll, you know, that's a lot of veggies to eat, on the sandwich, and then the salad. Might be overloading the boat."

Baring her teeth, she assures me that she's up to the job: "See, I'm part rabbit."

"O. So where are your long ears?"

"I had them clipped. But I'll manage." I'm check-mated.

Both the old folks want the bratwurst sandwich, with a cup of our goulash soup. "And I'd like some coffee," the old fellow moans. His wife wants some too.

"Would you like cream with that?"

He does not. But she has a unique idea: "Would you mind if I used my own?" she asks with a coy smile.

"Well, no, but you look a bit past the age."

Dang, another wisecrack slipped off the uncontrollable waiter's tongue.

It doesn't take long to produce two bratwurst sandwiches and a veggie sub. I deliver them, refill the old folks' coffees, and discover that the lady's 'own' cream comes from a little plastic cup labeled French Vanilla. How risqué.

Pretty soon, with signs of satiation that may well be genuine, the elderly bratwurst couple turn down my offer of hot apple-huckleberry strudel, and the rabbit-daughter triumphantly shows me her plate: not a green speck left on it. I congratulate her, run her dad's credit card, and they are off, if ever so slowly and cautiously. As soon as they are out of sight, in walks a couple of the same vintage but in much better shape.

"We always look forward to stopping here," says the lady. She and her white-haired husband have barely looked at their menus before they close them: "Two of those schnitzel sandwiches," she says. "And I'll have it with a salad. With extra ranch dressing.

"Did you want yours the same way, sir?"

He does. And a Diet Coke. When I bring their sandwiches, I ask: "So where are you from?"

"Why, from Florence," he says, in a way that faintly suggests I should have known that since they've been in before.

"We love to stop in here," she adds.

They still have good appetites, that's for sure. Before long their plates are clean. "Last time we missed out on the apple strudel," the lady says with a hint of reproach.

"It's apple-huckleberry strudel, actually, with the black huckleberries that grow wild around here. A great combination. We stick it back in a hot oven, and it comes out just so." Touching thumb to index finger, I make the French chef's sign of perfection. Experience has taught me that often seals the deal. "Would you like one?"

"It's to take home," the husband says. OK; in that case I will still reheat it to restore the flakiness of the crust; it only takes two or three minutes, anyway. I put the hot strudel in a Styrofoam box lined with foil, and I fill a Styrofoam cup with whipped cream. Strudel has to have whipped cream.

"We have an appointment to get my hearing checked," the man says. "Right down there." He points toward Second Street, the first cross-street down Commercial Avenue, and the location of a hearing-aid store. "Ever since flying in World War II I've had ringing and buzzing in my ears. Over fifty years of ear problems."

He must have given up counting, because by now it could add up to seventy years. But what's the difference; either way that's a lot of misery.

"I never knew the V.A. took care of that," he adds.

"Well, if it was service-related they should. Where did you serve?"

"I was in east-Asia," he says.

"Did you fly B-17s?" I'm big on B-17s and B-24s these days.

"No, C-47s. We flew over the Hump."

The C-47 was the military version of the twin engine Douglas DC-3, also named the Dakota. And the Hump meant the Himalayas, between India and China. That route was a sort of air bridge, to supply American and Chinese forces fighting the Japanese, on the other side.

"They called it the aluminum trail," he muses. "On account of all the planes that were lost."

I start telling him about Chester's trouble with the 52-below temperatures on his B-17. "Did you have those electrically heated jackets?"

"We had sheepskin jackets," he says. "And I had sheepskin boots, over my shoes. I didn't have much trouble with the cold. My main problem was the noise. You got all the engine noise. And then the M-16s firing."

"I thought the C-47s were pressurized?" I can tell he's having trouble hearing me over the background music, so I go turn it off.

"Weren't the C-47s pressurized?"

"O no, and no insulation."

I'm surprised because the DC-3, the commercial passenger plane version, was pressurized. That's my ignorance.

"So, how long was the flight?"

"About four, four and-a-half hours." That's maybe half the length of Chester's missions; he didn't get to land at Ploesti. Then he adds, brightening: "But O boy, it was great to get there. We loved the food. In India we had nothing but powdered eggs and tea. In China we got real eggs, and bacon. And coffee, too. But about the noise, part of what got to me too was the pressure differences. And then, when we were finally repatriated, I went home on a Liberty Ship. One day they said they were gonna do some target practice, with the 40 caliber machine guns. That sounded fine, and I was sitting right under the 50 mm cannon. All of a sudden they started firing that too; you can't imagine the noise. I guess the sailors thought that was some kind of joke. But I couldn't hear anything for five days."

"I guess we'll go on down to our appointment now," she adds. They are at least half an hour early, but when you need relief for a problem that's been bothering you for over half a century, there's no point in waiting.

WELL, RUN ME DOWN

This afternoon, after spending the better part of an undisturbed hour tallying last month's cash expenses, I decide to settle down with a book until the dinner crew comes in. It's a lively biography of Bismarck, and the writer, A. J. P. Taylor, dishes out snappy snippets of political wisdom. Here's one: since Bismarck always sought to divide Germany's enemies, he continually played one European power against another. That was his way of avoiding a war on more than one front, a policy that later German statesmen should have emulated, but didn't.

Ironically, Bismarck's scheming often caused Russia to accuse him of favoring France or England or Austria, while those nations accused him of being partial to Russia. In reality he only favored Germany, while keeping his neighbors divided and confused. As Taylor summarizes it, a statesman who puts his own country's interests first will never be popular abroad, anyway. Chiseled on an immovable slab of granite, that truth ought to be kept in the Oval Office.

Around three an elderly single man comes in. Well – elderly – he's probably my age, and he still has his hair, which is all-white, but he carries a medium-sized spare tire in front and walks with a limp. He also uses a cane. But he's glad to find some European cuisine, and orders the Sauerbraten. While he is eating I sit at the bar, scanning today's newspaper. But since I have trouble finding anything worth reading, I don't mind his interrupting me.

"Say, what part of Germany are you from?"

How many times have I been asked this question? "Ah – I'm not from Germany, actually. I came from the Netherlands."

"Ha. The Netherlands. You know, it was in 1960 when a buddy and I discovered a deal on Holland-America Line. Round trips for 300 dollars. So we decided to go over there and hitchhike around."

"Did you have any trouble getting rides? I did some hitchhiking myself, back then."

"Well, here's the thing," he says, pushing his plate aside. "I figured Americans would be popular over there. So my buddy and I, we sewed American flags on our backpacks, thinking that would help us get rides. But when we started from Amsterdam, or was it Rotterdam, it didn't seem to make a lot of difference. Not everybody was friendly, but as we got further south, they got outright hostile. Finally in France somebody tried to run us down. So this friend of mine who lived there took us aside. 'Take that flag off your bag,' he said, 'and sew something else on it. Anything but the stars and stripes.' So my buddy, his mom was Canadian so he sewed on a Canadian flag. And my family is Norwegian, so I put on a Scandinavian flag. That solved the problem."

"Well," I say soothingly, "the French seem to be cross with a lot of people. I hitchhiked with a Dutch flag on my bag, so they'd pick me up thinking I was French. My flag had the same colors as theirs except the stripes are horizontal, not vertical. So once I got in the car they'd get hostile because they heard my accent and thought they'd accidentally picked up a German. After I explained that I was Dutch, they'd settle down."

"Yeah, well, we were real disappointed."

"Look, I grew up in Europe, so I know how they look at Americans. I've seen German propaganda from 1944 that showed pictures of Frenchmen jeering and throwing garbage at American POWs being marched down the street, because of all the destruction they had caused during the invasion. That did not happen in the Netherlands, even though in our area entire villages were destroyed. People accepted it."

"Yeah, well, I didn't care for the French. I liked the Germans better."

"I've heard other Americans say that. I've even heard a World War I veteran say it. But about the Europeans, the French in particular, and how they like Americans, you've got to think of it as a family conflict. A lot of families have a wealthy and a poor branch. Sometimes the wealthy cousins do nice things for the relatives that live on the wrong side of the track. But will the low-life cousins ever love the fat cats, as they think of 'em? Not too likely."

"But they're not as poor as they used to be."

"Sure, economically they've caught up pretty well. But I'm also talking about the American military going over there twice to pull their chestnuts out of the fire. It's the rage of the impotent, you see. And to make up for it they indulge in hostility and snobbery. We used to sit on the outdoor terraces near Amsterdam's Central Station and make fun of the American servicemen on leave from Germany. You could always tell them apart; their slacks were too short and their socks were white. No self-respecting Dutchman would have dressed that way. It was like the British attitude about clothes back then; even brown shoes were suspect, let alone suede. One fellow who worked at my office, I still remember him carrying on about American misbehavior at a classical concert the night before. At the Concertgebouw they simply wore their raincoats inside the auditorium and draped them over the back of their chairs. 'Can you imagine?' he said, rolling his eyes."

"Uh – what – what's wrong with that?"

"They didn't follow the example of the clever Dutchmen, who would leave their coats at the coat-check counter, so after the concert they could wait in line for twenty minutes to get them back, and tip the coat-check girl too."

"It doesn't sound practical to me."

"It isn't. But I'd like to tell you about a hitch-hiking experience of my own. That was in 1961, or in '62, I can't remember which. I hitch-hiked to Spain through Belgium and France, and back through

Germany. France was rough. I always made sure I was shaved and didn't look like a bum, but even so, I might stand beside that road all day, with my thumb out. 'Course the French had small cars, that's true, and they were pretty full. I had much better luck in Germany, on the way home. And then some German, driving a VW Bug like a bat out of hell, dropped me off at an Autobahn-junction near Frankfurt. I'm just climbing out of his bug, and here this cop comes running from behind the bushes, you know, with his Donald Duck hat on and blowing his whistle like a banshee. It was illegal to stop for hitch-hikers on the Autobahn, so he fined the driver on the spot. Cash on the barrelhead; you don't get to go to court over there. I felt bad about that, but I was pretty-near-broke myself.

Well, this intersection was close to the big Rhein-Main air base and it was getting late in the day, so I pitched my little tent on the grass near a tall cyclone fence. Behind the fence was housing for the American families stationed at the base. I went to sleep, and first thing in the morning I woke up to another German police whistle, this time two cops with Donald Duck hats. Turns out they had been called by the women living at the base, because there'd been a child molester active in the area, so they came to check me out. Well, they could see I didn't fit the profile, so they wished me a good trip and they left.

But then, not much later, one of the American ladies came over and apologized for having called the cops on me. And she brought me food, delicious food. She thought I had camped close to their fence because I needed something, and she cared. I think she brought some kind of casserole. Mrs. Johnson, the wife of Staff Sgt. Johnson. She had a boy of five or six who was totally fascinated with my tent, and with camping, and we visited. That was not the end of it either. I stayed there a couple of days, while the ladies on the base had a kind of contest going, who could bring me the most food. Very generous people, Americans. The Europeans don't appreciate them, but that's life. There's an old saying in the Netherlands: *Doe wel en zie niet om.* It means: 'Do good and don't look back.' "

A few other people come in, he pays, and he's on his way. And then, a variant on A .J. P. Taylor's observation occurs to me: A statesman who does *not* put his own country's interests first is unlikely to be popular abroad, either. At best he may draw contempt. Particularly if he's American statesman.

CLARA SCHWARZ'S WAR

Just south of the Luzk area of Volhynia, where Lilli Kirschbaum-Clausen was born, is a region called Galicia, not to be confused with Spanish Galicia. Galicia's largest city is called L'viv by the citizens of the western Ukraine, to which it belongs today. But like virtually every city in that part of the world it's also known by other names, given to it by foreign armies that conquered it; and an awful lot of conquerors have come and gone. To the Poles and the Russians L'viv is known as Lvov or Lwów, while to the Germans and the Austrians it's Lemberg. To the Turks it was Ilbav or Lemberk. One more name, Leopoli, was coined by the Italians, in their case not because they conquered the place but because like other cities in that part of the world, L'viv hired architects and craftsmen from Italy to design the town in a handsome Renaissance style, back in the sixteenth century. Although it needs work after so many decades of Soviet neglect, L'viv is worth visiting for its quaint, Mediterranean-looking town center. But from here on, not to offend the people of the Ukraine but because the book I want to discuss refers to L'viv by its Polish name, Lvov, I will call it Lvov.

Some fifteen miles north of Lvov you will find a much smaller town called Zhovkva in Ukrainian, Zholkva in Yiddish and Żółkiew in Polish. History warrants using its Polish name, Żółkiew, because of its founder Stanisław Żółkiewski, a great warrior who once was the most powerful man in the Polish empire after the king. After a long string of victories against the Austrians, the Tatars, the Turks, the Cossacks, the Swedes, the Moldovans and the Russians (the latter while seizing both Moscow and the Czar), Żółkiewski was killed in a battle with the Turks, when he was well into his seventies. The town of Zolkiew, which he founded and owned outright, developed next to a castle he built there

Part of Zolkiew from the air. To the right of the square castle built by Stanislaw Zolkiewski is the city hall, built against the old town wall; to the right of it is one of the town gates; far right the St. Lawrence Church. On the big square in front of the church markets were held.

around 1600. Unfortunately, the 20th century would be extremely unkind to a place that had such a promising start, given to it by forward-looking statesmen like Żółkiewski. One Zolkiew landmark, the St. Lawrence Church, built during his lifetime by Italian architects from Lvov, would become a pantheon to Poland's military golden age, sheltering numerous battle mementos plus the graves of Żółkiewski and other Polish heroes. After the Soviets abused this elegant structure as a warehouse, it's being restored today with Polish funds. That's how important it is to the Poles, even though Zolkiew is now inside the Ukraine. And in World War II, the Nazi occupiers used the nearby courtyard of Żółkiewski's castle to hold the town's rounded-up Jews, before they were hauled off to be killed.[1]

---

[1] According to *Żółkiew - Encyclopedia of Jewish Communities in Poland, Volume II - (Zhovka, Ukraine)*, the Jews were held there in mid-March of 1942. This is also stated in *Mosty Wielki Organization - About Zolkiew*, which adds that the "courtyard of the citadel" was used again for the same purpose in November. These details are not in the book that is the subject of this chapter, *Clara's War, one girl's story of survival*, by Clara Kramer and Stephen Glantz, New York: HarperCollins, 2009. For quotations from *Clara's War* in this review I will mention the page number at the end of each one.

From its earliest days Zolkiew's population had been a mixture of Poles, Ukrainians and Jews; the first mention of Jews in Galicia dates from 1030 AD. The ancestors of most Jews in that part of the world had come from German lands, in a centuries-long process that paralleled the eastward movement of Germanic farmers, but for different reasons. The Jewish treks were more often caused by persecutions, and Jews settled in cities because they were traders and artisans, choices originally dictated by widespread prohibitions on Jews owning land. Before World War II about a third of the greater Ukraine's urban population consisted of Jews, who had developed many of today's best-known Jewish cultural and religious traditions there.

Galicia was well-located on trade routes, and for centuries Poland was a decentralized country in which local nobles held most of the power, along with the land. This included the authority to grant privileges to population groups that could help develop a nobleman's territories. To promote the growth of his own town Żółkiewski had actively encouraged Jews to settle there by granting them freedom of worship, the right to build a synagogue as well as their own homes, and more. Of course, big landowners like him were not solely motivated by altruism. They knew that Jews were more likely than the local peasants to have sophisticated skills, enterprise, and money. They wanted to see their towns grow, and to profit by leasing land and gaining tax revenues as a result. Żółkiewski's enticements caused numerous Jews from Lvov to move to Zolkiew. The Jews' privileges were maintained and expanded when the town was acquired from the Żółkiewskis by Jan Sobieski, another Polish warrior who is most famous for defeating the Turks besieging Vienna in 1683. Legend says that after his Vienna victory a donut-shaped bread was created as an imitation of Sobieski's stirrup, with the German word for stirrup, *Steigbügel*, becoming 'bagel'. Jan Sobieski was elected King of Poland, and like other Polish kings he appointed Jews to important positions. During his ownership of Zolkiew he helped pay for the construction of the fortress-like Grand Synagogue, a building whose secondary purpose seems to have been a last defense against foreign armies. Sobieski also donated the first gravestone for Zolkiev's Jewish cemetery.

During the centuries that followed, the fortunes of Zolkiew's Jews slowly waned, partly because of the never-ending wars in that part of the world, and partly because of increasingly oppressive taxation that indebted them. Still, before World War II Zolkiew had between 4,500 and 5,000 Jewish residents, almost half the town's population.

Both Galicia, which had been Austrian during Poland's non-existence of over a century, and Volhynia, which had been Russian, had been made part of resurrected Poland after World War I. And because both were in the eastern part of Poland they were, in accordance with the deal struck between Hitler and Stalin, invaded by Russian troops in September 1939. The Jews of Zolkiew rejoiced because Jewish refugees from Nazi-invaded western Poland had made them aware of what was happening there. "All the Jewish families of Zolkiew got down on their hands and knees to thank God for his mercy." (10) But if God's mercy was at work, it was not bountiful. The Soviet communists were far worse than the Czar's government that many of the locals had learned to hate in World War I. They started a big campaign of rounding up and banishing people to places in the east, or executing them outright. For this reign of terror they did not single out the Jews, but anybody who was rumored to have independent ideas, along with 'capitalist' business owners, 'bourgeois' individuals and those in positions of leadership. Goaded by covetous neighbors who saw a chance to enrich themselves, the Soviet commissars had no trouble finding suspects to arrest. This caused the local economy to turn very bad, but the Jews who were still there thought they could tough it out.

But of course, less than two years later, in June 1941, Hitler trashed his contract with Stalin and invaded the USSR, including Soviet-held Poland. In its train the German Army brought SS troops and *Einsatzgruppen* (special groups) whose business was ethnic cleansing, meaning wiping out Zolkiew's Jews as well as the Russian commissars, who quickly withdrew. Before they left they massacred everyone held in the prison at Lvov. But the fact that the commissars had banished a lot of the locals to places like Siberia proved a blessing in disguise, because the many Jews among them would miss out on the Nazis' mass-killings.

Mainly as a result of that process later called the 'holocaust', less than a hundred of Zolkiev's 4,500 to 5,000 Jews survived the war, and the number may be as low as fifty. Of those, 18 had hidden in a hole under one house during the final 20 months of the German occupation, and during all that time they had been provisioned and protected, with near-superhuman shrewdness, daring and tenacity, by a *Volksdeutscher* by the name of Valentin Beck. That doesn't mean Beck was some sort of saint. He was a notorious drinker, a womanizer, a deadbeat, and worse. Yet Clara Schwarz-Kramer, who published the eighteen Jews' story in 2008, wrote: "They say there are no angels here on earth. But they didn't know Beck." (232). One plausible-sounding explanation for Beck's daring actions was that he "was driven by his enormous contempt for any and all in positions of authority" (181), something that makes me suspect he and I could have gotten along. Among the lessons of this story, then, may be the worthlessness of gossip and the surprisingly unlikely instruments whom God still picks to do his work, as He did throughout the Bible. Moses didn't want the job. Jacob was a mama's boy. David was considered the least important member of his family. And Jesus – let's just say opinions varied. Valentin Beck, one of Zolkiew's least reputable residents, made it his life's priority to preserve the Jewish families under his house, not only while Zolkiew was under the Nazi jackboot but even when the Russians were about to take it back and he and his family, as *Volksdeutsche*, faced almost certain deportation to a Soviet gulag. The Russians assumed, not without reason, that all the local *Volksdeutsche* had been Nazi-collaborators, which was why all except the Becks had fled to Germany by then.

All this is related in a book called *'Clara's War'*, which in turn is based on a very detailed diary kept by Clara Kramer, born in 1927 who, as fifteen year-old Clara Schwarz, went into hiding with her parents and Jewish friends in November 1942.

It was only a couple of weeks after Hitler launched his June 1941 invasion of the USSR when the first German troops arrived in Zolkiew. The Wehrmacht soldiers didn't bother anybody. They behaved much like tourists, taking pictures and handing out candy to the kids and cigarettes to the adults. But two days later the SS and the Gestapo arrived. Shooting Jews at random and at will, they entered the town and Zolkiew's ancient Grand Synagogue. After stripping it of all its gold and silver while the Jews outside tore their clothes at the desecration, they set the building on fire but instead of collapsing it stood, probably thanks to its massive brick construction approved by Jan Sobieski, three centuries earlier:

> The SS officer became furious and ordered his men to throw the lamenting Jews on the embers to feed the fire, as if the heat of burning Jewish flesh would be enough to turn brick to ash. A Wehrmacht officer driving by in a Mercedes reacted in stunned horror. He ordered his men to pull the Jews from the flames. The SS officer was outranked, so a few Jews were saved for who knows how long. As soon as the Wehrmacht left, the SS tried to burn the synagogue down a second time, but the walls still held firm. [42]

According to other sources, the SS ended up dynamiting the building.

On the left: SS soldiers plundering the Zolkiev synagogue. One is holding a Star of David. Right: the building on fire. The synagogue's present condition is shown below.

After this, it took some time for the mass-killings and deportations to begin. At first the SS's priority was to bleed the Jewish community dry by stealing all its wealth, which they did by taking hostages and levying fines for violations of the customary anti-Jewish laws, although instant death by shooting was a common enough penalty. The anti-Jewish laws included mandatory wearing of the yellow star, prohibitions on using vehicles and bicycles, being out after curfew, using parks, schools and sidewalks, confiscation of homes and businesses, and forced labor. But among the worst humiliations may have been the destruction of the Jews' graves. The Nazis forced the Jews to smash all the gravestones in their cemetery, even the one donated by Jan Sobieski, and pave the streets with them.

Adding to the Jews' despair in the fall of 1941, the war news was always bad. By now the Germans had taken major cities east of Galicia; they had even occupied the Crimea. Clara Schwarz's family's livelihood had been a factory which turned the local farmers' produce into vegetable oil. With two other Jewish families by the names of Melman and Patrontasch, they were co-owners of the plant. The Nazis had confiscated it, but it soon turned out that those left in charge were clueless about how to keep it running. Everybody including the German army needed oil, so Clara's dad Meir Schwarz was ordered to manage the mill, "at no salary of course." (45) The three partners then ran the mill all day and all night while Mr. Patrontasch, who seems to have been the most multi-talented partner, developed contacts in the black market. Soon they had a lively trade going in oil, often not for money but for farmer's produce and anything else that was tradable for money. At least for now the three families had plenty to eat.

But by March 1942 the SS's thievery of valuables had about run its course, so all the Jews considered least able to work were collected into the castle courtyard, and from there taken to the train station, to be pushed into cattle cars that carried them to Belzec, one of the infamous death camps in occupied Poland. This occurred with a great deal of violence; blood ran down the streets. Now everyone who was left tried to get papers to leave the area or to go into hiding, mostly without success; it was too late. To Clara's dad's despair, her mother insisted on running a soup kitchen for the many destitute Jews still in town; it took most of the money he made from the oil business. As grim reminders of their fate the Jews watched a packed death train a day pass through Zolkiev on the Lvov-Lublin line; in both those cities the Nazis had created ghettos, the preparatory step for deportation. By this time three family members including "Dzadzio," the family patriarch, had been killed in various incidents, and more would be killed by the occupiers. Life had become pathetically cheap.

To prepare for the expected knock on the door, the three fathers decided to dig a temporary hiding place under the Melmans' house, the largest of the three family homes. First Mr. Patrontasch, who was also a skilled carpenter, constructed a hatch in the parquet floor of the main bedroom. He did such a good job, it was impossible to spot the seam. Next a crawl space, something on the order of a small ditch, needed to be excavated from this access hole to a remote corner of the house where a pit would be dug for everyone to hide in. Because there was so little room under the floor this first part, the crawl space, was to be excavated by the children, who themselves could barely fit between the floor and the dirt:

> It was high summer and hot in the crawl space. There was no ventilation, so we were dressed only in our underwear. . . . We dug for two weeks straight with our hands and then with pots and pans and shovels. My hands looked like those of a peasant, raw with blisters and broken fingernails, dirt wedged under the nails and tattooed in the lines of my palms. We had to dig to Mr. Patrontasch's exact specifications. We couldn't take the dirt outside, so we had to lay it out evenly all over the rest of the crawl space. We worked by the light of kerosene lamps, which fought us for every molecule of oxygen. There were times I almost passed out. . . .
> The bunker was three metres [between 9 and 10 feet] square and a metre and a half [less than 5 feet] deep. There was just enough space for the ten of us to lie next to each other. . . . Mr. Patrontasch designed a cover to disguise the underground bunker perfectly. . . . Once it was in place we couldn't tell the cover from the dirt floor. We had built a tomb. Inside it we placed matches, candles and water. (53/54)

The "bunker" under the Melmans' house was intended to be an emergency refuge only. All through the fall of 1942 Meir Schwarz kept trying to find someone to take them in and permanently hide them from the expected manhunt, but with no results. In the meantime there were rumors of an impending *aksja* – the Polish version of the word action, meaning a raid to seize the rest of Zolkiev's Jews. Those always came out of the blue, without warning, and usually very early in the morning because the victims would be most disoriented. As a precaution all three families started spending the night in the Melmans' house. And in the early morning of November 22 an *aksja* did come, with the Germans and the Jewish police banging on doors and shooting people trying to escape. The families, six adults and four children, crawled through the trapdoor and into the "bunker." It was hot in there with all ten, and it was dark. They sat there for two days and nights, until they learned that the death train had left. Once they ventured outside they learned of friends and relatives who had been killed while trying to hide or escape. The whole town was in mourning, but everyone knew it was only a matter of time before the man-hunters returned to catch those they had missed. Clara's 13-year-old sister Zosia was taken in by a Polish lady, but she was back the next day; she had cried all night and wanted her mom. Then the Nazis issued a new decree. Within a week, by December 1, all the Jews remaining in Zolkiev would have to move into a ghetto they had created, basically a very small part of town, too small to accommodate them comfortably and surrounded by barbed wire, concentration-camp style. Everyone knew that meant death, either by starvation and disease in the jam-packed ghetto or, if they survived, by assassination in a death camp. Two days after the decree there was a knock on the door:

> Papa opened it to find Pavluk standing on the step. He was a strong man whose giant hands were curled around his hat. His pants were shabby and he wore a soiled homespun linen shirt. He had one of those big moustaches that so many of the Ukrainian peasants had. Pavluk was a murderer. After being released from jail he had come to the factory looking for a job. Papa had gone to my grandfather for advice. Dzadzio hadn't hesitated for a second. He said, 'Hire the man. I promise you, you will have a grateful man your entire life.'
> Pavluk told Papa he wanted to hide us. Papa didn't say a word. He just took Pavluk's hand and invited him into the house.
> "Thank you. You don't know what this means to us. But we can't."
> I didn't understand why Papa was refusing the offer. Mania and me all looked at each other and at him. I could see the protest forming on my sister's lips. Her dark eyes expressed the most profound disappointment. Papa went on in a kind voice: "You have six children, Pavluk. And your house. Two rooms with no place for us to hide." As much as we wanted him to say yes, we knew Papa was right. We couldn't put six children at risk. Out of all the Poles and Ukrainians that my family knew and had helped for generations, Pavluk was the only one who had come forward to help us.
> Pavluk was upset that he hadn't properly thought through his plan for our survival. He muttered, "I want to do something, anything to help." Mama was moved by his sadness. Even though we had already put everything of value we had left behind the stuccoed false wall in the basement of our spinster neighbors, Mama gave him two down pillows and a featherbed to keep for us.
> Our down bedding would survive the Nazis. [60-61]

Here, desperation starts to rise from the book's pages; but then comes an unexpected breakthrough. For years the Schwarz family had employed a housekeeper, Julia Beck, who used to spend several days each month cleaning house and doing the laundry. "Together with Mama, she would boil the kilos of sheets and laundry in huge pots and then crank them through the wringer by hand." [65/66] I included this detail because on Mondays I saw my mother do exactly that, when I was little. I believe my dad lifted the huge pots of laundry on and off the heat. Even so, that was very hard work

By now it was November 1942:

. . . Julia Beck and her husband had agreed to hide us, the Melmans and the Patrontasches. We couldn't believe what we were hearing. The Becks of all people. We hadn't even considered approaching them because Mr. Beck had such a bad reputation. My parents discussed the implications of going under their protection. I had never met Beck. Everything I knew about him I had picked up from whispered conversations. He was a drunk. A philanderer. Couldn't hold on to a job. Owed money to everyone and never paid back a zloty. He was also reputed to be an anti-Semite. Could we risk putting our lives in the hands of a man who was known for a vicious tongue, his anti-Semitism, for his affection for drink and his failed businesses?

The decision was made to accept the offer. We knew that hiding only meant a reprieve. But we didn't have any other alternative, and we trusted Julia Beck. She had been our housekeeper and her mother had been my grandmother's before that. . . . And now this Polish woman and her Volksdeutscher husband were saving our lives. [65-66]

With the removal of all of Zolkiev's Jews mere days away, the local *Volksdeutsche* were given the pick of the Jews' houses, so it was agreed that while the families enlarged the hiding place, Mr. Beck would ask the German authorities to be given the Melmans' house that sat on it. This was easily accomplished. Initially eleven people would be living in the bunker: the Schwarz family, which meant the parents plus Clara and her sister Mania; the Melmans and their son Igo; the Patrontasches and their daughter Klarunia; plus Mr. Patrontasch's widowed sister Klara, a last-minute addition. Klara Patrontasch, not to be confused with Clara Schwarz our diarist, was a beautiful woman who had lost her husband and her daughter not long before the war.

The eleven arranged their damp space as well as humanly possible, and they set rules. Those unavoidably included the abolition of privacy. Given the primitive sanitary facilities, it had to be so. Perhaps to make up for that they mandated a formal politeness, which included addressing everyone as Mr. and Mrs. Complaining was prohibited; there would be plenty to complain about, but it would only make things worse. Each family would be responsible for its own food and water; not sharing would avoid disputes. And lastly, there was to be no talking unless absolutely necessary. Since the underground dwellers could hear the Becks' conversations upstairs, they figured anyone in the house would be able to hear theirs, and very likely the neighbors could too. Clara's mom, Salka, told her to start keeping a diary Why? "If they kill us, somebody will find the diary and they will know what we went through." Clara had no writing paper but she did have a pencil, so she started writing notes in the margins of her books. She found it was good therapy.

After they had been in their hiding place for three weeks, under what was now Beck's house, Christmas Eve came and they were invited upstairs for an enormous dinner:

> Beck had made a dancing bear for little Igo and Ala [Beck's daughter] gave Klarunia one of her stuffed dolls. Beck had packs of cigarettes for the men and in no time at all the packs were ripped open, matches lit, and the room full of smoke, the men puffing and sucking like there was no tomorrow, content, full, drunk, and happy. Ala had given Mania one of her combs, which she immediately put in her hair. She ran to the mirror to see how it looked. Beck gave me a package wrapped in newspaper. It was flat and at first I hoped it might be a book. I was crazy for a new book. I opened it. Inside was a composition book with a black cover and filled with lined paper, just like all the many composition books I had used in all my years in school and never given a thought to.
>
> "For our little writer," he said. "I know you'll be a famous writer some day, Clarutchka, I just beg that you only say nice things about me." Mr. Beck knew that I was keeping a diary and had no book to write in. He also gave me a blue pencil, which he had sharpened to a fine point with his penknife. . . .
>
> Beck was emerging from the circumscription and diminution of gossip and prejudice and becoming someone in my life who knew me. [91]

Since Beck was entertaining relatives on Christmas Day, they had to spend that day in the 'bunker'. The people below were not paying much attention to the boisterousness upstairs when a few words caught their attention. Beck, in an apparent fit of Dutch courage, bragged that he was hiding three Jewish families below. His brother told him he was crazy and suicidal. That he didn't owe the Jews anything. That he should remember he was a *Volksdeutscher*, and show loyalty to the German cause. Beck only became militant. He reminded his brother of the fall of 1939, when the Soviets had just taken over and were going to ship him off to Siberia:

> ". . . and you know who buys me out?"
> Now his voice was starting to rise again.
> "You, my beloved brother? You, my fellow Volksdeutscher? NO! IT WAS THE JEW MELMAN DOWNSTAIRS WHO BRIBED THE FUCKING COMMUNISTS! I ABANDON THEM, I ABANDON MY HONOR! I HATED JEWS ALL MY WHOLE LIFE. I STILL DO, WHY? HOW THE HELL SHOULD I KNOW? But it was a Jew saved my worthless-piece-of-shit life, my sacred wife and my beloved daughter ... Come here Ala, sit

by your father, I want my Ala to look at her father and see a man, not a coward. They can kill me ten times over ..."

Beck's Christmas visitors wasted no time leaving, and the majority opinion downstairs was that they were done for. But they were not. As readers we may speculate that Beck's dressing-down of his brother had a salutary effect, so he kept his mouth shut. But soon, with Beck's blessing, more Jewish friends and relatives joined the eleven in the bunker. In March 1943 Beck brought Lola Elefant, a woman only in her twenties whose hair had turned white at the beatings and mass-murders she had seen in the ghetto. Later that month, right after the Nazis had gathered the rest of Zolkiev's Jews, shot them in the woods and dumped them in a mass grave, Beck took in the Steckels. They were a childless couple and Professor Steckel, as he was addressed, had been Zolkiev's only pharmacist. This was the reason he'd been able to live outside the ghetto for some time – but he'd finally seen the light. The Steckels were well off. Beck had never asked the initial three families for money, although they had given what they could. But with the Steckels, Beck's primary motivation was financial; and they expected value in return.

While the other families were eating the first food they'd had in days – boiled potatoes – there was a knock on the trap door:

> *But even before Patrontasch opened the hatch, the smell of roasted chicken and pirogies [an east-European version of potato-stuffed ravioli] assaulted us. I can't describe it any other way. Julia kneeled at the hatchway with a tray in her hand. Chicken, pirogies, vegetables and bread. Fresh bread. The tray had to be passed from hand to hand, from family member to family member. The tray had to run the gauntlet of starving human beings, past the noses of Igo and Klarunia, two starving children, to the Steckels, who took the tray eagerly and started to eat without a word or a look at any of us. Why we didn't take their food, I can't tell you. . . . Poor Igo and Klarunia, their eyes bigger than their shrunken stomachs. What must they have been thinking? . . . to deny these children a bite of their food told me everything I needed to know about the Steckels and their character. (128/129)*

Not much later came two of Mr. Patrontasch's brothers, who had been able to escape from a nearby work camp that was clearly becoming a death camp. Soon after them came Zygush and Zosia, the small children of one of Clara's mother's sisters. Their dad had been killed during the German assault, and now their mom had been killed by the

SS, even though the children didn't know it yet. The Steckels clearly felt they had the right to demand that Zygush and Zosia not be admitted. For one thing, they might be noisy, but:

> "Beck looked right at the Steckels. 'The children are staying.' . . . Professor Steckel couldn't get a single word out before Beck cut him off. 'Throw the children out? If God brought them here, who is Beck to turn them away? Whatever will be will be.' It was Beck who brought God into the conversation and it was through the miracle of Beck that God had answered our prayers. The children were with us." (144)

So now, even though Beck had sworn he would not take in anyone besides the original eleven, the hole in the ground held eighteen people.

Then, in April, disaster struck. A house on their street caught on fire, the conflagration spread, and about twenty houses all around theirs burned down. In the confusion and panic Clara's sister Mania ran off, was caught and killed. Beck was as devastated as the families were, and worse: his own courage failed him, and he announced they would have to leave since Mania's killers would come looking for them also. But he soon got hold of himself, and bluffed his way through interrogations by the SS. They were not terribly persistent, and gullible enough to swallow Beck's stories.

In the meantime a novel problem developed. On numerous occasions Beck had been calling the beautiful widow Klara upstairs to perform some sort of domestic chore, but it became obvious that those assignments were really assignations; the two were having an affair. For one thing, this always happened as soon as Beck's wife Julia had left the house. But what could anyone do? The men tried talking to Klara but she blew them off; and we may guess that if Klara had ended the affair at their behest, that would not have endeared them to Beck, on whose goodwill everyone was utterly dependent. Still, his wife Julia was equally important, and she was bound to find out sooner or later. When she did her fury was memorable, especially when Beck defended himself by throwing punches and furniture; but again, the hidden Jews were powerless to intervene. Eighteen lives were in the hands of the Becks, all three of whom stormed out of the house. For three days and three sleepless nights the eighteen sat in their bunker, out of food and running out of water. If they ventured out they'd be killed. If they stayed and the Becks didn't come back, they would die of starvation or by their own hand; the Steckels carried vials of poison for just that reason. But in the end things settled down, and I should not tell how because this is meant to be a book review, not a Reader's Digest condensation.

September came, bringing some good war news. It also brought Yom Kippur, the Jewish Feast of Atonement and Forgiveness, which the eighteen conducted with all possible faithfulness, in the dirt and in their underwear on account of the heat under the house. Clara's father, who in his youth had almost become a rabbi instead of a businessman, chanted anancient prayer composed by a rabbi, possibly in medieval Spain. I have to quote part of it, for its beauty and for its connections to Psalm 8:4/5 and Job 7:17:

> Lord, what is Man that you recognize him?
> The son of a frail human that you reckon with him?
>
> Man is like a breath; his days are like a fleeting shadow.
> In the morning it blossoms and is rejuvenated,
> by evening it is cut down and brittle.
>
> According to the count of our days, so may You teach us;
> then we shall acquire a heart of wisdom.

After the traditional "Amen. Next year in Jerusalem," there was a knock on the trap door. The Becks were bringing them their post-fast meals. By this time the Schwarz family had almost run out of money and valuable objects to give to the Becks, and – in a strict application of house rules – nobody had given anything to cover the cost of feeding the youngest children, Zygush and Zosia. But here was Julia Beck, bringing a big pot of chicken soup, "filled with noodles and pirogies." (196/197)

By November 1943 they had been underground for a year. It had also been a whole year since the *Aksja* that had cost the lives of so many friends and relatives. The war, it seemed, would never end. Food was scarce; their mainstays were small amounts of potatoes and bread, with the latter becoming increasingly scarce. Everybody was skin and bones. Electricity in Zolkiew had become intermittent, so with little to do in the dark they spent more and more time sleeping. "We had become animals. Our skin was beyond pale. It was grey, the color of dirty sheets, and our hollowed-out eyes, even the children's, were ringed with the darkest of circles." (225) Beck had started another affair, this time with a widowed sister-in-law, and was gone a lot, while Julia's presence in the house became as unpredictable as the electric supply. But once again, the bunker's occupants were powerless. And when Beck entertained buddies at the house, to drink and play cards, they could do even less, for fear their presence might be noticed through talking, snoring, cooking, or using their primitive bathroom.

Their second Christmas came; Beck threw a noisy party upstairs, laughing uproariously while the entire assembly sang Christmas carols with adapted lyrics, such as "Joy to the World, the Yids are dead" and worse, while the children downstairs cringed in panic. The party ran very late. As soon as his last guest left, Beck asked all of them to come upstairs:

> He apologized profusely for having gone along with the singing. It had been an act. All the Becks were ashamed. That after all they had done for us, they would even worry about such a thing was a testament to their goodness. Mr. Beck cried and apologized and kissed each of the children. (216)

The year 1944 brought endless new hazards since elements of the slowly-retreating German war machine were being billeted at Beck's house, one after another. First came two German train operators who worked erratic schedules. Disposing of the bunker occupants' bodily wastes had been facilitated by the house's flush toilet, a rarity in those days. Going to an outside privy to dump buckets filled by eighteen people would have been extremely risky. But now, with the trainmen sometimes not leaving the house for days, disposal became a terrible problem. They could not empty the buckets in the trainmen's presence, but if they kept them too long the stench would give them away. So the Becks directed fast, military-style bucket-dumping maneuvers while the trainmen were being diverted by cheery, pretty Ala. Then half a dozen SS-troops moved in too, but fortunately they stayed only a week. Ala's boyfriend, a German pilot, also spent a great deal of time in the house. Part of the bunker was under the upstairs bathroom, so someone using it would be able to hear almost any noise from below. The group stationed a sound-guard in that area, to control all noises including snoring by any member of the party.

One night, as soon all the unwelcome guests were asleep, Mr. Melman started bringing up full buckets, for Mr. Patrontasch to dump them in the toilet. Evidently the flushing awoke one of the trainmen, who decided to go to the bathroom himself. He saw Patrontasch, but in his drunken drowsiness didn't react right away. Patrontasch jumped through the hatch, closing it after himself: "One of the trainmen, he saw me." Everyone downstairs prepared for the worst; this was the end. Soon a great commotion started upstairs, with the trainman screaming about the man he'd just seen, feet stomping all over to find him, Julia claiming it must have been a burglar who had stolen her silver. The trainman left to return with several policemen, but they pooh-poohed the incident and left.

April 1944 brought the front closer than ever. One night, as a sort of morale booster, Beck brought them upstairs to watch the explosions in Lvov, which the Russians were now bombing. Later that month four German soldiers who needed lodging showed up; their names were Norbert, Dieter, Richard and Hans. Getting rid of the downstairs waste now became utterly impossible; there was always someone in the house. The men dug a hole in the back of the bunker and covered it with wood, but everyone feared the smell would give them away.

One of the soldiers, Norbert, had a wonderful singing voice. Down below Clara was enthralled by his renditions of popular songs as well as classical ones from Schubert's *Die schöne Müllerin* – ' The Beautiful Miller's Daughter.' They also overheard Hans competing with a visiting local policeman, also named Hans, in bragging about how many Jews each Hans had killed. Joining in, Norbert contributed the thought that hacking them to pieces would be better than just shooting them.

Afterwards Norbert told Julia Beck that while lying on his bed he'd heard noises from down below, and wondered if they might have Jews down there. Julia laughed it off. But soon the next crisis occurred, when the Ukrainian police swarmed into the house, looking for Jews. By that time the Ukrainians, many of whom had welcomed the Germans as liberators, were determined to get rid of the local Poles as well as the remaining Jews, to create a future Ukraine for Ukrainians only. And to them the Becks qualified as Poles. The policemen ransacked the house, screaming at Julia:

"Where are they? Tell us and we won't kill you. You Polish bitch. Everybody knows they're here. We know how many! You've got 14 Jews! The whole town knows it!" I thought they would start beating her. I was afraid Julia would give us away, or worse, that they would kill her. But Julia was holding her own, screaming back, "There are no Jews here! We have Nazis living here!"

A familiar voice joined the screaming. It was our anti-Semitic soldier Hans, yelling at the top of his huge lungs: "SWINE! How do you dare search where German soldiers are living?"

> The Ukrainian shouted, "They're here! We have reports!"
> Hans must have taken out his gun. "You blue-coat, thieving sons of bitches, search, search all you want because there's no one here! But if I find one thing missing, I'll track you down and shoot you where you stand." . . .
> Hans had only come back to pick up something he had forgotten. Again, fate had intervened on our behalf. I didn't know what to make of it. (281/282)

Weeks later Mr. Steckel, who ordinarily never spoke, said he had something important to tell the rest of the bunker's residents.

> He cleared his throat.
> 'My pallet is right under the soldiers' room ... The first week they were here, Hans the policeman bragged to Norbert that he had killed 72 Jews with his own hands. The next day when Norbert came home he sang and whistled as usual until the Becks walked into his room to say hello. But Norbert was upset and he said to the Becks, "Papa, the bloody policeman Hans visited me in my office today. He shook my hand. I had to wash it ten times. I felt so dirty, Papa. I have it good here. I don't want to know what's going on in your house. I don't see anything. I don't hear anything and the Jews in Brody I didn't betray either." . . .
> Richard had also been in the room when Norbert had made this confession to Mr. Beck. . . . We couldn't comprehend it. . . . Our lives were in the hands of these soldiers.
> They had been protecting us and we didn't even know it. We were so sure Norbert was the most foul of the Nazis and now we owed him our lives. I didn't know now if his anti-Semitism was just a ruse like that of Beck. . . .
> I wasn't angry at Steckel for not telling us. He hadn't even told his wife. She seemed more surprised than any of us. We all knew instinctively that he had been trying to save our lives. If we had known and had let up our guard for one moment, it might have led to our deaths as well as that of the Becks. We were either vigilant all the time or not. . . . I didn't know anyone who would have been so wise as Mr. Steckel as not to report the conversation. (295/296)

Finally, in July all the Becks' lodgers left. The German retreat was on in earnest. Russian artillery damaged the house, while the Becks themselves had taken cover in a bunker dug in their back yard by the now departed German soldiers. Once a day Valentin Beck ran over to bring the bunker-people some water, but summers in Zolkiew get unbearably hot, and the starving, dehydrated group on their sweat-soaked pallets was feeling close to death. But then, after three days, Beck banged on the hatch, shouting that the Russians had arrived.

When the bunker-people ventured out of the house for the first time in eighteen months, their emaciated, under-used legs crumpled under them. The Russian soldiers gave them bread, asking over and over if they were Jews:

> *We were afraid to say yes, until one with a kind face, no more than a boy himself, told us it was all right and we were safe now. I nodded. I heard a commotion and looked back at the house.*
> *Mr. Melman staggered out of the house, barely able to hold the Torah. He handed it to Papa. He stripped the wrappings off it, until the bright white of the satin covering, the gold and silver of the handle coverings and the golden thread dazzled in the sunlight. I helped the children up and we walked over to Mr. Melman. The men walked inside and came out with coverings for their heads. We started to say the prayers of thanksgiving.* (303)

The three families (the Steckels vanished right away, without even a goodbye) experienced joyful reunions with surviving fellow-Jews – but very, very few. Clara's book says that 'Out of 5,000 Jews in Zolkiew, there were only 50 left.' (310)

For a month or two the Russians ran Zolkiew in a laissez-faire way. Army units constantly moved through town, setting up on the gigantic market place overnight, where the soldiers lit bonfires and did a great deal of singing and dancing. Going there became everyone's favorite pastime.

But one early September morning the NKVD, later called the KGB, arrested the Becks and took them to Lvov for questioning. Even though everyone in town knew they were the heroes who had enabled the survival of eighteen Jews, the Soviet secret police decided they were German spies, left behind by the Nazis to commit acts of sabotage. Their evidence consisted of some rifles Beck had kept at his house, a house the survivors had officially given him by now. Those survivors also made trips to Lvov, beseeching the Soviet officials and bribing them. They paid and they prayed.

"Please, a man and his wife are about to be killed. They saved our lives and 14 other people's as well. They're heroes."

That was Clara Schwarz, begging the soldiers guarding the office of Zolkiew's new Communist Party Secretary to allow her see him. They brought her, Lola and the two children, Zygush and Zosia, to his office. The Party Secretary, now Zolkiew's most powerful man, told her the Becks were German spies. She beseeched him to read her diaries, all four volumes of which she had brought. He promised to do so.

Two or three days later one of the soldiers returned the diaries, without a message. But a few evenings later the Becks were at their door. They looked terrible, but in no time at all they were the center of a boisterous reunion party. After some time Beck took Clara aside:

"Clarutchka, they told me about the diary. I guess you said some nice things about me after all."

Clara Schwarz-Kramer in 2009, at home in New Jersey.

Photo: Elaine Durbach

TOYOKA OKA'S WAR

"Hello Del. How are you set for food today?"

"(Giggle). O, my cupboard is getting bare. Some food would be nice."

"Fine, I'll be there after four. You want the usual, as usual?"

"O yes, that would be lovely!"

These are the telephone preliminaries for my weekly dinner delivery to Del, which is short for Delpha, my former mother in law. Yes, I confess; while I missed being a boomer baby, I did take part in another notorious demographic trend, the divorce boom of the 'eighties. And for years afterwards my relationship with Del was a frigid stand-off, for which I can't entirely blame her. Call it the mother-bear syndrome. Hey, she almost died while bringing Karen into the world, her only child. So it must have hurt when after twenty years of marriage I decided that I could no longer live with her daughter. But all that's water under the bridge. My two boys are living in Portland, supporting themselves, though neither one seems inclined to start a family. That could be my fault, who knows. And Del, now 88, lives alone on Coos Bay's most fashionable hill, in an apartment with a fine view of a bay once full of lumber ships, but now empty.

"Hulloo – "

"Come on in!"

As usual I find her sitting in her easy-chair, in her blue robe. Getting dressed was always a chore, and more so these days. When I started the food deliveries three or more years ago she still cooked occasionally, but she's given that up too although she may scramble an egg now and then. And no, she's not paying me; we don't do food deliveries commercially. But through the years I have brought free meals to other elderly people.

"Nice to see you!" she says, and I'm sure she means it. After I tried her on several of our more interesting (in my view) German specialties she decided on fish & chips as her favorite, so I'm bringing an extra-large plate that will last her a couple of days. She will warm up the leftover fries and fish in her little convection oven. I'm also bringing a pint of cold clam chowder, a pint of our tangy cole slaw, and some of my sliced German rye bread, all for the fridge. My sourdough rye bread, she once confided, keeps her digestion lively, and I'm not surprised. Unless you freeze that kind of bread it gains sourness every day, proof that the bugs keep doing their digestive thing and are ready for more. I put the cold stuff in her fridge and take the aluminum foil off the dinner plate of fish & chips. Eating off a real plate beats Styrofoam.

"This looks good," she sighs as she seats herself at the table, half-full coffee mug at her side. I settle down for a visit.

"You know," I say as she covers her first piece of fried fish with tartar sauce, "the other day I was reading about the Japanese internment, during World War II. They're commemorating it again this month. I was reading about the legality of it – although illegality would be closer to the truth. I mean, that order by Roosevelt was based on one of John Adams' Alien and Sedition Laws, way back from 1798. But there was nothing in that law that allowed FDR to lock up American citizens who had done nothing wrong. And a lot of 'em were American citizens."

"O yes, they were."

"Reason I bring this up, your dad told me once that a Japanese farmer friend came to see him when this was happening. He gave him $10,000 in cash. 'Keep this for me,' he said, 'because they are going to lock me up because of the color of my skin.' Do you know who that might have been?"

"Hm. Might have been Mr. Oka. But he never told me anything about that."

"Well, he told me, and he was proud of it. 'That's how that man trusted me,' he bragged, and he had reason to. But I was hoping you might know more."

"No, I don't." She takes another bite, and then a thought hits her:

"But when he died in 1986 I went down to settle the estate, and he always kept very good books. Very accurate books. And one thing that struck me in his ledger was a notation, 'Japanese relocation'. But it didn't say anything else."

"Maybe a note to himself," I speculate. "Something nobody else would understand."

"I suppose. I don't know."

There is not much else we can be sure of except that Herb Gardner, her father, was a man of few words and a man of his word, straight as an arrow, thrifty, generous and incorruptible. Even though he voted Democrat much of the time, he took a dim view of 'people who think that the world owes them a living'; but even so, he was always ready to help them. Looking back, I know he was a substitute father-figure for me. The Gardner family's story was the story of America. Herb's ancestors came from Nantucket Island, part of a 'colony' that included the family names Macy, Starbuck, Folger, Coffin and Gardner, all of whom intermarried and produced prominent achievers in American life. The first Gardner on the island was Captain John Gardner (1624-1706) invited to settle there in 1672. Although not highly educated, he was a man of 'physical courage and rugged honesty', and is remembered as a true leader of the colony.

I always thought Herb Gardner's taciturnity must hail back to that hardscrabble island off the Atlantic coast. The same may have been true of his attitude towards religion, which was neutral. Unlike most early colonies including nearby Massachusetts, 17th Century Nantucket did not require any religious adherence. As a result the island also became a refuge for persecuted Quakers, who in due course persecuted other Quakers.

Herb's branch of the Gardners had come to California by way of an Iowa dairy farm: one morning after one of those violent midwestern thunder storms, Grandpa Gardner had found all his cows dead on the field, I believe near the barbed wire, and decided to move on to the golden state, where farming proved to be more rewarding. And by 1942, when FDR issued Executive Order 9066, enabling the forcible removal of anyone of Japanese ancestry from the western states as an alleged war risk, his son Herb didn't need Mr. Oka's $10,000; he was becoming prosperous himself. During the depression he'd quit running a farm and gone to work as a salesman for Union Oil Company, driving a truck and delivering bulk oil. His wife Hattie ran the cafeteria for the local school, so they were not destitute. He had a way with people too, Herb did. When money got scarce during the Depression, Union Oil had instituted a rule that all delivery customers had to pay within 30 days or else they would be C.O.D. But Herb's predecessor had not passed that on, so when Herb took over he met a lot of irate former customers. "I didn't pay in 30 days, and now I'm C.O.D.? To hell with Union Oil! I'll get it some place else!" But he didn't argue; a former orchardist himself, he promised he'd drop in every week for a chat, not to promote Union Oil but to talk about the weather, about the apricot crop, about baseball, or whatever else a farmer in the Santa Clara Valley might want to talk about. And in time he restored his accounts.

Those were tough times, of course, and price supports for California fruit were not part of FDR's New Deal. Farms all over that insanely fertile valley south of San Francisco were being repossessed by the banks. Then Herb took his dad's advice. Grandpa Gardner had lost a lot of money in the crash of 1929 and didn't trust the stock market, but he urged his son: "Buy land! They quit makin' it years ago!" Since

Herb's credit was good and buyers were few, the banks were glad to let him have the land just for paying the interest. And then, not many years later, California started its meteoric development. First came the military-industrial build-up for World War II, and next the wartime boom, which drew lots of people to California and multiplied Herb's responsibilities, since he was on call 24 hours for oil deliveries to the shipyard and cement plant of Henry Kaiser, whom he knew well. The post-war economic boom put another premium on his properties. By 1946, when he was 48, Herb quit Union Oil and retired on his real-estate profits. Not long afterwards Del's husband persuaded him to put his gains into the stock market, and again his timing proved to be excellent.

"So – this Mr. Oka – did you know him?"

"I was friends with his daughter, Toyoka. We were classmates in fourth grade. Mr. Oka's wife had come from Japan, but he had met her here. There were just six of us in fourth grade, including me and Toyoka and her brother Isamo. They'd been born here. You see, along the San José-Los Gatos road, that was just a little winding road then,

The Gardner-Coffin clan in the 'thirties in Campbell, California. Herb Gardner, with prematurely white hair, is sitting in front on the right, his wife "Dede" (Hattie Bohnett) standing behind him. They had two daughters, Delpha (standing next to Dede) and Connie, standing next to Herb.

there were 8 acres that grandpa Bohnett had donated for a school. He wanted it named Cambrian school, and so it was."

"I can imagine that the Pearl Harbor attack spooked people pretty badly.

Herb and Hattie in the 'seventies, near the old storage buildings in back of their house. According to Del he had built them partly to store the possessions of Japanese-American friends.

And when people are in a panic they do weird things. Like putting fellow-citizens in concentration camps."

"O yes -- I was living in Berkeley, ready to go to work at 10 o'clock that Sunday morning, to my waitress job. I was still in the bathroom when the radio broke into a music program to announce this terrible thing that happened in Hawaii. So to get to work from our apartment on Dana Street I walked up to Telegraph, where the restaurant was. So I was walking along, it was a gorgeous, sunny day. And on my way I came to this intersection with four churches."

"I've only ever seen an intersection with four gas stations. Back in the 'sixties."

"Ha. There were four all right, and one I believe was a Methodist church that was just letting out. They must have announced the Japanese attack from the pulpit, because people were coming out in bunches, and it was like an explosion, with young fellows bouncing down the steps yelling how they were going to thrash those dirty sonsabitches. I had to laugh, and they were kind of indignant. You know: 'It's not funny!' But I just had to laugh because it sounded kind of odd, just coming out of church. You don't expect to hear that kind of talk from a church bunch."

"I've noticed that conservative Christians are pretty patriotic."

"And when I got to the restaurant, people were just stunned. Everybody talked to everybody. It does that to people."

"So, was everybody of Japanese descent hauled off to the desert?"

"Yes, but it was several months before that happened. And they never touched Hawaii. There was a tremendous Japanese population in Hawaii, but they had no restrictions at all. But Earl Warren was California attorney general, and he was pushing for it. It was a land grab, a rigged tragedy."

"That's funny, about Earl Warren. Because later on he became such a liberal darling, after he got on to the Supreme Court. I remember those bumper stickers, 'Impeach Earl Warren', on account of his desegregation orders."

"Yeah, well, Earl Warren had no political clout in Hawaii then. But there were a lot of people in California who wanted the Japanese farmland, and Warren wanted to be governor. That marvelous land is all under concrete now, but the realtors and the businessmen and the speculators made money off it. It was a big fire sale; those people had to dispose of their property in no time at all."

"So everybody – citizens and non-citizens – they were all hauled off to these camps?"

"Mmm. At first they were kept at three race tracks in the valley. There was Tanferan, and Bay Meadows, and another one I don't remember the name of. And they stayed there quite a while, while these camps were being built in the desert. Whole families were sleeping in the horse stalls, so you can imagine, it was bad. People did try to help out, bringing food and such. And Toyoka and her family wound up in a large camp near Tule Lake. They spent the entire war there. And Mr. Oka, he was a bitter man. Mrs. Oka died there, and he may have come back but Toyoka went to Detroit."

I should do more of the talking so she can eat her food while it's still warm. So I talk a little more about the illegality of the whole scheme, which has of course been accepted, but much later. Much too late for people whose lives had been destroyed. A couple of the Japanese-Americans challenged FDR's policy in court, but the Supreme Court said that under war circumstances he could pretty much do as he pleased. I guess that's one good reason for keeping the peace: in wartime domestic freedoms come under attack, but not from the enemy. And most judges are hesitant to swim against strong political currents. I excuse myself to go home.

> *"Silent enim leges inter arma."*
>
> "In times of war, of course, the law falls silent."
>
> Marcus Tullius Cicero

"Remember to take your plate," she says. As usual last week's dinner plate is waiting in the entry, washed and properly packaged in a sturdy paper grocery bag held by an oversized rubber band. No plastic bags for Delpha.

Back home I do an internet search on the interest groups behind Executive Order #9066. Besides Earl Warren they included all the newspapers and most of the politicians in California, Oregon and Washington, along with prominent business organizations like the California Farm Bureau. There was also a general DeWitt, an undistinguished warrior who had been put in charge of civil defense on the coast, and made up a lot of alarming stories about the Japanese domestic threat.

And then, to my surprise, there was Walter Lippmann, the famous pacifist journalist, steadfast opponent of the Cold War and a thorn in Lyndon Johnson's side during Vietnam. In February 1942, soon after Pearl Harbor, Lippmann was singing a very different tune. In a highly influential column entitled "The Fifth Column on the Coast", he warned that America's West Coast was "in imminent danger of a combined attack from within and from without." The fact that West Coast Japanese-Americans had not committed any significant sabotage meant nothing, he scoffed, but was proof positive that they were up to no good:

> "… this is not, as some have liked to think, a sign that there is nothing to be feared. It is a sign that the blow is well organized and that it is held back until it can be struck with maximum effect."

Earl Warren used the same illogical logic while testifying before the U.S. Congress, which then rubber-stamped Roosevelt's order. Was the post-war liberal turn of both Warren and Lippmann based on something else they shared -- a wish to atone for inciting that wartime persecution?

Pearl Harbor's a jewel of sunshine and sea,
where winters are balmy and fair;
but once upon a December's morn,
was felt a strange nip in the air!

C. L. Grove

HEIDE FUNKE'S WAR

"I have something for you," says Heide Cummings. She opens her freezer and takes out a foil-wrapped package that makes quite a plunk on her kitchen counter. "It's a loaf of bread I baked yesterday. It's not a rye bread like what you gave me, but it's an all-whole wheat bread. I never bake white breads, like Wonder Bread. This is heavy, like the German breads."

"Thank you. I'm looking forward to it." And I am. Whenever I'm talking to people of German background, we are unanimous in our disdain for American white bread. German bread is real bread. Although – I didn't actually grow up with it. Not until I was 18 or 19 did I get acquainted with traditional, dense, German sourdough rye. In the late 1950s, hitchhiking through the Eifel on the way home, I had stopped at a village bakery to spend my last few Pfennigs on a loaf of bread. Without asking what kind, the lady sold me a round, dark loaf; and as soon as I sat down along the road to eat, I thought I'd been sold a pig in a poke. Dutch bakers don't use rye much. They do bake wholesome bread, but it's all yeast-risen wheat, which tends to be on the sweet side, never sour like German rye. And the farther east you go in Europe, the more rye replaces wheat. It has something to do with the shorter growing seasons, I guess.

Even though the sourness of the Eifel rye bread intimidated me at first, it grew on me, and when I got into the food business I wanted to find out how to make it. And that took years, with too many results that looked suspiciously like sick-cow pies. But in the end I got it, and nobody else within hundreds of miles makes anything like my rye bread. Some local Germans are addicted to it; one elderly lady swears that one slice a day keeps her from having *Klo-Probleme*. *Klo* is German slang for the john. In other words, its live content keeps her digestion going.

Still and all, I don't want to create the impression that Heide has never ever used white bread, as she is careful to explain: "Years ago when we were fishing in northern Alberta, I used white bread once, and used it for bait. We were at a lake where people were throwing out bread for the ducks, white bread of course, and we noticed trout coming up to eat it. So I rolled up some of it into little balls, and used it for bait. I used a Cheerio to hold it together, and it worked. But here comes the game warden: "What are you using for bait?" So I told him, and he said there was no rule against it."

North SCHLESWIG
to Denmark
WW I

POMERANIA
to Poland
WW II

DANZIG
to Poland
WW II

MEMEL
to Lithuania – WW I

to Russia – WW II

EAST PRUSSIA
to Poland – WW II

CORRIDOR

Berlin

MALMEDY-
EUPEN
to Belgium
WW I

INTERNAL
GERMAN
BORDER
1945-1991

West
PRUSSIA
& POSEN
to Poland
WW I

SILESIA
to Poland
WW II

East UPPER
SILESIA
to Poland
WW I

ALSACE-
LORRAINE
to France
WW I

**GERMAN TERRITORIAL
LOSSES 1919-1945**

Territories lost at
Treaty of Versailles, 1919

Territories annexed by
Poland, 1945

Free City of Danzig,
1919-1939

Territories annexed by
Soviet Union, 1945

Five generations of Heide's family had owned a farming estate in East Prussia, the easternmost German land that the 1919 Treaty of Versailles had separated from the rest of Germany by creating the "Polish Corridor". This Corridor, part of resurrected Poland, had been carved out of the German-ruled lands of West Prussia and Posen. One reason had been to give Poland access to the Baltic, but another that a majority of the inhabitants of the Corridor already spoke Polish and had lived there for centuries, albeit under Prussian administrations since the late 1700s. Next, as we know, after the Nazis invaded Poland in 1939 they decided to forcibly Germanize these majority-Polish lands by expelling the Poles and re-settling *Volksdeutsche* families like Lilli Clausen's there. And as we also know, that story did not end well.

Unlike the Corridor, East Prussia had been conquered as far back as the 13th century by the Teutonic Knights, an order of German nobles who fought for Christianity, but in due course pursued more worldly goals. As a result the area had long been German-speaking, with only a small Polish-speaking minority. But as is usually true of east-European geographic history, things were more complicated. The Prussians, today considered the most German of Germans, started out as a Baltic tribe that after its defeat by the Teutonic Knights had gradually been Christianized and absorbed into the German nation. So in the end, whether people were considered German or not mainly depended on

the language they spoke. As reminders of the Knights' centuries-long Germanization process, many of East Prussia's cities still contain large castles they built, of which the most impressive one is the Marienburg, located on a branch of the Vistula River.

It's been three or four years since Heide and her husband Grant came into the restaurant and introduced themselves. Grant had fought in World War II. "In Patton's Army, 817th TD battalion, company B,

1st platoon," he explained proudly. "TD means Tank Destroyer. I drove a tank-killer. And I drove all other kinds of vehicles too. Reconnaissance jeeps, and armored cars for the brass."

Then Grant notices my car's license plate: TKT 817. "The 817th battalion!" he exclaims. That was mine!"

"Ah, well, the TKT part is more meaningful to me. It reminds me not to get so many tickets." But this goes over his head, because his hearing is pretty bad. Then he explains to me that M36 tank destroyers like the one he drove started out with a 76 mm cannon, which was inadequate against the German Tiger tanks. But in the summer of 1944 they were equipped with 90 mm guns. "Even the Tigers didn't have a chance," he muses contentedly. I can imagine your hearing doesn't have much of a chance against a 90 mm gun, either.

Grant was also at Omaha Beach on D-day, driving a floating tank.

"Did you ever see Patton?"

"O yes, right before D-Day he gave a big speech. I remember him saying: 'All I want to see is white flags. But if I see you shooting at any white flags, I'll shoot at you.' And he'd be there to do it, too. O, the rear echelon hated him. They never knew where he'd be next – usually in front."

"I had never heard that. So he went easy on the Germans?"

"O yes, the Germans, they were all right. The ones we captured, we gave them a hot meal and dry socks. And many spoke better English than we did."

"Were you wounded?"

"Yes, I got a one-week vacation in Switzerland that way. I got hit by shrapnel, and my teeth were hurt."

Grant and Heide didn't meet in Germany. Heide's family had come to America in 1950, after they had lost the family estate, a spread of 250 hectares (about 620 acres) in the war. Large ' estate' farms were typical of the eastern territories, while small peasant farms were more common in western Germany. But before the end of World War II, Roosevelt and Churchill had agreed to Stalin's demand that the German and Polish borders be drastically moved westward. This meant that Poland would not only regain the Corridor, but more German territory west of the Corridor besides. That new territory consisted of Pomerania and Silesia. At the same time Stalin would get to keep the eastern half of Poland that his infamous 1939 deal with Hitler had gained him. East Prussia would not remain German, either. The northern half would become Russian, the southern half Polish. And after the war all the local Germans who had not fled, or had returned after the war ended, were expelled unless they accepted their new nationality.

Heide has enjoyed traveling not just in Alberta but also in Minnesota, because both remind her of the former East Prussia: mostly flat with lots of lakes, fir and pine forests and heaths, and predominantly rural. The Masurian Lake District where they lived was famous for the very expensive Trakehner breed of horses. The main city in their *Kreis*, or district, was Allenstein, a town of about 50,000 which dates from the mid-fourteenth century and also contains a castle built by the Teutonic Knights. (Today, because of all the border changes after World War II, Allenstein, now called Olsztyn, is located in the northeastern-most corner of Poland.) The Funke family's estate was near a village called Daumen. Both the estate and Daumen were located east of Allenstein, and both bordered on a lake called Daumen See or Daumensee.

Time for a minor linguistic digression: usually, when Germans talk about a *See* (German nouns are capitalized, and this one is pronounced "zay"), they mean what an English speaker would call a lake, and a Dutchman would call a *meer*: an enclosed body of fresh water. But when

Daumensee, the lake near the family estate.

Germans talk of a *Meer*, they usually mean what an English speaker would call a sea and a Dutchman would call *zee* (again, pronounced "zay"). Examples are the German terms for the

East Prussia (Ostpreußen)
1923 - 1939

Lithuania

Memel

Memel - land

Heydekrug

Curic Lagoon

Tilsit

Memel River

Königsberg

Pillau

Pregel River

Gumbinnen

Insterburg

Vistula Lagoon

Braunsberg

Frauenburg

Pr. Eylau

Danzig

Elbing

Heilsberg

Angerburg

Marienburg

Rastenburg

Wartenburg

Bischofsburg

Vistula River

Daumen

Allenstein

Marienwerder

Osterode

Ortelsburg

Poland

Mediterranean (*das Mittelmeer*), the Black Sea (*das Schwarze Meer*), and the Caribbean (*das Karibische Meer*). But it gets even more confusing, and that's entirely the fault of the Germans, because they call the North Sea *Nordsee* and the Baltic *Ostsee* (East Sea). Maybe this muddle is due to the fact that for centuries most Germans never saw a sea or ocean, so they called any sizable body of water, salty or not, a *See*.

With Königsberg and Memel (see map), East Prussia included 14,300 square miles, more than the Netherlands, but much less densely populated with 2.5 million residents. Even so, East Prussia produced many famous people. The philosopher Immanuel Kant (1724-1804) was from Königsberg, as was the composer Werner Heymann (1896-1961) whose music is still being used in movies, notably 'Chocolat' and

'The Green Mile'. But no doubt East Prussia's most famous resident was the astronomer and all-around genius Copernicus (1473-1543) who lived at the castle in Allenstein and died in Frauenburg, east of Danzig. The claim that he was Polish is true mostly in a political sense. Back then East Prussia was controlled by the Polish Kingdom, which had allied itself with German-speaking free cities like Danzig against the Teutonic Knights, who by then behaved a lot like worldly robber barons. And

Downtown Königsberg, East Prussia, before the war. By early 1945, 90% of the city had been destroyed. Renamed Kaliningrad, it is now part of Russia.

Copernicus' family, although they were from Kopernik in then-German Silesia, favored the cause of the Polish king, and even fought for him.

But one of the former East Prussia's sweetest bequests to the world was a simple song. In 1636 Simon Dach, a poet born in Memel, was invited to the wedding of a 17 year old girl named Anna from Tharau, near Königsberg. At the wedding he was so smitten by her that he wrote a poem, 'Ännchen von Tharau.' He wrote it in the dialect then spoken in the eastern part of Prussia, which was closer to Dutch than High German because a lot of Dutch farmers had settled there. In 1778 the poet Johann Herder, also from East Prussia, re-wrote 'Ännchen' in *Hochdeutsch*, and in 1827 Friedrich Silcher, a composer of German *Volkslieder*, wrote its present melody. Though literally a folk song, a *Volkslied* is not like the ones popularized in America in the 1960s, by singers like Joan Baez. *Volkslieder* are immortal, very singable German favorites with simple but highly evocative lyrics. Some were created by unknown poets and composers, others by famous ones like Goethe and Heine, Schubert and Glück. On Youtube you can find performances of the *Hochdeutsch* version of 'Ännchen von Tharau', sung by German

choirs and by famous vocalists. Many people think that the late Fritz Wunderlich's rendition is the best.

In 1989 exiles from Memelland raised a statue of Ännchen in Memel.

Anke van Tharaw *(Plattdeutsch)*

Anke van Tharaw öß, die my geföllt,
se öß mihn Lewen, mihn Goet on mihn Gölt.
Anke van Tharaw heft wedder eer Hart
op my geröchtet ön Löw' on ön Schmart.
Anke van Tharaw mihn Rihkdom, mihn Goet,
Du mihne Seele, mihn Fleesch on mihn Bloet.

Ännchen von Tharau *(Hochdeutsch)*

Ännchen von Tharau ist, die mir gefällt,
sie ist mein Leben, mein Gut und mein Geld.
Ännchen von Tharau hat wieder ihr Herz
auf mich gerichtet in Lieb' und in Schmerz.
Ännchen von Tharau, mein Reichthum, mein Gut,
du meine Seele, mein Fleisch und mein Blut!

The only English translation of Ännchen that I know of is by Longfellow. It's second rate because it lacks the powerful plainness of the original, and it's garbled to boot. Instead of surrendering to him (line 4), Dach wrote that 'Annie' had *gerichtet* (aimed) her heart at him:

Annie of Tharaw

Annie of Tharaw, my true love of old,
she is my life, and my goods, and my gold.
Annie of Tharaw, her heart once again
to me has surrendered in joy and in pain.
Annie of Tharaw, my riches, my good,
Thou my soul, my flesh and my blood!

Erich Koch (between bowler-hatted local official and Hitler) welcoming the Führer to East Prussia in August 1939, days before the German attack on Poland that started World War II. Part of that attack was launched from East-Prussian territory.

While telling the story of the family's flight from East Prussia, Heide consults a stack of notes written by her mother, Lore Funke. Lore had been left in charge of the Funke estate while her husband, Hans-Werner, served on the eastern front which, by Nazi logic, made her the 'leader' of a food-producing organization for the *Reich*. This was so even though she was not a farm girl (she had no idea how to milk a cow), and she had relied on a manager to run the farm. But because of her 'leader' position, and despite the ever-closer threat of the advancing Russian armies, she (and many more) could not leave East Prussia.

And when permission finally came it was much too late, thanks to the dawdling of the *Gauleiter* (district leader) Erich Koch, a greedy bully whom the Poles later tried for war crimes and locked up for life in the jail in Wartenburg (now called *Barczewo)*, after commuting his original death sentence. Hitler's *Gauleiters* competed in nastiness with the great *Führer* himself, with Koch even sporting an authentic Hitler-mustache. And during the winter of 1944/45, when Germany's imminent defeat was obvious to everyone except the Nazi régime's bosses, those bosses saw to it that desertion and even simple expressions of hopelessness (called "defeatism") were punished by death, often by being shot or hanged on the spot. But unlike Hitler, Koch did not kill himself when the Russians were finally closing in. After ordering wounded soldiers about to be repatriated on a German vessel to be put back on shore, he escaped to western Germany by way of the icy Baltic.

Danzig, February 1945: a shop window carries warning posters. Left: <u>Soldiers, report to the nearest Army office. Whoever joins civilian refugees or loiters in private quarters is considered a deserter.</u> Right: <u>Danzigers, maintain discipline! Panic and rumor-mongering are the bolshevists' best allies</u>

But he had waited until January 20 to approve the evacuation of the East Prussians who had not yet fled. That cost a lot of lives, because Russian armies already blocked the overland way to the West, refugees were being attacked indiscriminately, and the weather was terrible.

Heide remembers that in addition to crop land, the Funke estate had about forty milk cows. Twelve years old at the time of their flight to the west, she was the eldest of five children. The estate/farm had provided a good income while it was being run by their manager Ziermann, who had spent his entire life on the place. After the early death of Heide's father, her mother Lore had remarried his cousin Hans-Werner Funke, thus keeping the Funke name connected to the estate. In quick succession, she and Hans-Werner then had four more children: Gerda, 4 ½ years old at the time, Werner, 3 ½, Vickie, 2 ½ and baby Lore, 1 ½. But like most German men her new husband had been drafted, and had been wounded on the eastern front. In September 1944 he'd come home on furlough. The handwriting was on the wall, he said:

"Don't spend any more of your strength and heart on this place. Our estate is lost – everything is lost. The Russians will be here soon, just try to get out before they come."

Winter 1944/45: East Prussian residents being evacuated through the frozen harbor of Pillau, at the exit of the Vistula lagoon east of Danzig.

Excellent advice as it was, Lore Funke felt powerless to take it. If she left without permission she might be accused of 'leaving her post' or 'defeatism' or both, and face Nazi justice. Another impediment was the estate's work crew, which by then consisted of 28 Russian POWs who were guarded by 3 or 4 disabled German soldiers. Those people had to be fed and housed, so the family's absence would be noticed right away. Before the end of Hans-Werner's furlough they decided, as a fallback plan, to meet in Stuttgart, Lore's hometown, in the western part of Germany, which they expected to be occupied by the Americans. They would meet at the family home of the children's nanny in that city. But until war conditions allowed her to leave the estate, Lore would have to stay. The children called their nanny *Tante* (Aunt) Lotte.

And that was the Funkes' situation in December 1944, when the first refugees from Tilsit, in the easternmost part of East Prussia, came rushing in. The peasants brought their livestock, which had to be fed along with the people. Communications including telephone and mail service had collapsed, so late at night, when Lore was sure no one else was awake, she tuned in to the forbidden London news broadcast to find out what was going on. Everyone dreaded what was to come, even the Russian POWs at the estate. The Soviet logic was even simpler than the Nazis' and just as brutal: any captured Russian soldier who had worked for the enemy was Russia's enemy, deserving of instant death or slightly delayed death in a Siberian labor camp.

Heide's mom found watching the hurry of the retreating German army units a strange experience. Their arrival not long before had given her the feeling of being protected. But this time they were just rushing through, hardly taking time to stop. She had her laborers and Novak the local blacksmith bring her seven farm wagons into top condition, and put spikes on the horses' shoes to cope with the abundant snow and ice. Finally, after word spread of the informal approval to leave on January 20, she spent all of that night packing her possessions. An army officer on his way through stayed up to help her, but he warned that in the end, the only good it might do was help her pass the night. Even if she managed to take all her things with her, most likely she would have to abandon them along the road, he predicted. The next morning a local policeman told her that the Russians were already in Frögenau, some forty miles to the west. That meant they would soon reach the coast at the Bay of Danzig, blocking all roads and railroads to western Germany. The only way out now was across the Baltic Sea, leaving by ship from Pillau. She doubted that would be possible, and it may have been a good thing she didn't try. Conditions were frigid in the extreme, there was no assurance of getting a place on a departing vessel, and Russian submarines in the Baltic were sinking German ships. Then an army sergeant came and ordered her Russian POW laborers and their German guards to be moved to Allenstein. Lore told them to butcher a couple of pigs and to take their meat with them on sleighs, along with some bread. For 3 ½ years they had been conscientious workers, who took good care of the stock; and when they said their goodbyes they had tears in their eyes. That night Allenstein fell into Russian hands. She never knew what became of them.

The next day, Sunday January 21, most of the people of the tiny village of Daumen descended on the estate. They included Novak the blacksmith and Ziermann the farm manager. The estate's seven wagons would carry fourteen families in all, plus the Funkes' domestic personnel who included, besides Tante Lotte, Mia the cook and a maid called Hilla. Throughout her story, Lore Funke described all of them as 'my people.' These constant mentions of 'my people' are touching echoes of days gone by, when the ancient 'noblesse oblige' relationship between a country landlord and the locals meant a great deal to both. It still did

Russian tanks in East Prussia, January 1945.

then, but Lore was in constant despair at her inability to protect 'her people' once the Russians arrived. When on January 21 'her people' from Daumen had brought their cows, chickens and pigs, she had a hard time explaining that they would be lucky to save their own lives on the road, let alone their animals. But then, Lore herself was just as attached to her personal possessions, if not to her livestock; and she would lose both as well.

Before abandoning the estate, the farm hands set most of the animals free so they could feed at the huge hay stacks and drink from the brook behind the farm. Dusk was already setting in when the caravan of seven horse-drawn wagons plus the Funke family's car (also pulled by horses, to save gasoline) started moving towards the public road that bordered the property. Since the way out ran uphill and was not plowed, just reaching the road was a struggle. Temperatures were -20°Celcius (-4° Fahrenheit), and once on the road Heide's mom had trouble seeing through her icy windshield. Not having slept for two nights, she soon got drowsy and landed the car in the ditch. Hiking up the road, she found an army corporal good at handling horses, who kindly managed to get the car back onto the pavement, and in the next village they found a warm house already crowded with refugees.

The next morning, snippets of war news and the sound of nearby gunfire convinced everyone that proceeding further was useless. But where could they go? She thought of a refuge, a small chicken farm located deep in the forest, where they might be safe from the attacking

Russians. Despite being strafed by Russian fighter planes, they made it safely into the woods. When they reached the chicken farm they found the owner's wife, Mrs. Gerull, still there. Her husband had been terminally ill for a long time, and the thought of leaving him behind while still alive was more than she could bear. But he had just died, and she needed help burying him in the frozen ground. That done, Lore told Heide she had done the very best she could. "This is where we will live or die. . . . I now lay our burdens in the hands of the Lord."

While listening to the London newscast again on Saturday January 27, she contentedly mused that she no longer needed to worry about the Nazis finding out about that illegal activity. They were, so to speak, between bosses, and for a little while could do as they pleased. Radio London confirmed that the Russians had reached the Vistula lagoon to the west, so the refugee caravan had been wise to turn around.

And shortly after midnight the following Tuesday morning, a couple of dozen Russians arrived at Mrs. Gerull's chicken farm. They set up a communications center in the house, while constantly ordering food to be cooked and engaging in pervasive property theft: watches, jewelry, clothes, plus anything edible. But there was no violence, there were no personal assaults – yet. Then all of a sudden they were gone, leaving a huge mess in their wake. It turned out they had also helped themselves to anything they pleased from the packed household goods stored in the barns, and much of what they didn't want, they had trashed.

Exhausted, the refugees didn't even consider cleaning up the mess because after their all-night ordeal they needed food. But no sooner had they started preparing it when another group of Russians appeared, and another after that, each one seedier and greedier than the last one. Soon the chicken farm had hardly any chickens left. Heide's mom had heard that Stalin had promised his men that as soon as they crossed the German border they could have everything they wanted, including every German woman. She had doubted it, but what was going on convinced her it must be true. The fervor with which they grabbed everything and every woman was incredible. Somehow, through guile or charm or sheer determination, she herself avoided it – but considering what was done to so many other women, she was a rare exception.

Although Stalin was one of history's most ruthless tyrants, I have not come across anything that would qualify as a written promise to his troops along the lines Heide's mom described. Most likely that was a rumor like the one that spread across East Prussia not long afterward, that the area would be in the American-administered sector of Germany.

On the other hand, just because an order was not written doesn't prove it was not issued. History's most notorious example may be the lack of a written order by Hitler authorizing the Jewish 'Final Solution'. On another hand yet, that January a Soviet order was promulgated that called on the Red Army to punish rape and robbery. Part of that may have been a cover for Stalin's informally condoning huge amounts of outrageous behavior by his armies. He *has* been quoted verbally excusing plunder, violence and rape as to be expected from millions of unpaid men who had grown up in circumstances far below those prevailing in Germany, who had been at war without a break for 3 ½ years, and who were furious about the atrocities committed by German troops in their homeland. Also, Stalin had left Russian propagandists like the writer Ilya Ehrenburg free to direct tirades at his troops, calling for plunder and rape of the enemy.

> "When the military man approaches, the world locks up its [silver] spoons and packs off its womankind."
>
> *George Bernard Shaw*

There are huge differences between historians' estimates of the numbers of rapes committed by the Russian soldiers – from tens of thousands to millions – with the higher numbers furiously disputed by Russian historians as slander against the heroic Red Army. But most western historians have come down on the side of the millions, and the fact that the rapes continued long after war's end provides support. After the summer of 1945 the Soviet military did start prosecuting rapists, but without achieving much since they continued until winter 1947/48, when the troops were finally confined to strictly guarded bases inside the Soviet Zone, the future 'German Democratic Republic' that the Kremlin was grooming to become a Soviet satellite.

There is much less dispute about the Russian soldiers' massive thievery, which has been standard procedure throughout the history of warfare, anyway. Besides, the Russian government itself was setting the example, dismantling and hauling off entire German industries.

Even so, other known facts suggest that there is a danger of painting the Russians as robbers and rapists, and the allied soldiers as saints – not to mention the Germans. To start with the latter, it is well known that Nazi officials used their positions to grossly enrich themselves, the most conspicuous example being Hermann Göring's looting of thousands of great works of art all over Europe. Compared with overlords like Göring, the average German soldier behaved pretty well, at least in western Europe. Recent scholarship even suggests that he behaved better than the average allied soldier. That's because even if the looting, violence and rape committed by American, British and French soldiers on the western front did not reach Russian proportions, they were still substantial, if not publicized much. The Americans made themselves especially notorious in recently-liberated France. Apparently before the troops went overseas US Army propaganda had pictured France as an erotic Nirvana, and many GIs behaved accordingly. But it is a fact that the U.S. Army conducted trials for rape, and that close to a hundred GIs were executed for it. (Over 80% of those executed were black; but therein lies another tale.) The fact that so much American misbehavior occurred in allied France creates a curious analogy between the two big wartime allies, since besides their wholesale rapes of German women, Russian soldiers also committed lots of rapes in Poland and Yugoslavia, both of which were Russian allies. They even raped Russian and Polish women they had liberated from German concentration camps.

These posters were not shown in America: Don't catch VD, or you won't go home.

As is true of society at large, a certain percentage of any army's soldiers will have criminal inclinations. Moreover, men in their late teens and early twenties commit more crimes than older age groups. Making things worse, when America went to war some authorities had pressed convicted criminals into military service, as an alternative punishment. Add the careless peer pressure inside a mob carrying guns, and it is clear that any army in wartime will do bad things unless it is superbly disciplined and meticulously controlled. In armies quickly created out of millions of conscripted men, that is not easily achieved.

The people at the chicken farm spent the remainder of Tuesday night wondering what would be coming next, in pitch dark so as not to attract any more visitors. At dawn some of the villagers sneaked in, to see if they had survived. The Russians had a particular hatred of 'capitalists', a category that included anybody who had a business or owned property. This was a serious concern for Lore Funke, as a large property owner. Her early-morning visitors carried the news that Russians had barged into an estate home across the lake that was owned by two elderly ladies, friends of hers. A few days earlier she had visited them, to have tea in their huge home surrounded by all their luxuries while listening to their puzzlement about why their navy-commander son-in-law had not sent a plane to rescue them. Later, when the Russians came, they refused to give them the keys to their silver closet. In response they had been dragged to the cellar and shot.

Yet another group of Russians reached the chicken farm, in a sleigh. This particular group was especially eager to find German soldiers, so they questioned every man present. Their procedure made it obvious that being an officer was a crime even worse than being a capitalist, but under questioning Lore told them (truthfully) that her husband was only a first sergeant, and (falsely) that he was not serving on the eastern front. More rapes followed. Heide recalls her mother's agony caused by the repeated ravishing of Mia the cook and of 'poor, bewildered Trudi,' Mrs. Gerull's maid. After this the Russian intrusions at the chicken farm diminished, but more were happening at the village. The Russian soldiers seemed indifferent to a female's. They didn't even care if people of either sex were watching, and seemed to enjoy making husbands watch their wives being raped. It was understandable that some husbands resisted until they were shot. Death must have seemed an easier choice.

After several days some local refugees returned who had fled ahead of the Funkes, and had continued traveling north until they had to give up. Their ordeal had terribly aged them, with some changed almost beyond recognition. While telling Lore they had lost count of the number of children who lay frozen in the woods, they praised her for having had the good judgment to turn around sooner. Others reported that the Russians were massacring the Germans' French POWs who had worked on the local farms. This was hard to understand, but evidently to them, French POWs who had worked for the Germans were traitors just as much as the Russian ones.

At the chicken farm days turned into weeks, many weeks. The Funke household came close to going home to the estate, but they changed their minds when they learned of yet more atrocities. Russian pilots frequently landed their planes on the frozen lakes, for no other purpose than to commit robbery and worse at lakefront homes like theirs. Returning still looked too dangerous.

But when on March 10 another sleigh arrived, carrying two Russians with the customary agendas, Lore Funke decided she'd had enough. As soon as they were gone she took the children and some live chickens Mrs. Gerull gave her, and left for home. The old lady herself refused to

leave her farm. Afterwards they heard that the Russians had put her to work on a distant railroad, and that she had died there, in the fall.

At the estate they found abandoned trenches and a lot of destruction. Evidently German troops had made a last stand on the grounds, killing 23 Russians whom the manager and the blacksmith had already buried. Inside the house nearly everything that had not been stolen had been destroyed; only the tiled heating stoves, which were nearly indestructible, still stood. But it was home, so they felt safer. And by now many of the Russian soldiers who passed through seemed harmless. They even made friends with an old Russian sergeant, who would stay for a meal of fish from the lake, holding the baby on his knee and grumbling if the help didn't say grace first: 'You always expect the Lord to grow things for you, but you don't thank Him,' he chided them. He always said grace himself; and this reminded Lore that most of her Russian POW laborers had worn crucifixes hidden under their coats. Diehard Russian communists were all atheists. Religious Russians, on the other hand, like believers all over the world, were bearable antagonists even in war.

But the unbearable ones returned, repeatedly gang-raping her cook Mia again. After a couple of weeks the Funkes were told to leave because their house was going to be blown up as a reprisal for some German attack. They decided that Nerwigk, a small village hidden in a government forest, might be the safest refuge, so they abandoned the estate again. By now the weather had turned spring-like, and on a hill above Nerwigk they found an abandoned house that might work. But their first order of business was a massive cleanup, since the departed Russian troops had pooped in every pot and pan and dish and plate in the house which, according to the general impression, seemed to be a cherished custom of theirs. It also seems to be one of those primitive human urges that would have fascinated Sigmund Freud: the fact is, desecration by defecation was not unique to Russian troops. At the time of the German invasion in May 1940, the French and Belgian soldiers who were in our part of the southern Netherlands to defend us did the same thing, but instead of filling pots and pans they did it in the evacuated local population's beds, which made cleanup even more of a challenge. *Merci bien pour ça!*

Unfortunately it did not take long for the refugees in their new abode to be found by the Russians, again. After avoiding the rapists by hiding in the woods for some time, Tante Lotte was rounded up along with cook Mia, manager Ziermann and Novak the blacksmith. They were to be taken away to a labor camp.

At the Yalta conference held in early February, Stalin had made clear to his allies-of-convenience Roosevelt and Churchill that, as part of war reparations owed by Germany, he intended to deport ethnic Germans from the areas held by his armies, to be used as forced laborers for the reconstruction of Russian heavy industry. (In fact, the process had started months earlier.) Despite the popular worship of both Roosevelt and Churchill, I believe that Lord Acton correctly observed that "great men are almost always bad men," with the exceptions being a small number of great men who just happened to become great by a stroke of luck, with events going their way even though they didn't have a clue. I leave it for the reader to decide in which category Roosevelt and Churchill belonged, but maybe it was both. Neither one objected to Stalin's slavery scheme, mostly because of their naïve eagerness to accept the sly tyrant's

> "In their own countries Roosevelt and Churchill are honored as embodiments of statesmanlike wisdom. To us, in our Russian [gulag] prison conversations, their consistent shortsightedness and stupidity stood out as astonishingly obvious. How could they ... fail to secure any guarantees whatever of the independence of Eastern Europe? ... And what was the military or political sense in their surrendering to destruction at Stalin's hands hundreds of thousands of armed Soviet citizens [Vlasovites] determined not to surrender? They say it was the price they paid for Stalin's agreeing to enter the war against Japan. With the atom bomb already in their hands ... What bankruptcy of political thought!"
>
> Alexander Solzhenitsyn, *The Gulag Archipelago*, paperback, 1973, Vol. 1, footnote, p. 259

vapid promises about things they cared about more, such as his participation in the future United Nations, his entering the war against Japan in the Pacific later that year, and his support for the creation of a 'strong, independent Poland.' Adding to the absurdity, at the post-war Nuremberg trials the allies, including Russia, tried and executed Nazi officials for having run German industries with forced labor from the occupied countries. That was bad all right, but Stalin's version of it was worse – and they had approved it.

As to the first of Stalin's three "concessions" to his western allies, he probably saw their eagerness to have him participate in the U.N. as too good a deal to pass up because that would give him a veto over that organization's decisions, and history has shown that he used it.

As a second concession, Stalin had promised to enter the Pacific war against Japan 90 days after Germany's final defeat. That turned out to be May 8, 1945, and true to his word, he declared war on a very weak Japan on August 8. Two days earlier the Enola Gay had dropped the first atomic bomb. But Stalin had been promised additional territories in the Far East for his trouble, and with very little effort he seized the Kuril Islands, Sakhalin and North Korea. There can be little doubt that Russian control of those lands led to the Korean war, five years later.

Probably worst of all, Stalin's idea of a 'strong, independent Poland' was quite different from that of his western allies, but it was just another of the craven concessions that let him take over and dominate several middle-European nations bordering the USSR – for two generations.

Of the other Yalta agreements, decency compels me to mention that all Russian citizens who had been held on German territory must go back to Russia, willingly or not. For those people that spelled their end, because by Stalin's logic, surrender and any kind of cooperation with the Germans were criminal; many of those people chose suicide.

To sum up, since two generations of central Europeans had to live with the consequences of Churchill and Roosevelt's inept horse-trading, they have rightly described the Yalta conference as 'the western betrayal'. That term may also apply to Stalin's forced labor plan. While getting nothing in return, Roosevelt and Churchill had approved a Russian version of the Nazi concentration camp system, for German POWs and others unlucky enough to have been 'repatriated'.

And yet Stalin's previous experiences with forced labor, particularly the collectivization of Russian agriculture, should have taught him that slavery is not a very efficient economic system, so perhaps his real reason was simple vengeance. In any event, the Russians soon

Yalta, early February 1945. Seated, left to right, Churchill, Roosevelt and Stalin.
Roosevelt died two months later.

discovered that their 271,700 German slaves (German estimates put the
total 100,000 higher) were not high achievers. Harsh treatment,
starvation diets and hopelessness made for low productivity, while the
women and the older men were simply unable to perform the heavy
work. That very same year the Russians started releasing deported
Germans, and by 1950 they claimed that most had returned to
Germany. But of course that was without those who had perished in
the camps. Soviet archives put those at 24%, while several post-war
German studies produced estimates twice as high.

(The fact that 200,000 ethnic Germans originally from Russian
territories, who had been resettled in Poland during the war, were
"returned" to the USSR after the Russian victory, proves that Lilli
Clausen's family was among the lucky ones who slipped through that
net. The death rate of the 'resettled' was very high as well.)

According to what Heide was told, Tante Lotte and Mia didn't mind
leaving their Nerwigk home very much, since they considered a labor
camp preferable to being constantly raped. But the labor camp Mia was

taken to was a coal mine in the Ural mountains, where conditions were even more appalling than we can imagine.

Those left in Nerwigk were thoroughly dispirited. They found some solace in prayer, the Catholics and the Protestants each in their own way. The next day another Russian soldier came to take one more of the refugee women, who had to abandon three children including a two-year-old and a great aunt of 91. Lore urged her to talk to the first Russian officer she met, asking for pity for her children and her aged relative. After two days the woman came back; the officer had let her go. It was an early sign of the Russian fury waning a bit.

Even so, it was far from over. The women in Nerwigk village and the refugees above developed a new protective tactic. As soon as Russian trucks appeared the women below would dash uphill and hide behind haystacks in the fields. This served as a signal for the refugees to rush into the woods above them. But now the official Russian strategy seemed to have evolved to collectivizing the local farms and forcing everyone they could find to work on them, milking cows and harvesting crops. At this news, and because they were out of food anyway, Lore decided they might as well go home again and make the best of it. If the Russians had a need for them, they might be better off there.

They arrived back in Daumen on May 1, the traditional Labor Day for communists. This seemed to explain why they had not been raped by Russians on the way; they must have been celebrating. It also turned out that the *Gutshaus* at the estate had not been blown up, but the Russian commander was living there, so Lore and her family moved into what she described as the barracks above the village. Instead of barracks the building seems to have been a jail; it still had bars on the windows. After three weeks of living there very quietly they were found, and she was told that, if she and her children didn't want to be thrown into the lake, she'd better be at the estate's milking barn at 3:30 the next morning.

That was it; there was nothing else for it. Before the crack of dawn she trudged down to her former milking yard, where pandemonium reigned. Germans and Russians and cows of all descriptions milled around, with bucket-carrying women grabbing cows at random and milking them as long as they could hold on, then grabbing another cow's udders. Lore was clueless about milking cows, so she just stood there with her bucket, but in the confusion nobody noticed that she was doing nothing. To keep up appearances, 'her women' occasionally poured a bit of milk from their buckets into hers. It was a ridiculous scene, but nobody laughed.

After a few weeks she was given a different chore, mending fishing nets on the bank of the lake. She was good at that job, which included bringing in the fish caught by an elderly German whom the Russians had appointed their fisherman. But women who tried to steal a fish for themselves were whipped mercilessly.

In the meantime Berlin had been taken by the Russians, Hitler had killed himself, and peace came; but lines of Russian trucks still filled the road, around the clock. Westbound trucks were empty, while eastbound ones were filled with a boundless array of everything that Russians coveted: sewing machines, mirrors, theater chairs, overstuffed furniture. In the meantime at the estate everyone labored without a break, and without recompense or nourishment. What little the women had to eat they had to forage for, so they sent their children into the woods to collect mushrooms and berries, and they gleaned small amounts of grain or potatoes. In the meantime the Russians took all the local crops, but Lore noticed that they made absolutely no provisions for the future, such as planting, and whatever task they gave the locals was marked by a total lack of organization. Chaos was the order of the day.

Finally Lore and another lady were ordered to start baking rye bread for the Russians. They would bake two batches of sourdough rye a day. In the morning they started with 150 pounds of rye flour. They sifted half of it, mixed it with water, salt and sourdough, and kneaded the dough in a big wooden trough they'd found. When the first 18 loaves came out of the oven at three in the afternoon, a second batch was already rising, to be baked in the early evening. Lore thought it was the best job she could have hoped for, since it enabled her to be with her children, and she could slip them a few extra calories. But of course,

she had to do that on the sly. When the women brought their loaves to the kitchen in their 'bread buggy', they saw how the Russians ate: French fries, lots of eggs, fried pike swimming in butter, and pitchers of cream (The Russians threw away the milk). But considering everything, they were glad to have their plain rye bread, and their children, still alive.

But now they had a new worry, because the 'victors of Berlin' were streaming back to Mother Russia, passing by on the road above the estate. Their transit revived the plunder and atrocities of a few months earlier, so during the day the women who were not working in the fields, including the bakers, made themselves scarce again. It caused Lore to wonder if slaving in the fields would not be preferable after all. Her nights were also filled with fear. They were still living on the upper floor of the "barracks," keeping all the doors locked, but on one occasion a Russian forced his way in. She had quickly collected her children from their beds and into her lap, and was sitting there in the dark, frozen with fear. After shining his flashlight on them he left without a word. But the next night another one barged in, and he made clear what he expected. Instead of giving in, she furiously cussed him out in German. This made him equally furious, but without paying attention she put the smallest children in the bread buggy and, with the others hanging on, pulled it past him on the way out. He did not stop her, and she spent the night with a neighbor. The way Heide relates the incident suggests that her mom was surprised at her own audacity.

One worry piled on top of another. Lore's little girl Vickie, now 3, got an ear infection, but there was no medical help in the immediate area. Leaving to search for a doctor was extremely dangerous with the roads still full of Russians, so she couldn't do that until the homeward migration had abated. Between baking and hiding, it was also difficult to make time to wash the children's hair to get rid of the abundant lice that the Russians had brought. Besides all that, they developed open sores from being underfed. Finally five women got leave to go see a doctor

St. Joseph's Hospital in Bischofsburg.

at the hospital in Bischofsburg, a ten-mile walk. When they got there they learned that the Catholic sisters had been raped by the Russians too, and had been put to work doing menial labor. But now that the hospital had re-opened they were back, except that they had no supplies. The doctor confirmed that their skin sores were caused by malnutrition, but all he could do was give them a small jar of black ointment. He mentioned that shortly before, an American commission had arrived to check on local conditions. They had advised him to leave for West Germany, where he would at least make a living. But the Russian-Polish régime would not let him go without a replacement. Still, this started Lore thinking. If she got a chance to leave, she would take it.

Then, in the kind of random luck that happens in war, they learned that the four rounded up for forced labor had not all been hauled off to Russia. Ziermann had made his way back from an East Prussian estate where the Russians had put him to work. He thought Novak the blacksmith and Mia had been taken to a Siberian labor camp, but Tante Lotte might still be in the province. Since he had brought an official transfer slip, he was promptly put to work as a foreman at the estate. Conditions started to loosen up a bit more. The Russians let the women have a bit of skim milk and some flour, and they were allowed more freedom to come and go. A tiny bottle of Lysol came as a godsend to Lore. They had discovered that a few drops of Lysol on the doorstep would keep the Russians away, because they associated its smell with the typhus rampant in every war zone. The Lysol also worked against the lice, but Lore had to use it sparingly.

Now some of the Russians started leaving, on the heels of the Ukrainian people who had been put to work in East Prussia during the war. The Ukrainians had been ordered to drive the local cows east. Their women were inconsolable, because they knew this would be their end. Back in Russia they would be accused of having worked for the enemy, receive a mock trial, and be killed.

Then, suddenly, Russian army units moved in to harvest the grain, and work for the locals became sporadic, although Lore was still baking bread. But then they heard some good news. The United Nations Relief and Rehabilitation Administration (UNRRA), mostly funded by the U.S., Switzerland and Sweden, had started bringing relief to war victims in many countries, though not to Germans. But the Poles who had taken over East Prussia had received UNRRA supplies, and Lore and her friends might be able to buy some if they sold their unbroken dishes and knick-knacks because the Poles would give them zlotys for

Silhouettes of Allenstein castle and church, before World War II.

those. Barefoot, they made the twenty-mile trip to Allenstein, and returned successful. Lore brought back a pint of oil, a loaf of white bread and some tomatoes. It made for a feast to celebrate Heide's birthday that evening. It was September 5, 1945.

While in Allenstein Lore also had learned that train tickets to travel west cost 155 zlotys, and that the minister who had married them and baptized their children had returned to nearby Wartenburg. A few days later she walked to Wartenburg, where she met former friends, many now aged and sick, and learned of others who had died of typhus or been killed, by strafing planes or because they looked official. The Russians had a habit of shooting anyone who wore some kind of uniform, even forest rangers and jail wardens. The minister had been put to work at City Hall, and he had aged terribly. Frail and weak as he was, he conducted a brief service at his home; Lore marveled how well he did it. While his wife lay dying of typhus Russians had barged in, looking for jewelry. In their frantic search they had turned over her mattress and dumped her on the floor, but finally they had found their hidden wedding rings, and left in triumph.

Back in Daumen Lore collected all the courage she had left to ask a Russian officer if he saw any chances of her traveling to the western part of Germany, to see friends and relatives. To her big surprise, he was very encouraging and told her she should be able to reach Stuttgart, in the American Zone, where she'd be much better off.

Ziermann fell deathly ill with typhus, a new troop of Russians moved in, and committed a deadly atrocity on a woman. Now Lore's mind was made up. By next Sunday, September 30, she would be gone. And so she was. Around noon that day she left with not much more than the clothes on her back, pulling the two smallest children in the bread buggy

Wartenburg

to Wartenburg. But before leaving she had secured a train ticket from Allenstein to the west, by bartering her children's coats. Pulling the buggy through soft sand was hard work, and it was evening when she got to her minister's manse, where she stayed for some time. Then she learned that Ziermann had died, and next the Polish militia barged in to haul off the minister. This left her and her children alone in the house until another group of militia told her to report to a "collective train" with an undisclosed destination. And they took away her train ticket.

This part of the story needs to be seen against the background of recent decisions by the victorious – but soon to be former – allies. Well before the war's end they had agreed that the nations to the east of Germany should be made 'ethnically homogeneous'. In a cruel twist of irony, this was the allied version of Hitler's program of ethnic cleansing; and by today's standards it has been called that. But at that time the big decision-makers saw the war as having been caused by the very problem they were trying to solve: conflicts between different ethnic groups living inside the same borders. That many of those conflicts had been inconsequential until they were virtually created by Hitler (and by Stalin) doesn't seem to have received much consideration. In any case, the allies had agreed that after the war, the millions of Germans living outside the greatly shrunk borders of Germany proper would be forcibly 'repatriated'. It was now early September 1945. At the Potsdam conference in late July, it had been ponderously agreed that:

"The Three Governments, having considered the question in all its aspects, recognize that the transfer to Germany of German populations, or elements thereof, remaining in Poland, Czechoslovakia and Hungary, will have to be undertaken. They agree that any transfers that take place should be effected in an orderly and humane manner."

Even though 'orderly and humane' manners were rare at first, this huge expulsion of between 10 and 12 million people would be largely completed by 1950. With regard to East Prussia, the allies had already agreed that its northern half would become Russian, with the southern half to become Polish. Along with the other Polish border adjustments, this left 4.5 million Germans

1945: Germans expelled from eastern territories.

living in areas under Polish control. Communications were bad or nonexistent in those war-torn areas, so many locals were not aware of the allied plan, as shown by other things we know. For example, after hostilities ended a large number of East Prussians who had fled to the west came backto their homes, only to be expelled by the Poles and the Russians. Another example is the curious rumor, mentioned by Lore more than once, that East Prussia was to become part of American-occupied Germany. The allies had never entertained that notion, as anybody who had access to the news should have known. But obviously a lot of people were flying blind. It even seems possible that the train Lore was ordered to board would have brought her to Germany. But we will never know, and it might not have.

The key fact, apparently still unknown by the time Lore decided to leave Daumen, was that the Potsdam-approved 'transfer' of Germans from East Prussia had already begun. At first run by Polish communist militias, it started out quite disorganized, marred by arbitrary detentions in labor camps, abuse and violence similar to that perpetrated by the Russians. There are also reports of 'forced divorces' of women

> "The communist regime in the East could stand and grow due to the enthusiastic support from an enormous number of Western intellectuals who felt a kinship and refused to see communism's crimes."
>
> *Alexander Solzhenitsyn*

whose husbands were already in Germany, but why I don't know. It's reported that the treatment of the Germans by the Poles varied from brutal to kind; clearly a lot depended on the Poles' personal experiences. While many had been brutalized and dispossessed themselves, others who had been well treated by Germans were of a better disposition.

Lore and her children were taken to Wartenburg's Polish militia headquarters, where they sat waiting all night while more people were brought in. About midnight one of the guards, speaking German, invited her to come into a different room, where it would be warm. Surprised by this kindness, she asked him where in Saxonia he had lived; and that surprised *him*. During the war millions of Poles had been hauled off to Germany to perform forced labor, and his accent had told her he must have picked up his German in Saxonia. She asked him about his employers there, and they chatted the rest of the night. By morning, she noted with considerable satisfaction, she had him softened up enough so he gave her back the train ticket that they had taken from her. But she barely had it when an officer stormed in, with a written order for her to board a 'collective train' from Allenstein. Since that was where she wanted to go anyway, she did not object, but he insisted she leave immediately, and it was pouring buckets outside.

So they left, and in no time were soaked to the bone. Since she was greatly worried about someone finding the written order she had been given, she got rid of it along the road. After going two or three miles in the downpour they came to a village. She noticed that Poles had been moving into homes formerly owned by Germans, so she must have had some awareness of the population movements going on. To find Germans, she looked for a house with a 'neat and tidy yard,' and found one. It turned out that the German people who lived there knew the Funkes, and were glad to provide hospitality. Drying everyone's clothes took days, and because it kept on raining they ended up staying for an entire week. After that she decided to go check out the situation in Allenstein. Her hosts had told her of a friend of hers who was hiding at a farm about halfway there. When her friend recognized her she rushed out of the house, showing 'nothing but the deepest compassion' for Lore and her children. But she herself had been through worse, since her baby had died of starvation while she was forced to work for the Russians on one of the estates.

At the office of the newly-installed Polish government in Allenstein, a sympathetic clerk told her in hushed German that there was no chance of her staying on what was now Polish soil. That was for three reasons:

she was not born in East Prussia, she didn't speak Polish, and she was not a Catholic. At the Allenstein train station she also found out that a west-bound train left every morning at 7:30. Returning to the village, she stopped at the house of her friend, who was thinking of fleeing west herself. They agreed that during her final walk from the village to Allenstein she would stop in to find out what she had decided; and so she returned to her hosts.

On that final trek to Allenstein she found that her friend had been unable to come to a decision, which meant she would stay. She endured 'three more horrible years before she made the break with her children.'

But in Allenstein Lore connected with a German mother with two children who also wanted out, and would bring food to share. It was still dark on the morning of October 30 when they walked to the station together. There they found a long line of people waiting to get a date stamped on their tickets. By the time theirs were stamped the train was gone, but they boarded the next morning, for a trip that took many days, alternating between freight and passenger trains, all moving very slowly. There were no timetables, so while waiting for the next train they never strayed far, sleeping where they could, with the 'most luxurious accommodation' being the wooden floor of a waiting room. It was getting quite cold, they ran out of food, and a lot of the time they were harassed and insulted by both Poles and Russians.

But finally they arrived in Frankfurt on the Oder, in a boxcar. The station was receiving POWs and other German prisoners from Siberia, all of whom arrived in rags, looking pitiful and emaciated. In a Red Cross facility they got a bit of food and a cot, and at 4 AM were ordered out to catch the Berlin train at the station. They waited ten hours in the bitter cold for what turned out to be another freight train, but it meant progress. In the boxcar they sat next to an army nurse who had just returned from a Siberian POW camp. When she was captured, she had been gang-raped by ninety Russians.

They reached west Berlin, now a virtual island surrounded by Russian-held territory, on November 6. They had left Allenstein on October 31, for a trip that in normal times might have taken nine hours at most. Needless to say they were all very hungry but they were given a loaf of American-style bread. While putting it down as 'balloon bread', Heide thinks it came from the Red Cross. Her mom thought it could not possibly provide them with enough nourishment but, lucky for them, American-style bread was greatly in demand just then, probably because during the war German bread had gradually become unpalatable because of all the fillers, like potato starch and even sawdust being added. To save flour, the government had ordered bakers to use ever-larger amounts of such fillers. Some reports connect this practice with widespread intestinal distress, even affecting the army, which in the later stages of the war contained many companies of 'stomach patients'. Lore traded her balloon bread for a *Kommißbrot*, a heavy loaf of dark rye traditionally baked in a pan. That was real food for them; it had substance. Besides the *Kommißbrot*, Heide remembers getting some soup, also from the Red Cross.

Because the Russians had removed a lot of train tracks, it took considerable time to get on a westbound train, and they ended up traveling west by way of Leipzig. After some time in Leipzig they finally left again. To get to the west they bribed one of the East German border guards to waive inspection of their boxcar, and on the 26th of November they were electrified when someone in the train noticed that they were just crossing into the American Zone.

Moments later they pulled into Hof-Moschendorf, which had become a major receiving center for German refugees and DPs. They were awed by the large number of nurses and other people who were there to receive them, by their kindness, and by the fact that before the new arrivals went anywhere they were given a big bowl of hearty soup. The children were overwhelmed, and Heide noticed that while her mom inhaled her soup, tears ran down her face. Then they were directed to the nearby camp, which was very well equipped to deal with masses of people who might be starving, ill, and vermin-infested. Even though the

Refugees arriving at Moschendorf.

Funkes had gone through delousing stations in the Russian Zone, they had never gotten rid of them completely. But this time, both their persons and their clothes were made louse-free. After living with the critters for such a long time, it felt as if something was missing.

After several enjoyable days in the camp, they caught a train to Nuremberg. At the Nuremberg station Lore showed her Polish train ticket to the man at the window, but he could not read it. When she explained her situation, he immediately handed her tickets for the train to Stuttgart. He also told her where in the station they could get food and milk at no charge. While waiting for the Stuttgart train, a momentary flashback occurred when the children spotted some American soldiers and went into hiding from 'the Russians'. She had trouble explaining that these uniforms would do them no harm. But they soon forgot their fear while marveling at the comfort of the upholstered seats and the speed of the train, which took only two hours to reach Stuttgart.

During the trip Lore wondered if a dream she'd had back in February might have been a sign of a happy ending. In her dream she had seen Hans-Werner, dressed in civilian clothes and crouching on the floor with a big smile, ready to catch toddling baby Lore in his arms. Did it mean he had made it to the West, and they would soon be reunited? So many people had been killed or deported without a trace. Getting her hopes up could make the disappointment worse.

On the first of that month the German postal service had resumed operations, and during their time between trains in Leipzig Lore had written to Tante Lotte, care of her Stuttgart parents, and also to a friend in Stuttgart, asking if she could stay with her for a few days, so as not to

Welcoming returning POWs in Camp Moschendorf.

burden Tante Lotte's parents. But of course, being on the move all the time, she had not received any answers and could only hope.

Stuttgart, her old hometown, looked like a different world. It had sustained much less bomb damage than Berlin, the lights were on, traffic was moving, and people were going about their business. What she noticed particularly was that they moved fearlessly, without the anxious, oppressed look of people in the east.

From the train station they took a streetcar to her friend's house, which luckily was still there. She and her son had received her letter that morning, and were terribly excited to see them. Since her friend was related to Tante Lotte, she first asked about her, and learned there had been no news. Then her friend added: "But you probably know that your husband is here in town?" Lore nearly fainted. Even so, when she learned that he was staying at Tante Lotte's parents, she decided not to go there that day. It was already late, and the sight of their re-united family might worsen Lotte's parents' own sorrows.

The next morning her friend's son went to collect Hans-Werner, with the story that his family would be arriving soon, and he needed his help preparing a room. Standing in the doorway, Lore had hoped to surprise him, but the shouts of the children upstairs gave away the secret. It was the kind of reunion that could only happen once in a lifetime. The only real hitch in the plan was that little Lore did not recognize her daddy and spurned him. But then, it had been over a year.

The very night when she had her encouraging dream, February 18, Hans-Werner had been wounded during his unit's retreat through East Prussia. But that had turned out to be his lucky break. After an emergency operation on a table to remove shrapnel from his shoulder and knee, he had been evacuated on a hospital ship, and after his recovery in a south German hospital he was on a ten-day furlough when the war ended. After holding him for one hour, the Americans had sent him home.

In time they received news about other friends and relatives, not much of it good. Hans-Werner's parents had perished during their flight in East Prussia, and had been buried in a mass grave. His sister had managed to flee to Denmark, but she died there soon afterward.

All this added to the reasons why a telegram sent by Tante Lotte to her parents, from Berlin, was greeted with exultation. Ever since she was taken away she had been held in a camp, in the now Russian-owned northern part of East Prussia. It had been a continuous nightmare of starvation and brutality, while she nursed the sick, hundreds of whom died every day. She had caught typhus herself, was treated by the Funkes' family doctor and survived, but he was later shot while trying to escape. Then, around Christmas 1945, she was interrogated about her family and their politics. After she swore that they had never wanted anything to do with the Nazis she had been released, but it took a long time and many reversals before she reached Berlin, covered with the customary malnutrition sores. She recovered in a hospital in the British sector, and ended up working for the Lutheran church in Stuttgart.

Poor Mia the cook never returned. In 1948 she had sent a postcard from a Siberian camp where she died not much later, though the date is unknown. No wonder: the Russians took better care of their horses than of their slave laborers, whom they simply worked to death. At first she had to work underground mining coal, then logging, and finally loading rocks onto rail cars.

After being held by the Russians for two years, Novak the blacksmith was released but forced to stay in former East Prussia. They corresponded, but Lore knew that the more the Novaks wrote about how great they were doing, the more miserable they were. Their state of fear had become permanent. For Novak and the others left behind, Lore fervently hoped they would be able to find a place where they might live without fear.

Allenstein's Market Place today.

Heide quotes her final lines: "It has happened to us. Here in this generous and beautiful America we have found freedom and peace." In America both Lore and Heide worked teaching German. That was well after the family realized that their American sponsor for emigration assumed that they had come as his personal indentured servants.

After Grant retired from working in the woods for Weyerhaeuser company, Heide and Grant ran a plant nursery, which they sold when her eyesight started failing.

Today in the former East Prussia, the little village of Daumen is known as Tumiany to the Poles, who thought it essential to change all of the local place names. For that same reason Allenstein is known as *Olsztyn*, Bischofsburg as *Biskupiec*, and Wartenburg as *Barczewo*. Danzig goes by *Gdansk*. And Königsberg, being Russian now, is *Kaliningrad*. The dialects formerly spoken in the province are nearly extinct, as is inevitable when a population is uprooted and scattered throughout German lands that have a different speech.

And when you do a search for *Immobilien* in *Ostpreußen* (real estate in East Prussia), you're likely to find a number of rural spreads with a formerly German *Gutshaus*, most of them *renovierungsbedürftig und daher preiswert* (in need of restoration and therefore a good deal).

"Behold," said Ecclediastes, "all is vanity and vexation of the spirit"; and he levied that judgment on "all the works that are done under the sun". Surely those include the works of the 20th century dictators who

thought so highly of themselves, and who set out to do such great things. Whatever they achieved was dwarfed by what they destroyed.

And what were the rationales behind their grand plans?

One was the notion that you can make no real economic progress unless you steal somebody else's property. That was Hitler's reason for attacking Poland and the USSR. He wanted not only their land but their minerals, including Russian oil, even though the Russians were happy to trade those resources for German products, as they still are today.

But the other justification for the dictators' nation-building-schemes was their belief that people who speak a different language cannot possibly get along inside the same country, so to keep the peace they must change their language or be forcibly separated. It's an idea that's been disproved in other places and at other times, in places like Switzerland and, yes, in the United States, which has always had linguistic minorities. And historically, when population groups clashed it had far more to do with differing customs, with religion and other outlooks on life, and of course with the ambitions of reckless politicians.

> "Germany is a great nation only because its people have so much Polish blood in their veins."
>
> *Friedrich Nietzsche*

When we study German and Polish history, we find many eras when Germans and Poles living in Prussian territories got along fine, and other times when they did not, and resentments accumulated. During the centuries when the Prussian kings were in charge, the relationship seemed to depend on the monarch, since through the years authoritarians alternated with more enlightened rulers.

Karl vom Stein zum Altenstein (1770-1840) who served as the Prussian king's Minister for Education from 1817 until his death,

became famous as a social innovator who – among other reforms –
introduced compulsory elementary education for both Polish and
German-speaking Prussians. Now nearly two centuries ago, in 1823,
Altenstein stated:

> 'Concerning the spread of the German language it is most important to
> get a clear understanding of the aims, whether it should be the aim to
> promote the understanding of German among Polish-speaking subjects
> or whether it should be the aim to gradually and slowly Germanize the
> Poles. According to the judgement of the minister only the first is
> necessary, advisable and possible, the second is not advisable and not
> achievable. To be good subjects it is desirable for the Poles to
> understand the language of government. However, it is not necessary
> for them to give up or postpone their mother language. The possession
> of two languages shall not be seen as a disadvantage but as a benefit
> instead because it is usually associated with a higher flexibility of the
> mind. . . . Religion and language are the highest sanctuaries of a nation
> and all attitudes and perceptions are founded on them. A government
> that . . . is indifferent or even hostile against them creates bitterness,
> debases the nation and generates disloyal subjects.'

And just as this book first went to press, Lech Walesa, the near-
legendary union organizer, fomenter of Polish independence and past
Polish president, proposed that Germany and Poland become one
nation. Needless to say, not everyone was pleased. But people rarely
are, with what far-sighted prophets have to say.